THE RHINE—CHIEF WATERWAY OF GERMANY

Because of its importance as a commercial waterway, serving a vast industrial area, and its far-famed romantic beauty, the Rhine has always occupied a special place in German life. This picture is taken from the steep vineyard terraces above the little town of Bacharach, in the picturesque 80-mile gorge through which the river flows.

GERMAN

HOW TO SPEAK
AND WRITE IT

An informal conversational method
for self study with 330 illustrations

by Joseph Rosenberg

DOVER PUBLICATIONS, INC.
New York

This new Dover edition, first published in 1962, is a slightly revised version of the work first published by Odhams Press Limited. The revision consists of minor editing to adapt the book for the American audience.

International Standard Book Number: 0-486-20271-2

Library of Congress Catalog Card Number: 63-358

Manufactured in the United States of America
Dover Publications, Inc.
31 East 2nd Street
Mineola, N.Y. 11501

FOREWORD

THE German language is more than the language of Germany. It is, in the same way as French, one of the great international tongues, widely understood and forming, as it were, a common denominator among many states. In Austria and in the majority of the Swiss cantons it is the official language, and throughout Central Europe it has enjoyed for centuries a very wide use both in speech and in writing.

Thus, the man or woman who is equipped with even a slight working knowledge of German has the means of direct contact with a variety of peoples and cultures—the means of access to ways of thought and life which must be experienced at first hand to be really appreciated and understood. A little learning becomes, therefore, not a dangerous but a delightful thing, yielding a potential store of fascinating and often amusing experiences which must otherwise be denied.

The study of a living language should not be a dull and onerous task, though too often the method of presentation makes it so. Feats of deliberate memorization, and the academic unravelling of complex rules, may produce excellent results in some cases, but the average student will find a lighter treatment more to his taste. His knowledge will grow more readily and pleasantly if a process of easy absorption is followed, and it is in this firm belief that the present Course has been prepared. The aim throughout has been to keep interest alive by stressing the human scene and by passing so frequently from one subject to another as constantly to stimulate the mind. A generous use of illustrations, in which objects and actions are clearly related to their equivalent German words, plays an essential part in the scheme.

In learning German, the student should not lose sight of the fact that beyond his studies there lies a whole literature. In the writings of Goethe, Schiller, Heine, Thomas Mann, and other great figures of the German-speaking world of letters there is a rich field for exploration in leisure hours, a field of which the scope and content are admirably summarized in Dr. Richard Friedenthal's Study Guide in the later pages of the book.

The author is indebted for criticism and useful suggestions to Mr. Max Reingwitz of Paris, and to Mr. Kurt Ronau of London.

JOSEPH ROSENBERG

CONTENTS

HEIDELBERG AND ITS 13TH-CENTURY CASTLE

Germany's foremost university town stands on the Neckar near its confluence with the Rhine. For nearly six hundred years it has enjoyed a world-wide reputation as a seat of learning, and it still retains many old buildings which preserve the medieval appearance of the town. The ruined castle is one of the chief monuments of Germany.

HOW TO USE THE COURSE

THERE ARE TWO WAYS of learning a foreign language by self-tuition. The first is to learn words; rules for grouping these words; exceptions to the rules; and then to practise putting these words together according to the rules, while remembering the exceptions.

It is most difficult to acquire fluency by this method. When speaking or writing the language you have no time to think what rule ought to be applied, or what exception remembered. Fluency in a language means that phrases are on the tip of your tongue when you need them.

This can be achieved far better by means of the second method, which is to memorize the most useful sentences so that they may come automatically to your lips at a moment's notice.

How did you learn your own English language? Did you study it? Of course not. You first began to understand it, then to speak it, by constantly hearing it spoken and by its daily repetition. You did not study the language—you absorbed it.

This Course has been devised with a view to assisting this process of natural absorption. The most useful words and expressions of the language are repeated so often and in such a variety of contexts that you will assimilate most of them simply by reading each Lesson carefully, perhaps several times.

METHOD OF STUDY

Each Lesson consists of a text, simple grammatical explanations, exercises and illustrations. In order to obtain the greatest benefit from them, the following order and method of study—in conjunction with a thorough revision after every four or five Lessons—are recommended:

(1) THE TEXT must be thoroughly understood and its correct pronunciation mastered with the help of the translations and equivalent pronunciations provided. Read it aloud over and over again until you can understand the German text without looking at the translation, and until you can pronounce it correctly without reference to the guide to pronunciation. It would be a good plan to study with a friend, who could check your pronunciation while you tried to read the text with the guide to pronunciation covered by a piece of paper. (It would be ideal, of course, if you could be assisted by a German-speaking friend.)

Remember that both translation and guide to pronunciation are provided only as a temporary assistance towards the proper understanding and correct pronunciation of the German text, and that as soon as these are achieved you must do without them. The aim is always to fuse the foreign word or expression with the object or action which it denotes; and from the very outset the student should train himself to avoid, as far as possible, the use of the English translation.

(2) THE GRAMMATICAL EXPLANATIONS. These are always preceded by examples, which are more important than the rules. It is advisable to memorize these examples.

(3) THE EXERCISES. You can check your answers by reference to the key given at the end of the book. If you find the translations into German too difficult, there is no harm in first looking up the German in the key. Then try again without looking, and again a few days later, until you are able to say the German instantly, fluently and quite correctly.

(4) THE ILLUSTRATIONS. These are designed to help you in a variety of ways. The photographic illustrations, apart from presenting characteristic aspects of life in German-speaking countries, are accompanied by descriptions in German which will enable you to absorb new words and phrases. With the aid of the brief vocabulary which is given in each case, you should have little difficulty in understanding these descriptions, but in cases of doubt you can refer to the key given on pages 374 to 380 in order to be absolutely clear as to the meaning of a particular phrase. Remember, however, that the key is provided only in order to resolve doubtful points, and if you can avoid using it, so much the better.

In the special word-building drawings which are scattered throughout the book the various objects depicted are clearly related to the corresponding German words. The English equivalents are, therefore, intentionally omitted; but, here again, such doubts as may arise can be settled by reference to the key on page 367. Do not refer to the key more often than you need, for the essence of the system is the natural absorption of words by direct association with the objects themselves.

Some of the illustrations take the form of test-pictures, by means of which you can test your knowledge in a number of ways. No key is given and their value is dependent upon your own keenness, but you will find them well worth while in helping you to attain fluency in thought and expression.

Finally, the small sketches which are interspersed on nearly every page fulfil a valuable purpose in giving prominence to everyday phrases and in exemplifying rules. Their value is enhanced by the omission of English translations, the meaning of the German words being perfectly clear from the picture itself and its context.

GERMAN PRONUNCIATION

Compared with English, German pronunciation is simple and consistent. In English the same letter may be pronounced in various ways; e.g. the letter *a* is pronounced differently in the words *tar*, *gate*, *hall*, *at*, *woman*. Conversely, the same sound may be represented by several different spellings; e.g. the vowels in *keen*, *machine*, *bean* and *scene*, although spelt differently, are all pronounced the same.

German has almost completely a phonetic spelling, i.e. one in which each letter or combination of letters corresponds to one sound only. In most cases German words are pronounced as spelt. There are a few cases of unusual or irregular pronunciation, but these irregularities are not nearly so confusing as in English.

To make the task of the beginner as easy as possible, we have introduced a system of equivalent pronunciation in the first part of this Course.

Neither this book nor any other can teach you an absolutely correct pronunciation of German. It can help you to acquire it and can explain the difficulties, but it cannot speak German to you. Fortunately, there are other ways for you to hear German spoken—the radio, for instance. Even if you do not understand the full meaning of the words at first, listening-in will gradually attune your ear to German sounds and intonation.

Differences between German and English

CLEARNESS OF PRONUNCIATION. German words are pronounced more clearly and forcibly than English words. There is less mumbling, less slurring together of syllables than there is in English. Take the word *general*, which is common to both languages. Although a word of three syllables, in English it is often pronounced as a word of two, of which the second becomes an almost indistinct mumble. In the German word **General** all three syllables are clearly pronounced: gay-nĕ-rahl′, with the stress on the last syllable.

Kuh is pronounced *coo*

THE VOWEL SOUNDS. German vowels are pure. When you say *me* or *fee* in English the sound *ee* always remains the same, and so does the position of your lips. In other words, this *ee* is a pure vowel. But if you watch your lips when you say *home*, you will notice that they gradually close, and that what you actually say is a kind of double sound (called a diphthong), like *ho-oom*.

Now, in German, **a, e, i, o, u** are invariably pure sounds, and in each case the sound remains the same from beginning to end: **a** is pure *ah*, **e** is pure *eh*, **i** as in *machine*, **o** pure *oh*, and **u** is pronounced as it is in the English word *rude*. (There are also shorter pronunciations of the vowels, but these likewise are pure sounds.)

There are only three diphthongs:

au, which is always pronounced like *ou* in *house;*

ei (in some words spelt **ai**), which is pronounced as in English *height;* and

eu (sometimes **äu**), which is sounded like *oy* in *boy.*

SILENT LETTERS. There are practically no silent letters in German. Every letter and every combination of letters is sounded, and with the exception of **ch** is always sounded in the same way.

The letters that are sometimes silent are:

h, which, when placed after a vowel, merely serves as an indication that the vowel is a long one; and

e, when used in the combination **ie**, which is pronounced as in *field.*

The letter **p**, when it appears before an **f**, is almost but not quite inaudible. In our phonetic rendering of such words as **Pfund** (*pound*) and **Pfennig** (*penny*) the *p* is therefore shown, but care should be taken to avoid giving it too much emphasis.

Pronunciation of ch

The usual pronunciation of **ch** is very similar to an exaggerated *h* as in the English words *hue, huge, Hugo.*

After **a, o** and **u**, (but *not* after **äu, eu, ä, ö,** and **ü**) **ch** acquires a hard guttural sound, as in the pronunciation of the Scottish word *loch*. (There is also a German word **Loch**, which means *hole*.)

In some words of foreign origin, like

ein Loch

Christ, Charakter and a few others, **ch** is sounded like *k*, as in the corresponding English words.

The combination **chs** sounds like *x*. Thus, the German word for *ox* is **Ochse**, and it sounds almost like the English word, except that the **e** at the end is sounded. Here it should be noted that an unstressed **e** is almost silent, but not completely so. It has nearly the same sound as *e* in *open* or *a* in *sofa*, and is shown in our system of pronunciation by the symbol **ĕ**.

Two Sounds with no English Equivalents

So far we have been able to explain German sounds by giving you the nearest English (or, in the case of **ch**, Scottish) equivalent. There are two sounds, however, which have no English counterparts.

müde

THE GERMAN **ü**. If you say *ee* with your lips right out, as though you were going to whistle, you will produce the right sound. To indicate the rounding of the lips we represent this sound in our guide to pronunciation by **e͡e**. The German word for *tired* is **müde** and is pronounced mē͡e′-dĕ.

This is rather a long vowel. As it is somewhat difficult to sound a long vowel before two or more consonants, a shorter pronunciation of **ü** is used in such cases. For instance, the German for *Munich* is **München**. In this word the **ü** is much shorter —more like *i* pronounced with the lips rounded. Therefore, we represent the short **ü** by **į**.

THE GERMAN **ö**. This is similar to *ay,* said with rounded lips. If you say *ale* with

WINTER IN THE SWISS ALPS

German is the basic language of nearly three-quarters of the four million inhabitants of Switzerland, though in certain parts of the country French and Italian predominate. In the picture above a ski-ing party from Gstaad, in the German-speaking Bernese Oberland, enjoy a meal on the Hornberg, making the most of the mid-winter sunshine.

Öl

rounded lips you will get the right pronunciation of the German word **Öl**, which means *oil*. In our guide to pronunciation we represent this vowel sound by ôȳ.

The corresponding shorter form of **ö** before two or more consonants sounds almost like *ea* in *earth*, or *e* in *her*. We therefore represent this sound in our guide to pronunciation by ẹ.

The Umlaut

The vowels **a, o, u,** and the diphthong **au,** change their sounds when bearing a sign called the Umlaut (¨). Whereas the long German **a** is sounded as in English *part*, the Umlaut changes the sound to *a* as in *gate*.

The pronunciation of **ö** and **ü** has been explained above, and we have also seen that **äu** is sounded like *oy* in *boy*.

Double Letters

DOUBLE VOWELS (**aa, oo, ee**) are sounded exactly like the single vowels, but they are invariably long. Thus, **Aal** (*eel*) is pronounced like *ahl;* **Klee** (*clover*) like *clay;* and **Boot** (*boat*) like the English word *boat*, but with a pure *oh*.

DOUBLE CONSONANTS are pronounced as single consonants; the doubling of the consonant merely serves as an indication that the preceding vowel is short.

Stress

One syllable, usually the first, is stressed more heavily than the others. We show this syllable by means of a stress mark (′).

Many words of foreign origin retain their original pronunciation and stress, e.g. **General** = gay-nĕ-rahl′; **Banane** = bah-nah′-nĕ; **Restaurant**=res-toh-rang′.

The Glottal Stop

In English the final consonant of a word is often telescoped with the next word, if the latter begins with a vowel (*ham and eggs* sounds like one word, *hamaneggs*). This is not done in German. There must be a complete break between the words and, if a word begins with a vowel, the vowel must be preceded by a brief pause, the so-called glottal stop. It is used even in the middle of a word, to prevent a consonant from joining on to a following vowel, e.g. **unangenehm** (*unpleasant*) must be pronounced thus: **un—angenehm.**

KEY TO PRONUNCIATION

The following table forms a key to the system of equivalent pronunciation used in this book. You will be well advised to make frequent reference to it until you become thoroughly familiar with the system.

ah	as in *father*
a	the same, only shorter
ay	as in *gay*
ôȳ	the same, with rounded lips
e	as in *let*
ĕ	as in *open*
ẹ	as in *her*
ee	as in *see*
ẽẽ	the same, with rounded lips
ī	as in *time*
i	as in *tin*
ị	the same, with rounded lips
oh	as in *no*
o	like the *aw* in *lawyer.*
oo	as in *food*
ŏŏ	as in *good*
ou	as in *house*
oy	as in *joy*
g	as in *go*
s	as in *so*
y	as in *yes*
ch	as *h* in *hue*, except after **a, o** and **u,** when it is pronounced as in Scottish *loch*
ng	as in *sing*

IM HAMBURGER HAFEN

Hamburg ist der grösste Handelshafen Deutschlands und einer der Haupthäfen des europäischen Kontinents. Hamburg liegt an der unteren Elbe und Alster, etwa 100 Kilometer von der Nordsee entfernt. Bei Flut fahren die Schiffe bis in den Hafen von Hamburg. Die Stadt hat über eine Million Einwohner und ist auch eine bedeutende Industriestadt. *(Translation on page* 374)

der Hafen, ··-	der Krieg, -e	der Handel	neben	der Haupthafen, ··-	unter
port, harbour	*war*	*commerce*	*next to*	*chief port*	*lower*
etwa	**entfernt**	**die Flut, -en**	**fahren**	**bis in**	**der Einwohner, -**	**bedeutend**
about	*distant*	*high tide*	*to travel*	*right into*	*inhabitant*	*important*

(Plurals of nouns are indicated by the method described on page 53)

ERSTE LEKTION: *FIRST LESSON*

Herr Wilhelm Schulz
herr[1] vil′-helm shoŏlts

Frau Anna Schulz
frou[2] a′-nah shoŏlts

Hans
hants

Grete
gray′-tĕ

Herr Schulz ist der Vater von Hans und Grete.
herr shoŏlts ist dayr fah′-tĕr fon hants oŏnt gray′-tĕ.
Mr. Schulz is the father of Hans and Grete.

Frau Schulz ist die Mutter.
frou shoŏlts ist dee moŏ′-tĕr.
Mrs. Schulz is the mother.

Hans ist der Sohn von Wilhelm und Anna Schulz.
hants ist dayr zohn fon vil′-helm oŏnt a′-nah shoŏlts.
Hans is the son of Wilhelm and Anna Schulz.

Grete ist die Tochter.
gray′-tĕ ist dee toch′[3]-tĕr.
Grete is the daughter.

Hans ist der Bruder von Grete.
hants ist dayr broŏ′-dĕr fon gray′-tĕ.
Hans is the brother of Grete.

Grete ist die Schwester von Hans.
gray′-tĕ ist dee schves′-tĕr fon hants.
Grete is the sister of Hans.

Herr und Frau Schulz sind die Eltern von Hans und Grete.
herr oŏnt frou shoŏlts zint dee el′-tĕrn fon hants oŏnt gray′-tĕ.
Mr. and Mrs. Schulz are the parents of Hans and Grete.

Hans und Grete sind die Kinder von Wilhelm und Anna Schulz.
hants oŏnt gray′-tĕ zint dee kin′-dĕr fon vil′-helm oŏnt a′-nah shoŏlts.
Hans and Grete are the children of Wilhelm and Anna Schulz.

---

[1] **err** as in *herring*.   [2] **ou** as in *house*.   [3] **ch** as in Scottish *loch*.

Er ist gross und sie ist klein
ayr ist grohs ōont zee ist klīn

Sie ist dünn und er ist dick
zee ist dĭn[1] ōont ayr ist dick

Herr Schulz ist dick.
herr shōolts ist dick.
Mr. Schulz is stout.

Frau Schulz ist auch dick, aber nicht so dick wie Herr Schulz.
frou shōolts is ouch dick, ah´-bĕr nicht zoh dick vee herr shōolts.
Mrs. Schulz is also stout, but not so stout as Mr. Schulz.

Grete ist klein und dünn.
gray´-tĕ ist klīn ōont dĭn.
Grete is small and thin.

Hans ist auch klein und dünn, aber er ist
hants ist ouch klīn ōont dĭn, ah´-bĕr ayr ist
Hans is also small and thin, but he is

nicht so klein wie Grete.
nicht zoh klīn vee gray´-tĕ.
not so small as Grete.

Die Familie Schulz wohnt in Hamburg.
dee fah-meel´-yĕ shōolts vohnt in ham´-bŏork.
The Schulz family lives in Hamburg.

Hamburg ist gross.
ham´-bŏork ist grohs.
Hamburg is large.

Wo ist Hamburg?
voh ist ham´-bŏork?
Where is Hamburg?

Es ist in Deutschland.
es ist in doytsh´-lant.
It is in Germany.

Berlin ist auch gross.
ber-leen´ ist ouch grohs.
Berlin is also large.

Bonn ist nicht so gross wie Berlin.
bon ist nicht zoh grohs vee ber-leen´.
Bonn is not as large as Berlin.

Bremen, Köln und Nürnberg sind auch in Deutschland.
bray´-mĕn, kêln ōont nĭrn´-berk zint ouch in doytsh´-lant.
Bremen, Cologne and Nuremberg are also in Germany.

Hamburg, Bremen, Köln und Nürnberg sind nicht so gross wie Berlin.
ham´-bŏork, bray´-mĕn, kêln ōont nĭrn´-berk zint nicht zoh grohs vee ber-leen´.
Hamburg, Bremen, Cologne and Nuremberg are not as large as Berlin.

---

[1]Say **din** with your lips rounded.

HOW TO TRANSLATE *THE*
(THE DEFINITE ARTICLE)

Singular

der Mann	**die Frau**	**das Kind**
dayr man	dee frou	das kint
the man	*the woman*	*the child*
der Vater	**die Mutter**	**das Bier**
dayr fah′-tĕr	dee moo′-tĕr	das beer
the father	*the mother*	*the beer*
der Sohn	**die Tochter**	**das Haus**
dayr zohn	dee toch′-tĕr	das hous
the son	*the daughter*	*the house*
der Bruder	**die Schwester**	
dayr broo′-dĕr	dee shvĕs′-tĕr	
the brother	*the sister*	

Plural

die Eltern	**die Kinder**
dee el′-tĕrn	dee kin′-dĕr
the parents	*the children*

Note.—(1) Above are three German equivalents for English *the* : **der, die, das.** **Der** is *the* in connection with masculine nouns; **die** is *the* in connection with feminine nouns; **das** is *the* in connection with neuter nouns. (2) **Die** is also used for the plural, no matter whether the noun is masculine, feminine or neuter. (3) All nouns are spelt with an initial capital letter.

NUMERALS

eins	**zwei**	**drei**	**vier**	**fünf**
īnts	tsvī	drī	feer	fĭnf
one	*two*	*three*	*four*	*five*

EXERCISES

I Read and Translate

Wer (=*who*) ist der Vater von Hans und Grete? Herr Schulz is der Vater.
Wer ist die Mutter? Frau Schulz ist die Mutter.
Wer sind die Eltern? Herr und Frau Schulz sind die Eltern.
Wer sind die Kinder? Hans und Grete sind die Kinder.
Was (=*what*) ist Herr Schulz von Hans und Grete? Er ist der Vater.

Was ist Frau Schulz von Hans und Grete? Sie ist die Mutter.
Was ist Hans von Grete? Er ist der Bruder von Grete.
Was ist Grete von Hans? Sie ist die Schwester von Hans.
Wo wohnt die Familie Schulz? Die Familie Schulz wohnt in Hamburg.
Wo ist Hamburg? Es ist in Deutschland.
Wo ist Berlin? Es ist auch in Deutschland.
Ist Berlin gross? Ja (=*yes*), es ist gross.
Ist Hamburg auch gross? Ja, es ist auch gross.
Ist Hans gross? Nein (=*no*), er ist klein.
Ist Herr Schulz dick? Ja, er ist dick.
Ist Hans auch dick? Nein, er ist nicht dick, er ist dünn.
Ist Grete die Schwester von Frau Schulz? Nein, sie ist nicht die Schwester von Frau Schulz.
Was ist Grete von Frau Schulz? Sie ist die Tochter.
Wer sind die Eltern von Hans und Grete? Herr und Frau Schulz sind die Eltern.

II Insert the missing words

1. Herr Schulz ist der ... 2. ... ist dick. 3. Frau Schulz ist die ... 4. ... ist auch dick. 5. Hans ist der ... 6. ... ist klein. 7. Grete ist die ... 8. ... ist dünn. 9. Herr und Frau Schulz sind die ... 10. Hans und Grete sind die ... 11. Hans ist ... Bruder von Grete. 12. Grete ist ... Schwester von Hans. 13. Herr Schulz ist ... Vater. 14. Frau Schulz ist ... Mutter. 15. Grete ist ... Tochter. 16. Hans und Grete sind ... Kinder.

III Answer in German

1. Wer ist der Bruder von Grete? 2. Wer ist die Mutter von Hans? 3. Was ist Herr Schulz von Hans? 4. Was ist Hans von Grete? 5. Ist Grete die Tochter von Frau Schulz? 6. Ist Hans der Vater von Grete? 7. Wer ist der Vater von Grete? 8. Wer ist die Schwester von Hans? 9. Wer sind die Eltern von Hans und Grete? 10. Ist Herr Schulz dick? 11. Ist Frau Schulz auch dick? 12. Ist Hans gross? 13. Ist Grete klein? 14. Wo ist Berlin? 15. Wo ist Hamburg?

(*Answers on page* 355)

WEINLESE

Die Weinlese findet in Deutschland im Oktober und November statt. Die Weintrauben werden in der Traubenmühle zerquetscht und dann in der Kelter ausgepresst. Die Arbeiter haben viel zu tun und müssen vom frühen Morgen bis zum späten Abend die Weintrauben abschneiden und zur Kelter tragen.

(*Translation on page* 374)

die Weinlese, -n	**findet . . . statt**	**die Weintraube, -n**	**die Traubenmühle, -n**
vintage	*takes place*	*grape*	*grape mill*
zerquetschen (zerquetscht)	**die Kelter, -n**	**auspressen (ausgepresst)**	**der Arbeiter, -**
to crush (crushed)	*wine-press*	*to squeeze (squeezed)*	*worker*

ZWEITE LEKTION: *SECOND LESSON*

der Mann
dayr man

die Frau
dee frou

das Kind
das kint

der Wein
dayr vīn

die Limonade
dee lee-moh-nah′-dĕ

das Bier
das beer

der Tee
dayr tay

die Milch
dee milch

das Wasser
das va′-sĕr

Das Bier ist gut.
das beer ist gōōt.
The beer is good.

Die Limonade ist kalt.
dee lee-moh-nah′-dĕ ist kalt.
The lemonade is cold.

Die Milch ist weiss.
dee milch ist vīs.[1]
The milk is white.

Der Wein ist rot.
dayr vīn ist roht.
The wine is red.

Der Tee und das Bier sind braun.
dayr tay ōōnt das beer zint broun.
The tea and the beer are brown.

Der Kaffee ist schwarz.
dayr ka′-fay ist shvarts.
The coffee is black.

THE DEFINITE ARTICLE
(*Continued from Lesson I*)

masc.: **der Mann, der Wein, der Tee**
fem.: **die Frau, die Milch, die Limonade**
neut.: **das Kind, das Bier, das Wasser.**

Masculine and feminine do not always mean male and female in German. The names of many *things* are masculine and therefore are used in connection with **der**. The names of many other things are feminine and therefore used with **die**. Many others are neuter and have **das** as their definite article.

Note.—Although most male beings are masculine and most females feminine in German, there are a few which are neuter. The most important ones are: **das Kind** (kint)—*the child;* **das Mädchen** (mayt′-chen) =*the girl, the maid;* **das Fräulein** (froy′-līn)=*the young lady, miss;* **das Weib** (vīp) =*the woman,* (sometimes *wife*).

---

[1] Pronounced like *vice.*

17

Wer trinkt Bier?
vayr trinkt beer?

Der Herr trinkt Bier
dayr herr trinkt beer

Was trinkt die Dame?
vas trinkt dee dah'-mĕ?

Die Dame trinkt Tee
dee dah'-mĕ trinkt tay

der Herr=*the gentleman.*
Herr Schmidt=*Mr. Schmidt.*
der Mann=*the man.*
die junge Dame=*the young lady.*

die Dame=*the lady.*
Frau Schmidt=*Mrs. Schmidt.*
die Frau=*the woman, wife.*
Fräulein Schmidt=*Miss Schmidt.*

Herr Schulz trinkt Bier.
herr shōōlts trinkt beer.
Mr. Schulz drinks beer.

Frau Schulz trinkt Kaffee.
frou shōōlts trinkt ka'-fay.
Mrs. Schulz drinks coffee.

Hans trinkt Limonade.
hants trinkt lee-moh-nah'-dĕ.
Hans drinks lemonade.

Grete trinkt Milch.
gray'-tĕ trinkt milch.
Grete drinks milk.

Was trinkt Herr Schulz?
vas trinkt herr shōōlts?
What does Mr. Schulz drink?

Er trinkt Bier.
ayr trinkt beer.
He drinks beer.

Was trinkt Frau Schulz?
vas trinkt frou shōōlts?
What does Mrs. Schulz drink?

Sie trinkt Kaffee.
zee trinkt ka'-fay.
She drinks coffee.

Wer trinkt Limonade?
vayr trinkt lee-moh-nah'-dĕ?
Who drinks lemonade?

Hans trinkt Limonade.
hans trinkt lee-moh-nah'-dĕ.
Hans drinks lemonade.

Wer trinkt Milch?
vayr trinkt milch?
Who drinks milk?

Grete trinkt Milch.
gray'-tĕ trinkt milch.
Grete drinks milk.

Wer trinkt Tee?
vayr trinkt tay?
Who drinks tea?

Die Dame trinkt Tee.
dee dah'-mĕ trinkt tay.
The lady drinks tea.

das Pferd trinkt Wasser
das pfayrt trinkt va'-sĕr

das Brot
das broht

das Fleisch
das flish

Herr Schulz isst[1] Fleisch.
herr shoolts ist flish.
Mr. Schulz eats meat.

Frau Schulz isst Obst.
frou shoolts ist ohpst.
Mrs. Schulz eats fruit.

Hans isst Brot mit Butter
hants ist broht mit boo'-těr
Hans eats bread with butter

und Käse.
oont kay'-zě.
and cheese.

Grete isst Wurst mit Salat.
gray'-tě ist voorst mit zah-laht'.
Grete eats sausage with salad.

Isst Herr Schulz Fleisch?   Ja.
ist herr shoolts flish?   yah.
Does Mr. Schulz eat meat? Yes.

Isst Frau Schulz Fleisch?
ist frou shoolts flish?
Does Mrs. Schulz eat meat?

Nein, sie isst nicht Fleisch.
nIn, zee ist nicht flish.
No, she doesn't eat meat.

Sie isst Obst.
zee ist ohpst.
She eats fruit.

die Wurst
dee voorst

das Obst
das ohpst

**(1) STATEMENTS   (2) QUESTIONS
(3) NEGATIONS**

(1) **Er isst Fleisch** = *He eats meat; he is eating meat.* **Sie trinkt Tee** = *She drinks tea; she is drinking tea.* No difference is made in German between *he eats* and *he is eating*, *he drinks* and *he is drinking*, etc.

(2) **Isst er Fleisch?** = *Does he eat meat?; is he eating meat?* **Was trinkt sie?** = *What does she drink?; what is she drinking?* For *does he eat?* say *eats he?* = **isst er?**; for *does she drink?* say *drinks she?* = **trinkt sie?** and so on for all similar sentences.

(3) **Er isst nicht** = *He does not eat; he is not eating.* **Sie trinkt nicht** = *She does not drink; she is not drinking. He does not eat* = *he eats not* = **er isst nicht**; *she does not drink milk* = *she drinks not milk* = **sie trinkt nicht Milch,** etc.

Note.—The verb *to do* is not used, as it is in English, to form questions and to make negative statements. *I do not smoke* must be turned into *I smoke not; she does not drink beer* into *she drinks not beer* (**sie trinkt nicht Bier**). *Does he smoke?* must be turned into *smokes he?* (**raucht er?**).

---

[1] There is no difference in pronunciation between **er isst** = *he eats* and **er ist** = *he is.*

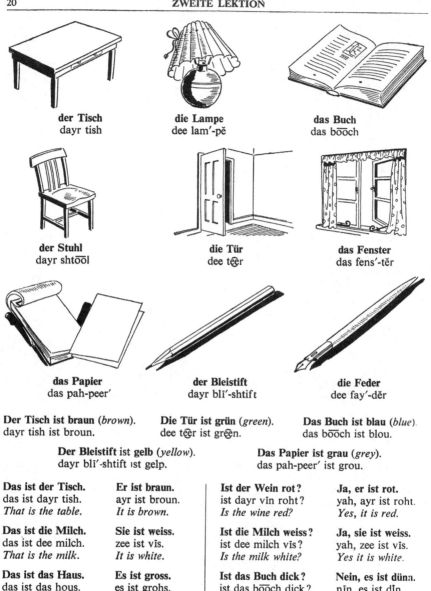

der Tisch
dayr tish

die Lampe
dee lam′-pĕ

das Buch
das bōōch

der Stuhl
dayr shtōōl

die Tür
dee tẽẽr

das Fenster
das fens′-tĕr

das Papier
das pah-peer′

der Bleistift
dayr blī′-shtift

die Feder
dee fay′-dĕr

Der Tisch ist braun (*brown*).
dayr tish ist broun.

Die Tür ist grün (*green*).
dee tẽẽr ist grẽẽn.

Das Buch ist blau (*blue*).
das bōōch ist blou.

Der Bleistift ist gelb (*yellow*).
dayr blī′-shtift ıst gelp.

Das Papier ist grau (*grey*).
das pah-peer′ ist grou.

Das ist der Tisch. das ist dayr tish. *That is the table.*	**Er ist braun.** ayr ist broun. *It is brown.*	**Ist der Wein rot?** ist dayr vīn roht? *Is the wine red?*	**Ja, er ist rot.** yah, ayr ist roht. *Yes, it is red.*
Das ist die Milch. das ist dee milch. *That is the milk.*	**Sie ist weiss.** zee ist vīs. *It is white.*	**Ist die Milch weiss?** ist dee milch vīs? *Is the milk white?*	**Ja, sie ist weiss.** yah, zee ist vīs. *Yes it is white.*
Das ist das Haus. das ist das hous. *That is the house.*	**Es ist gross.** es ist grohs. *It is big.*	**Ist das Buch dick?** ist das bōōch dick? *Is the book thick?*	**Nein, es ist dünn.** nīn, es ist dĭn. *No, it is thin.*
Das sind die Eltern. das zint dee el′-tĕrn. *Those are the parents.*	**Sie sind gross.** zee zint grohs. *They are big.*	**Sind die Kinder gross?** zint dee kin′-dĕr grohs? *Are the children big?*	**Nein, sie sind klein.** nīn, zee zint klīn. *No, they are small.*

HOW TO TRANSLATE
IT AND *THEY*

Der Tisch	ist	The table		
Er	gross.	It	} *is big.*	

Die Tür ⎱ ist   The door ⎱ is
Sie ⎰ grün.   It ⎰ *green.*

Das Papier ⎱ ist   The paper ⎱ is
Es ⎰ grau.   It ⎰ *grey.*

Die Kinder ⎱ sind   The children ⎱ are
Sie ⎰ klein.   They ⎰ *small.*

Singular			Plural
der	die	das	die
er	sie	es	sie

Care must be taken when translating *it*. As nouns may be masculine, feminine or neuter, use **er** when *it* stands for a masculine noun, **sie** when *it* stands for a feminine noun, and **es** for a neuter. For example, when translating *it is good* the translation of *it* will depend on the gender of the noun *it* stands for. If *it* stands for *the tea* you will have to say **er ist gut,** because *tea* is masculine in German: **der Tee.** If *it is good* refers to **die Milch** the correct German translation will be **sie ist gut.** If *it* stands for **das Bier** or **das Buch** you will have to say **es ist gut.**

Note that no such distinction is made for the translation of *they,* which is always **sie.** To know whether **sie** means *she* or *they,* look at the word that follows: **sie ist** means *she is;* **sie sind** means *they are.*

SENTENCE-BUILDING TABLE

		gut	good
Er		gross	large, tall
Sie	ist	klein	small
Es		dick	thick, stout
		dünn	thin
		rot	red
		gelb	yellow
		weiss	white
Sie sind		schwarz	black
		braun	brown
		grün	green
		grau	grey
		blau	blue

NUMERALS

sechs	sieben	acht	neun	zehn
zeks	zee′-bĕn	acht	noyn	tsayn
six	seven	eight	nine	ten

EXERCISES

I Read and Translate

1. Das ist der Stuhl. Er ist braun. 2. Das ist die Tür. Sie ist grün. 3. Das ist das Buch. Es ist blau. 4. Ist der Wein weiss? Nein, er ist rot. 5. Hans ist der Bruder von Grete. 6. Er isst Wurst. 7. Die Wurst ist gut. 8. Grete trinkt Wasser. 9. Das Wasser ist kalt. 10. Die junge Dame trinkt Kaffee. 11. Was isst der Herr? 12. Er isst Fleisch. 13. Wer isst Obst? 14. Was isst Frau Schulz? 15. Ist der Bleistift blau? Nein, er ist gelb.

II Answer in German

1. Ist Herr Schulz der Vater? 2. Isst er Fleisch? 3. Was isst Frau Schulz? 4. Was trinkt sie? 5. Wer trinkt Limonade? 6. Wer isst Brot mit Butter und Käse? 7. Was isst Grete? 8. Sind die Kinder gross? 9. Ist die Milch rot? 10. Was ist rot? 11. Was ist weiss?

III Nouns

Study carefully the nouns in Lessons I and II and then write out the following nouns with DER, DIE or DAS:

1. Vater. 2. Limonade. 3. Kind. 4. Milch. 5. Frau. 6. Buch. 7. Wein. 8. Wasser. 9. Tee. 10. Tisch. 11. Fenster. 12. Bleistift. 13. Feder. 14. Papier. 15. Lampe. 16. Dame. 17. Mutter. 18. Tür. 19. Stuhl. 20. Tochter.

IV Supply the missing words

1. Das ist der Bleistift. ... ist blau. 2. Das ist die Milch. ... ist weiss. 3. Ist der Wein rot? Ja, ... ist rot. 4. Ist das Papier grau? Ja, ... ist grau. 5. Ist der Kaffee schwarz? Nein, ... ist nicht schwarz. 6. Sind die Kinder klein? Ja, ... sind klein. 7. Ist Hans der Sohn? Ja, ... ist der Sohn.

(Answers on page 355)

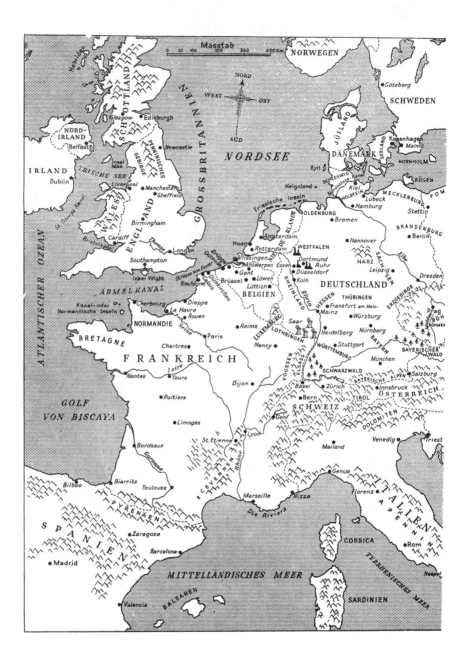

KARTE VON EUROPA—MAP OF EUROPE

This map will help you to become familiar with the German names of European countries and some of the places in them. Most of the names shown can be identified without difficulty, but, as you can see, there are many which undergo a considerable change and are not so easily linked with the English names that are familiar to us.

Here is an alphabetical list, with English equivalents, of some that are perhaps not so obvious:

Ärmelkanal	*English Channel (lit. Sleeve Channel)*
Bayern	*Bavaria*
Böhmen	*Bohemia*
Brügge	*Bruges*
Donau	*Danube*
Elsass	*Alsace*
Erzgebirge	*Ore Mountains*
Estland	*Esthonia*
Genf	*Geneva*
Köln	*Cologne*
Lettland	*Latvia*
Litauen	*Lithuania*
Lothringen	*Lorraine*
Löwen	*Louvain*
Lüttich	*Liége*
Mailand	*Milan*
Mähren	*Moravia*
Mittelländisches Meer	*Mediterraean Sea*
München	*Munich*
Neapel	*Naples*
Nizza	*Nice*
Nordostsee-Kanal	*Kiel Canal*
Nürnberg	*Nuremberg*
Pommern	*Pomerania*
Riesengebirge	*Giant Mountains*
Rokitno Sümpfe	*Pripet Marshes*
Sachsen	*Saxony*
Schlesien	*Silesia*
Schwarzwald	*Black Forest*
Venedig	*Venice*
Vlissingen	*Flushing*
Vogesen	*Vosges Mountains*
Weichsel	*Vistula*
Wien	*Vienna*

BAYERISCHES GASTHAUS

Dies ist ein Gasthaus in Dinkelsbühl, einem kleinen bayerischen Städtchen, das wegen seiner schönen, altertümlichen Häuser viel von Fremden besucht wird. Obwohl dieses Gasthaus kaum zu den altertümlichen Gebäuden gehört, passt es doch mit seinem hohen Giebel in den Rahmen der mittelalterlichen Stadt. (*Translation on page* 374)

das Gasthaus, ··-er	**wegen**	**altertümlich**	**der Fremde, -n**	**besuchen**	**obwohl**
inn	*on account of*	*ancient*	*stranger, tourist*	*to visit*	*although*

kaum	**das Gebäude, -**	**gehören**	**passen**	**der Giebel, -**	**der Rahmen, -**	**mittelalterlich**
hardly	*building*	*to belong*	*to fit*	*gable*	*frame*	*medieval*

24

DRITTE LEKTION: *THIRD LESSON*

Dies ist die Familie Lessing. Der Herr ist Herr Lessing, der Vater. Die Dame
dees ist dee fah-meel'-yĕ less'-sing. dayr herr ist herr less'-sing, dayr fah'-tĕr. dee dah'-mĕ
This is the Lessing family. The gentleman is Mr. Lessing, the father. The lady

ist Frau Lessing, die Mutter. Der junge Mann ist Herr Lessing junior, der Sohn.
ist frou less'-sing, dee moo'-tĕr. dayr yoong'-gĕ man ist herr less'-sing yoon'-yor, dayr zohn.
is Mrs. Lessing, the mother. The young man is Mr. Lessing junior, the son.

Die junge Dame ist Fräulein Lessing, die Tochter. Der Knabe ist Fritz, das
dee yoong'-gĕ dah'-mĕ ist froy'-līn less'-sing, dee toch'-tĕr. dayr knah'-bĕ ist frits, das
The young lady is Miss Lessing, the daughter. The boy is Fritz, the

Söhnchen. Das Mädchen ist Hilde, das Töchterchen. Herr Lessing ist ein Kaufmann.
záyn'-chĕn. das mayt'-chĕn ist hil'-dĕ, das tĕch'-tĕr-chĕn. herr less'-sing ist in kouf'-man.
little son. The girl is Hilda, the little daughter. Mr. Lessing is a business man.

Der junge Herr Lessing ist ein Student. Er studiert Medizin. Fräulein
dayr yoong'-gĕ herr less'-sing ist in shtoo-dent'. ayr shtoodeert' may-dee-tseen'. froy'-līn
Young Mr. Lessing is a student. He studies medicine. Miss

Lessing ist eine Studentin. Sie studiert moderne Sprachen. Fritz ist ein
less'-sing ist i'-nĕ shtoo-den'-tin. zee shtoo-deert' moh-der'-nĕ shprah'-chen. frits ist in
Lessing is a student. She studies modern languages. Fritz is a

Schüler. Hilde ist eine Schülerin. Sie lernen lesen, schreiben und rechnen.
shęę'-lĕr. hil'-dĕ ist i'-nĕ shęę'-lĕ-rin. zee ler'-nĕn lay'-zĕn, shri'-bĕn oont rech'-nĕn.
schoolboy. Hilda is a schoolgirl. They learn reading, writing and arithmetic.

ein Lehrer   **eine Lehrerin**
ĭn lāy'-rĕr   ī'-nĕ lāy'-rĕ-rin

**Herr Murdoch ist ein
Schotte** (sho'-tĕ)=*Scotsman.*

**Frau Murdoch ist eine
Schottin** (sho'-tin)=*Scotswoman.*

**Herr O'Connor ist ein
Ire** (ee'-rĕ)=*Irishman.*

**Frau O'Connor ist eine
Irin** (ɔe'-rin)=*Irishwoman.*

**Herr Griffiths ist ein
Walliser** (va-lee'-zĕr)=*Welshman.*

Frau Griffiths ist eine Walliserin
(va-lee'-zĕ-rin)=*Welshwoman.*

ein Kellner   **eine Kellnerin**
ĭn kel'-nĕr   ī'-nĕ kel'-nĕ-rin

MALE AND FEMALE

Der Lehrer=*the teacher* (man).

Die Lehrerin=*the teacher* (woman).

Der Kanadier=*the Canadian* (man).

Die Kanadierin=*the Canadian* (woman).

When you say in English *I am meeting a friend* you do not disclose whether it is a man or a woman you are meeting. Such ambiguity is rarely met in German. It is either **Freund** (froynt) or **Freundin** (froyn'-din); **Schüler** or **Schülerin**; **Engländer** or **Engländerin**; **Amerikaner** or **Amerikanerin**. Only the female counterpart to **Deutscher** does not take the ending **-in**; it is simply **Deutsche**.

ein Sänger   **eine Sängerin**
ĭn zɔng'-gĕr   ī'-nĕ zɔng'-gĕ-rin

Herr Jones ist ein Amerikaner (ah-may-ree-kah'-nĕr)=*American (man).*

Frau Jones ist eine Amerikanerin (ah-may-ree-kah'-nĕ-rin)=*American (woman).*

Herr Strauss ist ein Österreicher (āy'-stĕr-rīch-ĕr)=*Austrian (man).*

Frau Strauss ist eine Österreicherin (āy'-stĕr-rīch-ĕ-rin)=*Austrian (woman).*

Herr Steiner ist ein Schweizer (shvīts'-ĕr)=*Swiss (man)*

Frau Steiner ist eine Schweizerin (shvīts'-ĕ-rin)=*Swiss (woman).*

ein Spanier
in shpahn'-yĕr

eine Spanierin
ĭ'-nĕ shpahn'-yĕ-rin

ich bin ein Schotte
ich bin ĭn sho'-tĕ

Herr Schulz ist ein Deutscher. Auch Herr Lessing ist ein Deutscher. Frau Schulz ist eine
herr shōōlts ist ĭn doyt'-shĕr. ouch herr less'-sing ist ĭn doyt'-shĕr. frou shōōlts ist ĭ'-nĕ
Mr. Schulz is a German. Also Mr. Lessing is a German. Mrs. Schulz is a

Deutsche. Frau Lessing ist auch eine Deutsche. Ich bin ein Engländer. Sie sind ein Russe.
doyt'-shĕ. frou less'-sing ist ouch ĭ'-nĕ doyt'-shĕ. ich bin ĭn eng'-len-dĕr. zee zint ĭn rōō'-sĕ.
German. Mrs. Lessing is also a German.   I am an Englishman.   You are a Russian.

Was sind Sie, Herr Martino? Ich bin ein Italiener. Mein Freund, Herr Duval, ist ein
vas zint zee, herr martino? ich bin ĭn ee-tahl-yay'-nĕr. mīn froynt, herr dᴂ-val, ist ĭn
What are you, Mr. Martino? I am an Italian. My friend, Mr. Duval, is a

Franzose. Seine Frau ist eine Französin. Meine Freundin ist eine Kanadierin.
fran-tsoh'-sĕ. zī'-nĕ frou ist ĭ'-nĕ fran-tsᾱy'-zin. mī'-nĕ froyn'-din ist ĭ'-nĕ kah-nahd'-
Frenchman. His wife is a Frenchwoman. My lady friend is a Canadian woman.   [yĕ-rin.

ein Inder
in in'-dĕr

eine Inderin
ĭ'-nĕ in'-dĕ-rin

DIMINUTIVES

All nouns ending in **-chen** or **-lein** are neuter. Such words are called diminutives. **Ein Söhnchen**=*a little son;* **ein Töchterchen** =*a little daughter.*

One can add the endings **-chen** or **-lein** to almost every noun to form a diminutive; e.g.: **ein Buch**=*a book;* **ein Büchlein**=*a small book, booklet;* **ein Tischlein**=*a little table;* **ein Stühlchen**=*a little chair*, etc. (Compare English *lambkin, duckling, booklet,* etc.)

Note that when **-chen** or **-lein** is added, **a** usually changes to **ä, o** to **ö, u** to **ü** and **au**

die Katze	das Kätzchen	der Hund	das Hündchen
dee kat′-tsĕ	das kets′-chĕn	dayr hōont	das hĭnt′-chĕn

to **äu.** This modification is called **Umlaut** (pronounced ōōm′-lout).

Der Hund=*the dog;* **das Hündchen**=*the puppy;* **die Katze**=*the cat;* **das Kätzchen**= *the kitten;* **das Haus**=*the house;* **das Häuschen**=*the cottage.*

Whether **-chen** or **-lein** is added depends on whatever form is easier to pronounce. **-chen** is the more usual ending, but as it would be difficult to pronounce it after another **ch** the diminutive of **Buch** is invariably **Büchlein.**

You can also add **-chen** or **-lein** after proper names. **Hänslein** (hents′-lĭn) or **Hänschen** (hents′-chĕn) would be the endearing form for **Hans, Hildchen** for **Hilde,** etc. (Compare English *Jimmy, Tommy, Jackie, Rosie, Jenny,* etc.).

UMLAUT

a, o, u, or **au** with two dots on them are examples of **Umlaut.** The **Umlaut** changes the pronunciation of

a (*ah*) to **ä** (*a* as in *gate.* When ä is short it is like *e* in *get*).

o (*oh*) to **ö** (*ay* said with rounded lips: given in our imitated pronunciation as $\widehat{ay}$. When short, it is like *e* in *her,* shown in our system by ê).

u (*oo*) to **ü** (*ee* with rounded lips: given in our imitated pronunciation as $\widehat{ee}$. When short, it is like *i* with lips rounded, shown in our system by ĭ).

au (*ow* as in *how*) to **äu** (*oy* as in *joy*).

die Rose	das Röschen	das Haus	das Häuschen
dee roh′-zĕ	das rêz′-chĕn	das hous	das hoys′-chĕn

HOW TO TRANSLATE *A, AN* (THE INDEFINITE ARTICLE)

The indefinite article (*a, an*) is **ein** with masculine and neuter nouns, **eine** with feminines.

Masculine	Feminine	Neuter
ein Herr	eine Dame	ein Fräulein
ein Mann	eine Frau	ein Söhnchen
ein Sohn	eine Tochter	ein Töchterchen
ein Vater	eine Mutter	ein Mädchen
ein Student	eine Studentin	ein Kind
ein Schüler	eine Schülerin	ein Buch
ein Tisch	eine Lampe	ein Fenster

ein Glas	eine Tasse	ein Glas Wein	eine Tasse Kaffee
ĭn glas	ĭ'-nĕ ta'-sĕ	ĭn glas vĭn	ĭ'-nĕ ta'-sĕ ka'-fay

WAS KOSTET DER KOHL?

Kohl ist gesund und preiswert. Dieser Gemüsehändler sieht gewiss gut genährt aus und ist eine gute Reklame für seine Ware. *(Translation on page 374)*

der Kohl, -e	**gesund**	**preiswert**	**sieht ... aus**	**gut genährt**	**die Reklame, -n**	**die Ware, -n**
cabbage	*healthy*	*cheap*	*looks*	*well fed*	*advertisement*	*goods*

Herr Lessing raucht
        eine Zigarr⌒
herr less'-sing roucht
        ī'-nĕ tsee-gah'-rĕ

Seine Tochter raucht
        eine Zigarette
zī'-nĕ toch'-tĕr roucht
        ī'-nĕ tsee-gah-:e'-tĕ

EXERCISES

I   Read and Translate

Herr Lessing ist ein Mann. Frau Lessing ist eine Dame. Fräulein Lessing ist eine junge Dame. Fritz ist ein Knabe. Hilde ist ein Mädchen. Herr Schulz trinkt ein Glas Bier. Frau Schulz trinkt eine Tasse Kaffee. Herr Lessing raucht eine Zigarre. Frau Lessing raucht nicht. Fräulein Lessing raucht eine Zigarette. Raucht Fritz? Nein, er raucht nicht, er ist zu (tsōō = *too*) jung.

Wer ist der Vater? Herr Lessing ist der Vater. Wer ist der junge Herr? Er ist Herr Lessing junior. Wer ist ein Schüler? Fritz ist ein Schüler. Wer ist eine Studentin? Fräulein Lessing ist eine Studentin. Wer ist ein Schotte? Herr Murdoch ist ein Schotte. Wer sind Sie? Ich bin Herr Smith. Was sind Sie, Herr Smith? Ich bin ein Engländer. Sind Sie eine Engländerin, Frau O'Connor? Nein, ich bin eine Irin.

II   Answer in German

1. Was ist Herr Lessing? 2. Was ist Herr Lessing junior? 3. Was ist Fritz? 4. Was ist Hilde? 5. Was ist Fräulein Lessing? 6. Wer ist der Vater? 7. Wer ist eine Schülerin? 8. Wer ist ein Student? 9. Wer ist ein Engländer? 10. Wer ist eine Schottin? 11. Was ist der Sohn? 12. Was ist das Töchterchen? 13. Wer ist eine Studentin? 14. Wer ist ein Ire? 15. Wer ist eine Deutsche?

III   Supply the missing ein or eine

1. Herr Lessing ist ... Kaufmann. 2. Er ist ... Deutscher. 3. Er trinkt ... Glas Bier. 4. Das ist ... Bleistift. 5. Das ist ... Tür. 6. Hier sind ... Tisch und ... Stuhl. 7. Ich bin ... Engländer. 8. Sind Sie ... Deutsche? 9. Ist er ... Deutscher? 10. Fritz ist ... Schüler. 11. Fräulein Lessing ist ... Studentin. 12. Das ist ... Häuschen.

(*Answers on page* 355)

Sind Sie krank?
zint zee krank?

NUMERALS

elf	zwölf	dreizehn
elf	tsvĕlf	drī'-tsayn
eleven	*twelve*	*thirteen*
vierzehn	fünfzehn	sechzehn
feer'-tsayn	fĭnf'-tsayn	zech'-tsayn
fourteen	*fifteen*	*sixteen*

WO DIE ZEIT STILL STEHT

Hier ist der Marktplatz von Gengenbach, einem kleinen Städtchen im Schwarzwald mit schönen, alten Häusern. Ein Glockenturm erhebt sich über dem Stadttor am Ende des Marktplatzes, auf dem noch die langen Morgenschatten liegen. Charakteristisch für das Schwarzwaldhaus sind Fachwerk und hohe Giebel. Auto und Fahrrad passen schwer in das mittelalterliche Bild.

(*Translation on page* 374)

die Zeit,-en	der Glockenturm,¨-e	erheben	das Tor,-e	der Schatten,-	das Fachwerk,-e
time	*bell tower*	*to raise*	*gate*	*shadow*	*timber work*

VIERTE LEKTION: *FOURTH LESSON*

das Haus	**der Garten**	**die Strasse**
das hous	dayr gahr′-tĕn	dee shtrah′-sĕ

Dieses Haus ist klein.
dee′-zĕs hous ist klīn.
This house is small.

Dieser Garten ist gross.
dee′-zĕr gahr′-tĕn ist grohs.
This garden is large.

Diese Strasse ist lang.
dee′-zĕ shtrah′-sĕ ist lang.
This street is long.

Dieses Buch ist dick und schwer.
dee′-zĕs bōōch ist dick ōōnt shvayr.
This book is thick and heavy.

Der blaue Bleistift ist kurz.
dayr blou′-ĕ blī′-shtift ist kōōrts.
The blue pencil is short.

Das rote Buch ist dick.
das roh′-tĕ bōōch ist dick.
The red book is thick.

Das grüne Buch ist dünn.
das grēē′-nĕ bōōch ist dĭn.
The green book is thin.

HOW TO TRANSLATE *THIS*

Corresponding to the three German equivalents for *the*, there are three words for *this*: **dieser, diese, dieses.** They are used in connection with nouns, e.g., **dieser Stuhl** = *this chair;* **diese Frau** = *this woman;* **dieses Kind** = *this child.* For *this is* say **dies ist,** and for *that is* say **das ist,** no matter whether what follows is masculine, feminine or neuter, e.g.: **dies ist der Mann** = *this is the man;* **dies ist die Frau** = *this is the woman;* **das ist das Kind** = *that is the child.*

Masc.	Fem.	Neut.	
der	die	das	= *the*
dieser	diese	dieses	= *this*
er	sie	es	= *he, she, it*

Dieser Mann ist dick	**Diese Frau ist dünn**
dee′-zĕr man ist dick	dee′-zĕ frou ist dĭn

32

ENDINGS OF ADJECTIVES (I)

Dieser rote Bleistift ist gut.
This red pencil is good.

Der gute Bleistift ist rot.
The good pencil is red.

Die blaue Karte ist dick.
The blue card is thick.

Diese dicke Karte ist blau.
This thick card is blue.

Das dünne Buch ist grün.
The thin book is green.

Dieses grüne Buch ist dünn.
This green book is thin.

Dieser grosse Junge und dieses kleine Mädchen sind mein Neffe und meine Nichte.
This big boy and this little girl are my nephew and niece.

After **der, die, das,** or **dieser, diese, dieses** adjectives take the ending **-e.**

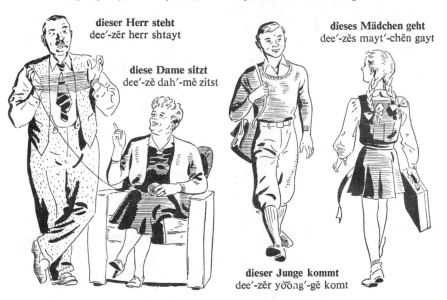

dieser Herr steht
dee′-zĕr herr shtayt

diese Dame sitzt
dee′-zĕ dah′-mĕ zitst

dieses Mädchen geht
dee′-zĕs mayt′-chĕn gayt

dieser Junge kommt
dee′-zĕr yōōng′-gĕ komt

Ich bin der Lehrer. Ich stehe. Sie sind der Schüler. Sie sitzen. Ich schreibe an
ich bin dayr lay′-rĕr. ich shtay′-hĕ. zee zint dayr shēē′-lĕr. zee zit′-tsĕn. ich shrī′-bĕ an
I am the teacher. I am standing. You are the student. You are sitting. I write on

die Tafel. Sie schreiben in das Heft. Schreibt dieser Junge? Nein, er schreibt nicht.
dee tah′-fĕl. zee shrī′-bĕn in das heft. shrīpt dee′-zĕr yōōng′-gĕ? nīn, ayr shrīpt nicht.
the blackboard. You write in the notebook. Is this boy writing? No, he is not writing.

Was tut er? Er spielt. Ich spiele Tennis. Herr Schulz spielt Billard. Hans
vas tōōt ayr? ayr shpeelt. ich shpee′-lĕ tennis. herr shōōlts shpeelt bil′-yahrt. hants
What is he doing? He is playing. I play tennis. Mr. Schulz plays billiards. Hans

spielt Fussball. Grete spielt Klavier. Was spielen Sie? Ich spiele Karten.
shpeelt fōōs′-bal. gray′-tĕ shpeelt klah-veer′. vas shpee′-lĕn zee? ich shpee′-lĕ kahr′-tĕn.
plays football. Grete plays the piano. What are you playing? I am playing cards.

Der Kellner bringt das Bier und die Milch
dayr kel′-nĕr bringt das beer o͝ont dee milch

Ich trinke Bier. Sie trinken Milch.
ich tring′-kĕ beer. zee tring′-kĕn milch.
I drink beer. You drink milk.

Kellner, bringen Sie das Bier für mich?
kel′-nĕr, bring′-gĕn zee das beer fe͡er mich?
Waiter, are you bringing the beer for me?

Ja, es ist für Sie, mein Herr. Die Milch ist
yah, es ist fe͡er zee, mīn herr. dee milch ist
Yes, it is for you, sir. The milk is

für das Kind. Danke, das ist richtig.
fe͡er das kint. dang′-kĕ, das ist rich′-tich.
for the child. Thanks, that is correct.

VERBS IN THE PRESENT TENSE

I		*You*		*He, She, It*			
ich	**komme**	Sie	**kommen**	er, sie, es	**kommt**	=	*come(s)*
	gehe		**gehen**		**geht**	=	*go(es)*
	sitze		**sitzen**		**sitzt**	=	*sit(s)*
	stehe		**stehen**		**steht**	=	*stand(s)*
	spiele		**spielen**		**spielt**	=	*play(s)*
	trinke		**trinken**		**trinkt**	=	*drink(s)*
	rauche		**rauchen**		**raucht**	=	*smoke(s)*
	bringe		**bringen**		**bringt**	=	*bring(s)*

Verbs used in connection with **ich** end in **-e;** those used with **Sie** (*you*) end in **-en;** those expressing what *he*, *she* or *it* is doing end in **-t.**

Exceptions to this rule are the following : **ich bin**=*I am;* **Sie sind**=*you are.*

Rauchen Sie?
rou′-chĕn zee?

Nein, danke, ich bin
nīn, dang′-kĕ, ich bin

Nichtraucherin.
nicht′-rou-chĕr-rin.

THIS AND THAT

Dieser Herr ist ein Lehrer.	**Jener Herr ist ein Kaufmann.**
dee′-zĕr herr ist in lay′-rĕr.	yay′-nĕr herr ist in kouf′-man.
This man is a teacher.	*That man is a business man.*
Diese Frau ist eine Lehrerin.	**Jene Frau ist eine Hausfrau.**
dee′-zĕ frou ist ī′-nĕ lay′-rĕ-rin.	yay′-nĕ frou ist ī′-nĕ hous′-frou.
This woman is a teacher.	*That woman is a housewife.*
Dieses Kind ist ein Knabe.	**Jenes Kind ist ein Mädchen.**
dee′-zĕs kint ist in knah′-bĕ.	yay′-nĕs kint ist in mayt′-chĕn.
This child is a boy.	*That child is a girl.*

Corresponding to the three German forms for *this* (**dieser, diese, dieses**) there are three words for *that*: **jener, jene, jenes**. Like **dieser, diese, dieses** they are used in connection with nouns, e.g., **jener Tisch**=*that table:* **jene Tür**=*that door:* **jenes Buch**=*that book.*

CAFÉTERRASSE AUF DEM KURFÜRSTENDAMM, BERLIN

Man trägt zwar noch den Wintermantel, sitzt aber schon auf der Caféterrasse, um den ersten Frühjahrssonnenschein zu geniessen.   *(Translation on page 374)*

tragen	**zwar**	**der Mantel, ···-**	**schon**	**das Frühjahr, -e**	**der Sonnenschein**	**geniessen**
to wear	*it is true*	*overcoat*	*already*	*spring*	*sunshine*	*to enjoy*

Sehen Sie diese Frau? Ist sie nicht schön? Welche Frau meinen Sie, die blonde oder
zay'-ĕn zee dee'-zĕ frou? ist zee nicht shāÿn? vel'-chĕ frou mī'-nĕn zee, dee blon'-dĕ oh'-dĕr

die schwarze? Die blonde. Ja, die blonde ist schön, aber die schwarze ist hässlich.
dee shvar'-tsĕ? dee blon'-dĕ. yah, dee blon'-de ist shāÿn, ah'-bĕr dee shvar'-tsĕ ist hes'-lich.

sehen = *to see*; schön = *beautiful*; meinen = *to mean*; schwarz = *dark*; hässlich = *ugly*.

WHICH?

Welcher Herr ist Herr Schulz? Der grosse, dicke. Welche Dame ist Frau Lessing?
vel'-chĕr herr ist herr shōŏlts? dayr groh'-sĕ, di'-kĕ. vel'-chĕ dah'-mĕ ist frou less'-sing?
Which man is Mr. Schulz? The tall stout one. Which lady is Mrs. Lessing?

Die kleine, dicke. Welches Haus ist älter, das grosse oder das kleine?
dee klī'-ne, di'-kĕ. vel'-chĕs hous ist el'-tĕr, das groh'-sĕ oh'-dĕr das klī'-nĕ?
The small stout one. Which house is older, the big one or the small one?

Dieses schöne, kleine Haus ist älter als jenes hässliche, grosse.
dee'-zĕs shāÿ-nĕ, klī'-nĕ hous ist el'-tĕr als yay'-nĕs hes'-li-chĕ, groh'-sĕ.
This beautiful little house is older than that ugly big one.

Welcher Stuhl, dieser oder jener? = *Which chair, this one or that one?* **Welche Tür, diese**
oder jene? = *Which door, this one or that one?* **Welches Fenster, dieses oder jenes?** = *Which*
window, this one or that one?

Welcher, welche, welches are the three German words for *which*, corresponding to the
three for *this* (**dieser, diese, dieses**) and the three for *that* (**jener, jene, jenes**).

Ich gehe in ein Café, eine Tasse Kaffee trinken. Kommen Sie mit? Hier ist ein Café.
ich gay'-ĕ in īn ka-fay', ī'-nĕ ta'-sĕ ka'-fay tring'-kĕn. ko'-mĕn zee mit? heer ist īn ka-fay'.
I am going to a café to drink a cup of coffee. Are you coming with me? Here is a café.

Kennen Sie dieses Café? Ja, ich kenne es gut. Der Kaffee ist sehr gut und auch
ke'-nĕn zee dee'-zĕs ka-fay'? yah, ich ke'-nĕ es gōōt. dayr ka'-fay ist zayr gōōt ōōnt ouch
Do you know this café? Yes, I know it well. The coffee is very good and also

der Kuchen ist nicht schlecht. Gehen wir hinein. Da ist ein Tisch frei.
dayr kōō'-chen ist nicht shlecht. gay'-ĕn veer hi-nīn'. dah ist īn tish frī.
the cake is not bad. Let us go in. There is a table free.

Note:—(1). There is a difference in both spelling and pronunciation between **der Kaffee**
(ka'-fay), *coffee*, and **das Café** (ka-fay'), *café*.

(2). There is no difference in German between *good* and *well*. Both are rendered by **gut,**
e.g.: **Der Kaffee ist gut** = *the coffee is good;* **ich kenne ihn gut** = *I know him well.*

(3). In **Kommen Sie mit?** (*Are you coming with me?*) *me* is not translated. Similarly **ich**
komme mit = *I am coming with you;* **er kommt mit** = *he is coming with me* (or *us*); **essen Sie**
mit? = *will you eat with us?* etc.

NUMERALS

sechzehn	**siebzehn**	**achtzehn**	**neunzehn**	**zwanzig**
zech'-tsayn	zeep'-tsayn	acht'-tsayn	noyn'-tsayn	tsvan'-tsich
sixteen	*seventeen*	*eighteen*	*nineteen*	*twenty*

EXERCISES

I Read and Translate

Ist dieser Garten gross? Nein, er ist
klein. Ist diese Strasse lang? Nein, sie ist
kurz. Ist das rote Buch dick oder dünn?
Es ist dünn. Ist der dicke Mann gross?
Nein, er ist klein. Welcher Bleistift ist lang,
der gelbe oder der blaue? Welches Buch ist
dick, das rote oder das grüne? Welche
Strasse ist schön, die lange oder die kurze?
Wie[1] ist Fräulein Lessing, dick oder dünn?
Sie ist dünn. Dieser Herr trinkt Bier. Jener
Herr trinkt Wein. Diese Dame spielt
Klavier, jene Dame spielt Karten. Dieser
Herr raucht eine Zigarre, jener Herr raucht
eine Zigarette. Dieses Kind ist ein Knabe,
jenes ist ein Mädchen.

Welche Frau ist schön, die blonde oder
die schwarze? Die blonde ist schön, aber
die schwarze ist hässlich. Meinen (*think*)
Sie nicht auch?

II Complete by adding one of the three endings: -er, -e, -es

1. Dies- Glas ist gross. Jen- Glas ist klein.
2. Dies- Strasse ist lang. Jen- Strasse ist
kurz. 3. Welch- Herr ist d- Lehrer, dies-
oder jen-? 4. Welch- Dame ist die Lehrerin,
dies- oder jen-? 5. Welch- Kind ist das
Söhnchen von Frau Schulz, dies- oder jen-?
6. Wer ist dies- Frau? 7. Ist dies- Garten
gross? 8. Ist jen- kleine Knabe der Sohn
von Frau Lessing? 9. Ist jen- kleine Mädchen ihr (*her*) Töchterchen? 10. Dies- Mann
ist ein Lehrer.

III Answer in German

1. Wer ist gross? 2. Wer ist klein und
dick? 3. Wer ist dünn? 4. Was ist lang?
5. Was ist kurz? 6. Was ist gut? 7. Wie ist
Herr Schulz? 8. Wie ist Frau Lessing?
9. Welcher Herr ist gross und dick? 10.
Welche Dame ist dünn?

(*Answers on page 356*)

---

[1] **Wie** means *how* or *what is ... like?*

NACH SCHWERER ARBEIT SCHMECKT DAS ESSEN UMSO BESSER

Diese Aufnahme stammt aus dem Berner Oberland in der Schweiz. Die Bauernfamilie nimmt das Mittagessen gemeinsam mit den Landarbeitern ein. Es scheint ihnen gut zu schmecken, weil sie in den Feldern und auf den Bergabhängen seit dem frühen Morgen gearbeitet haben.

(*Translation on page* 374)

schwer	**schmecken**	**das Essen**	**umso besser**	**die Aufnahme, -n**	**stammen**
hard, heavy	*to taste*	*meal*	*all the better*	*photograph*	*to originate*
die Bauernfamilie	**nimmt . . . ein**		**gemeinsam**	**scheinen**	**der Bergabhang, ¨-e**
farmer's family	*takes in, has (a meal)*		*together*	*to seem*	*hillside*

FÜNFTE LEKTION : *FIFTH LESSON*

| **der Apfel** | **die Birne** | **die Banane** |
| dayr ap′-fĕl | dee bir′-nĕ | dee ba-nah′-nĕ |

Ich esse Brot mit Butter und Käse. Wir essen Fleisch mit Gemüse oder Salat.
ich e′-sĕ broht mit bŏŏ′-tĕr ŏŏnt kay′-zĕ. veer e′-sĕn flīsh mit gĕ-mǖ′-zĕ oh′-dĕr zah-laht′.
I eat bread with butter and cheese. We eat meat with vegetables or salad.

Herr Schulz isst viel Fleisch. Er ist dick. Fräulein Lessing isst kein Fleisch.
herr shŏŏlts ist feel flīsh. ayr ist dick. froy′-līn less′-sing ist kīn flīsh.
Mr. Schulz eats a lot of meat. He is stout. Miss Lessing does not eat meat.

Sie ist Vegetarierin. Sie isst viel Obst und Gemüse. Hans isst Birnen und
zee ist vay-gĕ-tahr′-yĕ-rin. zee ist feel ohpst ŏŏnt gĕ-mǖ′-zĕ. hants ist bir′-nĕn ŏŏnt
She is a vegetarian. She eats lots of fruit and vegetables. Hans eats pears and

Bananen. Er isst keine Äpfel. Herr Lessing isst Wurst. Er ist nicht Vegetarier.
ba-nah′-nĕn. ayr ist kī′-nĕ ep′-fĕl. herr less′-sing ist vŏŏrst. ayr ist nicht vay-gĕ-tahr′-yĕr.
bananas. He doesn't eat apples. Mr. Lessing eats sausage. He is not a vegetarian.

THE NEGATIVE
(*Continued from Lesson* 2)

Ich rauche nicht.   **Sie trinkt kein Bier.**   **Es regnet nicht.**
I don't smoke.   *She doesn't drink beer.*   *It is not raining.*

Es ist kein Stuhl frei.   **Ich rauche keine englische**
There is no vacant chair.   *I am not smoking an English*

Zigarette, ich rauche eine amerikanische.
cigarette, I am smoking an American one.

Ich habe kein Geld
ich hah′-bĕ kīn gelt

If the verb or an adjective is put in the negative, *not* is translated by **nicht**. If a noun is negatived you must use **kein** or **keine** (=*no* or *not a*), which is used like **ein**, e.g.:

ein Tisch=*a table*   **kein Tisch**=*no table*
eine Frau=*a woman*   **keine Frau**=*no woman*
ein Buch=*a book*   **kein Buch**=*no book*

39

Ich trinke Kaffee mit Milch und Zucker. Ich trinke Tee mit Milch, aber ohne
ich tring'-kĕ ka'-fay mit milch ōont tsōō'-kĕr.   ich tring'-kĕ tay mit milch, ah'-bĕr oh'-nĕ
I drink coffee with milk and sugar.   I drink tea with milk, but without

Zucker. Die Deutschen trinken Tee ohne Milch, aber manchmal mit Zitrone.
tsōō'-kĕr. c̆ee doyt'-shĕn tring'-kĕn tay oh'-nĕ milch, ah'-bĕr manch'-mahl mit tsee-troh'-nĕ
sugar. The Germans drink tea without milk, but sometimes with lemon.

Trinken sie viel Tee? Nein, sie trinken wenig Tee, aber sie trinken viel Kaffee.
tring'-kĕn zee feel tay?   nīn, zee tring'-kĕn vay'-nich tay, ah'-bĕr zee tring'-kĕn feel ka'-fay.
Do they drink much tea?   No, they drink little tea, but they drink much coffee.

Nehmen Sie viel Zucker? Ich nehme wenig Zucker, nur ein Stück. Meine Frau
nay'-mĕn zee feel tsōō'-kĕr?   ich nay'-mĕ vay'-nich tsōō'-kĕr, nōōr īn shtĭk.   mī'-nĕ frou
Do you take much sugar?   I take little sugar, only one lump.   My wife

trinkt Tee mit viel Zucker. Sie nimmt drei Stück[1] Zucker.
trinkt tay mit feel tsōō'-kĕr.   zee nimt drī shtĭk tsōō'-kĕr.
drinks tea with lots of sugar.   She takes three lumps of sugar.

Die Kinder trinken Kakao mit viel Milch und Zucker.
dee kin'-dĕr tring'-kĕn kak-ah'-oh mit feel milch ɔ̄ont ts ɔ̄ō'-kĕr.
The children drink cocoa with lots of milk and sugar.

Sie trinken auch warme, frische Milch.
zee tring'-kĕn ouch vahr'-mĕ, fri'-shĕ milch.   **die Zähne**
They drink also warm fresh milk.   dee tsay'-nĕ

Zucker schmeckt süss. Kaffee ohne Zucker schmeckt bitter. Zitronen schmecken
tsōō'-kĕr shmekt zẽ̃s.   ka'-fay oh'-nĕ tsōō'-kĕr shmekt bi'-tĕr.   tsee-troh'-nĕn shme'-kĕn
Sugar tastes sweet.   Coffee without sugar tastes bitter.   Lemons taste

sauer. Fritz isst gern Schokolade. Schokolade ist sehr süss. Grete isst gern
zou'-ĕr.   frits ist gern shoh-koh-lah'-dĕ.   shoh-koh-lah'-dĕ ist zayr zẽ̃s.   gray'-tĕ ist gern
sour.   Fritz likes eating chocolate.   Chocolate is very sweet.   Grete likes eating

Bonbons. Es ist nicht gut für die Zähne, viele Bonbons zu essen. Essen Sie gern
bong-bongs'.   es ist nicht gōōt fẽr dee tsay'-nĕ, fee'-lĕ bong-bongs' tsōō e'-sĕn.   e'-sĕn zee
sweets.   It is not good for the teeth to eat lots of sweets.   Do you like eating   [gern

Äpfel? Ja, ich esse Äpfel sehr gern. Sie sind nicht zu süss.
ep'-fĕl?   yah, ich e'-sĕ ep'-fĕl zayr gern.   zee zint nicht tsōō zẽ̃s.
apples?   Yes, I like eating apples very much.   They are not too sweet.

TO *LIKE* DOING SOMETHING

Ich esse gern Äpfel.	**Gern** is an adverb meaning *gladly*. To say
I like eating apples.	that you like doing something, you have to
Ich trinke gern Rotwein.	say that you do it gladly. A word for word
I like drinking red wine.	translation of the examples given above is:
Er raucht gern türkische Zigaretten.	*I eat gladly apples; I drink gladly red wine;*
He likes smoking Turkish cigarettes.	*he smokes gladly Turkish cigarettes.*

---

[1] After cardinal numbers **Stück** is not put into the plural. This applies to all words (excep̆t
feminine nouns in -e) denoting measurements or quantity, e.g. : **zwei Pfund Äpfel** = *two pounds of
apples ;* **zwanzig Mark** = *twenty marks ;* **dreissig Meter von hier** = *thirty metres from here.* But
zehn Flaschen Bier = *ten bottles of beer ;* **zwei Tassen Tee** = *two cups of tea.*

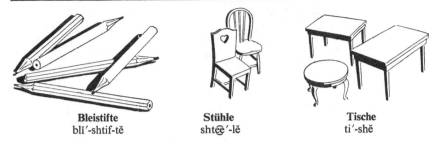

Bleistifte	**Stühle**	**Tische**
blī′-shtif-tĕ	shtēē′-lĕ	tī′-shĕ

Dies ist ein Bleistift. Dies sind zwei Bleistifte. Das ist eine Feder. Das sind drei Federn.
dees ist īn blī′-shtift. dees zint tsvī blī′- shtif-tĕ. das ist ī′-nĕ fay′-dĕr. das zint drī fay′-dĕrn.
This is a pencil These are two pencils. That is a pen. Those are three pens.

Hier ist ein Ei. Hier sind vier Eier. Da ist ein Glas. Da sind Gläser und Tassen. Ich
heer ist īn ī. heer zint feer ī′-ĕr. dah ist īn glas. dah zint glay′- zĕɪ ōōnt tas′-sĕn. ich
Here is an egg. Here are four eggs. There is a glass. There are glasses and cups. I

Federn	**Tassen**	**Türen**
fay′-dĕrn	tas′-sĕn	tēē′-rĕn

habe drei Bleistifte und zwei Federn. Wie viele Bücher haben Sie? Ich habe
hah′-bĕ drī blī′ -shtif-tĕ ōōnt tsvī- fay′-dĕrn. vee fee-lĕ bēē′-chĕr hah′-bĕn zee? ich hah′-bĕ
have three pencils and two pens. How many books have you? I have

vier. Herr und Frau Lessing haben vier Kinder, zwei Söhne und zwei Töchter.
feer. herr ōōnt frou less′-sing hah′-bĕn feer kin′-dĕr, tsvī zȳ′-nĕ ōōnt tsvī tĕch′-tĕr.
four. Mr. and Mrs. Lessing have four children, two sons and two daughters.

Sie essen gern Äpfel, Birnen, Pflaumen und andere Früchte.
zee e′-sĕn gern ep′-fĕl, bir′-nĕn, pflou′-mĕn ōōnt an′-dĕ-rĕ frēēch′-tĕ.
They like eating apples, pears, plums and other fruits.

Bücher	**Gläser**	**Häuser**
bēē′-chĕr	glay′-zĕr	hoy′-zĕr

VERBS IN THE PLURAL

wir kommen = *we are coming; we come*
wir bringen = *we are bringing; we bring*
wir rauchen = *we are smoking; we smoke*
sie essen = *they are eating; they eat*
sie trinken = *they are drinking; they drink*
sie spielen = *they are playing; they play*

Verbs used in connection with **wir** (*we*) and **sie** (*they*) end in **-en**. The endings for both singular and plural are:

$$
\begin{array}{lll}
I = \text{ich} & -e & we = \text{wir} \\
he = \text{er} & & you = \text{Sie} \\
she = \text{sie} & -t & they = \text{sie} \\
it = \text{es} & &
\end{array}
\quad \text{-en}
$$

Note:—*She, you* and *they* are all sounded alike. **Sie**, meaning *you*, is always spelt with a capital. To know whether **sie** means *she* or *they*, you have to look at the verb which follows. If it ends in **-t**, **sie** means *she*; if it ends in **-en**, **sie** means *they*.

sie nimmt = *she is taking; she takes*
Sie nehmen = *you are taking; you take*
sie nehmen = *they are taking; they take*

PLURAL OF NOUNS

There are three main rules for the formation of the plural of nouns in German:

(1) Most masculine and neuter nouns add **-e** to the singular. The masculines modify **a, o. u** and **au**; the neuters do not, e.g.:

der Tisch, die Tische = *table(s)*
der Stuhl, die Stühle = *chair(s)*
der Gast, die Gäste = *guest(s)*
der Rock, die Röcke = *skirt(s)*
der Zaun, die Zäune = *fence(s)*
das Jahr, die Jahre = *year(s)*
das Haar, die Haare = *hair(s)*
das Bein, die Beine = *leg(s)*

(2) Most feminine nouns add **-n** or **-en** to the singular, e.g.:

die Dame, die Damen = *lady (ladies)*
die Lampe, die Lampen = *lamp(s)*
die Strasse, die Strassen = *street(s)*
die Feder, die Federn = *pen(s)*
die Frau, die Frauen = *woman (women)*
die Tür, die Türen = *door(s)*
die Uhr, die Uhren = *watch(es)*

Die Herren spielen Karten
dee herr'-rĕn shpee'-lĕn kahr'-tĕn

Die Damen spielen Tennis
dee dah'-mĕn shpee'-lĕn ten'-nis

Hunde, Katzen und Pferde
ho͞on'-dĕ, kat'-tsĕn o͞ont pfayr'-dĕ

(3) Masculine and neuter nouns ending in **-el, -er,** or **-en** (also diminutives ending in **-chen** or **-lein**) take no additional ending, e.g.:

der Vater, die Väter	= *father(s)*
der Garten, die Gärten	= *garden(s)*
der Löffel, die Löffel	= *spoon(s)*
das Mädchen, die Mädchen	= *girl(s)*
das Messer, die Messer	= *knife (knives)*
das Fenster, die Fenster	= *window(s)*

Most German nouns form their plurals according to these rules. There are, however, many exceptions, e.g.:

Masculines adding -e, but not modifying

der Tag, die Tage	= *day(s)*
der Arm, die Arme	= *arm(s)*
der Hund, die Hunde	= *dog(s)*
der Schuh, die Schuhe	= *shoe(s)*

Masculines adding -en or -n

der Herr, die Herren	= *gentleman(men)*
der Soldat, die Soldaten	= *soldier(s)*
der Bär, die Bären	= *bear(s)*
der Löwe, die Löwen	= *lion(s)*
der Knabe, die Knaben ⎫ der Junge, die Jungen ⎬	= *boy(s)*
der Buchstabe, die Buchstaben	= *letter(s) of alphabet*
der Student, die Studenten	= *student(s)*
der Ochse, die Ochsen	= *ox(en)*

and all other masculines ending in **-e**.

Feminines adding ¨-e

die Kuh, die Kühe	= *cow(s)*
die Hand, die Hände	= *hand(s)*
die Stadt, die Städte	= *town(s)*

and some other feminines of one syllable.

Neuters adding -n or -en

das Auge, die Augen	= *eye(s)*
das Ohr, die Ohren	= *ear(s)*
das Bett, die Betten	= *bed(s)*
das Hemd, die Hemden	= *shirt(s)*

These four are the only nouns in this group.

Nouns adding ¨-er

das Buch, die Bücher	= *book(s)*
das Dach, die Dächer	= *roof(s)*
das Haus, die Häuser	= *house(s)*
das Kind, die Kinder	= *child (-ren)*

and some more neuters of one syllable.

There are only a few masculines in this group, e.g.:

der Mann, die Männer	= *man (men)*
der Wald, die Wälder	= *wood(s)*
der Wurm, die Würmer	= *worm(s)*

There are only two feminines with plurals ending in ¨-er:

die Mutter, die Mütter	= *mother(s)*
die Tochter, die Töchter	= *daughter(s)*

Note:—As we have already seen in Lesson 1, *the* in the plural is **die**.

NUMERALS—*(continued)*

21	einundzwanzig	ĭn'-ōōnt-tsvan-tsich		90	neunzig	noyn'-tsich
22	zweiundzwanzig	tsvī'-ōōnt-tsvan-tsich		100	hundert	hōōn'-dert
23	dreiundzwanzig	drī'-ōōnt-tsvan-tsich		101	hunderteins	hōōn'-dert-'ĭnts
24	vierundzwanzig	feer'-ōōnt-tsvan-tsich		200	zweihundert	tsvī'-hōōn-dert
30	dreissig	drī'-sich		1000	tausend	tou'-zent
40	vierzig	feer'-tsich		2000	zweitausend	tsvī'-tou-zent
50	fünfzig	fĭnf'-tsich		10 000	zehntausend	tsayn'-tou-zent
60	sechzig	zech'-tsich		100 000	hundert-	hōōn'-dert-tou-zent
70	siebzig	zeep'-tsich			tausend	
80	achtzig	acht'-tsich		1 000 000	eine Million	ī'-nĕ mil-yohn'

1960 **eintausendneunhundertundsechzig**
ĭn'-tou-zent-noyn-hōōn'-dert-ōōnt-zech-tsich

For numbers up to 20 see Lessons 1—4 (pages 15, 21, 30, 37)

Ober, die Rechnung, bitte
oh'-bĕr, dee rech'-nōōng, bi'-tĕ

EXERCISES

I Read and Translate

Was trinken Sie? Ich nehme eine Tasse Kaffee. Mit Milch oder ohne Milch? Mit viel Milch, bitte. Nehmen Sie Zucker? Zwei Stück, bitte. Was essen Sie? Fleisch mit Salat, bitte. Ober, zwei Tassen Kaffee, bitte. Eine Tasse ohne Milch und eine mit viel Milch. Eine Portion Fleisch mit Salat, und für mich ein Butterbrot (= *slice of bread and butter*) mit Käse.

II Answer in German

1. Trinken Sie Milch? 2. Trinken Sie viel Tee? 3. Trinken Sie Kaffee mit Milch und Zucker? 4. Wer isst viel Fleisch? 5. Essen Sie viel Fleisch? 6. Sind Sie Vegetarier? 7. Was essen Sie gern? 8. Trinken Sie gern Bier? 9. Rauchen Sie viel? 10. Schmeckt Milch mit Zucker gut? 11. Wie schmeckt Kaffee ohne Zucker? 12. Wie schmeckt Schokolade? 13. Ⱳ'as schmeckt sauer? 14. Essen Sie gern Oʋst? 15. Haben Sie viele Bücher? 16. Wie viele Bücher haben Sie? 17. Wie viele Kinder haben Herr und Frau Lessing? 18. Trinken Sie gern Kaffee? 19. Wieviel Stück Zucker nehmen Sie? 20. Nehmen Sie viel Milch?

III Give (a) the definite article and (b) the plural of

1. Tür. 2. Glas. 3. Fenster. 4. Tasse. 5. Sohn. 6. Tochter. 7. Buch. 8. Feder. 9. Zigarette. 10. Stuhl. 11. Haus. 12. Baum. 13. Garten. 14. Strasse.

(Answers on page 356)

TWO SIMPLE PROVERBS

In der Nacht sind alle Katzen grau.
In the night all cats are grey.

Es is nicht alles Gold was glänzt.
All is not gold that glitters.

A proverb = **ein Sprichwort;** *the proverbs =* **die Sprichwörter.**

SECHSTE LEKTION : *SIXTH LESSON*

eine Tasche
ī'-nĕ ta'-shĕ

eine Handtasche
ī'-nĕ hant'-ta-shĕ

Die Bilder auf Seiten 46 und 48 zeigen uns verschiedene Kleidungsstücke; sowohl
dee bil'-dĕr ouf zī'-ten 46 ōont 48 tsī'-gĕn ōons fer-shee'-dĕ-nĕ klī'-dōongs-stĭ'-kĕ; zoh-
The pictures on pages 46 and 48 show us various articles of clothing; [vohl'

Damenkleidung als auch Herrenkleidung. Ich habe vier Anzüge, drei Paar
dah'-mĕn-klī'-dōong als ouch her'-rĕn-klī'-dōong. ich hab'-bĕ feer an'-tsǣ-gĕ, drī pahr
women's clothing as well as men's clothing. I have four suits, three pairs

Schuhe und zwei Mäntel. Meine Frau hat viele Kleider, ein Kostüm und auch zwei
shōo'-ĕ ōont tsvī men'-tĕl. mī'-nĕ frou hat fee'-lĕ klī'-dĕr, īn kos-tēm' ōont ouch tsvī
of shoes and two overcoats. My wife has many dresses, one suit and also two

Mäntel. Ihr Sommermantel ist hell; der Wintermantel ist dunkel. Mein Hut ist blau,
men'-tĕl. eer zo'-mĕr-man-tĕl ist hel; dayr vin'-tĕr-man-tĕl ist dōong'-kĕl. mīn hōot ist blou,
coats. Her summer coat is light; the winter coat is dark. My hat is blue,

meine Krawatte ist rot. Meine Schuhe sind schwarz, und
mī'-nĕ krah-va'-tĕ ist roht. mī'-nĕ shōo'-ĕ zint shvarts, ōont
my tie is red. My shoes are black, and

meine Socken sind grau. Ihr Kleid ist grün. Ihre Handtasche
mī'-nĕ zo'-kĕn zint grou. eer klīt ist grǣn. ee'-rĕ hant'-ta-shĕ
my socks are grey. Your dress is green. Your handbag

ist braun. Wie sind Ihre Schuhe, weiss oder grau? Sie sind weiss.
ist broun. vee zint ee'-rĕ shōo'-ĕ, vīs oh'-dĕr grou? zee zint vīs.
is brown. What colour are your shoes, white or grey? They are white.

Dies ist Karls Anzug. Sein Anzug ist blau. Seine Hose
dees ist kahrls an'-tsōok. zīn an'-tsōok ist blou. zī'-nĕ hoh'-zĕ
This is Karl's suit. His suit is blue. His trousers

ist ein wenig zu lang. Seine Jacke ist zu kurz. Dies ist
ist īn vay'-nich tsōo lang. zī'-nĕ ya'-kĕ ist tsōo kōorts. dees ist
are a little too long. His jacket is too short. This is

Karls Anzug
kahrls an'-tsōok

Annas Kostüm. Ihre Bluse ist hellgrün; ihr Rock und ihre Jacke sind dunkelblau.
a'-nahs kos-tēm'. ee'-rĕ blōo'-zĕ ist hel-'grǣn; eer rock ōont ee'-rĕ ya'-kĕ zint dōong'-kĕl-
Anna's suit. Her blouse is light green; her skirt and jacket are dark blue. [blou.

Wir sind Engländer. Wir wohnen in Südengland. Unser Haus ist sehr alt. Wir
veer zint eng'-len-dĕr. veer voh'-nĕn in zǣt'-eng-lant. ōon'-zĕr hous ist zayr alt. veer
We are English. We live in Southern England. Our house is very old. We

HERRENKLEIDUNG—MEN'S CLOTHING
(English key on page 367)

der Anzug, ⸚-e

1. der Kragen, -
2. die Jacke, -n
3. der Aufschlag, ⸚-e
4. der Ärmel, -
5. die Weste, -n
6. die Hose, -n

die Reitkleidung

1. die Sportjacke, -n
2. die Tasche, -n
3. die Brusttasche, -n
4. die Reitpeitsche, -n
5. die Reithose, -n
6. der Reitstiefel, -

der Smoking, -s

Zum Smoking trägt man eine schwarze Krawatte

der Frack, ⸚-e

Zum Frack trägt man immer eine weisse Krawatte

der Mantel, ⸚-

Dieser Mann trägt einen Mantel ohne Gürtel

die Krawatte, -n

Dies ist eine gestreifte Krawatte

das Halstuch, ⸚-er

Dies ist ein wollenes Halstuch

der Regenmantel, ⸚-

Dieser Mann trägt einen Regenmantel mit Gürtel

haben auch eine kleine Villa in Südfrankreich. Unsere Villa ist neu. Schulzes
hah'-běn ouch ī'-ně klī'-ně vil'-lah in zē̠ēt-frank'-rīch. ōōn'-zě-rě vil'-lah ist noy. shōōl'-tsĕs
have also a small villa in the South of France. Our villa is new. The Schulzes

sind Deutsche. Sie wohnen in Hamburg. Sie haben kein Haus; sie haben eine
zint doyt'-shĕ. zee voh'-nĕn in ham'-bŏŏrk. zee hah'-bĕn kīn hous; zee hah'-bĕn ī'-ně
are Germans. They live in Hamburg. They have no house; they have a

Wohnung. Ihre Wohnung hat drei Zimmer, eine Küche und ein Badezimmer.
voh'-nŏŏng. ee'-rě voh'-nŏŏng hat drī tsi'-měr, ī'-ně kĮ'-chě ōōnt īn bah'-dě-tsi'-měr.
flat. Their flat has three rooms, a kitchen and a bathroom.

seine Eltern (unsere Grosseltern)   ihre Eltern (unsere Grosseltern)

sein Vater (unser Grossvater)   ihr Vater (unser Grossvater)

seine Mutter (unsere Grossmutter)   ihre Mutter (unsere Grossmutter)

unser Vater   Hier sind unsere Eltern   unsere Mutter

Hier bin ich. Ich bin ein Knabe   Hier ist meine Schwester. Sie ist ein Mädchen

Die Familie Schulz wohnt in Hamburg. Die Familie Lessing wohnt in Berlin.
dee fah-meel'-yĕ shōōlts vohnt in ham'-bŏŏrk. dee fah-meel'-yĕ less'-sing vohnt in ber-leen'.
The Schulz family lives in Hamburg. The Lessing family lives in Berlin.

Herr Schulz ist der Bruder von Frau Lessing. Frau Lessing ist die Tante von Hans
herr shōōlts ist dayr brōō'-děr fon frou less'-sing. frou less'-sing ist dee tan'-tě fon hants
Mr. Schulz is the brother of Mrs. Lessing. Mrs. Lessing is the aunt of Hans

und Grete. Herr Lessing ist ihr Onkel. Herr Schulz ist der Onkel von Fritz und
ōōnt gray'-tě. herr less'-sing ist eer ong'-kěl. herr shōōlts ist dayr ong'-kěl fon frits ōōnt
and Grete. Mr. Lessing is their uncle. Mr. Schulz is the uncle of Fritz and

Hilde. Frau Schulz ist ihre Tante. Fritz ist ein Vetter von Hans; Hilde ist seine
hil'-dě. frou shōōlts ist ee'-rě tan'-tě. frits ist īn fe'-těr fon hants; hil'-dě ist zī'-ně
Hilde. Mrs. Schulz is their aunt. Fritz is a cousin of Hans; Hilde is his

DAMENKLEIDUNG—LADIES' CLOTHING
(English key on page 367)

die Bluse, -n

die Falte, -n

der Rock, ¨ -e

der Gürtel, -

die Schnalle, -n

der Sweater, -

der Kragen, -

das Jäckchen, -

der Ärmel, -

der Hut, ¨ -e

die Kapuze, -n

die Jacke, -n

der Rock, ¨ -e

das Kleid, -er

das Kostüm, -e

der Regenmantel, ¨ -

der Wintermantel, ¨ -

der Pelzkragen, -

der Muff, -e

der Pelzmantel, ¨ -

das Abendkleid, -er

Kusine. Fritz ist ein Neffe und Hilde eine Nichte von Wilhelm und Anna Schulz.
kōō-zee′-nĕ. frits ist in nĕ′-fĕ ōōnt hil′-dĕ ĭ′-nĕ nich′-tĕ fon vil′-helm ōōnt a′-nah shōōlts.
(girl) cousin. Fritz is a nephew and Hilde a niece of Wilhelm and Anna Schulz.

Dies ist der alte Herr Schulz und dies ist
dees ist dayr al′-tĕ herr shōōlts ōōnt dees ist
This is old Mr. Schulz and this is

seine Frau. Der alte Herr Schulz ist der
zī′-nĕ frou. dayr al′-tĕ herr shōōlts ist dayr
his wife. Old Mr. Schulz is the

Vater von Wilhelm Schulz und der
fah′-tĕr fon vil′-helm shōōlts ōōnt dayr
father of Wilhelm Schulz and the

Grossvater von Hans und Grete. Die
grohs′-fah-tĕr fon hants ōōnt gray′-tĕ. dee
grandfather of Hans and Grete. Old

alte Frau Schulz ist ihre Grossmutter.
al′-tĕ frou shōōlts ist ee′-rĕ grohs′-mōō-tĕr.
Mrs. Schulz is their grandmother.

Der alte Herr Schulz und die alte Frau
dayr al′-tĕ herr shōōlts ōōnt dee al′-tĕ frou
Old Mr. Schulz and old Mrs.

Der alte Herr Schulz und seine Frau
dayr al′-tĕ herr shōōlts ōōnt zī′-nĕ frou

Schulz sind auch die Eltern von Frau Lessing. Sie sind also auch die Grosseltern von
shōōlts zint ouch dee el′-tĕrn fon frou less′-sing. zee zint al′-zoh ouch dee grohs′-eltĕrn fon
Schulz are also the parents of Mrs. Lessing. They are therefore also the grandparents of

Fritz und Hilde. Fritz, Hilde, Grete und Hans sind ihre Enkelkinder (der Enkel;
frits ōōnt hil′-dĕ. frits, hil′-dĕ, gray′-tĕ ōōnt hants zint ee′-rĕ en′-kel-kin-dĕr (dayr en′-kĕl;
Fritz and Hilde. Fritz, Hilde, Grete and Hans are their grandchildren (the grandson;

die Enkelin). Der alte Herr Schulz ist der Schwiegervater von Anna Schulz,
dee en′-kĕ-lin). dayr al′-tĕ herr shōōlts ist dayr shvee′-gĕr-fah-tĕr fon a′-nah shōōlts,
the granddaughter). Old Mr. Schulz is the father-in-law of Anna Schulz,

und die alte Frau Schulz ist ihre Schwiegermutter. Anna ist ihre Schwiegertochter.
ōōnt dee al′-tĕ frou shōōlts ist ee′-rĕ shvee′-gĕr-mōō-tĕr. a′-nah ist ee′-rĕ shvee′-gĕr-toch-tĕr.
and old Mrs. Schulz is her mother-in-law. Anna is her daughter-in-law.

Herr Lessing ist ihr Schwiegersohn. Die Eltern von Frau Schulz leben nicht mehr.
herr less′-sing ist eer shvee′-gĕr-zohn. dee el′-tĕrn fon frou shōōlts lay′-bĕn nicht mayr.
Mr. Lessing is her son-in-law. The parents of Mrs. Schulz live no more.

Sie sind beide tot. Herr Lessing ist ein Schwager von Frau Schulz. Herr Schulz und
zee zint bī′-dĕ toht. herr less′-sing ist in shvah′-gĕr fon frou shōōlts. herr shōōlts ōōnt
They are both dead. Mr. Lessing is a brother-in-law of Mrs. Schulz. Herr Schulz and

Frau Lessing sind Geschwister. Frau Schulz und Frau Lessing sind Schwägerinnen.
frou less′-sing zint gĕ-shvis′-tĕr. frou shōōlts ōōnt frou less′-sing zint shvay′-gĕ-ri-nĕn.
Frau Lessing are brother and sister. Frau Schulz and Frau Lessing are sisters-in-law.

das Baby
das bay'-bee

das kleine Kind	der Knabe	das Mädchen	der junge Mann	die junge Dame
das klī'-ně kint	der knah'-bě	das mayt'-chěn	dayr yōōng'-gě man	dee yōōng'-gě dah'-mě

der Mann (der Herr)	die Frau (die Dame)	der alte Herr	die alte Dame
dayr man (dayr herr)	dee frou (dee dah'-mě)	dayr al'-tě herr	dee al'-tě dah'-mě

MY, HIS, HER, YOUR, Etc.

Masculine, singular

mein Hut=*my hat*
sein Hut=*his hat*
ihr Hut=*her hat*
sein Preis=*its cost*
unser Garten=
  our garden
Ihr Hut=*your hat*
ihr Garten=
  their garden

Neuter, singular

mein Buch=*my book*
sein Buch=*his book*
ihr Buch=*her book*
sein Alter=*its age*
unser Haus=*our house*

Ihr Buch=*your book*
ihr Haus=*their house*

Feminine, singular

meine Frau=*my wife*
seine Krawatte=*his tie*
ihre Handtasche=
  her handbag
seine Farbe=*its colour*
unsere Strasse=*our street*
Ihre Tochter=
  your daughter
ihre Stadt=*their town*

Plural (all genders)

meine ⎫
seine ⎪
ihre ⎪
    ⎬ Hüte
seine ⎪ Bücher
unsere ⎪ Federn
Ihre ⎪
ihre ⎭

From the above examples it will be seen that the masculine and neuter forms of the possessive adjectives are identical, and that the feminine and plural forms also correspond with each other. The following summary will help you to remember them:

	Masc.	Fem.	Neut.	Plural
my	mein	meine	mein	meine
his	sein	seine	sein	seine
her	ihr	ihre	ihr	ihre
its	sein	seine	sein	seine
our	unser	unsere	unser	unsere
your	Ihr	Ihre	Ihr	Ihre
their	ihr	ihre	ihr	ihre

HOW TO TRANSLATE *TO LIVE*

Wo wohnen Sie? = *Where do you live?*
Er lebt nicht mehr = *He is no longer alive*
(lit.: *He lives no more.*)

To live is **wohnen** when meaning *to dwell*, *to reside;* **leben** in the sense of *to be alive*.

NATIONALTRACHT

In vielen Gegenden Deutschlands haben sich noch alte Nationaltrachten erhalten. Das obige Bild zeigt den Kopfputz der Bückeburger Bäuerinnen.

Das untere Bild zeigt eine Modenschau in einem Café auf dem Kurfürstendamm in Berlin.

(*Translation on page* 374)

die Nationaltracht, -en
  national costume

erhalten
  to preserve

der Kopfputz, -e
  head-dress

die Bäuerin, -nen
  peasant woman

die Modenschau, -en
  fashion show

FALSE FRIENDS

Examples of the deceptive similarity between some words common to English and German.

Words spelt alike or almost alike in English and in German have not necessarily the same meaning. Thus **bekommen** does not mean *to become* but *to get;* **also** is to be translated by *so,* *thus* or *therefore;* **altern** does not mean *to alter,* but *to be getting old;* **fast** is not the English *fast* but means *almost.* **Die Glocke** means *the bell* and not *the clock;* **der Knabe** (*knave*) is *the boy;* **die Hose** not *hose,* but *pair of trousers;* **locken** does not mean *to lock,* but *to allure;* **der Rat** is not *the rat* but *the advice;* and **damit** is not a swear word, but is to be translated by *with it* or *with them.*

ein Paar Schuhe
în pahr shoo'-ĕ

ein Paar Handschuhe
în pahr hant'-shoo-ĕ

SEINE SCHWIEGERMUTTER

Fröhlich tänzelte Heinrich die Strasse entlang, als ihn sein Freund Paul traf.

"Was ist nur los mit Ihnen, Heinrich?"

"Ich war am Bahnhof, meine Schwiegermutter ist weggefahren, sie war vier Wochen bei uns."

"Aber Menschenskind, Sie haben ja kohlschwarze Hände."

Heinrich betrachtete seine Hände und murmelte dann leise: "Wissen Sie, ich habe die brave Lokomotive gestreichelt!"

Tänzeln, *to skip;* **entlang,** *along;* **traf,** *met;* **was ist los?** *what is the matter?;* **der Bahnhof,** **··-e,** *station;* **die Schwiegermutter,** **··,** *mother-in-law;* **Menschenskind,** *my dear chap;* **kohlschwarz,** *pitch black;* **betrachten,** *to look at;* **murmeln,** *to mumble;* **brav,** *good;* **die Lokomotive, -n,** *engine;* **streicheln,** *to stroke.*

COLOURS

Welche Farbe hat ihr Kleid? **Es ist blau.**
What colour is her dress? It is blue.

Wie ist sein Hut, braun oder schwarz?
What colour is his hat, brown or black?

Er ist weder braun noch schwarz, er ist grau.
It is neither brown nor black, it is grey.

In German there are two ways of asking what colour something is:

Welche Farbe hat ......? or **Wie ist ......?**

Welche Farbe hat ......? literally means *what colour has ......?* but in answering always use **er (sie, es) ist grün (blau, rot,** etc.) or, in the plural, **sie sind grün (blau, gelb,** etc.). **Wie ist?** literally means *how is?* but it often means *what is ... like?* and it can also be used for asking what the colour of something is provided the context makes it clear that the question refers to colour.

Note:—Do not use **wie ist?** when asking *How are you? How is he?* etc. The expressions for these phrases are in Lesson 13.

zwei Paar Schuhe
tsvī pahr shoo'-ĕ

zwei Paar Handschuhe
tsvī pahr hant'-shoo-ĕ

DER SCHÖNE MANN

Dame: "Es ist doch komisch, dass schöne Männer immer so schrecklich eingebildet sind."

Herr: "Oh, doch nicht immer! Ich zum Beispiel gar nicht!"

Doch, *really, indeed, yet, but;* **komisch,** *funny;* **schrecklich,** *terribly;* **eingebildet,** *conceited;* **zum Beispiel,** *for instance;* **gar nicht,** *not at all.*

NEW NOUNS

	Anzug, ···-e	*suit*
	Mantel, ···-	*overcoat*
	Rock, ···-e	*skirt*
	Schuh, -e	*shoe*
DER	Engländer, -	*Englishman*
	Bruder, ···-	*brother*
	Onkel, -	*uncle*
	Enkel, -	*grandson*
	Schwager, ···-	*brother-in-law*

	Tasche, -n	*pocket, bag*
	Handtasche, -n	*handbag*
	Seite, -n	*page*
	Kleidung	*clothing*
	Jacke, -n	*jacket*
	Krawatte, -n	*tie*
	Socke, -n	*sock*
	Hose, -n	*pair of trousers*
DIE	Bluse, -n	*blouse*
	Villa, Villen	*villa*
	Wohnung, -en	*flat*
	Küche, -n	*kitchen (or cook-*
	Familie, -n	*family ing)*
	Tante, -n	*aunt*
	Nichte, -n	*niece*
	Enkelin, -nen	*granddaughter*
	Schwägerin, -nen	*sister-in-law*
	Farbe, -n	*colour*

	Bild, -er	*picture*
	Kleidungsstück, -e	*article of clothing*
DAS	Paar, -e[1]	*pair*
	Kleid, -er	*dress*
	Kostüm, -e	*ladies' suit*
	Zimmer, -	*room*

Note.—In the above and later lists of nouns the plural forms are shown for convenience as follows: -e, -n, etc., indicate that the plural is formed by adding these letters to the singular (**der Schuh, die Schuhe**); ···- indicates that the root vowel is modified, without any addition to the end of the word (**der Mantel, die Mäntel**); - indicates that there is no change (**der Onkel, die Onkel**).

Where no symbols or letters follow the singular, the noun has no plural form (**die Kleidung**).

EXERCISES

I Answer in German

1. Wieviel Paar Schuhe haben Sie? 2. Welche Farbe hat Ihr Mantel? 3. Welche Farbe haben Ihre Schuhe? 4. Ist dieses Buch gelb? 5. Sind Ihre Handschuhe grün? 6. Wo wohnt die Familie Lessing? 7. Wohnen Sie auch in Berlin? 8. Wo wohnen Sie? 9. Was ist Frau Lessing von Hans und Grete? 10. Wer ist der Onkel von Fritz und Hilde? 11. Was ist Fritz von Hans? 12. Wer ist der Grossvater von Hans und Grete? 13. Was ist die alte Frau Schulz von Hans und Grete? 14. Was ist Hilde von Fritz? 15. Was ist die alte Frau Schulz von Anna Schulz? 16. Leben die Eltern von Frau Schulz noch? 17. Was ist Herr Lessing von Frau Schulz?

II Replace the ellipses by the German for my, your, his, her, their, our

1. ... Vater und ... Mutter sind ... Eltern. 2. ... Haus ist gross. 3. ... Hut ist braun, ... Schuhe sind schwarz. 4. ... Bluse ist weiss. 5. ... Flasche ist voll Wasser. 6. ... Taschen sind voll Äpfel.

III Translate into German

1. This little girl is my niece. 2. This little boy is my cousin. 3. That old man is our grandfather. 4. He likes to drink wine. 5. What does he like to eat? 6. He likes fish. 7. Do you like eating sweets? 8. I don't like them, they are not good for the teeth. 9. She eats a great deal of meat. 10. They have five children: two sons and three daughters. 11. What colour is your suit? 12. It is grey. 13. Are your shoes also grey? No, they are black; but my hat is grey. 14. My grandfather is no longer living. 15. My parents live in the South of England. 16. Where do you live? 17. Is your grandfather still (=noch) alive? 18. Have you many brothers and sisters? 19. My parents-in-law do not live in a flat, they have a villa. 20. Her grandmother is no longer alive.

(*Answers on page 357*)

---

[1] *Two pairs of trousers* = **zwei Paar Hosen** (see footnote on page 40)

IN DEN BAYERISCHEN ALPEN:

Oberammergau ist ein Dorf in Oberbayern, in dem sich eine Schule für Holzschnitzerei befindet. Das Dorf ist berühmt durch die Passionsspiele, die infolge eines während einer Pestepidemie getanen Gelübdes alle zehn Jahre von Einwohnern aufgeführt werden.

die Holzschnitzerei, -en	sich befinden	berühmt	das Passionsspiel, -e	während
wood carving	*to be situated*	*famous*	*Passion play*	*during*

TOTALANSICHT VON OBERAMMERGAU

Hier sieht man eine Totalansicht des Dorfs mit der Kirche links und dem Passions-
theater rechts. Im Hintergrund erheben sich die steilen, baumbedeckten Abhänge der
Alpen. Die drei Berggipfel heissen Not, Kofel und Rappenkopf. *(Translation on page 374)*

die Pest	das Gelübde, -	aufführen	steil	baumbedeckt	der Berggipfel, -	heissen
plague	*vow*	*to perform*	*steep*	*tree-covered*	*mountain peak*	*to be called*

SIEBENTE LEKTION: *SEVENTH LESSON*

Vorgestern war Sonntag der erste Juli. Gestern war Montag der zweite
fohr'-ges-tĕrn vahr zon'-tak dayr ayr'-stĕ yōō'-lee, ges'-tĕrn vahr mohn'-tak dayr tsvī-tĕ
The day before yesterday was Sunday the first of July. Yesterday was Monday the second of

Juli. Heute ist Dienstag der dritte Juli. Morgen ist[1] Mittwoch der vierte
yōō'-lee. hoy'-tĕ ist deens'-tak dayr dri'-tĕ yōō'-lee. mor'-gĕn ist mit'-voch dayr feer'-tĕ
July. To-day is Tuesday the third of July. To-morrow will be Wednesday the fourth of

Juli. Übermorgen ist[1] Donnerstag der fünfte Juli.
yōō'-lee. ẽ'-bĕr-mor-gĕn ist do'-ners-tak dayr fĭnf'-tĕ yōō'-lee.
July. The day after to-morrow will be Thursday the fifth of July.

KALENDER

	JANUAR					FEBRUAR					MÄRZ			
S	-	7	14	21	28	-	4	11	18	25	-	-	4	11	18	25	-
Mo	1	8	15	22	29	-	5	12	19	26	-	-	5	12	19	26	-
Di	2	9	16	23	30	-	6	13	20	27	-	-	6	13	20	27	-
Mi	3	10	17	24	31	-	7	14	21	28	-	-	7	14	21	28	-
Do	4	11	18	25	-	1	8	15	22	-	1	8	15	22	29	-
F	5	12	19	26	-	2	9	16	23	-	2	9	16	23	30	-
S	6	13	20	27	-	3	10	17	24	-	3	10	17	24	31	-

	APRIL					MAI					JUNI			
S	1	8	15	22	29	-	6	13	20	27	-	-	3	10	17	24	-
Mo	2	9	16	23	30	-	7	14	21	28	-	-	4	11	18	25	-
Di	3	10	17	24	-	1	8	15	22	29	-	-	5	12	19	26	-
Mi	4	11	18	25	-	2	9	16	23	30	-	-	6	13	20	27	-
Do	5	12	19	26	-	3	10	17	24	31	-	-	7	14	21	28	-
F	6	13	20	27	-	4	11	18	25	-	1	8	15	22	29	-
S	7	14	21	28	-	5	12	19	26	-	2	9	16	23	30	-

	JULI					AUGUST					SEPTEMBER			
S	1	8	15	22	29	-	5	12	19	26	-	2	9	16	23	30
Mo	2	9	16	23	30	-	6	13	20	27	-	3	10	17	24	-
Di	3	10	17	24	31	-	7	14	21	28	-	4	11	18	25	-
Mi	4	11	18	25	-	1	8	15	22	29	-	5	12	19	26	-
Do	5	12	19	26	-	2	9	16	23	30	-	6	13	20	27	-
F	6	13	20	27	-	3	10	17	24	31	-	7	14	21	28	-
S	7	14	21	28	-	4	11	18	25	-	1	8	15	22	29	-

	OKTOBER					NOVEMBER					DEZEMBER			
S	-	7	14	21	28	-	4	11	18	25	-	2	9	16	23	30
Mo	1	8	15	22	29	-	5	12	19	26	-	3	10	17	24	31
Di	2	9	16	23	30	-	6	13	20	27	-	4	11	18	25	-
Mi	3	10	17	24	31	-	7	14	21	28	-	5	12	19	26	-
Do	4	11	18	25	—	1	8	15	22	29	-	6	13	20	27	-
F	5	12	19	26	-	2	9	16	23	30	-	7	14	21	28	-
S	6	13	20	27	-	3	10	17	24	-	1	8	15	22	29	-

Eine Woche hat sieben Tage.
ī'-nĕ vo'-chĕ hat zee'-bĕn tah'-gĕ.
A week has seven days.

Die sieben Tage heissen :
dee zee'-bĕn tah'-gĕ hī'-sĕn :
The seven days are called:

Sonntag (zon'-tak)	Sunday
Montag (mohn'-tak)	Monday
Dienstag (deens'-tak)	Tuesday
Mittwoch (mit'-voch)	Wednesday
Donnerstag (do'-ners-tak)	Thursday
Freitag (frī'-tak)	Friday
Sonnabend (zon'-ah-bent)	Saturday

Note:—In Austria and Southern Germany *Saturday* is **Samstag** (zams'-tak).

Ein Jahr hat zwölf Monate.
īn yahr hat tsvĕlf moh'-na-tĕ.
A year has twelve months.

Die Monate heissen:
dee moh'-na-tĕ hī'-sĕn:
The months are called:

Januar (ya'-nōō-ahr)	January
Februar (fay'-brōō-ahr)	February
März (merts)	March
April (a-pril')	April
Mai (mī)	May
Juni (yōō'-nee)	June
Juli (yōō'-lee)	July
August (ou-gōōst')	August
September (zep-tem'-bĕr)	September
Oktober (ok-toh'-bĕr)	October
November (noh-vem'-bĕr)	November
Dezember (day-tsem'-bĕr)	December

---

[1]Although these expressions refer to the future, in colloquial German the present tense is usual with expressions of time such as **morgen**=*to-morrow*; **nächste Woche**=*next week*.

56

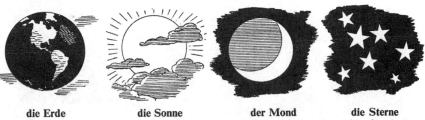

die Erde	die Sonne	der Mond	die Sterne
dee ayr'-dĕ	dee zo'-nĕ	dayr mohnt	dee shter'-nĕ

Wir sind jetzt im Juli. Heute ist Dienstag der dritte. Dieser Monat hat
veer zint yetst im yōō'-lee. hoy'-tĕ ist deens'-tak dayr drī'-tĕ. dee'-zĕr moh'-nat hat
We are now in July. To-day is Tuesday the third. This month has

einunddreissig Tage. Nicht jeder Monat hat so viele Tage. April, Juni,
īn'-ōōnt-drī-sich tah'-gĕ. nicht yay'-dĕr moh'-nat hat zoh fee'-lĕ tah'-gĕ. a-pril', yōō'-nee,
thirty-one days. Not every month has as many days. April, June,

September und November haben jeder nur dreissig Tage. Januar
zep-tem'-bĕr ōōnt noh-vĕm'-bĕr hah'-bĕn yay'-dĕr nōōr drī'-sich tah'-gĕ. ya'-nōō-ahr
September and November have only thirty days each. January

ist der erste Monat, Februar der zweite, März der dritte, April der vierte,
ist dayr ayr'-stĕ moh'-nat, fay'-brōō-ahr dayr tsvī'-tĕ, merts dayr drī'-tĕ, a-pril' dayr feer'-tĕ,
is the first month, February the second, March the third, April the fourth,

u.s.w. (und so weiter). Dezember ist der letzte Monat, November der vorletzte.
ōōnt zoh vī'-tĕr. day-tsem'-bĕr ist dayr lets'-tĕ moh'-nat, noh-vem'-bĕr dayr fohr'-lets-tĕ.
etc. (and so on). December is the last month, November the last but one.

Der letzte Monat war Juni, der vorletzte war Mai. Der nächste Monat
dayr lets'-tĕ moh'-nat vahr yōō'-nee, dayr fohr'-lets-tĕ vahr mī. dayr naych'-stĕ moh'-nat
(The) last month was June, the last but one was May. The next month

ist August, der übernächste ist September. Der wievielte ist heute? Heute ist
ist ou-gōōst', dayr ē̄'-bĕr-naych-stĕ ist zep-tem'-bĕr. dayr vee'-feel-tĕ ist hoy'-tĕ? hoy'-tĕ ist
is August, the next but one is September. What is to-day's date? To-day is

der dritte. Welcher Wochentag ist heute? Heute ist Dienstag.
dayr drī'-tĕ. vel'-chĕr vo'-chĕn-tak ist hoy'-tĕ? hoy'-tĕ ist deens'-tak.
the third. What day of the week is it (to-day)? To-day is Tuesday.

Das Jahr hat vier Jahreszeiten. Sie heissen:
das yahr hat feer yah'-rĕs-tsī-tĕn. zee hī'-sĕn:
The year has four seasons. They are called:

der Frühling (frē̄'-ling) *Spring*	**der Herbst** (herpst)	*Autumn*
der Sommer (zo'-mĕr) *Summer*	**der Winter** (vin'-tĕr)	*Winter*

Wir sind jetzt im Sommer. Im Sommer sind die Tage lang und die Nächte kurz.
veer zint yetst im zo'-mĕr. im zo'-mĕr zint dee tah'-gĕ lang ōōnt dee naych'-tĕ kōōrts.
We are now in summer. In summer the days are long and the nights short.

Im Frühling blühen die Obstbäume
im fręę'-ling blęę'-hĕn dee ohpst'-boy-mĕ

Im Sommer reift das Getreide
im zo'-mĕr rīft das ge-trī'-dĕ

Im Winter sind die Nächte lang und die Tage kurz. Ein Tag hat vierundzwanzig
im vin'-tĕr zint dee naych'-tĕ lang ōont dee tah'-gĕ kŏŏrts. in tak hat feer'-ōont-tsvan-tsich
In winter the nights are long and the days short. A day has twenty-four

Stunden. Eine Stunde hat sechzig Minuten. Dreissig Minuten sind
shtōōn'-dĕn. i'-nĕ shtōōn'-dĕ hat zech'-tsich mee-nōō'-tĕn. drī'-sich mee-nōō'-tĕn zint
hours. An hour has sixty minutes. Thirty minutes are

eine halbe Stunde, und fünfzehn Minuten sind eine Viertelstunde.
i'-nĕ hal'-bĕ shtōōn'-dĕ, ōont fĭnf'-tsayn mee-nōō'-tĕn zint i'-nĕ feer'-tel-shtōōn-dĕ.
half-an-hour, and fifteen minutes are a quarter of an hour.

Eine Minute hat sechzig Sekunden.
i'-nĕ mee-nōō'-tĕ hat zech'-tsich zay-kŏŏn'-dĕn.
A minute has sixty seconds.

Der Februar hat nur achtundzwanzig Tage. Ein Jahr hat dreihundertfünf-
dayr fay'-brŏŏ-ahr hat nōōr acht'-ōont-tsvan-tsich tah'-gĕ. in yahr hat drī'-hŏŏn-dert-fĭnf-
February has only twenty-eight days. A year has three hundred

undsechzig Tage. Alle vier Jahre hat der Februar neunundzwanzig Tage und
ōont-zech-tsich tah'-gĕ. a'-lĕ feer yah'-rĕ hat dayr fay'-brŏŏ-ahr noyn'-ōont-tsvan-tsich
and sixty-five days. Every four years February has twenty-nine days and   [tah'-gĕ ōont

das Jahr dreihundertsechsundsechzig Tage. Ein solches Jahr heisst ein Schaltjahr.
das yahr drī'-hŏŏn-dert-zeks-ōont-zech-tsich tah'-gĕ. in zol'-chĕs yahr hīst in shalt'-yahr.
the year three hundred and sixty-six days. Such a year is called a leap year.

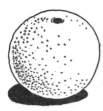

Eine ganze Apfelsine
ī'-nĕ gan'-tsĕ ap-fĕl-
zee'-nĕ

Eine halbe Apfelsine
ī'-nĕ hal'-bĕ ap-fĕl-
zee'-nĕ

$\frac{1}{2}$ = **ein halb**[1] (īn halp);

$\frac{1}{4}$ = **ein Viertel** (īn feer'-tĕl);

$\frac{3}{4}$ = **drei Viertel** (drī feer'-tĕl).

EACH ; EVERY

Jeder Soldat hat eine Uniform.
Every soldier has a uniform.

Jede Schülerin hat ein Buch.
Each schoolgirl has a book.

Jedes kleine Mädchen hat eine Puppe.
Every little girl has a doll.

Nicht jeder Soldat ist tapfer.
Not every soldier is brave.

Alle Kinder spielen gern.
All children like to play.

Each (or *every*) is rendered by **jeder,
jede, jedes,** according to the gender of the
noun it precedes, in the same way as
dieser, diese, dieses and **jener, jene, jenes.**
The plural of **jeder, jede, jedes** is **alle** (*all*).

Im Herbst reifen die Äpfel, die Birnen,
im herpst rī'-fĕn dee ep'-fĕl,dee bir'-nĕn,

die Pflaumen und andere Früchte
dee pflou'-mĕn ŏŏnt an'-dĕ-rĕ frĭch'-tĕ

Im Winter sind die Felder, die Bäume
im vin'-tĕr zint dee fel'-dĕr, dee boy'-mĕ

und die Häuser mit Schnee bedeckt
ŏŏnt dee hoy'-zĕr mit shnay be-dekt'

---

[1] The word **halb** can be used as an adverb or as an adjective, but the noun is **eine Hälfte.** As
an adjective, **halb** always follows the article : **ein halber Apfel**= *half an apple* ; **eine halbe Stunde**
= *half an hour* ; **ein halbes Jahr**= *half a year.*

DAS OBST UND DIE NÜSSE—FRUIT AND NUTS

(English key on page 367)

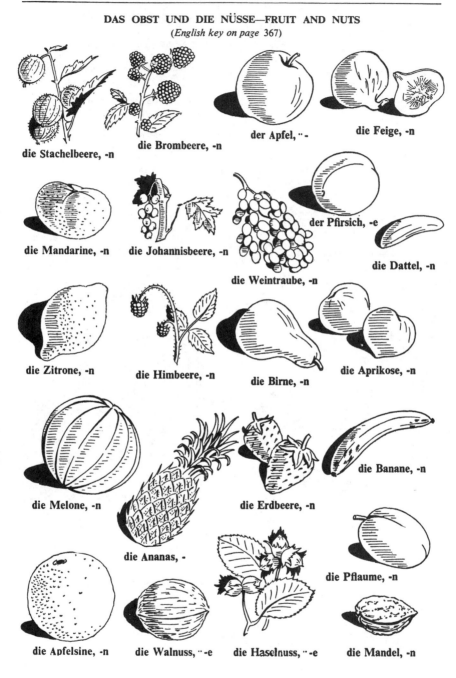

die Stachelbeere, -n

die Brombeere, -n

der Apfel, " -

die Feige, -n

die Mandarine, -n

die Johannisbeere, -n

der Pfirsich, -e

die Weintraube, -n

die Dattel, -n

die Zitrone, -n

die Himbeere, -n

die Birne, -n

die Aprikose, -n

die Melone, -n

die Erdbeere, -n

die Banane, -n

die Ananas, -

die Pflaume, -n

die Apfelsine, -n

die Walnuss, " -e

die Haselnuss, " -e

die Mandel, -n

ORDINAL NUMBERS

1st	erste (der, die, das)
2nd	zweite
3rd	dritte
4th	vierte
5th	fünfte
6th	sechste
7th	sieb(en)te
8th	achte
9th	neunte
10th	zehnte
11th	elfte
12th	zwölfte
13th	dreizehnte
14th	vierzehnte
15th	fünfzehnte
16th	sechzehnte
17th	siebzehnte
18th	achtzehnte
19th	neunzehnte
20th	zwanzigste
21st	einundzwanzigste
22nd	zweiundzwanzigste
23rd	dreiundzwanzigste
30th	dreissigste
40th	vierzigste
100th	hundertste
101st	hundert und erste
120th	hundertzwanzigste
1000th	tausendste
2000th	zweitausendste

Note that the ordinals are formed by adding -te to the numbers from **1** to **19**, and -ste to the numbers from **20** upwards. The usual abbreviation for ordinals is the figure followed by a full stop, thus: **1.** (*first*); **2.** (*second*); **3.** (*third*), etc. There are special words only for *the first* and *the third*.

TO BE CALLED

Wie heissen Sie?
What is your name?

Wie heisst er?
What is his name?

Ich heisse Walter.
My name is Walter.

Wie heisst sie?
What is her name?

Wie heisst Ihre Schwester?
What is your sister's name?

Wie heisst das auf Deutsch?
What is that in German?

ORDER OF WORDS   (1)

Ich g e h e heute ins Theater.
Heute g e h e ich ins Theater.

Die Kinder s p i e l e n im Garten.
Im Garten s p i e l e n die Kinder.

Die Tage s i n d im Sommer lang.
Im Sommer s i n d die Tage lang.

Die Äpfel r e i f e n im Herbst.
Im Herbst r e i f e n die Äpfel.

The verb stands in the second place but, as you see in the examples, it is not necessarily the second word in the sentence.

This rule does not apply :

(1) In questions: **Gehen Sie heute ins Theater?**=*Are you going to the theatre to-day?* **Schlafen die Kinder?**=*Are the children asleep?*

(2) With **und, aber, oder** and similar words, which merely connect words or phrases and have no effect on the order of words.

Er ist gross, und sie ist klein.
Er ist dick, aber sie ist dünn.

(3) In subordinate clauses (Lesson 12).

VERGISSMEINNICHT

Es blüht ein schönes Blümchen
auf uns'rer grünen Au';
sein Aug' ist wie der Himmel,
so heiter und so blau.

Es weiss nicht viel zu reden,
und alles, was es spricht,
ist immer nur dasselbe,
ist nur: Vergissmeinnicht.

Hoffmann von Fallersleben

Das Vergissmeinnicht, -, *forget-me-not;* **es blüht,** *there blooms;* **die Aue, -n,** *meadow;* **das Auge, -n,** *eye,* **der Himmel,** *heaven, sky;* **heiter,** *serene, cheerful;* **es weiss,** *it knows;* **reden,** *to say;* **alles,** *everything;* **immer,** *always;* **nur,** *only;* **dasselbe,** *the same.*

HIER BRAUCHT NIEMAND ZU VERDURSTEN

Der Wagen mit den Bierfässern hält vor der Post-Stiftsstube in der Stiftstrasse in Stuttgart. Vorher hat schon ein anderer Wagen Eis abgeladen, um das Bier kühl zu halten. Wer lieber etwas Warmes trinkt, kann sich nebenan in das Café im ersten Stock des Gasthofs setzen.

(*Translation on page* 375)

verdursten	**das Fass, ⁝-er**	**halten**	**vorher**	**das Eis**	**abladen**
to die of thirst	*barrel*	*to stop*	*previously*	*ice*	*to unload*
wer lieber trinkt		**nebenan**	**der Stock, -werke**		**der Gasthof, ⁝-e**
whoever prefers to drink		*next door*	*storey, floor*		*inn*

NEW NOUNS

DER
Tag, -e	day
Monat, -e	month
Kalender, -	calendar
Mond, -e	moon
Stern, -e	star
Baum, "-e	tree
Apfel, "-	apple
Schnee	snow
Soldat, -en	soldier

DIE
Woche, -en	week
Stunde, -n	hour
Minute, -n	minute
Sekunde, -n	second
Erde, -n	earth
Sonne, -n	sun
Jahreszeit, -en	season
Nacht, "-e	night
Birne, -n	pear
Pflaume, -n	plum
Apfelsine, -n	orange
Uniform, -en	uniform
Puppe, -n	doll

DAS
Jahr, -e	year
Viertel, -	quarter
Feld, -er	field
Theater, -	theatre

EXERCISES

I Read and Translate

Heute ist Freitag, der achtundzwanzigste März. Gestern war Donnerstag, der siebenundzwanzigste. Übermorgen ist Sonntag, der dreissigste. Freitag ist der sechste Tag. Der März ist der dritte Monat. Der Januar ist der erste Monat. Der Mai ist der fünfte Monat. Der November ist der elfte (oder der vorletzte) Monat. Wir sind jetzt im Sommer. Der November ist ein Herbstmonat. Die Wintermonate heissen Dezember, Januar und Februar.

II Answer in German

1. Wie heissen Sie? 2. Wie heisst dieses Buch? 3. Der wievielte ist heute? 4. Der wievielte war vorgestern? 5. Welcher Tag war gestern? 6. Wie viele Tage hat Juli? 7. Hat jeder Monat einunddreissig Tage?

8. Hat jede Frau lange Haare? 9. Hat jeder Schüler ein Buch? 10. Sind alle Engländer gross? 11. Wie heissen die 12 Monate? 12. Wie viele Tage hat ein Jahr? 13. Wie viele Tage hat der Februar? 14. Ist dieses Jahr ein Schaltjahr? 15. Wie heissen die sieben Wochentage?

III Re-write the following

Place the words in bold type at the beginning (e.g. Der Oktober ist der zehnte Monat = Der zehnte Monat ist der Oktober).

1. Die Äpfel sind **im September** reif. 2. Wir sind **jetzt** im Sommer. 3. Im Sommer sind **die Tage** lang. 4. Die Tage sind **im Winter** kurz. 5. Die Bäume sind **im Winter** mit Schnee bedeckt. 6. Der April ist der **vierte Monat.** 7. Dieser Monat hat **dreissig Tage.** 8. Das Getreide reift **im Sommer.** 9. Ich heisse **Walter Müller.** 10. Die Obstbäume blühen **im Frühling.**

(*Answers on page 357*)

DIE ERKLÄRUNG

Wenn Schleiermacher in Berlin seine berühmten Predigten hielt, war die Kirche meist bis auf den letzten Platz gefüllt. Seine Zuhörer bestanden jedoch überwiegend aus Studenten, Offizieren und jungen Damen.

Ein Kollege des berühmten Theologen wollte wissen, wieso sich immer das gleiche Auditorium bei seinen Predigten einfinde.

"Nichts einfacher als das," gab Schleiermacher Auskunft. "Die Studenten kommen, weil ich in der Prüfungskommission sitze, die jungen Mädchen kommen wegen der Studenten und die Offiziere der Mädchen wegen."

Schleiermacher, *famous preacher and professor of theology;* **berühmt,** *famous;* **die Predigt, -en,** *sermon;* **die Kirche, -n,** *church;* **die Zuhörer** (m. pl.), *audience;* **bestanden aus,** *consisted of;* **jedoch,** *however;* **überwiegend,** *predominantly;* **wollte wissen,** *wanted to know;* **wieso,** *why;* **gleich,** *same;* **das Auditorium,** *audience;* **sich einfinden,** *to be present;* **einfach,** *simple;* **die Auskunft, "-e** *information;* **die Prüfung, -en,** *examination;* **wegen,** *on account of.*

BERN: DER ZEITGLOCKENTURM

Der Zeitglockenturm, das alte Wahrzeichen der schweizer Hauptstadt Bern, war bis
zum dreizehnten Jahrhundert das westliche Tor der Stadt. Er wurde mehrmals erneuert
und im Jahre 1930 mit Fresken geschmückt. Auf der Ostseite ist eine merkwürdige Uhr,
die jede volle Stunde durch das Krähen eines Hahnes verkündet.

(*Translation on page* 375)

der Zeitglockenturm, ''-e		**das Wahrzeichen, -**		**das Jahrhundert, -e**		**mehrmals**
clock tower		*landmark*		*century*		*several times*

wurde erneuert	**schmücken**	**merkwürdig**	**das Krähen**	**der Hahn, ''-e**	**verkünden**
was restored	*to decorate*	*curious*	*crowing*	*cock*	*to announce*

ACHTE LEKTION: *EIGHTH LESSON*

WIEVIEL UHR IST ES? — WHAT TIME IS IT?

Es ist fünf (Minuten) vor vier
es ist fĭnf (mee-noō´-tĕn) fohr feer

Es ist vier (Uhr)
es ist feer (ōōr)

Es ist drei Minuten nach vier
es ist drī mee-noō´-tĕn nach feer

Es ist (ein) Viertel fünf
es ist (ĭn) feer´-tĕl fĭnf

Es ist halb fünf
es ist halp´-fĭnf

Es ist drei Viertel fünf
es ist drī´-feer-tĕl fĭnf

TELLING THE TIME

There are different ways of telling the time in German. *A quarter past four* can be, as shown above, **ein Viertel fünf** or **ein Viertel nach vier** or **fünfzehn (Minuten) nach vier** or **vier Uhr fünfzehn**. *A quarter to five* can be **drei Viertel fünf** or **ein Viertel vor fünf** or **vier Uhr fünfundvierzig**. When Germans say **ein Viertel fünf** they mean to say that one quarter of the hour between four and five has passed; **halb fünf** means that half the hour to five has passed, and **drei Viertel fünf** that three quarters of the way to five has passed.

To have so many ways of telling the time is rather confusing, but we have to mention them as they are all in general use. To be on the safe side you can start with the full hour and add the minutes, but be sure to remember **halb sieben**=*half past six;* **drei Viertel neun**=*a quarter to nine;* **ein Viertel elf**=*a quarter past ten*, etc. The 24-hour system is widely used, but never with **Viertel, halb, vor** or **nach:**

3.05 p.m.=15 (**fünfzehn**)	Uhr 5 (**fünf**)	
3.30 p.m.=	„	Uhr 30 (**dreissig**)
3.45 p.m.=	„	Uhr 45 (**fünfund-** **vierzig**)

Ich habe eine gute Uhr. Sie geht richtig. Es ist genau zehn Uhr (und) achtzehn
ich hah´-bĕ ī´-nĕ goō´-tĕ ōōr. zee gayt rich´-tich. es ist gĕ-nou´ tsayn ōōr (ōōnt) acht´-tsayn
I have a good watch. It is right. It is exactly ten o'clock (and) eighteen

(Minuten). Ihre Uhr geht nicht richtig. Sie geht drei Minuten nach. Unsere
(mee-noō´-tĕn). ee´-rĕ ōōr gayt nicht rich´-tich. zee gayt drī mee-noō´-tĕn nach. ōōn´-zĕ-rĕ
(minutes). Your watch is not right. It is three minutes slow. Our

Wanduhr geht vor. Sie geht fünf Minuten vor. Meine Taschenuhr geht nicht.
vant´-ōōr gayt fohr. zee gayt fĭnf mee-noō´-tĕn fohr. mī´-nĕ ta´-shĕn-ōōr gayt nicht.
(wall) clock is fast. It is five minutes fast. My (pocket) watch does not go.

UHREN—CLOCKS AND WATCHES

(English key on page 367)

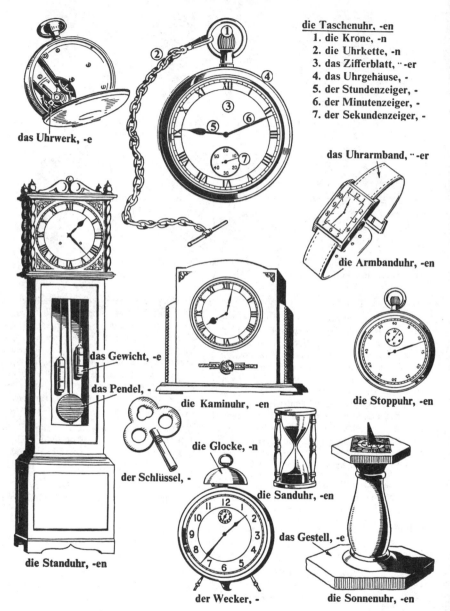

das Uhrwerk, -e

die Taschenuhr, -en
1. die Krone, -n
2. die Uhrkette, -n
3. das Zifferblatt, ¨-er
4. das Uhrgehäuse, -
5. der Stundenzeiger, -
6. der Minutenzeiger, -
7. der Sekundenzeiger, -

das Uhrarmband, ¨-er

die Armbanduhr, -en

das Gewicht, -e

das Pendel, -

die Kaminuhr, -en

die Stoppuhr, -en

die Glocke, -n

der Schlüssel, -

die Sanduhr, -en

das Gestell, -e

die Standuhr, -en

der Wecker, -

die Sonnenuhr, -en

Ich muss sie aufziehen. Meine Taschenuhr ist aus Silber. Ihre Armbanduhr ist aus
ich mōōs zee ouf'-tsee'-ĕn. mĭ'-nĕ ta'-shĕn-ōōr ist ous zil'-bĕr. ee'-rĕ arm'-bant-ōōr ist ous
I must wind it up. My (pocket) watch is (out of[1]) silver. Your wrist-watch is (out of)

Gold. Unsere Wanduhr ist aus Holz. Die Uhr hat zwei Zeiger. Der grosse Zeiger
golt. ōōn'-zĕ-rĕ vant'-ōōr ist ous holts. dee ōōr hat tsvī tsī'-gĕr. dayr groh'-sĕ tsī'-gĕr
gold. Our clock is (out of) wood. The watch has two hands. The big hand

zeigt die Minuten, der kleine die Stunden. Viele Uhren zeigen die Sekunden.
tsīgt dee mee-nōō'-tĕn, dayr klī'-nĕ dee shtōōn'-dĕn. fee'-lĕ ōō'-rĕn tsī'-gĕn dee zay-
shows the minutes, the small (one) the hours. Many watches show the seconds. [kōōn'-dĕn.

A.M. AND P.M. — CORRECT GREETING

der Morgen
mor'-gĕn
the morning

morgens
mor'-gĕns
in the (early) morning

Guten Morgen!
>gōō'-tĕn mor'-gĕn!
Good morning !

der Vormittag
fohr'-mit-tak
before noon

vormittags
fohr'-mit-taks
in the (later) morning

der Mittag
mi'-tak
noon

mittags
mi'-taks
at noon

Guten Tag!
>gōō'-tĕn tak!
Good day !

der Nachmittag
nach'-mi-tak
the afternoon

nachmittags
mach'-mi-taks
in the afternoon

der Abend
ah'-bent
the evening

Guten Abend!
>gōō'-tĕn ah'-bent!
Good evening !

abends
ah'-bents
in the evening

die Nacht
nacht
the night

nachts
nachts
at night

Gute Nacht!
>gōō'-tĕ nacht!
Good night !

5 a.m. = **fünf Uhr morgens**
11 a.m. = **elf Uhr vormittags**
noon = **zwölf Uhr mittags**
3 p.m. = **drei Uhr nachmittags**
7 p.m. = **sieben Uhr abends**
10 p.m. = **zehn Uhr abends**
midnight = **zwölf Uhr nachts**

heute morgen	= *this morning*
heute vormittag	= *this forenoon*
heute nachmittag	= *this afternoon*
heute abend	= *this evening; to-night*
heute nacht	= *to-night*
morgen abend	= *to-morrow evening*
morgen früh	= *to-morrow morning*
gestern morgen	= *yesterday morning*
gestern abend	= *yesterday evening;*
	last night
vorgestern	= *day before yesterday*

Note:—At eight or nine p.m. you still say **Guten Abend.** You say **Gute Nacht** only before you go to bed. *I am going to the theatre to-night* = **Ich gehe heute abend ins Theater. Der Morgen** spelt with a capital M is *the morning*, but **morgen** with a small m means *to-morrow;* **morgens** — *in the morning. To-morrow morning* = **morgen früh,** i.e. *to-morrow early.*

---

[1] *made* is understood.

Hans und Grete gehen in die Schule. **Die Schule beginnt um acht Uhr und endet**
hants ŏont gray'-tĕ gay'-ĕn in dee shōō'-lĕ. dee shōō'-lĕ bĕ-gint' ŏom acht ōor ŏont en'-dĕt
Hans and Grete go to school. *The school begins at eight o'clock and ends*

um eins. **Um halb zwei kommen sie nach Hause zum Mittagessen.** **Am Nachmittag**
ŏom ints. ŏom halp tsvī ko'-mĕn zee nach hou'-zĕ tsŏom mi'-tak-e-sĕn. am nach'-mi-tak
at one. *At half past one they come home for lunch.* *In the afternoon*

Sie sind zu Hause
zee zint tsōō hou'-zĕ

Sie gehen nach Hause
zee gay'-ĕn nach hou'-zĕ

Sie kommen von Hause
zee ko'-mĕn fon hou'-zĕ

gehen sie nicht in die Schule. **Sie bleiben zu Hause und machen ihre Schularbeiten.**
gay'-ĕn zee nicht in dee shōō'-lĕ. zee blī'-bĕn tsōō hou'-zĕ ŏont ma'-chĕn ee'-rĕ shōōl'-
they do not go to school. *They stay at home and do their homework.* [ar-bī-tĕn.

Ich stehe um sieben Uhr auf. **Dann gehe ich ins Badezimmer und wasche mich.**
ich shtay'-ĕ ŏom zee'-bĕn ōor ouf. dan gay'-ĕ ich ints bah'-dĕ-tsi-mĕr ŏont va'-shĕ mich.
I get up at seven o'clock. *Then I go to the bathroom and wash (myself).*

Ich wasche mich mit Wasser und Seife. **Dann gehe ich ins Schlafzimmer zurück und**
ich va'-shĕ mich mit va'-sĕr ŏont zī'-fĕ. dan gay'-ĕ ich ints shlahf'-tsi-mĕr tsōō-rĭk' ŏont
I wash (myself) with water and soap. *Then I go back into the bedroom and*

Sie kommt ins Esszimmer
zee komt ints es'-tsi-mĕr

Sie ist im Esszimmer
zee ist im es'-tsi-mĕr

Ich gehe ins Kino
ich gay'-ĕ ints kee'-noh

Ich bin im Kino
ich bin im kee'-noh

kleide mich an. Um acht Uhr esse ich Frühstück. Ich frühstücke im Esszimmer. Um
klī'-dĕ mich an. ōōm acht ōōr e'-sĕ ich frĕ͡e'-shtĭk. ich frĕ͡e'-shtĭ-kĕ im es'-tsi-mĕr. ōōm
dress (myself). At eight o'clock I eat breakfast. I breakfast in the dining room. At

halb neun gehe ich von Hause fort. Um neun Uhr komme ich im Büro an.
halp noyn gay'-ĕ ich fon hou'-zĕ fort. ōōm noyn ōōr ko'-mĕ ich im bĕ͡e-roh' an.
half past eight I leave home. At nine o'clock I arrive at the office.

Ich arbeite von neun bis eins. Um ein Uhr habe ich eine Stunde Mittagspause.
ich ar'-bī-tĕ fon noyn bis ints. ōōm īn ōōr hah'-bĕ ich ī'-nĕ shtōōn'-dĕ mit'-taks-pou-zĕ.
I work from nine to one. At one o'clock I have one hour's lunch break.

Ich gehe in ein Restaurant, zu Mittag zu essen. Um zwei Uhr komme ich ins Büro
ich gay'-ĕ in īn res-toh-rang', tsōō mi'-tak tsōō e'-sĕn. ōōm tsvī ōōr ko'-mĕ ich ints
I go to a restaurant, to eat lunch. At two o'clock I come back to the [bĕ͡e-roh'

zurück. Ich arbeite dann noch dreieinhalb Stunden bis halb sechs. Dann gehe ich
tsōō-rĭck'. ich ar'-bī-tĕ dan noch drī'-īn-halp shtōōn'-dĕn bis halp zeks. dan gay'-ĕ ich
office. Then I work for another three and a half hours until half past five. Then I go

nach Hause, zum Abendessen. Abends gehe ich ins Theater, ins Kino
nach hou'-zĕ, tsōōm ah'-bĕnt-e-sĕn. ah'-bĕnts gay'-ĕ ich ints tay'-ah-tĕr, ints kee'-noh
home for supper. In the evening I go to the theatre, to the cinema,

Er geht ins Bett
ayr gayt ints bet

Er ist im Bett
ayr ist im bet

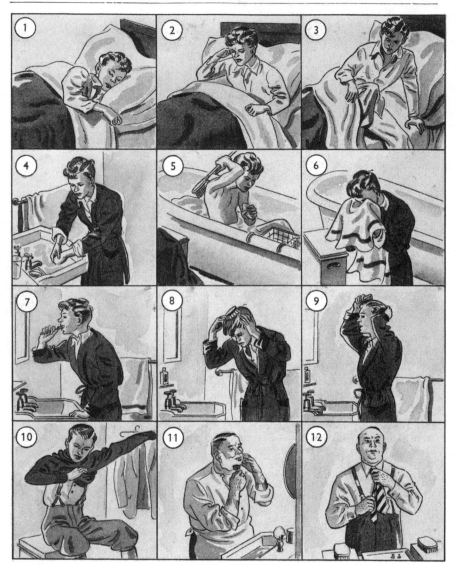

AUFSTEHEN--GETTING UP
(English key on page 367)

1. Karl schläft
2. Er wacht auf
3. Er steht auf
4. Er wäscht sich
5. Er nimmt ein Bad
6. Er trocknet sich das Gesicht ab
7. Er putzt sich die Zähne
8. Er bürstet sich das Haar
9. Er kämmt sich das Haar
10. Er kleidet sich an
11. Herr Schulz rasiert sich
12. Er bindet sich den Schlips um

oder in ein Konzert. **Oft bleibe ich abends zu Hause und höre Radio**
oh'-děr in in kon-tsert'. oft blī'-bě ich ah'-běnts tsōō hou'-zě ōont hāy'-rě rahd'-yoh
or to a concert. Often I stay at home in the evening and listen to the radio

oder lese ein Buch. **Ich gehe gewöhnlich um elf Uhr zu Bett, aber mein Vater**
oh'-děr lay'-zě in bōōch. ich gay'-ě ge-vāyn'-lich ōōm elf ōōr tsōō bet, ah'-běr min fah'-těr
or read a book. I usually go to bed at eleven o'clock, but my father

geht viel später zu Bett und liest
gayt feel shpay'-těr tsōō bet ōōnt leest
goes much later to bed and often reads

oder schreibt oft bis ein Uhr nachts.
oh'-děr shrīpt oft bis in ōōr nachts.
or writes until one o'clock at night.

Er braucht nicht viel Schlaf. Ich schlafe
ayr broucht nicht feel shlahf. ich shlah'-fě
He does not need much sleep. I sleep

acht Stunden, von elf bis sieben.
acht shtōōn'-děn, fon elf bis zee'-běn.
eight hours, from eleven to seven.

Er hört Radio
ayr hāyrt rahd'-yoh

REFLEXIVE VERBS

ich wasche mich = *I wash (myself)*
Sie waschen sich = *you wash (yourself or yourselves)*
er wäscht sich = *he washes (himself)*
sie wäscht sich = *she washes (herself)*
es wäscht sich = *it washes (itself)*
wir waschen uns = *we wash (ourselves)*
sie waschen sich = *they wash (themselves)*
Waschen Sie sich! = *Wash yourself!*

ich kleide mich an = *I dress (myself)*
Sie kleiden sich an = *you dress (yourself or yourselves)*
er kleidet sich an = *he dresses (himself)*
sie kleidet sich an = *she dresses (herself)*
es kleidet sich an = *it dresses (itself)*
wir kleiden uns an = *we dress (ourselves)*
sie kleiden sich an = *they dress (themselves)*
Kleiden Sie sich an! = *Get dressed!*

ich kleide mich aus = *I undress (myself)*
Kleiden Sie sich aus! = *Get undressed!*

Whereas in English it is sufficient to say *I wash* or *I dress* without adding *myself*, it is necessary in German to add **mich** for *myself*. **Ich wasche** by itself means *I do some washing* or *I wash something* or *somebody else*, e.g. **ich wasche meine Taschentücher** = *I wash my handkerchiefs.* Similarly, to **ich**

kleide . . . an words must be added to indicate *whom* you are dressing. If it is yourself you put **mich** between **kleide** and **an: ich kleide mich an.** Verbs like *to wash, to dress, to undress*, etc., where you do the action to yourself, are called reflexive verbs.

When a part of the body or an article of clothing is the direct object of the verb, the reflexive pronoun is the indirect object. **Ich wasche mir die Hände** = *I wash "to myself"* (indirect object) *the hands* (direct object). But **Ich wasche mich** = *I wash myself* (direct object).

Uns and **sich** are the same in form whether as direct or indirect objects.

ONE

um eins or **um ein Uhr** = *at one (o'clock)*
ein Bett = *a bed*
eine Uhr = *a watch, a clock*

Bitte, zählen Sie: eins, zwei, drei, u.s.w. = *Please count: one, two, three, etc. One is* **eins** if it stands by itself. If followed by a noun it is **ein** or **eine** according to the gender of the noun. But, as shown above, *one o'clock* is **ein Uhr,** thus distinguishing it from **eine Uhr** meaning *a watch* or *a clock*.

NEW NOUNS

DER	Morgen, -	*morning*
	Abend, -e	*evening*
	Mittag, -e	*mid-day, noon*

DIE	Uhr, -en	*clock, watch*
	Schule, -n	*school*
	Arbeit, -en	*work*
	Seife, -n	*soap*

DAS	Holz, ⋯-er	*wood*
	Wasser, -	*water*
	Büro, -s	*office*
	Kino, -s	*cinema*
	Konzert, -e	*concert*
	Haus, ⋯-er	*house*
	Bett, -en	*bed*
	Silber, Gold	*silver, gold*

Stehen Sie auf! Es ist schon halb zehn
shtay'-ĕn zee ouf! es ist shohn halp tsayn

EXERCISES

I   Answer in German

1. Wie viele Stunden hat ein Tag? 2. Wie viele Stunden arbeiten Sie? 3. Arbeiten Sie gern? 4. Arbeiten Sie viel? 5. Zeigt Ihre Uhr die Sekunden? 6. Wieviel Uhr ist es jetzt? 7. Um wieviel Uhr essen Sie Frühstück? 8. Um wieviel Uhr essen Sie zu Mittag? 9. Um wieviel Uhr essen Sie Abendbrot? 10. Was tun Sie abends? 11. Geht Ihre Uhr richtig? 12. Wie viele Zeiger hat Ihre Uhr? 13. Um wieviel Uhr kommen Sie nach Hause? 14. Essen Sie Abendbrot zu Hause oder im Restaurant? 15. Um wieviel Uhr gehen Sie zu Bett? 16. Wie viele Stunden schlafen Sie? 17. Um wieviel Uhr stehen Sie auf? 18. Wo waschen Sie sich?

II   Translate into German

1. What is this? It is a glass and it is full of water. 2. Not every glass is full. 3. How many glasses have you? I have eight. 4. Who is he? An Englishman. At what time is he coming here? 5. What time is it? It is twenty minutes past three. 6. At what time do you get up? I get up at half past six, but on Sunday I get up at nine. 7. What do you do then? I wash in the bathroom. I wash my hands and my face. Then I go back into the bedroom and dress myself. 8. At eight o'clock I go into the dining-room and have breakfast. 9. What is the date to-day? It is the 21st of March. 10. How many minutes are there in (say *has*) a quarter of an hour? Fifteen. Is that correct? 11. We have our breakfast at 7.30, lunch at 1, and supper at 6.45. 12. I work from 8 to 12.30 and from 2 to 6.15.

III   Write the following Times in German

1. 11.05 a.m. 2. 8.15 a.m. 3. 1.25 p.m. 4. 7.45 p.m. 5. Noon. 6. Midnight. 7. 11.55 a.m. 8. 11.55 p.m.

(*Answers on page* 357)

EINE ÄRZTLICHE GESCHICHTE

Ein gelehrter Professor der Medizin hatte ein sehr schwer verständliches wissenschaftliches Buch herausgegeben. Bei einem Ärzte-Kongress wurde Rudolf Virchow von einem Kollegen nach seiner Meinung über das neue Werk befragt.

"Wie denken Sie über dieses Buch, Herr Professor?"

Virchow lächelte und sagte: "Es ist ein ausgezeichnetes Werk. Es verdiente, ins Deutsche übertragen zu werden."

Ärztlich, *medical;* **die Geschichte, -n,** *story;* **gelehrt,** *learned;* **schwer verständlich,** *abstruse;* **wissenschaftlich,** *scientific;* **herausgeben,** *to publish;* **der Arzt, ⋯-e,** *doctor;* **Rudolf Virchow,** *a famous German medical man;* **die Meinung, -en,** *opinion;* **wurde . . . befragt,** *was asked;* **lächeln,** *to smile;* **ausgezeichnet,** *excellent;* **verdienen,** *to deserve;* **übertragen,** *to translate.*

NEUNTE LEKTION : *NINTH LESSON*

Hier sind fünf Häuser. Das erste Haus ist klein. Das zweite Haus ist auch klein, aber
heer zint fĭnf hoy´-zĕr.　das ayr´-stĕ hous ist klīn.　das tsvī´-tĕ hous ist ouch klīn, ah´-bĕr
Here are five houses. The first house is small. The second house is also small, but

nicht so klein wie das erste. Das erste Haus ist kleiner als das zweite. Das dritte
nicht zoh klīn vee das ayr´-stĕ.　das ayr´-stĕ hous ist klī´-nĕr als das tsvī´-tĕ.　das dri´-tĕ
not as small as the first. The first house is smaller than the second. The third

Haus ist so gross wie das vierte. Das fünfte Haus ist noch grösser. Es ist das grösste
hous ist zoh grohs vee das feer´-tĕ.　das fĭnf´-tĕ hous ist noch grāy´-sĕr.　es ist das grāys´-tĕ
house is as big as the fourth. The fifth house is still bigger. It is the biggest

Haus. Das erste Haus ist das kleinste.
hous.　das ayr´-stĕ hous ist das klīn´-stĕ.
house. The first house is the smallest.

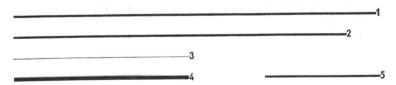

Dies sind fünf Linien. Die erste Linie ist sehr lang. Die zweite ist auch lang. Sie
dees zint fĭnf leen´-yĕn.　dee ayr´-stĕ leen´-yĕ ist zayr lang.　dee tsvī´-tĕ ist ouch lang. zee
These are five lines. The first line is very long. The second is also long. It

ist fast so lang wie die erste. Die dritte, die vierte und die fünfte Linien sind
ist fast zoh lang vee dee ayr´-stĕ.　dee dri´-tĕ, dee feer´-tĕ ŏŏnt dee fĭnf´-tĕ leen´-yĕn zint
is almost as long as the first. The third, the fourth and the fifth lines are

73

STRASSENBILD IN WIEN

Der Verkehrsschutzmann bringt den Verkehr zum Stehen, um es den Fussgängern zu ermöglichen, die Strasse zu überqueren. Das Kostüm des Mädchens mit den Zöpfen ist charakteristisch für die hübschen Trachten, die beim österreichischen Volke sehr beliebt sind.

(*Translation on page 375*)

der Verkehrsschutzmann, ···-er	**der Verkehr**	**der Fussgänger, -**	**ermöglichen**
traffic policeman	*traffic*	*pedestrian*	*to enable*
überqueren **der Zopf, ···-e**	**hübsch**	**die Tracht, -en**	**österreichisch**
to cross *braid*	*pretty*	*dress, costume*	*Austrian*

kurz. Die vierte Linie ist so kurz wie die dritte. Die erste Linie ist ein
kŏŏrts. dee feer'-tĕ leen'-yĕ ist zoh kŏŏrts vee dee dri'-tĕ. dee ayr'-stĕ leen'-yĕ ist īn
short. The fourth line is as short as the third. The first line is a

wenig länger als die zweite. Die zweite Linie ist ein wenig kürzer als die
vay'-nich leng'-gĕr als dee tsvī'-tĕ. dee tsvī'-tĕ leen'-yĕ ist īn vay'-nich kịr'-tsĕr als dee
little longer than the second. The second line is a little shorter than the

erste. Die dritte Linie ist sehr dünn. Sie ist dünner als die erste und die zweite.
ayr'-stĕ. dee dri'-tĕ leen'-yĕ ist zayr dịn. zee ist dị'-nĕr als dee ayr'-stĕ ŏŏnt dee tsvī'-tĕ.
first. The third line is very thin. It is thinner than the first and the second.

Die vierte Linie ist sehr dick. Die zweite Linie ist auch dick, aber nicht so dick wie
dee feer'-tĕ leen'-yĕ ist zayr dic. dee tsvī'-tĕ leen'-yĕ ist ouch dic, ah'-bĕr nicht zoh dic vee
The fourth line is very thick. The second line is also thick, but not as thick as

die vierte. Die vierte Linie ist die dickste, die dritte ist die dünnste. Die erste
dee feer'-tĕ. dee feer'-tĕ leen'-yĕ ist dee dix'-tĕ, dee dri'-tĕ ist dee dịns'-tĕ. dee ayr'-stĕ
the fourth. The fourth line is the thickest, the third is the thinnest. The first

Linie ist die längste, die fünfte die kürzeste.
leen'-yĕ ist dee lenx'-tĕ, dee fịnf'-tĕ dee kịr'-tsĕs-tĕ.
line is the longest, the fifth the shortest.

Hans ist zehn Jahre alt, sein Vetter Fritz ist zwölf Jahre alt, seine Kusine Hilde
hants ist tsayn yah'-rĕ alt, zīn fe'-tĕr frits ist tsvĕlf yah'-rĕ alt, zī'-nĕ kŏŏ-zee'-nĕ hil'-dĕ
Hans is ten years old, his cousin Fritz is twelve years old, his cousin Hilda

ist acht Jahre alt. Hans ist also zwei Jahre jünger als sein Vetter und zwei Jahre
ist acht yah'-rĕ alt. hants ist al'-zoh tsvī yah'-rĕ yịng'-gĕr als zīn fe'-tĕr ŏŏnt tsvī yah'-rĕ
is eight years old. Hans is therefore two years younger than his cousin and two years

älter als seine Kusine Hilde. Grete ist neun Jahre alt; sie ist also ein Jahr
el'-tĕr als zī'-nĕ kŏŏ-zee'-nĕ hil'-dĕ. gray'-tĕ ist noyn yah'-rĕ alt; zee ist al'-zoh īn yahr
older than his cousin Hilda. Grete is nine years old; she is therefore one year

jünger als ihr Bruder. Herr und Frau Lessing haben vier Kinder. Fräulein
yịng'-gĕr als eer brŏŏ'-dĕr. herr ŏŏnt frou less'-sing hah'-bĕn feer kin'-dĕr. froy'-līn
younger than her brother. Mr. and Mrs. Lessing have four children. Miss

Lessing ist das älteste Kind, Hilde das jüngste. Wie alt ist Herr Lessing? Er ist
less'-sing ist das el'-tĕs-tĕ kint, hil'-dĕ das yịngs'-tĕ. vee alt ist herr less'-sing? ayr ist
Lessing is the oldest child, Hilda the youngest. How old is Mr. Lessing? He is

vierundvierzig Jahre alt. Er ist zwei Jahre älter als seine Frau. Sie ist also
feer'-ŏŏnt-feer'-tsich yah'-rĕ alt. ayr ist tsvī yah'-rĕ el'-tĕr als zī'-nĕ frou. zee ist al'-zoh
forty-four years old. He is two years older than his wife. She is therefore

zweiundvierzig. Wer ist jünger, Frau Lessing oder ihr Bruder, Herr Schulz? Herr
tsvī'-ŏŏnt-feer-tsich. vayr ist yịng'-gĕr, frou less'-sing oh'-dĕr eer brŏŏ'-dĕr, herr shŏŏlts?
forty-two. Who is younger, Mrs. Lessing or her brother, Mr. Schulz? Mr. [herr

Schulz ist jünger als seine Schwester. Er ist ein Jahr jünger als sie. Er ist
shŏŏlts ist yịng'-gĕr als zī'-nĕ shves'-tĕr. ayr ist īn yahr yịng'-gĕr als zee. ayr ist
Schulz is younger than his sister. He is one year younger than she. He is

einundvierzig und seine Schwester zweiundvierzig.   **Ist Herr Schulz älter**
in'-ōōnt-feer-tsich ōōnt zī'-ně shves'-těr tsvī'-ōōnt-feer-tsich.   ist herr shōōlts el'-těr
forty-one and his sister forty-two.   *Is Mr. Schulz older*

oder jünger als seine Frau?   **Er ist drei Jahre älter.**   **Frau Schulz ist also**
oh'-děr yĭng'-gěr als zī'-ně frou?   ayr ist drī yah'-rě el'-těr.   frou shōōlts ist al'-zoh
or younger than his wife?   *He is three years older.*   *Mrs. Schulz is therefore*

achtunddreissig Jahre alt.   **Ja, das ist richtig.**
acht'-ōōnt-drī-sich yah'-rě alt.   yah, das ist rich'-tich.
thirty-eight years old.   *Yes, that is right.*

IN THE FRUIT SHOP

When you have studied the following conversation, imagine that you are a customer
in this shop trying to carry on a conversation with the shop assistant along similar lines.
You can refer where necessary to the names of fruit and vegetables given on pages 60 and
232. The labels shown in the picture speak for themselves, except perhaps **Heurige
Kartoffeln**, which is an Austrian expression meaning *new potatoes.*

Was kosten diese Äpfel?   **Neunzig Pfennig das Pfund.**   **Das ist sehr teuer.**   **Haben**
vas kos'-těn dee'-zě ep'-fěl?   noyn'-tsich pfe'-nich das pfōōnt.   das ist zayr toy'-ěr.   hah'-běn
How much are these apples?   *Ninety pfennigs a pound.*   *That is very expensive.*   *Haven't*

Sie nicht billigere?   **Wir haben auch billigere zu sechzig, aber sie sind nicht so**
zee nicht bi'-li-gě-rě?   veer hah'-běn ouch bi'-li-gě-rě tsōō zech'-tsich, ah'-běr zee zint
you cheaper ones?   *We have also cheaper ones at sixty, but they are not so*   [nicht zoh

gut.   **Was kostet eine Apfelsine?**   **Zehn Pfennig.**   **Das ist billig.**   **Ich nehme ein Dutzend.**
gōōt.   vas kos'-tět ī'-ně ap-fěl-zee'-ně?   tsayn pfe'-nich.   das ist bi'-lich.   ich nay'-mě īn dōō'-
good.   *How much is an orange?*   *Ten pfennigs.*   *That is cheap.*   *I (will) take a dozen.*   [tsěnt.

Herr Lessing hat viel Geld.   Er ist reich.   Er ist reicher als sein Schwager, Herr Schulz.
herr less'-sing hat feel gelt.   ayr ist rīch.   ayr ist rī'-chĕr als zīn shvah'-gĕr, herr shōōlts.
Mr. Lessing has much money.   He is rich.   He is richer than his brother-in-law, Mr. Schulz.

Die Familie Schulz ist nicht reich, sie haben nur eine Dreizimmerwohnung.
dee fah-meel'-yĕ shōōlts ist nicht rīch, zee hah'-bĕn nōōr ī'-nĕ drī'-tsi-mĕr-voh-nōōng.
The Schulz family is not rich, they have only a three-room flat.

Die Familie Lessing hat eine
dee fah-meel'-yĕ less'-sing hat ī'-ne
The Lessing family has a

schöne grosse Villa in einem
shāȳ'-nĕ groh'-sĕ vi'-lah in ī'-nĕm
beautiful large villa in a

Vorort von Berlin.
for'-ort fon ber-leen'.
suburb of Berlin.

Die Flasche ist halb voll
dee fla'-shĕ ist halp foll

Das Glas ist ganz voll
das glas ist gants foll

Karl, Erich, Walter, Heinrich und Wilhelm trinken Bier.   In Karls Glas ist viel
kahrl, ay'-rich, val'-tĕr, hīn'-rich ōōnt vil'-helm tring'-kĕn beer.   in kahrls glas ist feel
Charles, Eric, Walter, Henry and William are drinking beer. In Charles's glass there is much

Bier; sein Glas ist voll.   In Erichs Glas ist etwas weniger Bier, es ist fast voll.   Walters
beer; zīn glas ist foll.   in ay'-richs glas ist et'-was vay'-ni-gĕr beer, es ist fast foll.   val'-ters
beer; his glass is full. In Eric's glass (there) is a little less beer, it is almost full. Walter's

Glas ist halb voll.   In Heinrichs Glas ist nur wenig Bier.   Sein Glas ist fast leer.
glas ist halp foll.   in hīn'-richs glas ist nōōr vay'-nich beer.   zīn glas ist fast layr.
glass is half full. In Henry's glass there is only a little beer. His glass is almost empty.

Wilhelms Glas ist ganz leer; er hat kein Bier.
vil'-helms glas ist gants layr; ayr hat kīn beer.
William's glass is quite empty; he has no beer.

Fünf Glas Bier
fĭnf glas beer

SCHLOSS NEUSCHWANSTEIN

Dieses bei Hohenschwangau in Südbayern gelegene Schloss ist eines der schönsten bayerischen Königsschlösser. Wie andere Schlösser verdankt es seine Existenz den romantischen Neigungen Ludwigs des Zweiten. Die Lage des Schlosses ist unvergleichlich schön mit einer weiten Aussicht auf die bayerischen Alpen, die einen grossartigen Hintergrund bilden.

(*Translation on page* 375)

gelegen	**das Königsschloss, ⸱⸱⸱-er**	**verdanken**	**die Neigung, -en**	**die Lage, -n**
situated	*royal castle*	*to owe*	*inclination*	*position*
unvergleichlich	**die Aussicht, -en**	**grossartig**	**der Hintergrund, ⸱⸱⸱-e**	**bilden**
incomparable	*view*	*magnificent*	*background*	*to form*

78

COMPARISONS

Mein Buch ist so dick wie ihr Buch.
My book is as thick as her book.

Hamburg ist nicht so gross wie Berlin.
Hamburg is not as big as Berlin.

Hamburg ist grösser als München.
Hamburg is bigger than Munich.

Grete ist kleiner als Hans, aber sie ist intelligenter (in-tĕ-li-gen′-tĕr).
Grete is smaller than Hans, but she is more intelligent.

Diese Zeitung ist besser als jene.
This newspaper is better than that one.

Paris ist die grösste Stadt in Frankreich.
Paris is the largest city in France.

Die Wolga ist der längste Fluss in Russland.
The Volga is the longest river in Russia.

Viele sagen, Budapest ist die schönste Stadt in Europa.
Many say Budapest is the most beautiful city in Europe.

Der höchste Berg ist mit Schnee bedeckt
dayr hȳchs′-tĕ berk ist mit shnay bĕ-dekt′

Positive		Comparative	Superlative	
klein	= small	kleiner		kleinste
gross	= big	grösser		grösste
schön	= beautiful	schöner		schönste
lang	= long	länger	der	längste
alt	= old	älter		älteste
kurz	= short	kürzer	die	kürzeste
intelligent	= intelligent	intelligenter		intelligenteste
interessant	= interesting	interessanter	das	interessanteste
gut	= good	besser		beste
hoch	= high	höher		höchste
nah	= near	näher		nächste

German adjectives are compared by adding **-er** to form the comparative, **-ste** to form the superlative; and with most words of one syllable by modifying **a, o, u,** as well.

Note:—(1) An **-e-** is inserted before the **-ste** of the superlative after **z** or **t** (**der kürzeste, der älteste**).

(2) **-er** and **-ste** are added, no matter how long the adjective may be. Thus: *more interesting*=**interessanter**; *the most intelligent woman*=**die intelligenteste Frau**, etc.

(3) *Than*, after the comparative, is **als** (**älter als ich**=*older than I*).

(4) The comparison of **gut** is irregular; also the comparative of **hoch** and the superlative of **nah**.

(5) A few adjectives, although of one syllable, do not modify; among others, the following:

klar=*clear*	**klarer**	**der,**	⎰ **klarste**
voll=*full*	**voller**	**die, das**	⎱ **vollste**

DER OPTIMIST UND DER PESSIMIST

Der Optimist sagt:
    " Die Flasche ist halb voll."

Der Pessimist sagt:
    " Die Flasche ist halb leer."

DEFINITE ARTICLE
with Price Quotations, Measurements, etc.

Diese Birnen kosten sechzig Pfennig das Pfund.
These pears cost sixty pfennigs a pound.

Die Bananen kosten zehn Pfennig das Stück.
The bananas cost ten pfennigs apiece.

Er rechnet drei Mark für die Stunde.
He charges three marks an hour.

Dieser Stoff kostet vier Mark dreissig der Meter.
This material costs four marks thirty a metre.

Die Limonade kostet fünfzehn Pfennig das kleine Glas.
The lemonade costs fifteen pfennigs a small glass.

When giving price quotations, measurements, weights, etc., the definite article is used in German, instead of the indefinite article as used in English.

Note:—(1) **das Stück** is used for *apiece* or *each*. (2) **Mark, Pfennig, Pfund, Meter, Stück,** etc., are used for both singular and plural, when preceded by a cardinal number (see footnote on page 40).

NEW NOUNS

DER	Vetter, -n	*cousin (male)*
	Pfennig, -e	*penny*
	Berg, -e	*mountain*
	Optimist, -en	*optimist*
	Pessimist, -en	*pessimist*
	Fluss, ··-e	*river*
	Stoff, -e	*material*
DIE	Linie, -n	*line*
	Kusine, -n	*cousin (female)*
	Flasche, -n	*bottle*
	Stadt, ··-e	*town*
DAS	Geld, -er	*money*
	Geschäft, -e	*business, shop*
	Pfund, -e	*pound*
	Dutzend, -e	*dozen*
	Stück, -e	*piece*

EXERCISES

I Answer in German

1. Hat Herr Ford viel Geld? 2. Haben Sie so viel Geld wie er? 3. Haben Sie viele Taschentücher? 4. Was ist grösser, ein Herrentaschentuch oder ein Damentaschentuch? 5. Sind Damenschuhe so gross wie Herrenschuhe? 6. Sind Kinderschuhe kleiner als Herrenschuhe? 7. Welches ist die grösste Stadt in Amerika? 8. Ist der Rhein der längste Fluss in Europa? 9. Was ist grösser, eine Taschenuhr oder eine Armbanduhr? 10. Geht Ihre Uhr gut? 11. Was ist schöner, die Rose oder die Lilie? 12. Welches ist die schönste Blume, die Rose, die Nelke oder die Narzisse? 13. Wann sind die Tage länger, im Juli oder im September? 14. Welches ist der längste Tag? 15. Wann sind die Tage kürzer, im Herbst oder im Winter? 16. Welches ist der kürzeste Tag?

II Translate into German

1. They have a beautiful flat. 2. My book is thicker than your book. 3. How old are you? 4. I am older than you. 5. You are younger than my sister. 6. Who is the oldest here? 7. Are you the youngest? 8. Which is better, the red wine or the white wine? 9. Is this the best book? 10. Is this the shortest way? (der Weg, vayk). 11. Which way is shorter? 12. This way is as short as that (way). 13. Are you eating a whole orange or only a half? 14. Is this the biggest hotel? (das Hotel, hoh-tel'). 15. It is not the biggest, but it is the best. 16. How much are the pears? 17. They are too dear. 18. Are these cheaper?

III Insert the comparative or superlative of alt, jung, lang, dünn, gross, interessant, gut

1. Mein Bruder ist . . . als ich. 2. Ich bin das . . . Kind. 3. Diese Strasse ist . . . als jene. 4. Dies ist die . . . Strasse. 5. Welches Buch ist . . ., dieses oder jenes? 6. München ist die . . . Stadt in Süddeutschland. 7. Was ist . . ., der Rotwein oder der Weisswein? 8. Ist dies der . . . Wein? 9. Welches ist das . . . Buch? 10. Ist Frau Schulz . . . als ihr Mann?

(Answers on page 358)

ZEHNTE LEKTION: *TENTH LESSON*

Er liebt mich, er liebt mich nicht, er liebt mich
ayr leept mich, ayr leept mich nicht, ayr leept mich

Sie liebt ihn. Er liebt sie. Die Eltern lieben ihre Kinder. Unsere Eltern lieben
zee leept een. ayr leept zee. dee el'-tĕrn lee'-bĕn ee'-rĕ kin'-dĕr. ōōn'-zĕ-rĕ el'-tĕrn lee'-bĕn
She loves him. He loves her. The parents love their children. Our parents love

uns, und wir lieben sie. Ich liebe sie, und sie lieben mich.
ōōns ōōnt veer lee'-bĕn zee. ich lee'-bĕ zee ōōnt zee lee'-bĕn mich.
us and we love them. I love them and they love me.

DIRECT OBJECT (I)
(Me, Him, Her, Them, Us, You)

Er liebt sie
ayr leept zee

er hört mich = *he hears me*
sie hört ihn = *she hears him*
ich sehe sie = *I see her*
wir sehen Sie = *we see you*
Sie sehen sie = *you see them*
sie hören uns = *they hear us*

Subject: **ich**=*I*, **er**=*he*, **sie**=*she* or *they*, **wir**=*we*, **Sie**=*you*.

Direct object: **mich**=*me*, **ihn**=*him*, **sie**=*her* or *them*, **uns**=*us*, **Sie**=*you*.

There is no difference in German between *she, her, they* and *them*. These four words are rendered by **sie**. We have already seen that when **sie** is the subject it means *she* if the verb ends in **-t**, and *they* if the verb ends in **-en**. When **sie** is the direct object the only way to tell whether *her* or *them* is intended is by the context.

The subject usually precedes the verb and the object follows it, e.g. **sie kennt sie**=*she knows her* (or *them*). In questions, both forms follow the verb, but then the subject precedes the object. **Kennt sie sie?**=*does she know her* (or *them*)?

You will remember that **er** (*he*) and **sie** (*she*) are also pronouns for masculine and feminine names of things which are the subject of the verb. In the same way **ihn** (*him*) and **sie** (*her*) are also the pronouns for masculine and feminine names of things which are the direct object of the verb, and are translated then by *it*. *I see it* (den Bleistift)=**ich sehe ihn**; *I see it* (die Feder)=**ich sehe sie**.

81

eine Kaffeetasse
ĭ'-nĕ ka'-fay-ta-sĕ

ein Glas Bier
ĭn glas beer

eine Flasche Wein
ĭ'-nĕ fla'-shĕ vīn

ein Bierglas
ĭn beer'-glas

eine Tasse Kaffee
ĭ'-nĕ ta'-sĕ ka'-fay

eine Weinflasche
ĭ'-nĕ vīn'-fla-shĕ

COMPOUND NOUNS

das Blei (*lead*)   + der Stift (*stick*)   = der Bleistift (*pencil*)
die Lippen (*lips*) + der Stift (*stick*)   = der Lippenstift (*lipstick*)
das Haus (*house*) + die Tür (*door*)   = die Haustür (*house door*)
der Wein (*wine*)   + das Glas (*glass*)   = das Weinglas (*wine glass*)
der Wein (*wine*)   + die Flasche (*bottle*) = die Weinflasche (*wine bottle*)
der Wein (*wine*)   + der Berg (*mountain*) = der Weinberg (*vineyard*)

Note from the above examples that compound nouns have the gender of the last component; **das Streichholz** is neuter, but **die Schachtel** is feminine, therefore **die Streichholzschachtel** (*match box*) is also feminine because **Schachtel** is the last component.

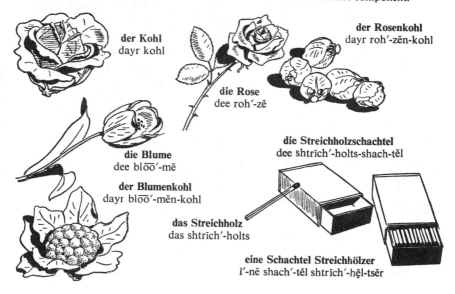

der Kohl
dayr kohl

der Rosenkohl
dayr roh'-zĕn-kohl

die Rose
dee roh'-zĕ

die Blume
dee blōō'-mĕ

die Streichholzschachtel
dee shtrīch'-holts-shach-tĕl

der Blumenkohl
dayr blōō'-mĕn-kohl

das Streichholz
das shtrīch'-holts

eine Schachtel Streichhölzer
ĭ'-nĕ shach'-tĕl shtrīch'-hĕl-tsĕr

das Gepäck
das gĕ-pek´

der Gepäckträger
dayr gĕ-pek´-tray-gĕr

der Brief
dayr breef

der Briefträger
dayr breef´-tray-gĕr

Die Tulpe ist eine schöne Blume. Die Nelke ist schöner, die Rose ist am
dee tōol´-pĕ ist ī´-nĕ shāy´-nĕ blōo´-mĕ. dee nel´-kĕ ist shāy´-nĕr, dee roh´-zĕ ist am
The tulip is a beautiful flower. The carnation is more beautiful, the rose is the most

schönsten. Ich habe Nelken gern, ich habe Tulpen lieber, aber ich habe
shāyns´-tĕn. ich hah´-bĕ nel´-kĕn gern, ich hah´-bĕ tōol´-pĕn lee´-bĕr, ah´-bĕr ich hah´-bĕ
beautiful. I like carnations, I like tulips better, but I like

Rosen am liebsten. Was trinken Sie lieber, Tee oder Kaffee? Ich trinke
roh´-zĕn am leeps´-tĕn. vas tring´-kĕn zee lee´-bĕr, tay oh´-dĕr ka´-fay? ich tring´-kĕ
roses best. Which do you prefer to drink, tea or coffee? I

Tee lieber, aber ich trinke auch gern Kaffee. Herr Schulz trinkt am liebsten
tay lee´-bĕr, ah´-bĕr ich tring´-kĕ ouch gern ka´-fay. herr shōolts trinkt am leeps´-tĕn
prefer (to drink) tea, but I also like (to drink) coffee. Mr. Schulz likes

Bier. Was trinken Sie am liebsten? Ich trinke am liebsten Rotwein. Essen Sie
beer. vas tring´-kĕn zee am leeps´-tĕn? ich tring´-kĕ am leeps´-tĕn roht´-vīn. e´-sĕn zee
beer best. What do you like best to drink? I like red wine best. Do you

gern Erdbeeren? Ich esse sie gern, aber ich esse Kirschen lieber.
gern ayrt´-bay-rĕn? ich e´-sĕ zee gern, ah´-bĕr ich e´-sĕ kir´-shĕn lee´-bĕr.
like strawberries? I like them, but I like cherries better.

das Rad
das rat

das Fahrrad
das fahr´-rat

das Motorrad
das mo-tohr´-rat

DER KAMPF UMS TÄGLICHE BROT

Der Schweizer Bauer hat manch ungewöhnliche Arbeit zu leisten. Er muss auf gefährlich steilen Bergabhängen pflügen und eggen; denn jedes Stückchen Erde, das irgendwie Ertrag hergibt, muss mühsam bebaut werden, damit die Lebensmittelversorgung des Landes aufrecht erhalten werden kann.

(*Translation on page* 375)

der Kampf, ··-e	**täglich**	**manch**	**ungewöhnlich**	**gefährlich**	**pflügen**	**eggen**
struggle	*daily*	*many a*	*unusual*	*dangerous*	*to plough*	*to harrow*

irgendwie	**mühsam**	**bebaut**	**die Lebensmittelversorgung, -en**	**aufrecht erhalten**
in any way	*laboriously*	*cultivated*	*food supply*	*to maintain*

Herr Lessing liest viel. Er liest gern Romane. Er liest gerade einen
herr less'-sing leest feel. ayr leest gern roh-mah'-nĕ. ayr leest gĕ-rah'-dĕ ī'-nĕn
Mr. Lessing reads a great deal. He likes reading novels. He is just reading a

Roman von Émile Zola. Lesen Sie auch gern Bücher von Zola? Ich
roh-mahn' fon ay-meel' zoh-lah'. lay'-zĕn zee ouch gern bę̄'-chĕr fon zoh-lah'? ich
novel by Émile Zola. Do you also like reading books by Zola? I

finde sie ganz interessant, aber ich lese lieber ein Buch von Galsworthy.
fin'-dĕ zee gants in-tĕ-rĕ-sant', ah'-bĕr ich lay'-zĕ lee'-bĕr īn bōōch fon gauls'-wor-thy.
find them quite interesting, but I prefer reading a book by Galsworthy.

Ich lese französische Romane ganz gern, aber ich lese englische
ich lay'-zĕ fran-tsā͞y'-zi-shĕ roh-mah'-nĕ gants gern, ah'-bĕr ich lay'-zĕ eng'-li-shĕ
I like reading French novels quite well, but I prefer to read English

Bücher lieber. Ich lese am liebsten die Romane von Dickens.
bę̄'-chĕr lee'-bĕr. ich lay'-zĕ am leeps'-tĕn dee roh-mah'-nĕ fon di'-kens.
books. I like reading the novels of Dickens best.

COMPARISON OF ADVERBS

Sie singt schön.
She sings beautifully.

Sie singt schöner als er.
She sings more beautifully than he.

Wer schreibt am schönsten?
Who writes best? (Who has the most beautiful handwriting?)

Das Fahrrad fährt schnell.
The bicycle is (lit., travels) fast.

Das Motorrad fährt schneller.
The motor-bicycle is faster.

Das Auto fährt am schnellsten.
The motor-car is fastest.

Rotwein schmeckt gut.
Red wine tastes good.

Weisswein schmeckt besser.
White wine tastes better.

Sekt schmeckt am besten.
Champagne tastes best.

Note.— As most adjectives can be used as adverbs, it follows that adverbs are compared like adjectives, but the superlatives take the form **am ...sten.**

Not only adverbs, but adjectives also, have a form of the superlative with **am ...sten.** Thus, there are two forms of the superlative: **der, die, das grösste** and **am grössten.**

The former is used when several objects of the same kind are compared: **Die Rose ist die schönste Blume** = *The rose is the most beautiful flower.*

The latter is used to express the idea that a thing is at its highest degree; it corresponds to the English superlative without the article: **Dort ist es am wärmsten**=*There it is warmest.* **Die Apfelsinen sind hier am süssesten**=*The oranges are sweetest here.*

		Positive			Comparative	Superlative
Regular	{	schnell	=	*quickly*	schneller	am schnellsten
		schön	=	*beautifully*	schöner	am schönsten
		wenig	=	*little*	weniger	am wenigsten
Irregular	{	gut	=	*well*	besser	am besten
		gern	=	*gladly*	lieber	am liebsten
		viel	=	*much*	mehr (*more*)	am meisten (*most*)
		hoch	=	*high*	höher	am höchsten
		nah	=	*near*	näher	am nächsten

VERBS CHANGING ROOT VOWEL IN THIRD PERSON SINGULAR

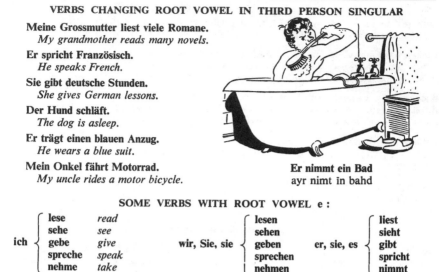

Meine Grossmutter liest viele Romane.
My grandmother reads many novels.

Er spricht Französisch.
He speaks French.

Sie gibt deutsche Stunden.
She gives German lessons.

Der Hund schläft.
The dog is asleep.

Er trägt einen blauen Anzug.
He wears a blue suit.

Mein Onkel fährt Motorrad.
My uncle rides a motor bicycle.

Er nimmt ein Bad
ayr nimt in bahd

SOME VERBS WITH ROOT VOWEL e :

ich
lese	read
sehe	see
gebe	give
spreche	speak
nehme	take

wir, Sie, sie
| lesen |
| sehen |
| geben |
| sprechen |
| nehmen |

er, sie, es
| liest |
| sieht |
| gibt |
| spricht |
| nimmt |

SOME VERBS WITH ROOT VOWEL a :

ich
schlafe	sleep
trage	carry (wear)
fahre	drive (ride)

wir, Sie, sie
| schlafen |
| tragen |
| fahren |

er, sie, es
| schläft |
| trägt |
| fährt |

Some verbs with e as their root vowel change it to i (or ie) in the third person singular, but not all verbs with e have this modification, as we know from **ich gehe, er geht; ich lebe, er lebt; ich stehe, er steht.**
Some verbs with a as their root vowel modify it to ä in the third person singular, but here again the modification does not apply to all verbs with a (**ich sage, er sagt; ich habe, er hat,** etc.).

Note.—(1) **Tragen** can mean both *to carry* and *to wear.* **Der Briefträger** = *the postman* (lit., *the letter carrier*). **Er trägt eine Uniform** = *he wears a uniform.* (2) **Fahren** is *to ride, to drive* or *to go by vehicle;* **gehen** is used only for *to walk. To go* (by car, ship. train, etc.) is **fahren.** *To ride a bicycle* = **Rad fahren;** *to drive a car* = **ein Auto fahren.** But **fahren** cannot be used for riding an animal, for which the verb is **reiten.**

der Radfahrer[1]
dayr rat'-fahr-ĕr

der Autofahrer
dayr ou'-toh-fahr-ĕr

der Reiter
rī'-tĕr

[1] In colloquial German **Rad** is often used for **Fahrrad** (*cycle*).

THE LESSINGS AT HOME

Can you describe in simple sentences what each member of the family is doing? *To knit* is **stricken,** *stocking* is **der Strumpf,** and *newspaper* **die Zeitung.** Remember to change the root vowels of **lesen** and **schlafen** in describing the actions of Herr Lessing and Hilde.

TO LIKE SOMEBODY OR SOMETHING
(See also Lesson 5)

Sie hat Rosen gern.
She likes roses.

Sie hat ihn gern.
She likes him.

Er hat sie nicht gern.
He does not like her.

Ich fahre gern Rad.
I like cycling.

Ich esse gern Fleisch.
I like (eating) meat.

Ich esse lieber Fisch.
I prefer fish.

Was trinken Sie am liebsten?
What do you like best to drink?

Ich tue es gern.
I like doing it.

Ich habe sie lieber als ihn.
I like her better than him.

In Lesson 5 we explained that in order to say that they like doing something, Germans say that they do it gladly. To like doing anything better is to *do it preferably* **(lieber),** and to like doing something best is to *do it most preferably* **(am liebsten).** From the examples given above you can see that to like somebody or something is rendered by **gern haben;** to like somebody (or something) *better* is **lieber haben;** and to like *best* is **am liebsten haben.**

A LOVE POEM

Keine Rose, keine Nelke
kann blühen so schön,
Als die Liebe von zwei Seelen,
wenn sie treu beisammen stehn.

Kein, *no;* **blühen,** *to bloom;* **die Seele, -n,** *soul;* **treu,** *true;* **beisammen,** *together.*

BLUMEN—FLOWERS
(English key on page 367)

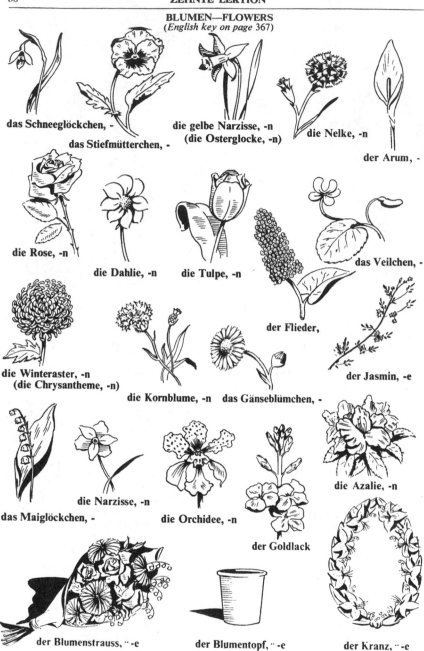

das Schneeglöckchen, -

das Stiefmütterchen, -

die gelbe Narzisse, -n
(die Osterglocke, -n)

die Nelke, -n

der Arum, -

die Rose, -n

die Dahlie, -n

die Tulpe, -n

das Veilchen, -

der Flieder,

die Winteraster, -n
(die Chrysantheme, -n)

die Kornblume, -n   das Gänseblümchen, -

der Jasmin, -e

das Maiglöckchen, -

die Narzisse, -n

die Orchidee, -n

der Goldlack

die Azalie, -n

der Blumenstrauss, ¨-e

der Blumentopf, ¨-e

der Kranz, ¨-e

NEW NOUNS

DER
- **Brief, -e** — *letter*
- **Briefträger, -** — *postman*
- **Gepäckträger, -** — *porter*
- **Schrank, ⋯-e** — *cupboard*
- **Roman, -e** — *novel*
- **Hund, -e** — *dog*
- **Radfahrer, -** — *cyclist*
- **Strumpf, ⋯-e** — *stocking*
- **Reiter, -** — *rider*

DIE
- **Schachtel, -n** — *box*
- **Blume, -n** — *flower*
- **Tulpe, -n** — *tulip*
- **Nelke, -n** — *carnation*
- **Rose, -n** — *rose*
- **Erdbeere, -n** — *strawberry*

DAS
- **Streichholz, ⋯-er** — *match*
- **Gepäck,** — *luggage, articles of*
- **Gepäckstücke** — *luggage*
- **Auto, -s** — *motor-car*
- **Rad, ⋯-er** — *wheel*
- **Fahrrad, ⋯-er** — *bicycle*
- **Bad, ⋯-er** — *bath*

10. Er ist Schotte. Er heisst Jock. Seine Frau ist aber Deutsche. 11. Sie essen gern Erdbeeren. 12. Meine Schwester isst am liebsten Kirschen.

II Answer in German

1. Lesen Sie gern Romane? 2. Was lesen Sie lieber, Kriminalromane oder Liebesromane? 3. Essen Sie gern Erdbeeren? 4. Was essen Sie lieber, Erdbeeren oder Kirschen? 5. Was essen Sie am liebsten? 6. Was trinken Sie am liebsten? 7. Finden Sie Bernard Shaws Bücher interessant? 8. Sprechen Sie Deutsch? 9. Haben Sie viele Bücher? 10. Lesen Sie viel? 11. Fahren Sie Rad? 12. Haben Sie ein Fahrrad?

III Translate into German

1. I love her. 2. She loves him. 3. He loves her. 4. She does not love me. 5. I do not love him. 6. We speak German. 7.

der Kleiderschrank
dayr klī′-dĕr-shrank

SCHRÄNKE
shreng′-kĕ

der Bücherschrank
dayr bĕ̄′-chĕr-shrank

der Küchenschrank
dayr kī′-chĕn-shrank

EXERCISES

I Read and Translate

1. Sprechen Sie Deutsch? 2. Ein wenig, nicht viel. 3. Spricht Ihre Frau Französisch? 4. Sie liest französische Bücher und Zeitungen, aber sie spricht nicht gut. 5. Sie nimmt französische Stunden. 6. Nehmen Sie deutsche Stunden? 7. Ich habe einen Freund. Er ist Lehrer. Er gibt deutsche Stunden. 8. Ist er Deutscher? 9. Er ist kein Deutscher, aber er spricht gut Deutsch.

They do not speak French. 8. What are you doing? 9. I am reading. 10. What is she doing? 11. She is reading a book. 12. I like eating strawberries. 13. I do not like cherries. 14. I like him. 15. She does not like him. 16. We do not like them. 17. Do you like him? 18. Do you read much? 19. Do you like writing letters? 20. Which do you prefer, tea or coffee? 21. I like tea better than coffee. 22. I don't like tea without milk.

(*Answers on page* 358)

ELFTE LEKTION : *ELEVENTH LESSON*

DIRECT OBJECT (II)
(continued from Lesson 10)

Ich schreibe einen Brief.
I am writing a letter.

Haben Sie eine Feder?
Have you a pen?

Haben Sie einen Bleistift?
Have you a pencil?

Nehmen Sie die Feder!
Take the pen.

Nehmen Sie den Bleistift!
Take the pencil.

Haben Sie einen Bogen Briefpapier?
Have you a sheet of notepaper?

Stecken Sie den Brief in den Umschlag!
Put the letter into the envelope.

Subject: **Der Bleistift (die Feder, das Buch)**
ist rot

Direct Object: **Ich nehme den Bleistift**
(die Feder, das Buch)

With masculine nouns, the article **der** indicates that the noun is the subject of the

Die Tür ist offen, das Fenster ist zu
dee tēēr ist o'-fĕn, das fens'-tĕr ist tsōō

sentence. When a masculine noun is used as the direct object, this is indicated by a change in the article, which becomes **den** instead of **der**. No difference between subject and object is made in the articles of feminine and neuter nouns, or of nouns in the plural.

The above sentences put in the plural would be as follows :

Subject: **Die Bleistifte (Federn, Bücher) sind rot.**

Direct Object : **Ich nehme die Bleistifte (Federn, Bücher).**

In grammar the subject is said to be in the nominative case, the direct object in the accusative case[1]. Thus **den Vater** is the accusative case of **der Vater**, but **die Mutter** and **das Kind** have no distinguishing forms for the accusative case, as this distinction is limited to masculine nouns in the singular.

Er öffnet das Fenster, sie schliesst die Tür
ayr ȇf'-nĕt das fens'-tĕr, zee shleest dee tēēr

Das Fenster ist jetzt offen und die Tür ist jetzt zu
das fens'-tĕr ist yetst o'-fĕn ŏŏnt dee tēēr ist yetst tsōō

---

[1] In English grammar the accusative of *he* is *him* ; of *I me* ; of *who, whom*, etc.

A similar change takes place in connection with the masculine form of the indefinite article (ein). Compare the following pairs of sentences:

Masculine, singular

Das ist ein Baum=*That is a tree;*
Ich sehe einen Baum=*I see a tree.*

Feminine, singular

Das ist eine Kirche=*That is a church;*
Ich sehe eine Kirche=*I see a church.*

Neuter, singular

Da kommt ein Kind=*There comes a child;*
Ich höre ein Kind=*I hear a child.*

Plural (all genders)

Da sind (die) Bäume, Kirchen, Männer.
Ich sehe (die) Frauen, Kinder, etc.

FURTHER EXAMPLES:

Dieser Stuhl ist besser als jener.
This chair is better than that one.

Nehmen Sie diesen, nicht jenen.
Take this one, not that one.

Ich nehme diesen Mantel, diesen Hut, dieses Kleid und diese Schuhe.
I am taking this overcoat, this hat, this dress and these shoes.

Sie haben meinen Stuhl, warum nehmen Sie nicht Ihren?
You have my chair, why don't you take yours?

Bitte, stecken Sie Ihren Regenschirm und seinen Stock in den Schirmständer.
Please put your umbrella and his walking-stick in the umbrella stand.

The accusative of **dieser** is **diesen;** of **mein, meinen;** of **sein, seinen;** of **ihr, ihren;** etc.

Note that the accusative is used after the verb **haben** (*to have*), the nominative case after **sein** (*to be*), e.g.

Es ist hier ein Hund.
There is a dog here.

Wir haben einen Hund.
We have a dog.

Er steckt den Brief in den Briefkasten
ayr shtekt dayn breef in dayn breef'-ka-stĕn

ENDINGS OF ADJECTIVES (II)
(continued from Lesson 4)

Er schreibt einen sehr langen Brief.
He is writing a very long letter.

Ich habe einen blauen Bleistift und Sie haben einen gelben.
I have a blue pencil and you have a yellow one.

Sie trägt einen grünen Hut, einen grauen Mantel und blaue Schuhe.
She is wearing a green hat, a grey coat and blue shoes.

Note that the adjective also takes the ending -en in the masculine singular form of the accusative.

Er öffnet den Geldschrank
ayr ĕf'-nĕt dayn gelt'-shrank

JUWELEN UND SCHMUCKSACHEN—JEWELLERY AND TRINKETS
(English key on page 367)

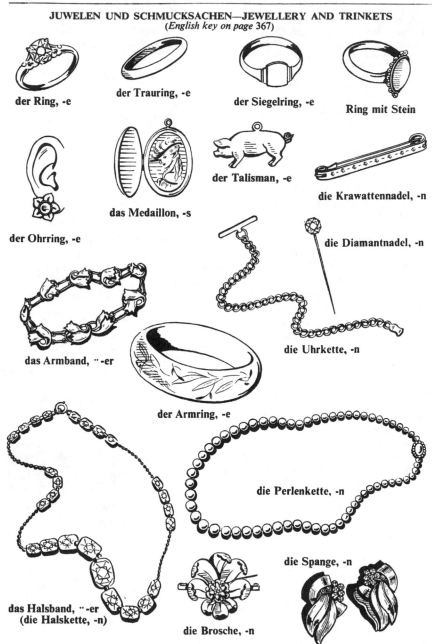

der Ring, -e

der Trauring, -e

der Siegelring, -e

Ring mit Stein

der Talisman, -e

die Krawattennadel, -n

das Medaillon, -s

die Diamantnadel, -n

der Ohrring, -e

die Uhrkette, -n

das Armband, ̈-er

der Armring, -e

die Perlenkette, -n

die Spange, -n

das Halsband, ̈-er
(die Halskette, -n)

die Brosche, -n

Ich habe eine sehr gute Uhr. Sie ist aus Gold. Goldene Uhren sind teuer. Sind
ich hah'-bĕ ĭ'-nĕ zayr gōō'-tĕ ōōr. zee ist ous golt. gol'-dĕ-nĕ ōō'-rĕn zint toy'-ĕr. zint
I have a very good watch. It is made of gold. Gold watches are expensive. Are

Uhren in Deutschland teuer? Goldene Uhren sind natürlich teuer. Sie können
ōō'-rĕn in doytsh'-lant toy'-ĕr? gol'-dĕ-nĕ ōō'-rĕn zint na-tȩr'-lich toy'-ĕr. zee kȩ'-nĕn
watches expensive in Germany? Gold watches are, of course, expensive. You can,

aber eine gute, silberne Uhr für dreissig oder vierzig Mark kaufen. Ich
ah'-bĕr ĭ'-nĕ gōō'-tĕ, zil'-bĕr-nĕ ōōr fȩr drī'-sich oh'-dĕr feer'-tsich mark kou'-fĕn. ich
however, buy a good silver watch for thirty or forty marks. I

finde das sehr billig. In England sind sie teuer. Uhren und Juwelen sind
fin'-dĕ das zayr bi'-lich. in eng'-lant zint zee toy'-ĕr. ōō'-rĕn ŏont yōō-vay'-lĕn zint
find that very cheap. In England they are expensive. Watches and jewellery are

in England teurer, aber gute Kleidung ist billiger.
in eng'-lant toy'-rĕr, ah'-bĕr gōō'-tĕ klī'-dŏong ist bi'-li-gĕr.
dearer in England, but good clothing is cheaper.

der Schlüssel
dayr shl̯ĭ'-sĕl

Der Ring ist aus Gold (das Gold = *gold*).
Die Uhr ist aus Silber (das Silber = *silver*).
Die Feder ist aus Stahl (der Stahl = *steel*).
Der Schlüssel ist aus Eisen (das Eisen = *iron*).
Der Spiegel ist aus Glas (das Glas = *glass*).
Möbel[1] sind aus Holz (das Holz = *wood*).
Der Ball ist aus Gummi
        (das Gummi = *rubber*).
Das Buch ist aus Papier (das Papier = *paper*).
Das Kleid ist aus Baumwolle
        (die Baumwolle = *cotton*).
Der Anzug ist aus Wolle (die Wolle = *wool*).
Die Bluse ist aus Seide (die Seide = *silk*).
Das Taschentuch ist aus Leinen
        (das Leinen = *linen*).
Die Schuhe sind aus Leder
        (das Leder = *leather*).

"Haben Sie einen Spiegel?"
"Einen Handspiegel?"
"Nein, einen für das Gesicht".
(Der Spiegel = *mirror;* das Gesicht = *face*).

DER SCHLÜSSEL
(*A verse by Friedrich von Schiller, 1759 - 1805*)

Willst du dich selber erkennen,
  so sieh, wie die andern es treiben.
Willst du die andern verstehn,
  blick in dein eigenes Herz.

Du, dich, dein, *thou, thee, thine;* selber,
self; erkennen, *to know;* andern, *other;*
treiben, *to do;* blicken, *to glance;* eigen,
own; das Herz, -en, *heart.*

(The uses of the familiar forms du, dich and dein are explained in Lesson 21.)

---

[1] Möbel (plural) = *furniture.* Das Möbel = *piece of furniture.*

WIESBADEN: DER BLUMENGARTEN VOR DEM KURHAUS

Die lateinische Inschrift über dem Portal des Kurhauses verkündet, dass man sich hier im Gebiet der schon den Römern bekannten heilkräftigen Quellen befindet. Der berühmte Badeort wird jährlich von tausenden aus allen Ländern besucht, die in seinen warmen Quellen Heilung gegen Gicht, Rheumatismus und Katarrhe suchen.

(*Translation on page* 375)

das Kurhaus, ¨-er	die Inschrift, -en	verkünden	das Gebiet, -e
pump room (*cure house*)	*inscription*	*to proclaim*	*region, sphere*

heilkräftig	die Quelle, -n	sich befinden	der Badeort, -e	die Gicht
healing	*spring*	*to find oneself*	*spa*	*gout*

94

Ich stelle
(die Flaschen auf den Tisch)

Ich lege
(die Bücher auf den Tisch)

Ich stecke
(den Brief in die Tasche)

HOW TO TRANSLATE *TO PUT*
Er stellt die Flasche auf den Tisch.
He puts the bottle on the table (i.e. in an upright position).
Sie legt Messer und Gabeln auf den Tisch·
She puts knives and forks on the table.
Stecken Sie das Geld in die Tasche.
Put the money in your pocket.

Legen Sie den Schlüssel hin.
Put the key down.
Stellen Sie den Schirm hin.
Put the umbrella down.

Stellen = to put in an *upright* position.
Legen = to put in a *horizontal* position.
Stecken = to put *into*, i.e., to slip in.

Da kommt Frau Müller.
da komt frou mǐ'-lĕr.

Sie hat einen schönen
zee hat ĭ'-nĕn shäⓨ'-nĕn

Pelzmantel, nicht wahr?
pelts'-man-tĕl, nicht vahr?

ISN'T IT? HASN'T HE? DON'T YOU?

Es ist kalt, nicht wahr?
It is cold, isn't it?

Sie kommen mit ins Kino, nicht wahr?
You are coming with us to the cinema, aren't you?

Sie spielen Klavier, nicht wahr?
You play the piano, don't you?

Er hat einen jüngeren Bruder, nicht wahr?
He has a younger brother, hasn't he?

Sie kommen morgen wieder, nicht wahr?
You'll come back to-morrow, won't you?

Er ist ein gescheiter Knabe, nicht wahr?
He is a clever boy, isn't he?

Sie kann gut schwimmen, nicht wahr?
She can swim well, can't she?

Nicht wahr is an abbreviation for **ist es nicht wahr?** = *is it not true?* It stands for the English: *do you? don't you? does he? doesn't he? are you? aren't you? is he? isn't he? won't you? can't you? etc.*

THE IMPERATIVE
(Commands, Requests and Exclamations)

Gehen Sie!=*Go!* Sehen Sie!=*Look!*
Warten Sie!=*Wait!* Warten Sie nicht!=
Don't wait! Setzen Sie sich!=*Sit down!*

The imperative in German has the same form as the question with Sie, but followed by an exclamation mark instead of a question mark. Compare the following:

Question:

Lesen Sie?=*Are you reading?*
Sagen Sie?=*Do you say?*
Lassen Sie es hier?=*Do you leave it here?*
Stehen Sie auf?=*Are you getting up?*

Command:

Lesen Sie!=*Read!*
Sagen Sie!=*Say!*
Lassen Sie es hier!=*Leave it here!*
Stehen Sie auf!=*Get up!*

To make a polite request, say bitte, either before or after the imperative, e.g. Bitte, tun Sie das für mich=*Please do this for me;* Setzen Sie sich, bitte=*Please sit down;* Geben Sie es mir, bitte=*Please give it to me.*

MISCELLANEOUS EXCLAMATIONS AND REQUESTS

Ach Gott!	*Oh dear!*
Wie schön!	*How nice!*
Wie merkwürdig!	*How strange!*
Unsinn! Quatsch!	*Nonsense!*
Ach Quatsch!	*Oh, nonsense!*
Wie schade!	*What a pity!*
Sehen Sie!	*Look!*
Schauen Sie her!	*Look here!*
Sehen Sie nicht her!	*Don't look!*
Kommen Sie!	*Come!*
Hören Sie!	*Listen!*
Herein!	*Come in!*
Zu Hilfe!	*Help! Help!*
Nehmen Sie Platz!	*Sit down!*
Machen Sie schnell!	*Hurry up!*
Bitte um Ruhe!	*Please be quiet!*
Achtung!	*Mind! Beware!*
Vorsicht!	*Careful!*
Gehen Sie hinein!	*Go in!*
Kommen Sie herein!	*Come in!*
Folgen Sie mir!	*Follow me!*
Hören Sie mal zu!	*Do listen to me!*
Vergessen Sie nicht!	*Don't forget!*

NEW NOUNS

DER	Bogen, -	*sheet (of paper); also bend, arch*
	Umschlag, ···-e	*envelope*
	Hut, ···-e	*hat*
	Mann, ···-er	*man, husband*
	Kasten, ···-	*box*
	Spiegel, -	*mirror*
	Ring, -e	*ring*
	Schlüssel, -	*key*
	Schirm, -e	*umbrella, screen*
DIE	Tür, -en	*door*
	Kirche, -n	*church*
	Bluse, -n	*blouse*
DAS	Fenster, -	*window*
	Gesicht, -er	*face*
	Juwel, -en	*jewel*
	Messer, -	*knife*

SEINE GRIPPE

"Wie geht es Karl mit seiner Grippe?"

"Na, er wird wohl noch längere Zeit im Krankenhaus bleiben."

"So, sagte das der Arzt?"

"Das nicht .. aber ich habe seine Pflegerin gesehen."

Die Grippe, *influenza;* wie geht es, *how is;* na, *well;* er wird .. bleiben, *he will remain;* noch längere Zeit, *still some time;* das Krankenhaus, ···-er, *hospital;* der Arzt, ···-e, *doctor;* die Pflegerin, -nen, *nurse.*

FREIE WAHL

"Ich sehe, Hans," sagte der Vater, "dass dein Brüderchen den kleinen Apfel isst und du den grossen! Hast du ihn denn selbst wählen lassen?"

"Natürlich, Papa," antwortete der Junge. "Ich sagte ihm: Entweder den kleinen Apfel oder gar keinen—und dann hat er den kleinen genommen."

Die Wahl, *choice;* wählen, *to choose;* lassen, *to let;* antworten, *to answer;* entweder .. oder, *either .. or;* gar keinen, *none at all;* er hat genommen (from nehmen), *he has taken, he took.*

EXERCISES

I Answer in German

1. Wie alt sind Sie? 2. Haben Sie einen Bruder? 3. Wie heisst Ihre Strasse? 4. Haben Sie eine Uhr? 5. Ist sie aus Gold? 6. Ist der Tisch aus Holz? 7. Was ist (a) aus Eisen, (b) aus Stahl, (c) aus Papier? 8. Wieviel kostet Ihr Bleistift? 9. Ist er teuer? 10. Was ist teurer, eine goldene Uhr oder eine silberne? 11. Schreiben Sie viele Briefe? 12. Wen (vayn—whom) lieben die Eltern?

II Replace the nouns by pronouns

1. Der Vater liebt seinen Sohn. 2. Die Lehrerin nimmt die Feder. 3. Mein Bruder schliesst die Tür. 4. Die Mutter öffnet das Fenster. 5. Die Kinder trinken die Milch. 6. Die Eltern lieben die Kinder. 7. Die Mutter sieht das Kind. 8. Der Kellner bringt den Wein. 9. Die Dame liest die Zeitung. 10. Die Schüler lesen die Bücher.

III Replace the blanks by legt, stellt, steckt

1. Er .. den Brief in den Briefkasten. 2. Er .. das Buch auf den Tisch. 3. Er .. das Geld in die Tasche. 4. Er .. das Glas auf den Tisch. 5. Er .. den Bleistift auf den Tisch. 6. Er .. den Bleistift in die Tasche.

IV Translate into German

1. The teacher opens the book. 2. The students open their books also. 9. One student reads. 4. He takes the book, opens it and reads. 5. Please open a window. 6. Please shut the door. 7. Please don't take my hat, take yours. 8. Put this letter into the letter-box. 9. Take this chair, it is better. 10. Put it down. 11. What is the name of your teacher? 12. Where does he live? 13. Please write his address (die Adresse, -n) on this bit of paper. 14. Put this in your pocket. 15. Watches are expensive now, aren't they?

(*Answers on page* 359)

WHAT IS YOUR NAME?

A selection of girls' names and their German equivalents. Boys' names are on page 108.

Adela	Adelheid, Adele	*Ellen*	Lene	*Katharine*	Katharina
Agnes	Agnes	*Elsie*	Else, Ilse	*Lilian*	Lilli
Alice	Alice, Alexia	*Emily*	Emilie	*Louise*	Luise, Ludwiga
Amanda	Amanda	*Emma*	Emma	*Margaret*	Margarete, Grete
Amelia	Amalie	*Erica*	Erika	*Marjory*	Gretchen
Ann	Anna	*Evelyn*	Eveline	*Martha*	Martha
Annie	Annchen	*Frances*	Franziska	*Mary*	Marie
Audrey	Ethelried	*Freda*	Frieda	*Matilda*	Mathilde
Beatrice	Beatrix	*Gertrude*	Gertrud	*Nelly*	Lenchen
Betty	Lieschen, Elschen	*Gertie*	Trude, Trudchen	*Pauline*	Paula
Blanche	Blanka	*Hetty*	Jette	*Peggy*	Meta
Bridget	Brigitte	*Hedda*	Hedwig	*Phoebe*	Phöbe
Cecily	Cäcilie	*Helen*	Helene	*Rachel*	Rahel
Charlotte	Charlotte, Lotte	*Henrietta*	Henriette	*Rosalind*	Rosalinde
Constance	Konstanze	*Hilda*	Hilde	*Sarah*	Sara
Dolly	Dorchen	*Isobel*	Isabella	*Sibyl*	Sibylle
Dorothy	Dora, Dorette	*Jane*	Johanna	*Sophia*	Sophie
Edith	Edith	*Janet*	Jutta	*Theresa*	Therese
Eleanor	Eleanore	*Jenny*	Hannchen	*Ursula*	Ursula
Elizabeth	Elisabeth, Lisbeth	*Kate*	Käte	*Winifred*	Winfreda

The following names, which have no equivalents in English, are also commonly used in Germany: **Annaliese, Erna, Irmgard, Elfrieda, Inge.**

ZONS AM RHEIN

Das kleine Städtchen Zons, nordöstlich von Dormagen am Rhein, ist mit seinen zahlreichen Türmen und Toren eine der besterhaltenen, mittelalterlichen Festungen des Rheinlands. Wie die meisten linksrheinischen Städte ist es eine römische Gründung. Sontium nannten es die Römer.

Köln hiess ursprünglich Colonia Agrippina, Trier Augusta Treverorum, Mainz Mogontiacum, und Koblenz Confluentes, d.h. die am Zusammenfluss mehrerer Flüsse (Rhein, Mosel, Lahn) gegründete Stadt.

Diese Städte waren durch Landstrassen verbunden und hatten Wasserleitungen, Bäder und Brücken. Die Besetzung durch die Römer war in der Hauptsache eine militärische und hatte die Aufgabe, die ausgedehnten Grenzen des römischen Imperiums zu schützen.

Der Anbau des Weins, für den das Rheinland so berühmt ist, soll durch die Römer eingeführt worden sein.

(*Translation on page 375*)

zahlreich	**der Turm, ···-e**	**besterhalten**
numerous	*tower*	*best preserved*
die Festung, -en	**die Gründung, -en**	
fortress	*foundation*	
ursprünglich	**d.h. (das heisst)**	
originally	*that is*	
der Zusammenfluss, ···-e		**gründen**
confluence		*to found*
verbinden	**die Wasserleitung, -en**	
to join	*aqueduct*	
das Bad, ···-er	**die Besetzung, -en**	
bath	*occupation*	
die Hauptsache, -n		**die Aufgabe, -n**
chief point		*task*
ausgedehnt	**die Grenze, -n**	**schützen**
extended	*frontier*	*to guard*
der Anbau	**soll .. sein**	**einführen**
cultivation	*is supposed to be*	*to introduce*

ZWÖLFTE LEKTION: *TWELFTH LESSON*

Die Katze will hinausgehen, aber sie kann die Tür nicht öffnen
dee kat′-sĕ vil hi′-nous-gay-ĕn, ah′-bĕr zee kan dee tͤr nicht ĕf′-nĕn

Ich will das Brot schneiden, aber ich habe kein Messer. Ohne ein Messer kann ich
ich vil das broht shnī′-dĕn, ah′-bĕr ich hah′-bĕ kīn me′-sĕr. oh′-nĕ īn me′-sĕr kan ich
I want to cut the bread, but I have no knife. Without a knife I

das Brot nicht schneiden. Hans will einen Brief schreiben, aber er hat weder einen
das broht nicht shnī′-dĕn. hants vil ī′-nĕn breef shrī′-bĕn, ah′-bĕr ayr hat vay′-dĕr ī′-nĕn
cannot cut the bread. Hans wants to write a letter, but he has neither a

Bleistift noch eine Feder. Ohne Schreibmaterial kann er seinen Brief nicht schreiben.
blī′-shtift noch ī′-nĕ fay′-dĕr. oh′-nĕ shrīp′-ma-tayr′-i-ahl kan ayr zī′-nĕn breef nicht
pencil nor a pen. Without writing material he cannot write his letter. [shrī′-bĕn.

Frau X will einen neuen Hut kaufen.
frou iks vil ī′-nĕn noy′-ĕn hoͦot kou′-fĕn.
Mrs. X wants to buy a new hat.

Der Hut kostet zwölf Mark, und sie hat
dayr hoͦot kos′-tĕt tsvͤlf mark, oͦont zee hat
The hat costs twelve marks, and she has

nicht so viel Geld. Er ist zu teuer.
nicht zoh feel gelt. ayr ist tsoͦo toy′-ĕr.
not so much money. It is too expensive.

Er will durch das Fenster steigen
ayr vil doͦorch das fens′-tĕr shtī′-gĕn

Dieser Mann hat seinen Hausschlüssel verloren. Er kann die Tür nicht aufschliessen.
dee′-zĕr man hat zī′-nĕn hous′-shlͤ-sel fer-loh′-rĕn. ayr kan dee tͤr nicht ouf′-shlee-sĕn.
This man has lost the key of his house. He cannot unlock the door.

Niemand ist zu Hause. Er will durch das offene Fenster steigen. Er kann es
nee′-mant ist tsoͦo hou′-zĕ. ayr vil doͦorch das o′-fĕ-nĕ fens′-tĕr shtī′-gĕn. ayr kan es
No one is at home. He wants to climb through the open window. He cannot do

nicht. Das Fenster ist zu klein, und er ist zu dick. Seine Frau ist im Kino. Er
nicht. das fens'-tĕr ist tsōō klīn ōōnt ayr ist tsōō dik.   zī'-nĕ frou ist im kee'-noh.   ayr
it. The window is too small and he is too stout. His wife is in the cinema. He

muss warten, bis sie nach Hause kommt.
mōōs vahr'-tĕn, bis zee nach hou'-zĕ komt.
must wait until she comes home.

Dies ist die zwölfte Lektion. Sie können jetzt schon ein wenig Deutsch sprechen.
dees ist dee tsvęlf'-tĕ lek-tsyohn'.   zee kę'-nĕn yetst shohn īn vay'-nich doytsh shpre'-chĕn.
This is the twelfth lesson. You can now already speak a little German.

Deutsch ist eine Sprache. Andere Sprachen sind Englisch, Französisch,
doytsh ist ī'-nĕ shprah'-chĕ.   an'-dĕ-rĕ shprah'-chĕn zint eng'-lish, fran-tsặy'-zish,
German is a language. Other languages are English, French,

Russisch, Spanisch, Italienisch und so weiter. Können Sie Französisch
rōō'-sish, shpah'-nish, i-tal-yay'-nish ōōnt zoh vī'-tĕr.   kę'-nĕn zee fran-tsặy'-zish
Russian, Spanish, Italian and so on. Can you speak

sprechen? Nur sehr wenig. Ich kann lesen und schreiben, aber nicht
shpre'-chĕn?   nōōr zayr vay'-nich.   ich kan lay'-zĕn ōōnt shrī'-bĕn, ah'-bĕr nicht
French? Only very little. I can read and write, but not

sprechen. Ich kann Franzosen verstehen, wenn sie nicht zu schnell sprechen.
shpre'-chĕn.   ich kan fran-tsoh'-zĕn fer-shtay'-ĕn, ven zee nicht tsōō shnel shpre'-chĕn.
speak it. I can understand Frenchmen, if they don't speak too fast.

Verstehen Sie mich, wenn ich Deutsch spreche? Bitte, sprechen Sie langsam
fer-shtay'-ĕn zee mich, ven ich doytsh shpre'-chĕ?   bi'-tĕ, shpre'-chĕn zee lang'-zahm
Do you understand me when I speak German? Please speak slowly

und deutlich, dann kann ich Sie verstehen. Finden Sie Deutsch leicht oder schwer?
ōōnt doyt'-lich, dan kan ich zee fer-shtay'-ĕn.   fin'-dĕn zee doytsh līcht oh'-dĕr shvayr?
and distinctly, then I can understand you. Do you find German easy or difficult?

Wenn Sie wollen, können wir zusammen üben. Sie kennen vielleicht das Sprichwort:
ven zee vo'-lĕn, kę'-nĕn veer tsōō-za'-mĕn ę'-bĕn.   zee ke'-nĕn fee'-līcht das shprich'-vort:
If you wish, we can practise together. Perhaps you know the proverb:

"Übung macht den Meister". Nein, ich kenne es nicht. Können Sie es bitte an die
ę'-bōōng macht dayn mīs'-tĕr.   nīn, ich ke'-nĕ es nicht.   kę'-nĕn zee es bi'-tĕ an dee
"Practice makes perfect". No, I don't know it. Can you please write it on the

Tafel schreiben? Ich will es gern an die Tafel schreiben, aber ich kann die Kreide
tah'-fĕl shrī'-bĕn?   ich vil es gern an dee tah'-fĕl shrī'-bĕn, ah'-bĕr ich kan dee krī'-dĕ
blackboard? I will gladly write it on the blackboard, but I cannot find the

nicht finden. Hier ist ein Stück Kreide. Der Lehrer schreibt den Satz an die
nicht fin'-dĕn.   heer ist īn shtįk krī'-dĕ.   dayr lay'-rĕr shrīpt dayn zats an dee
chalk. Here is a piece of chalk. The teacher writes the sentence on the

Tafel. Der Schüler versteht es immer noch nicht. Er sagt: "Ich verstehe diesen
tah'-fĕl.   dayr shę'-lĕr fer-shtayt' es i'-mĕr noch nicht.   ayr zahkt: ich fer-shtay'-e dee'-zĕn
blackboard. The scholar even yet does not understand it. He says: "I don't understand

Satz nicht. Wollen Sie ihn mir bitte erklären!" "Übung macht den Meister"
zahts nicht. vo′-lĕn zee een meer bi′-tĕ er-klay′-rĕn! ḝ′-bŏong macht dayn mīs′-tĕr
this sentence. Will you please explain it to me." "Übung macht den Meister"

heisst auf Englisch: "Practice makes perfect." Wörtlich übersetzt heisst es "Practice
hīst ouf eng′-lish: vĕrt′-lich ḝ′-bĕr-zétst hīst es
is in English: "Practice makes perfect." Literally translated it is "Practice

makes the master." Ich will es aufschreiben. Können Sie mir bitte einen Bleistift
         ich vil es ouf′-shrī-bĕn. kḝ′-nĕn zee meer bi′-tĕ ī′-nĕn blī′-shtift
makes the master." I will write it down. Can you please lend me a pencil

oder eine Feder leihen? Hier ist mein Füllfederhalter, und da ist mein Bleistift.
oh′-dĕr ī′-nĕ fay′-dĕr lī′ĕn? heer ist mīn fĭl′-fay-dĕr-hal-tĕr ŏont dah ist mīn blī′-shtift.
or a pen? Here is my fountain pen and there is my pencil.

Bitte, nehmen Sie, was Sie wollen. Danke, ich nehme den Bleistift.
bi′-tĕ, nay′-mĕn zee vas zee vo′-lĕn. dang′-kĕ, ich nay′-mĕ dayn blī′-shtift.
Please take what you want. Thanks, I'll take the pencil.

Ist der erste Buchstabe ein A oder ein U? Ich habe meine Brille nicht
ist dayr ayrs′-tĕ bŏŏch′-shtah-bĕ īn ah oh′-dĕr īn ŏŏ? ich hah′-bĕ mī′-né bri′-lĕ nicht
Is the first letter an A or a U? I haven't (got) my spectacles

hier und kann nicht gut sehen. Der erste Buchstabe ist ein Ü (U Umlaut).
heer ŏont kan nicht gŏŏt zay′-ĕn. dayr ayr′-stĕ bŏŏch′-shtah-bĕ ist īn ḝ (ŏŏ ŏŏm′-lout).
here and cannot see well. The first letter is a Ü (U modified).

Ich buchstabiere das ganze Wort. U Umlaut, b, u, n, g. Das zweite Wort:
ich bŏŏch-shtah-bee′-rĕ das gan′-tsĕ vort. ŏŏ ŏŏm′-lout, bay, ŏŏ, en, gay. das tsvī′-tĕ vort:
I am spelling the whole word. U modified, b, u, n, g. The second word:

m, a, c, h, t. Das dritte: d, e, n.
em, ah, tsay, hah, tay. das dri′-tĕ: day, ay, en.
m, a, c, h, t. The third: d, e, n.

Das vierte: m, e, i, s, t, e, r.
das feer′-tĕ: em, ay, ee, es, tay, ay, er.
The fourth: m, e, i, s, t, e, r.

Das ist ein Buchstabe: t.
Das sind Buchstaben: a, h, n, r.

Das ist ein Wort:
         kalt.—Dieses Wort hat vier Buchstaben.
Das sind Wörter:
         heute, Strasse, Papier, Brille.

Das ist ein Satz:
         Ich muss einen Brief schreiben.—Dieser
         Satz hat fünf Wörter. Auf Englisch
         heisst dieser Satz: *I must write a letter.*

     Der Lehrer schreibt das deutsche A B C an die Tafel
dayr lay′-rĕr shrīpt das doyt′-shĕ ah bay tsay an dee tah′-fĕl

GOBELIN—WEBERINNEN

Die Kunst des Handwebens ist nicht ganz ausgestorben. In vielen Teilen Deutschlands wird sie noch geübt. Das Bild zeigt Thüringer Gobelin-Weberinnen bei der Arbeit.

(Translation on page 375)

die Kunst, ···-e	weben	aussterben	üben	zeigen	die Arbeit, -en
art	*to weave*	*to die out*	*to practise*	*to show*	*work*

CAN, WILL, MUST

Ich kann das nicht tun.
I cannot do that.

Können Sie es für mich tun?
Can you do it for me?

Er kann nicht kommen.
He cannot come.

Sie können uns nicht verstehen.
They cannot understand us.

Ich will einen Brief schreiben.
I want to write a letter.

Wollen Sie rauchen?
Do you want to smoke?

Er will es nicht tun.
He doesn't want to do it.

Sie wollen morgen kommen.
They want to come to-morrow.

Ich muss jetzt gehen.
I must go now.

Sie müssen bald wieder kommen.
You must soon come again.

Er muss eine Brille tragen.
He has to wear a pair of spectacles.

Müssen wir das tun?
Must we do that?

ich, er, sie, es	kann	**wir, Sie, sie**	können	=	*can (am able)*
	will		wollen	=	*will (want)*
	muss		müssen	=	*must (have to)*

Note that these three verbs add neither -e nor -t when used with **ich, er, sie, es.**

IM SCHWARZWALD

Der Schwarzwald wird durch das tiefe Kinzigtal in zwei Teile geteilt. Der nördliche Teil hat eine durchschnittliche Höhe von 700 Metern. Der höchste Berg, der Feldberg (1493 m.), liegt im Süden. Der Schwarzwald ist dicht mit Wald bedeckt. Eichen und Buchen in den niederen Regionen und Kiefern in den oberen liefern das Material für die berühmte Holz- und Uhrenindustrie.

(*Translation on page* 375)

teilen	**durchschnittlich**	**die Eiche, -n**	**die Buche, -n**	**die Kiefer, -n**
to divide	*average*	*oak*	*beech*	*fir*

Ich kann diesen Hut nicht tragen. Er ist zu gross
ich kan dee′-zĕn hōōt nicht trah′-gĕn.   ayr ist tsōō grohs
I cannot wear this hat.   It is too big

für mich. Ich kann ihn nicht tragen, weil er zu gross
fḙr mich.   ich kan een nicht trah′-gĕn, vĭl ayr tsōō grohs
for me. I cannot wear it because it is too big

für mich ist.   Marie kann das neue Kleid nicht tragen.
fḙr mich ist.   mah-ree′ kan das noy′-ĕ klīt nicht trah′-gĕn.
for me. Mary cannot wear the new dress.

Es ist zu lang für sie.   Sie kann es nicht tragen, weil es zu lang für sie ist.   Die Katze
es ist tsōō lang fḙr zee.   zee kan es nicht trah′-gĕn, vĭl es tsōō lang fḙr zee ist.   dee kat′-sĕ
It is too long for her.   She cannot wear it because it is too long for her.   The cat

will hinaus, aber die Tür ist zu.   Sie kann nicht hinaus, weil die Tür zu ist.   Ich kann
vil hi′-nous, ah′-bĕr dee tḙr ist tsōō.   zee kan nicht hi′-nous, vĭl dee tḙr tsōō ist.   Ich kan
wants to get out, but the door is shut.   It cannot (get) out because the door is shut.   I cannot

das Brot nicht schneiden.   Warum nicht?   Weil ich kein Messer habe.
das broht nicht shnī′-dĕn.   vah-rōōm′ nicht?   vĭl ich kīn me′-sĕr hah′-bĕ.
cut the bread.   Why not?   Because I have no knife.

Warum können Sie den Hut nicht tragen?   Weil er zu gross für mich ist.
vah-rōōm′ kḙ′-nĕn zee dayn hōōt nicht trah′-gĕn?   vĭl ayr tsōō grohs fḙr mich ist.
Why can't you wear the hat?   Because it is too big for me.

Warum kann Frau X den Hut nicht kaufen?   Weil er zu teuer ist.   Warum
vah-rōōm′ kan frou iks dayn hōōt nicht kou′-fĕn?   vil ayr tsōō toy′-ĕr ist.   vah-rōōm′
Why cannot Mrs. X buy the hat?   Because it is too expensive.   Why

kann Marie das neue Kleid nicht tragen?   Weil es zu lang ist.   Was will die Katze?
kan mah-ree′ das noy′-ĕ klīt nicht trah′-gĕn?   vĭl es tsōō lang ist.   vas vil dee kat′-sĕ?
can't Mary wear the new dress?   Because it is too long.   What does the cat want?

Sie will hinaus.   Was will Frau X kaufen?   Sie will einen Hut kaufen.   Kann die Katze
zee vil hi-nous′.   vas vil frou iks kou′-fĕn?   zee vil ī′-nĕn hōōt kou′-fĕn.   kan dee kat′-sĕ
It wants (to get) out.   What does Mrs. X want to buy?   She wants to buy a hat.   Can the cat

hinaus?   Nein, sie kann nicht hinaus.   Warum nicht?   Weil die Tür zu ist.
hi-nous′?   nīn, zee kan nicht hi-nous′.   vah-rōōm′ nicht?   vĭl dee tḙr tsōō ist.
(get) out?   No, it cannot (get) out.   Why not?   Because the door is shut.

ORDER OF WORDS (II)

Ich will lesen, während Sie schreiben.
  I want to read while you are writing.

Ich kann das Fleisch nicht schneiden, weil ich
  kein Messer habe.
  I cannot cut the meat because I have no knife.

Sie können nicht hinein, wenn Sie keinen
  Schlüssel haben.
  You cannot get in if you haven't a key.

While you are writing; because I have no knife; if you haven't a key are dependent clauses; i.e. they are not complete in themselves and depend on the principal clause.

In Lesson 7 you learned that the verb occupies the second place in a German sentence. This rule, however, applies to principal clauses only. *In dependent clauses the verb is placed at the end.*

TO HAVE

Nehmen Sie noch eine Tasse Tee.
Have another cup of tea.

Nehmen Sie, was Sie wollen.
Have what you want.

Ich nehme einen Apfel.
I'll have an apple.

Haben Sie Apfelsinen?
Have you any oranges?

Ich habe keine.
I haven't got any.

In English, *to have* is sometimes used in the sense of *to take* or *to partake of.* In

German, **haben** cannot be used in this way. **Nehmen, essen, trinken,** or other verbs will render the particular meaning of *have* according to the circumstances.

Have a cigarette = **Nehmen Sie** (or **Rauchen Sie**) **eine Zigarette,** but *never* **haben Sie eine Zigarette,** which can *only* mean *have you got a cigarette?*

Note that the English *got,* used in colloquial English in connection with *have,* remains untranslated in German. If, however, the English *get* is used in the sense of *to obtain, to receive,* it is rendered by **bekommen** or **erhalten.**

RADRENNEN DURCH DIE ALPEN

Die Teilnehmer an einem durch Deutschland und Österreich führenden Radrennen nähern sich dem schwersten Teil ihrer Aufgabe: der Fahrt über den Arlbergpass (1802 m.) auf dem Wege von Innsbruck nach Friedrichshafen.

(*Translation on page 376*)

das Radrennen,-	**der Teilnehmer,-**	**führen**	**sich nähern**	**die Fahrt, -en**
cycle race	*participant*	*to lead*	*to approach*	*ride, drive*

IN (HEREIN) AND OUT (HERAUS)

Er kann nicht herein.
He cannot get in.

Sie will heraus.
She wants to get out.

Warum kommen Sie nicht herein?
Why don't you come in?

Wollen Sie nicht hereinkommen?
Won't you come in?

Ich kann nicht heraus.
I can't get out.

Führen Sie den Hund heraus.
Bring the dog outside.

Herein (*in*) and **heraus** (*out*) are adverbs, and are used only in combination with verbs. They are always placed at the end of a sentence unless the infinitive is there, in which case they precede it.

herauskommen = *to come out*
herausnehmen = *to take out*
hereinkommen = *to come in*
hereinnehmen = *to take in*

Note that **herein** and **heraus**, like other adverbs and prepositions, can be combined in one word with the infinitive which they precede. (Compare English: *to outgrow, to infiltrate, to upset,* etc.)

Er kann nicht herein is short for **er kann nicht hereinkommen**; **er will heraus** for **er will herauskommen** (*he wants to come out*); to someone knocking at the door you say: **Herein,** which is short for **Kommen Sie herein.**

Notes.—(1) **Herein** and **heraus** are both adverbs and should not be used for the prepositions *in* and *out*, which are rendered by **in** and **aus.** Adverbs are used in connection with verbs, prepositions with nouns or pronouns. Thus, in the sentence *Why don't you come in?* **in** is an adverb; in *in the garden* it is a preposition. The first is therefore rendered by **herein,** the second by **in.**

(2) **hin und her** = *hither and thither, to and fro;* **hin und hergehen** = *to go and come back;* **drei Stunden hin und drei her** = *three hours there and three back.*

NEW NOUNS

DER	**Franzose, -n**	*Frenchman*
	Meister, -	*master*
	Satz, ·-e	*sentence*
	Lehrer, -	*teacher*
	Schüler, -	*schoolboy, pupil*
	Buchstabe, -n	*letter (of the alphabet)*

DIE	**Katze, -n**	*cat*
	Lektion, -en	*lesson*
	Übung, -en	*practice, exercise*
	Tafel, -n	*blackboard*
	Kreide, -n	*chalk*
	Brille, -n	*pair of spectacles*

DAS	**Material, -ien**	*material*
	Sprichwort, -e	*proverb*
	Wort, ·-er	*word*

ERFOLG

Man sprach über Erfolge.

Der Mann aus Amerika erzählte:

"Ich habe ganz unten angefangen und bin jetzt oben angekommen."

"Wirklich?"

"Ja. Ich war Schuhputzer und bin jetzt Frisör."

Der Erfolg, -e, *success;* **erzählen,** *to tell;* **ganz unten,** *right at the bottom;* **anfangen,** *to start;* **oben,** *on top;* **ankommen,** *to reach;* **wirklich,** *really;* **der Schuhputzer, -,** *shoeblack;* **der Frisör, -e,** *hairdresser.*

SEINE FREUNDE

Der weitgereiste Mann erzählte von der fernen Welt.

"Und Asien! Wundervoll! Nie werde ich auch die Türkei, Indien und Japan vergessen! .. Und China, das himmlische Reich .."

"Und die Pagoden? Haben Sie welche gesehen?"

"Gesehen? Mein Lieber, ich habe mit ihnen zu Mittag gegessen!"

Weitgereist, *far-travelled;* **fern,** *distant;* **nie werde ich .. vergessen,** *never shall I forget;* **das himmlische Reich,** *the Celestial Empire;* **welche,** *some, any.*

EXERCISES

I Read and Translate

1. Ich muss Briefe schreiben. Kann ich Ihre Feder haben? 2. Sie können sie haben. Hier ist sie. 3. Ich will lesen, während Sie schreiben. 4. Haben Sie etwas zu lesen? 5. Wollen Sie ein Buch lesen, oder die Zeitung? 6. Hier ist eine deutsche Zeitung. Können Sie sie lesen? 7. Ich kann Deutsch lesen, aber nicht sprechen. 8. Können Sie mich verstehen? 9. Ich kann Sie verstehen, wenn Sie nicht zu schnell sprechen. 10. Sie müssen nicht so schnell sprechen.

II Answer in German

1. Können Sie Russisch sprechen? 2. Kann ich (der Lehrer) Deutsch sprechen? 3. Wie viele Sprachen können Sie sprechen? 4. Wollen Sie Russisch lernen? 5. Ist Russisch leicht zu lernen? 6. Finden Sie Deutsch schwer? 7. Müssen Sie deutsche Stunden nehmen, wenn Sie die Sprache lernen wollen? 8. Was müssen wir haben, wenn wir Brot schneiden wollen? 9. Können Sie die Tür aufschliessen, wenn Sie keinen Schlüssel haben? 10. Wollen Sie heute ins (= in das) Kino gehen?

III Translate

1. Can you speak German? 2. I can read German, but not speak it. 3. Do you want to smoke? 4. What do you want to drink? 5. Must you go? 6. I don't want to, but I have to. 7. Here is a newspaper. Read it while I write this letter. 8. Why don't you open that door? Because I haven't got the key. 9. Why don't you eat your meat? 10. I can't eat it because it is too cold. 11. I can't drink my milk because it is too hot. 12. You can't come in now.

(Answers on page 359)

WHAT IS YOUR NAME?

A selection of boys' names and their German equivalents. Girls' names are on page 97

Adolphus	Adolf	*Ferdinand*	Ferdinand	*Leonard*	Leonhard
Albert	Albert, Albrecht	*Francis, Frank*	Franz	*Louis, Lewis*	Ludwig
Alfred	Alfred	*Fred*	Fritz	*Matthew*	Matthäus
Aloysius	Alois	*Frederick*	Friedrich	*Maurice*	Moritz
Alphonse	Alfons	*Geoffrey*	Gottfried	*Michael*	Michel
Andrew	Andreas	*George*	Georg	*Nicholas*	Nikolaus, Klaus
Anthony	Anton	*Gerald*	Gerold, Gerhard	*Paul*	Paul(us)
Arthur	Arthur	*Godfrey*	Gottfried	*Percival*	Parzival
Aubrey	Alberich	*Gregory*	Gregor	*Peter*	Peter, Petrus
Augustus	August	*Gustavus*	Gustav	*Ralph*	Rudi
Bartholomew	Bartholomäus	*Guy*	Guido	*Raymond*	Raimund
Bernard	Bernhard	*Henry*	Heinz, Heinrich	*Reginald*	Reinhold
Bruno	Bruno	*Herman*	Hermann	*Richard*	Richard
Charles	Karl	*Hugh, Hugo*	Hugo	*Roderick*	Roderich
Christopher	Christoph	*Humphrey*	Humfried	*Roger*	Rüdiger
Clement	Klemens	*Jack*	Hans	*Rudolph*	Rudolf
Conrad	Konrad	*Jacob, James*	Jakob	*Rupert*	Ruprecht
Curtis	Kurt	*Joe*	Sepp, Pepi	*Stephen*	Stefan
Derek	Dietrich	*John*	Hans, Johann	*Timothy*	Timotheus
Edward	Eduard	*Johnnie*	Hänschen	*Tony*	Toni
Eric	Erich	*Joseph*	Josef	*Walter*	Walther
Ernest	Ernst	*Julius*	Julius	*Wilfred*	Wilfried
Eugene	Eugen	*Laurence*	Lorenz	*William*	Wilhelm

The following names which have no equivalents in English are also commonly used in Germany: **Manfred, Otto, Siegfried, Siegmund.**

DREIZEHNTE LEKTION : *THIRTEENTH LESSON*

Er bringt ihr Blumen
ayr bringt eer bloo´-měn

Sie gibt ihm einen Kuss
zee geept eem i´-něn koos

Können Sie mir bitte etwas zu trinken geben? Warten Sie einen Moment,
kę´-něn zee meer bi´-tě et´-vas tsoo tring´-kěn gay´-běn? wahr´-těn zee i´-něn moh-ment´,
Can you please give me something to drink? Wait a moment,

ich bringe Ihnen eine Tasse Kaffee. Können Sie mir bitte Feuer geben?
ich bring´-gě ee´-nen i´-ně ta´-sě ka´-fay. kę´-něn zee meer bi´-tě foy´-ěr gay´-běn?
I bring you a cup of coffee. Can you give me (a) light, please?

Ich kann Ihnen leider kein Feuer geben; ich habe keine Streichhölzer und
ich kan ee´-nen li´-děr kin foy´-ěr gay´-běn; ich hah´-bě ki´-ně shtrich´-hęl-tsěr oont
Unfortunately, I can't give you a light; I have no matches and

auch kein Feuerzeug. Kann ich Ihnen eine Tasse Tee anbieten, oder trinken
ouch kin foy´-ěr-tsoyk. kan ich ee´-něn i´-ně ta´-sě tay an´-bee-ten, oh´-děr tring´-kěn
no lighter, either. Can I offer you a cup of tea, or would you rather drink

Sie lieber Kaffee? Danke sehr; es ist mir ganz egal. Ich trinke beides gern.
zee lee´-běr ka´-fay? dang´-kě zayr; es ist meer gants ay-gahl´. ich tring´-kě bi´-děs gern.
coffee? Thank you very much; it is all the same to me. I like both.

Und Sie, gnädige[1] Frau? Ich trinke Kaffee lieber. Darf ich Ihnen eine Tasse
oont zee, gnay´-dee-gě frou? ich tring´-kě ka´-fay lee´-běr. darf ich ee´-něn i´-ně ta´-sě
And you, madam? I prefer (drinking) coffee. May I pour out a cup

eingiessen? Bitte, ich nehme nur wenig Milch und keinen Zucker. Hier ist
in´-gee-sěn? bi´-tě, ich nay´-mě noor vay´-nich milch oont ki´-nen tsoo´-kěr. heer ist
for you? Please, I take only a little milk and no sugar. Here is

Butterbrot, da ist Kuchen[2] und dort drüben sind Törtchen[2]. Bitte, bedienen
boo´-těr-broht, dah ist koo´-chěn oont dort drę̄´-běn zint tęrt´-chěn. bi´-tě, be-dee´-něn
the bread and butter, the cake is there and over there are pastries. Please help

---

[1] **Gnädige Frau** literally means *gracious lady*. It is the German equivalent for *Madam*, but is used only when addressing a married woman. The corresponding form of addressing an unmarried woman is **gnädiges Fräulein.**

[2] **Kuchen** is plain cake or fruit cake ; **Torte** is cream cake or any sort of fancy cake. **Törtchen** corresponds to what we call pastries.

DER KAFFEETISCH—THE COFFEE TABLE
(English key on page 368)

1. der Kaffeetisch, -e	11. der Eierbecher, -	21. der Brotkorb, ⸚-e
2. die Kaffeekanne, -n	12. der Eierlöffel, -	22. das Brötchen, -
3. die Zuckerdose, -n	13. die Zeitung, -en	23. die Käseglocke, -n
4. die Zuckerzange, -n	14. die Gabel, -n	24. das Törtchen, -
5. der Sahnengiesser, -	15. das Messer, -	25. der Kuchen, -
6. das Tablett, -e	16. der Teller, -	26. die Torte, -n
7. das Salzfass, ⸚-er	17. die Butterdose, -n	27. das Mädchen, -
8. die Tasse, -n	18. das Buttermesser, -	28. die Schürze, -n
9. die Untertasse, -n	19. die Marmeladendose, -n	29. die Türmatte, -n
10. der Kaffeelöffel, -	20. der Untersatz, ⸚-e	30. das Flügelfenster, -

110

Sie sich. Darf ich Sie bitten, mir die Marmeladendose herüberzureichen?
zee zich. darf ich zee bī'-těn, meer dee mahr-mě-lah'-děn-doh-sě he-rḝ'-běr-tsōō-ri-chěn?
vourself. May I ask you to pass the jam pot to me?

Aber gern. Darf ich Ihnen etwas auflegen? Nur ein klein wenig, bitte, auf diese
ah'-běr gern. darf ich ee'-něn et'-vas ouf'-lay-gěn? nōōr in klin vay'-nich, bi'-tě, ouf
(But) gladly. May I put some on for vou? Only very little, please, on this [dee'-zě

Scheibe Brot. Darf ich Ihnen noch eine Tasse eingiessen? Wenn ich bitten darf.
shī'-bě broht. darf ich ee'-něn noch ī'-ně ta'-sě īn'-gee-sěn? ven ich bi'-těn darf.
slice of bread. May I pour out another cup for you? If you will be so kind (if I may ask).

Ich giesse ein
ich gee'-sě in

Ich giesse aus
ich gee'-sě ous

INDIRECT OBJECT (I)—Pronouns

Er gibt mir deutsche Stunden.
He gives me German lessons.

Ich kann Ihnen leider nichts geben.
Unfortunately, I can't give you anything.

Können Sie uns etwas zu essen bringen?
Can you bring us something to eat?

Zeigen Sie ihr, was Sie haben.
Show her what you have.

Schreiben Sie ihnen oft?
Do you write to them often?

Wem gehört dieses Auto?
To whom does this car belong?

Es gehört mir	= *It belongs to me.*
Es gehört uns	=: *It belongs to us.*

Gehört es Ihnen? = *Does it belong to you?*
Gehört es ihm? = *Does it belong to him?*
Gehört es ihr? == *Does it belong to her?*
Gehört es ihnen? = *Does it belong to them?*

mir=(*to*) *me*, **Ihnen**=(*to*) *you*, **uns**=(*to*)
us, **ihm**=(*to*) *him*, **ihr**=(*to*) *her*, **ihnen**=(*to*)
them.

German has distinctive forms for most pronouns to distinguish the direct from the indirect objects. Compare the following:

Direct Object (*Accusative*)

Er sieht mich=*He sees me.*
Hören Sie ihn?=*Do you hear him?*
Ich kann sie sehen=*I can see her.*
Ich verstehe Sie=*I understand you.*
Sie hassen uns=*They hate us.*
Wir haben sie gern=*We like them.*

Indirect Object (*Dative*)

Es gehört mir=*It belongs to me.*
Schreiben Sie ihm?=*Are you writing to him?*
Ich bringe es ihr=*I bring it to her.*
Gehört das Ihnen?=
Does this belong to you?
Schreiben Sie uns=*Write to us.*
Wir schreiben ihnen oft=
We often write to them.

Note.—(1) The only form used for both the direct and indirect object is **uns**=*us.* For *me, you, him, her* and *them* different forms are used. (2) In English the indirect object is often not clearly expressed, *to* being omitted. We say *he gives me* and not *to me.* Care must be taken to use the German dative case wherever the indirect object is implied, e.g. *Tell me*=**Sagen Sie mir** (i.e. *say to me*).

Der Briefträger bringt dieser Familie die Post
dayr breef'-tray-gĕr brinkt dee'-zĕr fah-meel'-yĕ dee pohst

Der Briefträger gibt dem Vater einen Brief und der Mutter ein Paket.
dayr breef'-tray-gĕr geept daym fah'-tĕr ī'-nĕn breef ōont dayr mōō'-tĕr in pah-kayt'.
The postman gives (to) the father a letter and (to) the mother a parcel.

Der Brief ist von ihrem Sohn. Er bittet den Vater, ihm Geld zu senden. Das
dayr breef ist fon ee'-rĕm zohn. ayr bi'-tĕt dayn fah'-tĕr eem gelt tsōō zen'-dĕn. das
The letter is from their son. He asks the father to send him money. The

Paket ist von ihrer Tochter. Sie sendet der Mutter ein Geschenk. Die Kinder
pah-kayt' ist fon ee'-rĕr toch'-tĕr. zee zen'-dĕt dayr mōō'-tĕr in gĕ-shenk'. dee kin'-dĕr
parcel is from their daughter. She sends (to) the mother a present. The children

schreiben den Eltern oft. Der Sohn schreibt ihnen, wenn er Geld braucht (und das ist
shrī'-bĕn dayn el'-tĕrn oft. dayr zohn shrīpt ee'-nĕn, ven ayr gelt broucht (ōont das ist
write to the parents often. The son writes to them when he needs money (and that is

sehr oft). Die Tochter schreibt ihnen
zayr oft). dee toch'-tĕr shrīpt ee'-nĕn
very often). The daughter writes to them

regelmässig jede Woche. Sie gibt
ray'-gĕl-may-sich yay'-dĕ vo'-chĕ. zee geept
regularly every week. She gives

den Eltern einen Bericht über die
dayn el'-tĕrn ī'-nĕn bĕ-richt' ēē'-bĕr dee
her parents an account of the

Ereignisse der Woche, und sie vergisst nie,
er-īg'-ni-sĕ dayr vo'-chĕ ōont zee fĕr-gist' nee
events of the week, and she never forgets to

Grüsse an ihre Grosseltern zu senden.
grēē'-sĕ an ee'-rĕ grohs'-el-tĕrn tsōō zen'-dĕn.
send greetings to her grandparents.

Er gibt den Kindern Geschenke
ayr geept dayn kin'-dĕrn gĕ-sheng'-kĕ

INDIRECT OBJECT (II)—Nouns

Er gibt dem Lehrer ein Buch.
He gives the teacher a book.

This sentence has two objects, the teacher and the book. What we really give is the book, which is the direct object. We do not actually give the teacher, we give *to* the teacher. *To the teacher* is the indirect object. When a noun is used as the indirect object in German, this is indicated by a change in the article.

> **der** and **das** change to **dem**.
> **die** (fem. sing.) changes to **der**.
> **die** (plural) changes to **den** and an **n** is added to the noun.

Sie bringt der Lehrerin ein Glas Wasser
zee bringt dayr lay′-rĕr-in in glas va′-sĕr

Nominative

der Lehrer	=	*the teacher*
das Kind	=	*the child*
die Frau	=	*the woman*
die Lehrer	=	*the teachers*
die Kinder	=	*the children*
die Frauen	=	*the women*

Dative

dem Lehrer	=	*to the teacher*
dem Kind(e)[1]	=	*to the child*
der Frau	=	*to the woman*
den Lehrern	=	*to the teachers*
den Kindern	=	*to the children*
den Frauen	=	*to the women*

Dieses Haus gehört einem Engländer.
This house belongs to an Englishman.

Sagen Sie es einer Kellnerin.
Tell it to a waitress.

Ich schreibe
I am writing
- **meinem Vater,** *to my father*
- **meiner Mutter,** *to my mother*
- **meinen Eltern,** *to my parents*

Zeigen Sie es
Show it
- **Ihrem Lehrer,** *to your teacher (man)*
- **Ihrer Lehrerin,** *to your teacher (woman)*
- **Ihren Lehrern,** *to your teachers (men)*
- **Ihren Lehrerinnen,** *to your teachers (women)*

Geben Sie es
Give it
- **seinem (ihrem) Bruder,** *to his (her) brother*
- **seiner (ihrer) Schwester,** *to his (her) sister*
- **seinen (ihren) Brüdern,** *to his (her) brothers*
- **seinen (ihren) Schwestern,** *to his (her) sisters*

Er zeigt der Grossmutter seine Bücher
ayr tsikt dayr grohs′-mōō-tĕr zi′-nĕ bǣ′-chĕr

---

[1] Sometimes an e is added to masculine and neuter nouns of one syllable.

KOHLENGRUBENARBEITER NACH DES TAGES ARBEIT

In der Ruhr besitzt Deutschland ein Zentrum vielfältiger Industrie. Fabriken und Gruben aller Art sind über diese Gegend verstreut. Das Bild zeigt Kohlengrubenarbeiter beim Schichtwechsel am Ausgang einer Kohlengrube in der Nähe von Gelsenkirchen.

(*Translation on page* 376)

der Kohlengrubenarbeiter, -	**besitzen**	**das Zentrum**	**vielfältig**	**die Fabrik, -en**
coal miner	*to possess*	*centre*	*manifold*	*factory*
die Grube, -n	**aller Art**	**die Gegend, -en**	**verstreuen**	**der Schichtwechsel, -**
mine	*of every kind*	*region*	*to scatter*	*change of shift*

Schreiben Sie mit ⎰ diesem Bleistift,
Write with ⎱ dieser Feder,
           this pencil
           this pen

Von welchem Land
   From what country ⎱ kommen Sie?
Von welcher Stadt ⎰ *do you come?*
   From what town

Er schreibt seinem Lehrer.
He is writing to his teacher.

Sie schreibt mit einer Feder.
She is writing with a pen.

Er trinkt aus meinem Glas.
He is drinking out of my glass.

Trinken Sie aus Ihrem Glas!
Drink out of your glass!

Er isst mit seiner Gabel.
He eats with his fork.

Ich komme von Ihren Eltern.
I am coming from your parents.

The dative of **dieser** (masc. sing.) and **dieses** (neut. sing.) is **diesem; ein, einem; sein, seinem; kein, keinem**, etc.

The dative of **diese** (fem. sing.) is **dieser; eine, einer; seine, seiner; keine, keiner**, etc.

The dative of **diese** (plural) is **diesen; meine, meinen; seine, seinen; keine, keinen**, etc.—and **n** is added to the noun.

Note.—**Mit, von, aus,** and many other prepositions are followed by the dative case.

ASKING HOW SOMEBODY IS

Guten Morgen, Herr Schulz.
Good morning, Mr. Schulz.

Wie geht es?   Danke, es geht mir gut.
How are you?   *Thanks, I am well.*

Und wie geht es Ihnen?
And how are you?

Sehr gut, danke.
Very well, thank you.

Und wie geht es Ihrem Vater?
And how is your father?

Danke, es geht ihm auch gut.
Thank you, he is also well.

Geht es Ihrer Mutter auch gut?
Is your mother also well?

Es geht ihr leider nicht gut.
Unfortunately, she is not very well.

Sie liegt krank im Bett.
She is ill in bed.

Sie ist stark erkältet.
She has a very bad cold.

Und wie geht es Ihren Kindern?
And how are your children?

Danke, es geht ihnen ausgezeichnet.
Thank you, they are excellent.

I am well is Es geht mir gut = *It goes well with me*. *He is well* is Es geht ihm gut = *It goes well with him*, etc.

Er ist erkältet
ayr ist er-kel'-tĕt

Note the following idiomatic expressions:

Es tut mir leid.
I am sorry.

Tut es Ihnen leid?
Are you sorry?

Es tut ihm (ihr) leid.
He (she) is sorry, etc.

Was fehlt Ihnen?
What is wrong with you?

Was fehlt mir?
What is wrong with me?

Was fehlt ihm (ihr)?
What is wrong with him (her)?

NEW NOUNS

DER		
	Kuss, ̈-e	kiss
	Kuchen, -	cake
	Vater, ̈-	father
	Sohn, ̈-e	son

DIE		
	Torte, -n	fancy cake
	Dose, -n	pot, jar, box
	Scheibe, -n	slice
	Tochter, ̈-	daughter
	Kellnerin, -nen	waitress, barmaid

DAS		
	Feuer, -	light, fire
	Feuerzeug, -e	cigarette lighter
	Butterbrot, -e	bread and butter
	Törtchen, -	pastry
	Geschenk, -e	present
	Paket, -e	parcel

EXERCISES

I   Read and Translate

1. Ist in diesem Glas Wein? 2. Nein, in diesem Glas ist Wasser, aber in dem anderen (=other) ist Wein. 3. Kann ich Ihnen etwas zu trinken geben? 4. Was trinken Sie gern? Was trinken Sie am liebsten? 5. Können Sie mir bitte ein Glas Wasser geben? 6. Warten Sie einen Moment, ich bringe Ihnen eine Tasse Kaffee. 7. Trinken Sie Kaffee mit Milch und Zucker? Mit Milch bitte, aber ohne Zucker. 8. Bitte, bringen Sie meiner Mutter ein Glas Milch und etwas zu essen.

II   Replace the words in italics by the appropriate pronouns

1. *Dieses Buch* gehört meinem Vater. 2. Schreiben Sie *meiner Schwester*? 3. Der Briefträger bringt *die Briefe*. 4. Können Sie *den Briefträger* sehen? 5. *Die Eltern* geben *den Kindern* Geschenke. 6. *Der junge Mann* bringt *meiner Schwester* Blumen. 7. Ich gebe *meinem Vetter* eine Uhr.

III   Translate into German

1. What are you doing? 2. I am writing a letter. 3. To whom are you writing? 4. To my brother, to my sister and to my parents. 5. Do they often write to you? 6. To whom does this fountain pen belong? 7. It belongs to me. 8. This bag belongs to that lady. Give it to her. 9. Take this bottle to your mother. 10. How is she? 11. How is your son? 12. What is wrong with her daughter?

(*Answers on page* 360)

SPRICHWÖRTER

Was ich nicht weiss, macht mich nicht heiss.
What the eye does not see, the heart does not grieve over.

Jeder ist seines Glückes Schmied.
Each man is master of his fate.

Rette sich wer kann.
Every man for himself.

Frisch gewagt, ist halb gewonnen.
Well begun is half done.

Jung gewohnt, alt getan.
The child is father to the man.

Ein Spatz in der Hand ist besser als eine Taube auf dem Dach.
A bird in the hand is worth two in the bush.

Hunger ist der beste Koch.
Hunger is the best sauce.

Man muss das Eisen schmieden, so lange es heiss ist.
Strike while the iron is hot.

Kleider machen Leute.
Fine feathers make fine birds.

Eine Hand wäscht die andere.
One good turn deserves another.

Stille Wasser sind tief.
Still waters run deep.

Der Apfel fällt nicht weit vom Stamm.
Like father, like son.

Der Mensch denkt, Gott lenkt.
Man proposes, God disposes.

Ein Prophet gilt nichts in seinem Vaterland.
A prophet is without honour in his own country.

FRÜHLING IM OBERENGADIN

Das Engadin ist ein 60 Meilen langes Tal, das sich vom Maloja Pass bis nach Tirol erstreckt und von hohen Bergen umgeben ist. Der höher gelegene Teil des Tales, das Oberengadin oberhalb von St. Moritz, ist der schönste Teil mit seinen schneebedeckten Berggipfeln und tiefklaren Seen. (Translation on page 376)

der Frühling, -e	**das Tal, ⸱⸱⸱-er**	**sich erstrecken**	**umgeben**
spring	*valley*	*to stretch, extend*	*to surround*
oberhalb	**der Berggipfel, -**	**tief** **klar**	**der See, -n**
above	*mountain top*	*deep* *clear*	*lake*

117

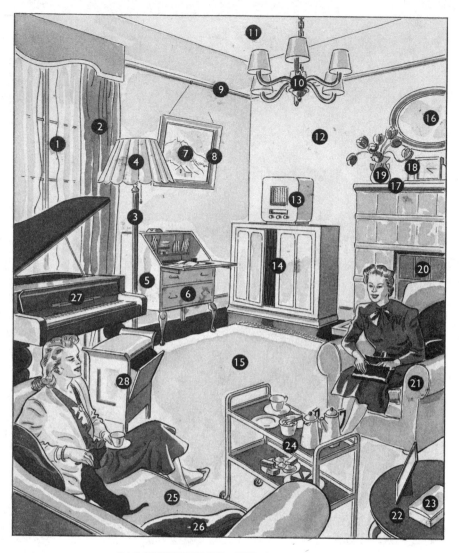

DAS WOHNZIMMER—THE SITTING ROOM
(English key on page 368)

1. das Fenster, -
2. der Vorhang, ⋯-e
3. die Stehlampe, -n
4. der Lampenschirm, -e
5. der Schreibtisch, -e
6. die Schublade, -n
7. das Bild, -er
8. der Bilderrahmen, -
9. die Leiste, -n

10. der Lüster, -
11. die Decke, -n
12. die Wand, ⋯-e
13. das Radio, -
14. der Bücherschrank, ⋯-e
15. der Teppich, -e
16. der Spiegel, -
17. das Kaminsims, -e
18. die Uhr, -en

19. die Blumenvase, -n
20. der Kamin, -e
21. der Sessel, -
22. der Tisch, -e
23. der Kasten, ⋯-
24. der Teewagen, -
25. das Sofa, -s; 26. das Kis-
27. das Klavier, -e   [sen, -
28. der Klavierstuhl, ⋯-e

118

VIERZEHNTE LEKTION : *FOURTEENTH LESSON*

USE OF PREPOSITIONS

After studying the text below, cover it over and describe what you see in the picture, using as many prepositions as possible; then check your result with the printed text.

Auf dem Tisch sind Bücher, ein Tintenfass und ein Kasten. In dem Kasten sind
ouf daym tish zint bę̄'-chĕr, ĭn tin'-tĕn-fas ōont ĭn kas'-tĕn. in daym kas'-tĕn zint
On the table are books, an inkpot and a box. In the box are

Federn und Bleistifte. Das Tintenfass steht zwischen dem Kasten und den
fay'-dĕrn ōont blī'-shtif-tĕ. das tin'-tĕn-fas shtayt tsvi'-shĕn daym kas'-tĕn ōont dayn
pens and pencils. The inkpot stands between the box and the

Büchern. Unter dem Tisch steht ein Papierkorb. Über dem Tisch hängt eine
bę̄'-chĕrn. ōon'-tĕr daym tish shtayt ĭn pah-peer'-korp. ę̄'-bĕr daym tish hengt ī'-nĕ
books. Under the table stands a waste-paper basket. Above the table hangs a

Lampe. Hinter dem Tisch ist ein Spiegel. Vor dem Spiegel steht ein Mann.
lam'-pĕ. hin'-tĕr daym tish ist ĭn shpee'-gĕl. fohr daym shpee'-gĕl shtayt ĭn man.
lamp. Behind the table is a mirror. In front of the mirror stands a man.

Neben dem Spiegel ist ein Schrank. Es ist ein Bücherschrank.
nay'-bĕn daym shpee'-gĕl ist ĭn shrank. es ist ĭn bę̄'-chĕr-shrank.
Beside the mirror is a cupboard. It is a bookcase.

Ein kleiner Junge sitzt an dem Tisch. Vor ihm liegt ein Buch, in dem er liest.
ĭn klī'-nĕr yōong'-gĕ zitst an daym tish. fohr eem leekt ĭn bōoch, ĭn daym ayr leest.
A little boy sits at the table. Before him lies a book, in which he reads.

119

MORE PREPOSITIONS

This text, based on the picture above, introduces many more prepositions. Cover over the text when you have thoroughly mastered it and describe the scene in your own words. Comparison with the text will show whether you have used the prepositions correctly.

Auf diesem Bild sehen wir ein Zimmer. Es ist ein Wohnzimmer. In diesem Zimmer
ouf dee´-zĕm bilt zay´-ĕn veer in tsi´-mĕr. es ist in vohn´-tsi-mĕr. in dee´-zĕm tsi´-mer
In this picture we see a room. It is a sitting room. In this room

sind sechs Personen (vier Erwachsene und zwei Kinder), und zwei Tiere (ein Hund
zint zeks per-zoh´-nĕn (feer er-vak´-sĕ-nĕ ŏŏnt tsvi kin´-dĕr), ŏŏnt tsvi tee´-rĕ (in hŏŏnt
are six persons (four adults and two children), and two animals (a dog

und eine Katze). In der Mitte ist ein Tisch. An dem Tisch sitzt eine Frau. Sie hat eine
ŏŏnt i´-nĕ kat´-sĕ). in dayr mi´-tĕ ist in tish. an daym tish zitst i´-nĕ frou. zee hat i´-nĕ
and a cat). In the middle is a table. At the table sits a woman. She has a

Feder in der Hand und schreibt einen Brief. Auf dem Tisch liegen Briefbogen
fay´-dĕr in dayr hant ŏŏnt shript i´-nĕn breef. ouf daym tish lee´- gĕn breef´-boh-gĕn
pen in her hand and writes a letter. On the table lie note paper

und Umschläge. Links vorn, in der Ecke, ist ein Ofen. Es ist ein Kachelofen.
ŏŏnt ŏŏm´-shlay-gĕ. links forn, in dayr e´-kĕ, ist in oh´fĕn. es ist in ka´-chĕl-oh-fĕn.
and envelopes. In the left hand corner, in front, is a stove. It is a tiled stove.

Neben dem Ofen steht ein Mann. Er hat eine Zigarre im Mund und eine
nay´-bĕn daym oh´-fĕn shtayt in man. ayr hat i´-nĕ tsee-gah´-rĕ im mŏŏnt ŏŏnt i´-nĕ
Next to the stove stands a man. He has a cigar in his mouth and a

Zeitung in der Hand. Im Moment liest er nicht, sondern spricht zu der Frau,
tsī'-tŏŏng in dayr hant. im moh-ment' leest ayr nicht, zon'-dĕrn shpricht tsŏŏ dayr frou,
newspaper in his hand. At this moment he does not read, but speaks to the woman,

die am Tisch sitzt. Unter dem Tisch liegt ein Hund. Er hat einen Knochen im Maul.[1]
dee am tish zitst. ŏŏn'-tĕr daym tish leekt īn hŏŏnt. ayr hat ī'-nĕn kno'-chĕn im moul.
who sits at the table. Under the table lies a dog. He has a bone in his mouth.

Hinter dem Tisch ist ein Fenster. Vor dem Fenster steht ein Lehnstuhl. In dem
hin'-tĕr daym tish ist īn fens'-tĕr. fohr daym fens'-tĕr shtayt īn layn'-shtŏŏl. in daym
Behind the table is a window. In front of the window stands an armchair. In the

Lehnstuhl sitzt der Grossvater und raucht seine Pfeife. Ein kleines Mädchen
layn'-shtŏŏl zitst dayr grohs'-fah-tĕr ŏŏnt roucht zī'-nĕ pfī'-fĕ. īn klī'-nĕs mayt'-chĕn
armchair sits the grandfather and smokes his pipe. A little girl

steht an dem Fenster und schaut hinaus.
shayt an daym fens'-tĕr ŏŏnt shout hi -nous.'
stands by the window and looks out.

Rechts an der Wand steht ein Klavier. Die junge Dame sitzt vor dem Klavier
rechts an dayr vant shtayt īn klah-veer'. die yŏŏng'-gĕ dah'-mĕ zitst fohr daym klah-veer'
On the right by the wall stands a piano. The young lady sits in front of the piano

und spielt eine Sonate von Schubert. Neben dem Klavier ist ein Sofa.
ŏŏnt shpeelt ī'-nĕ zoh-nah'-tĕ fon shŏŏ'-bert. nay'-bĕn daym klah-veer' ist īn zoh'-fah.
and plays a sonata by Schubert. Next to the piano is a sofa.

Auf dem Sofa liegen Kissen. Hinter dem Sofa steht eine Stehlampe. Das
ouf daym zoh'-fah lee'-gĕn ki'-sĕn. hin'-tĕr daym zoh'-fah shtayt ī'-nĕ shtay'-lam-pĕ. das
On the sofa are cushions. Behind the sofa stands a standard lamp. That

ist eine grosse Lampe, die auf dem Fussboden steht, und die man im Zimmer
ist ī'-nĕ groh'-sĕ lam'-pĕ, dee ouf daym fŏŏs'-boh-dĕn shtayt, ŏŏnt dee man im tsi'-mĕr
is a big lamp which stands on the floor and which one can carry

herumtragen und da hinstellen kann, wo man sie haben will. Die grosse
he-rŏŏm'-trah-gĕn ŏŏnt dah hin'-shte-lĕn kan, voh man zee hah'-bĕn vil. dee groh'-sĕ
about in the room and put down where one wants it. The big

Lampe, die an der Decke hängt, ist ein Lüster. Die Decke ist oben, und der
lam'-pĕ, dee an dayr de'-kĕ henkt, ist īn lĭs'-tĕr. dee de'-kĕ ist oh'-bĕn ŏŏnt dayr
lamp which hangs from the ceiling is a chandelier. The ceiling is above and the

Fussboden ist unten. Auf dem Fussboden liegt ein Teppich. Der kleine Junge
fŏŏs'-boh-dĕn ist ŏŏn'-tĕn. ouf daym fŏŏs'-boh-dĕn leekt īn te'-pich. dayr klī'-nĕ yŏŏng'-gĕ
floor is below. On the floor lies a carpet. The little boy

bringt seiner Mutter etwas zu trinken. Die Katze geht aus dem Zimmer.
bringt zī'-nĕr mŏŏ'-tĕr et'-vas tsŏŏ tring'-kĕn. dee kat'-sĕ gayt ous daym tsi'-mĕr.
brings his mother something to drink. The cat goes out of the room.

---

[1] **Der Mund** is the mouth of a human being. The mouth of an animal is **das Maul** (plural **Mäuler**).

DER ESSTISCH—THE DINNER TABLE
(*English key on page* 368)

1. der Tisch, -e
2. das Tischbein, -e
3. das Tischtuch, ···-er
4. die Gemüseschüssel, -n
5. die Kartoffelschüssel, -n
6. der Brotkorb, ···-e
7. das Weinglas, ···-er
8. die Serviette, -n
9. der Suppenteller, -
10. die Suppenterrine, -n

11. das Salzfass, ···-er
12. der Pfefferstreuer, -
13. der Senf
14. der Essteller, -
15. die Karaffe, -n
16. die Sauciere, -n
17. der Suppenlöffel, -
18. das Messer, -
19. das Fischmesser, -
20. der Kompottlöffel, -

21. die Gabel, -n
22. der Serviettenring, -e
23. die Anrichte, -n
24. die Obstschale, -n
25. die Kompottschale, -n
26. der Kompotteller, -
27. die Weinflasche, -n
28. die Fleischschüsse!, -n
29. die Tranchiergabel, -n
30. das Tranchiermesser, -

BEI TISCH—*AT TABLE*

Um halb eins deckt die Mutter den Tisch. Vor jeder Person steht ein Teller.
ŏŏm halp ĭns dekt dee mŏŏ'-tĕr dayn tish. fohr yay'-dĕr per-zohn' shtayt ĭn te'-lĕr.
At half-past twelve the mother lays the table. In front of each person stands a plate.

Neben jedem Teller liegen ein Messer und eine Gabel; hinter jedem Teller liegt ein
nay'-bĕn yay'-dĕm te'-lĕr lee'-ĕn ĭn me'-sĕr ŏŏnt ī'-nĕ gah'-bĕl; hin'-tĕr yay'-dĕm te'-lĕr
Beside each plate lie a knife and a fork; behind each plate lies a [leekt ĭn

Löffel. Auf dem Tisch stehen auch ein Salzfass, der Brotkorb, die Gemüseschüssel,
lāy'-fĕl. ouf daym tish shtay'-ĕn ouch ĭn zalts'-fas, dayr broht'-korp, dee gĕ-mêê'-zĕ-shḹ-sĕl,
spoon. On the table stand also a salt-cellar, the bread basket, the vegetable dish,

die Suppenterrine, u.s.w. Wir essen Suppe mit einem Löffel, dem
dee zŏŏ'-pĕn-tĕ-ree'-nĕ, ŏŏnt-zoh-vī'-tĕr. veer e'-sĕn zŏŏ'-pĕ mit ī'-nĕm lāy'-fĕl, daym
the soup tureen, etc. We eat soup with a spoon, the

Suppenlöffel. Wir essen Fleisch mit einer Gabel und schneiden es mit einem Messer.
zŏŏ'-pĕn-lāy-fĕl. veer e'-sĕn flīsh mit ī'-nĕr gah'-bĕl ŏŏnt shnī'-dĕn es mit ī'-nĕm me'-sĕr.
soup spoon. We eat meat with a fork and cut it with a knife.

Die Engländer trinken Tee aus Tassen, die Deutschen aus Gläsern. Bier trinkt man
dee eng'-lĕn-dĕr tring'-kĕn tay ous ta'-sĕn, dee doyt'-shĕn ous glay'-zĕrn. beer trinkt man
The English drink tea out of cups, the Germans out of glasses. One drinks beer

aus einem Bierglas, und Wein aus einem Weinglas. Das Fleisch liegt auf einer
ous ī'-nĕm beer'-glas, ŏŏnt vīn ous ī'-nĕm vīn'-glas. das flīsh leekt ouf ī'-nĕr
out of a beer glass, and wine out of a wine glass. The meat lies on a

Fleischplatte, wenn man es auf den Tisch bringt. Das Gemüse ist in der Gemüseschüssel,
flīsh'-pla-tĕ, ven man es ouf dayn tish bringt. das gĕ-mêê'-zĕ ist in dayr gĕ-mêê'-zĕ-shḹ-sĕl,
meat dish when one brings it on the table. The vegetable is in the vegetable dish,

und die Suppe in der Suppenterrine. Das Essen ist fertig. Setzen wir uns.
ŏŏnt dee zŏŏ'-pĕ in dayr zŏŏ'-pĕn-tĕ-ree'-nĕ. das e'-sĕn ist fayr'-tich. zc'-tsĕn veer ŏŏns.
and the soup in the soup tureen. The meal is ready. Let us sit down.

Nehmen Sie Suppe?	**Ein klein wenig, wenn ich bitten darf.**
Do you take soup?	*Just a little, if I may (ask).*
Nein, danke.	**Wie schmeckt Ihnen der Braten?**
No, thank you.	*How do you like the joint?*
Essen Sie gern Fisch?	**Er ist ausgezeichnet.**
Do you like fish?	*It is excellent.*
Danke, ich esse Fisch sehr gern.	**Noch etwas Kompott?**
Thanks, I like fish very much.	*Some more stewed fruit?*
Bedienen Sie sich!	**Danke, ich habe genug.**
Help yourself!	*Thanks, I have (had) enough.*
Nach Ihnen, bitte.	**Nehmen Sie Bratkartoffeln oder Kartoffelbrei?**
After you, please.	*Do you take fried potatoes or mashed?*
Bitte, reichen Sie mir das Brot.	**Möchten Sie Senf zum Fleisch?**
Please pass the bread.	*Would you like mustard with your meat?*
Möchten Sie noch etwas?	**Darf ich um das Salz und den Pfeffer bitten?**
Would you like more?	*May I ask for salt and pepper?*

PREPOSITIONS (I)

A preposition is a word placed before a noun or pronoun to show in what relation that person or thing stands to something else.

Dieses Telegramm ist für meinen Bruder.
This telegram is for my brother.

Gehen Sie nicht ohne Ihren Mantel!
Don't go without your coat.

Der kleine Junge schaut durch das Schlüsselloch.
The little boy looks through the keyhole.

Es ist schwer, gegen den Strom zu schwimmen.
It is difficult to swim against the current.

Note from these examples that the prepositions **für**=*for*, **ohne**=*without*, **gegen**=*against*, and **durch**=*through*, are all followed by the accusative case.

Schreiben Sie nicht mit dem Bleistift.
Don't write with the pencil.

Schreiben Sie mit der Feder.
Write with the pen.

Wollen Sie ein Stück von diesem Kuchen haben?
Do you want a piece of this cake?

Trinken Sie nicht aus der Flasche!
Don't drink from the bottle!

Trinken Sie aus einem Glas!
Drink from a glass!

From these further examples it will be seen that **mit**=*with*, **von**=*from*, and **aus**=*out of*, are followed by the dative case.

Other prepositions which we have met so far are **auf**=*on*, **unter**=*under*, **über**=*over*, **zwischen**=*between*, **an**=*at, by*, **neben**=*near, next to*, **in**=*in*, **vor**=*before*, **hinter**=*behind*. These are followed by the accusative case in answer to the question *Where to?* and by the dative case in answer to the question *Where?* They are more fully dealt with in Lesson 25.

Some prepositions can be contracted with the definite article: **im** is a contraction of **in dem**; **am** is a contraction of **an dem**; **vom** is a contraction of **von dem**.

SOMETHING, NOTHING; SOMEBODY, NOBODY

Dieser Mann hat etwas in der Hand

Auf diesem Stuhl sitzt jemand

Dieser Mann hat nichts in der Hand

Auf diesem Stuhl sitzt niemand

etwas (et'-vas)=*something*
nichts (nichts)=*nothing*

jemand (yay'-mant)=*somebody, someone*
niemand (nee'-mant)=*nobody, no one*

DER MARKTPLATZ IN TRIBERG

Triberg ist ein Schwarzwaldstädtchen von 4500 Einwohnern. Es ist Kurort, Wintersportsplatz und Zentrum der Uhrenindustrie.

(*Translation on page* 376)

der Einwohner, -	der Kurort, -e	das Zentrum	die Uhrenindustrie, -n
inhabitant	*spa*	*centre*	*clock industry*

ORDER OF WORDS (III)

Sie schreibt ihrer Tochter einen Brief.
She is writing a letter to her daughter.

Er zeigt seinem Schüler Bilder.
He is showing pictures to his pupil.

Wir senden unseren Kindern ein Paket.
We send our children a parcel.

When a verb has two objects, both of which are nouns, the dative object normally precedes the accusative object.

If the dative object is specially stressed or enlarged, it can follow the accusative object, e.g.:

Er bringt die Blumen nicht seiner Mutter, sondern seiner Tante = *He brings the flowers not to his mother but to his aunt.*

Sie senden das Geld ihrem Onkel, der sehr arm ist = *They send the money to their uncle, who is very poor.*

If one object is a pronoun and the other a noun, the pronoun comes first, e.g.:

Er sendet mir das Geld = *He sends me the money.*

Er sendet es seinem Vater = *He sends it to his father.*

Sie bringt uns das Fleisch = *She brings us the meat.*

If both objects are pronouns, the accusative pronoun precedes, e.g.:

Ich gebe es ihm — *I give it to him.*

Sie gibt ihn mir nicht = *She does not give it (any masculine object) to me.*

Sie zeigen sie ihr = *You show it (the pen or any other feminine object) to her.*

HOW TO TRANSLATE *BUT*

Ich spreche perfekt Deutsch, aber ich bin kein Deutscher.
I speak German perfectly, but I am not a German.

Ihr Haar ist nicht schwarz, sondern braun.
Her hair is not black but brown.

Aber is used in the sense of *however;* **sondern** in contradiction of a preceding negative statement.

DER MARKTPLATZ IN HAMELN

Hameln, eine altertümliche Kreisstadt in der Nähe von Hannover, ist durch die Sage vom Rattenfänger bekannt geworden: ein Fremder habe durch die Töne seiner Schalmei die Seelen der Kinder zusammen mit den Ratten herausgelockt, so dass die Kinder nun hinter ihm und den Ratten herlaufen müssen. (*Translation on page* 376)

die Kreisstadt, ̈-e	**die Nähe**	**die Sage, -n**	**der Rattenfänger, -**	**der Fremde, -n**
county town	*neighbourhood*	*legend*	*rat-catcher*	*stranger*
der Ton, ̈-e	**die Schalmei**	**die Seele, -n**	**herauslocken**	**herlaufen**
sound, melody	*shawm (pipe)*	*soul*	*to lure*	*to run off*

NEW NOUNS

DER
Korb, ⋯-e	*basket*
Erwachsene, -n[1]	*adult*
Ofen, ⋯-	*stove*
Knochen, -	*bone*
Sessel, -	*chair*
Stuhl, ⋯-e	*chair*
Lehnstuhl, ⋯-e	*armchair*
Fussboden, ⋯-	*floor*
Lüster, -	*chandelier*
Teppich, -e	*carpet*
Teller, -	*plate*
Löffel, -	*spoon*

DIE
Lampe, -n	*lamp*
Person, -en	*person*
Ecke, -n	*corner*
Zigarre, -n	*cigar*
Zeitung, -en	*newspaper*
Wand, ⋯-e	*wall*
Sonate, -n	*sonata*
Decke, -n	*ceiling, cover*
Gabel, -n	*fork*
Schüssel, -n	*dish*
Platte, -n	*plate*
Suppenterrine, -n	*soup tureen*
Kartoffel, -n	*potato*

DAS
Tintenfass, ⋯-er	*inkpot*
Klavier, -e	*piano*
Sofa, -s	*sofa, settee*
Kissen, -	*cushion*
Mittagessen, -	*lunch*
Salzfass, ⋯-er	*salt-cellar*
Gemüse, -	*vegetable*
Haar, -e	*hair*

EXERCISES

I Insert the appropriate endings -em, -er, -en.

1. Das Briefpapier liegt auf d— Tisch. 2. Der Stuhl steht hinter d— Bett. 3. Er sitzt auf d— Stuhl. 4. Sie steht an d— Tür. 5. Der Hund liegt neben d— Ofen. 6. Die Federn sind in d— Schachtel. 7. Die Kinder gehen mit ihr— Eltern. 8. Ich schreibe mit mein— Füllfeder. 9. Wir geben d— Kindern Geschenke. 10. Die Kinder sind in d— Schule. 11. Er hat die Zeitung in d— Hand. 12. Wir haben unsere Bücher in d— Händen. 13. Er kommt von d— Post. 14. Er schreibt sein— Vater. 15. Das Briefpapier gehört ihr— Mutter. 16. Der Schreibtisch steht zwischen ein— Fenster und ein— Tür. 17. Das Kätzchen spielt zwischen d— Stühlen. 18. Wir liegen unter d— Bäumen in dies— Garten. 19. Haben Sie etwas in Ihr— Händen? 20. Hängt das Bild an dies— oder jen— Wand?

II Answer in German

1. Wie viele Personen sind auf dem Bild auf Seite 120? 2. Was hat die Frau in der Hand? 3. Was ist auf dem Tisch? 4. Wo liegt der Hund? 5. Wo sitzt der Grossvater? 6. Wer steht neben dem Ofen? 7. Steht jemand an der Tür? 8. Liegt etwas auf dem Ofen? 9. Wo ist das Briefpapier? 10. Was tut die Katze?

III Answer the following questions, using pronouns in place of the nouns given in each question

1. Der Lehrer gibt dem Schüler ein Buch.

(*a*) Wer gibt das Buch? (*b*) Wem gibt der Lehrer es? (*c*) Was gibt der Lehrer dem Schüler?

2. Die Mutter sendet der Tochter das Paket.

(*a*) Wem sendet die Mutter das Paket? (*b*) Was sendet die Mutter der Tochter? (*c*) Sendet die Mutter der Tochter das Paket?

3. Die Kinder zeigen den Eltern die Bilder.

(*a*) Was zeigen die Kinder den Eltern? (*b*) Wer zeigt den Eltern die Bilder? (*c*) Zeigen die Kinder den Eltern die Bilder?

(*Answers on page* 360)

---

[1] This is not strictly a noun but an adjective. It can be either masculine or feminine, and whether used in the singular or plural it takes the appropriate adjectival ending. See "Adjectives used as Nouns ", page 304.

FÜNFZEHNTE LEKTION: *FIFTEENTH LESSON*

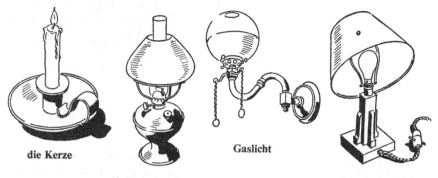

die Kerze

Gaslicht

die Petroleumlampe

elektrisches Licht

Die Sonne ist am Himmel. Am Tage können wir gut sehen, weil die Sonne uns
dee zo'-nĕ ist am hi'-mĕl. am tah'-gĕ kĕ̦'-nĕn veer gōōt zay'-ĕn, vīl dee zo'-nĕ ōōns
The sun is in the sky. In the daytime we can see well, because the sun gives us

Licht gibt. Es ist jetzt hell, weil die Sonne am Himmel ist. In der Nacht ist es dunkel.
licht geept. es ist yetst hel, vīl dee zo'-nĕ am hi'-mĕl ist. in dayr nacht ist es dōōng'-kĕl.
light. It is light now because the sun is in the sky. At night it is dark.

Wenn der Mond am Himmel steht, können wir ein wenig sehen. Das Mondlicht
ven dayr mohnt am hi'-mĕl shtayt, kĕ̦'-nĕn veer īn vay'-nich zay'-ĕn. das mohnt'-licht
When the moon is in the sky we can see a little. Moonlight

ist viel schwächer als das Sonnenlicht. Heute Abend wird der Mond scheinen. Wir
ist feel shve'-chĕr als das zo'-nĕn-licht. hoy'-tĕ ah'-bĕnt virt dayr mohnt shī'-nĕn. veer
is much weaker than sunlight. To-night the moon will shine. We

werden den Mond und die Sterne am Himmel sehen. Wenn wir in der Nacht
vayr'-dĕn dayn mohnt ōōnt dee shter'-nĕ am hi'-mĕl zay'-ĕn. ven veer in dayr nacht
shall see the moon and the stars in the sky. If we want to see at night

sehen wollen, müssen wir Licht machen. In diesem Zimmer haben wir
zay'-ĕn vo'-lĕn, mį'-sĕn veer licht ma'-chĕn. in dee'-zĕm tsi'-mĕr hah'-bĕn veer
we have to make light. In this room we have

elektrisches Licht. Wenn ich das Zimmer verlasse, schalte ich das elektrische Licht aus.
ay-lek'-tri-shĕs licht. ven ich das tsi'-mĕr fer-la'-sĕ, shal'-tĕ ich das ay-lek'-tri-shĕ licht ous.
electric light. When I leave the room, I switch off the electric light.

Der Schalter ist rechts von der Tür. Bitte, schalten Sie das Licht ein! In der Küche
dayr shal'-tĕr ist rechts fon dayr tür. bi'-tĕ, shal'-tĕn zee das licht īn! in dayr kį'-chĕ
The switch is on the right of the door. Please switch on the light! In the kitchen

haben wir Gaslicht. Gas schaltet man nicht ein, man zündet es mit einem Streichholz an.
hah'-bĕn veer gas'-licht. gas shal'-tĕt man nicht īn, man tsįn'-dĕt es mit ī'-nĕm shtrīch'-
we have gaslight. Gas is not switched on, it is lit with a match. [holts an.

128

Die Sonne gibt uns nicht nur Licht, sondern auch Wärme. Im Winter heizen wir
dee zo'-nĕ geept ōōns nicht nōōr licht, zon'-dĕrn ouch ver'-mĕ. im vin'-tĕr hī'-tsĕn veer
The sun gives us not only light but also warmth. In winter we heat

den Ofen, um uns zu wärmen. Man heizt den Ofen mit Holz und Kohlen.
dayn oh'-fĕn, ōōm ōōns tsōō ver'-mĕn. man hītst dayn oh'-fĕn mit holts ōōnt koh'-lĕn.
the stove in order to warm ourselves. One heats the stove with wood and coal.

Die Engländer haben Kaminfeuer in ihren Häusern. Die Amerikaner
dee eng'-lĕn-dĕr hah'-bĕn kah-meen'-foy-ĕr in ee'-rĕn hoy'-zĕrn. dee ah-may-ree-kah'-nĕr
The English have open fires in their houses. The Americans

haben Zentralheizung und die Deutschen Kachelöfen. Wenn es kalt ist, wärmen
hah'-bĕn tsen-trahl'-hī-tsōōng ōōnt dee doyt'-shĕn ka'-chĕl-ay-fĕn. ven es kalt ist, ver'-mĕn
have central heating and the Germans tiled stoves. When it is cold we warm

wir uns am Ofen. Wenn die Sonne scheint, haben wir gutes Wetter. Wenn es regnet
veer ōōns am oh'-fĕn. ven dee zo'-nĕ shīnt, hah'-bĕn veer gōō'-tĕs ve'-tĕr. ven es rayg'-nĕt
ourselves by the stove. When the sun shines, we have good weather. When it rains

oder schneit, ist das Wetter schlecht. Wenn das Wetter schlecht ist, ist der Himmel grau. Er
oh'-dĕr shnīt, ist das ve'-tĕr shlecht. ven das ve'-tĕr shlecht ist, ist dayr hi'-mĕl grou. ayr
or snows the weather is bad. When the weather is bad, the sky is grey. It

ist mit Wolken bedeckt. Der Himmel ist blau, wenn er wolkenlos ist. Im Winter
ist mit vol'-kĕn bĕ-dekt'. dayr hi'-mĕl ist blou, ven ayr vol'-kĕn-lohs ist. im vin'-tĕr
is covered with clouds. The sky is blue when it is cloudless. In winter

schneit es zuweilen. Der Schnee ist weiss, und er bedeckt die Strassen, die Häuser
shnīt es tsōō-vī'-lĕn. dayr shnay ist vīs ōōnt ayr. bĕ-dekt' dee shtrah'-sĕn, dee hoy'-zĕr
it snows sometimes. The snow is white and it covers the streets, the houses

und die Felder. Wenn es regnet, sind die
ōōnt dee fel'-dĕr. ven es rayg'-nĕt, zint dee
and the fields. When it rains, the

Strassen nass. Wenn die Sonne scheint, sind
shtrah'-sĕn nas. ven dee zo'-nĕ shīnt, zint
streets are wet. When the sun shines, are

Ein
Kachelofen

die Strassen trocken. Wie ist das Wetter
dee shtrah'-sĕn tro'-kĕn. vee ist das ve'-tĕr
the streets are dry. What is the weather

heute? Es ist schön. Die Sonne scheint,
hoy'-tĕ? es ist shayn. dee zo'-nĕ shīnt,
like today? It is fine. The sun is shining,

aber es ist nicht zu warm. Wie ist der Winter in England? Er ist gewöhnlich kalt
ah'-bĕr es ist nicht tsōō varm. vee ist dayr vin'-ter in eng'-lant? ayr ist ge-vayn'-lich kalt
but it is not too warm. What is the winter like in England? It is usually cold

und nass. In London ist es zuweilen neblig. Der Nebel ist manchmal sehr dicht.
ōōnt nas. in lon'-don ist es tsōō-vī-lĕn nayb'-lich. dayr nay'-bĕl ist manch'-mahl zayr
and wet. In London it is sometimes foggy. The fog is occasionally very dense. (dicht.

GC—E

The universe and the weather are the main subjects of study in this Lesson. To help you, the artist has brought together on these two pages some contrasting types of weather. With the aid of the vocabularies given below, try to describe what is happening in each

Above: **die Sonne,** *sun;* **der Sonnenstrahl, -en,** *sunray;* **die Hitze,** *heat;* **die Wolke, -n,** *cloud;* **der Sonnenschirm, -e,** *sunshade;* **der Kahn, ̈-e,** *punt;* **das Badekostüm, -e,** *bathing-dress;* **der Bademantel, ̈-,** *bathing-wrap.*

Below: **der Wind,** *wind;* **der Regen,** *rain;* **das Gewitter, -,** *thunderstorm;* **der Sturm, ̈-e,** *storm;* **der Donner,** *thunder;* **der Blitz,** *lightning;* **der Hagel,** *hail;* **der Nebel,** *fog;* **es regnet,** *it is raining.*

Es ist heiss, kalt, windig, neblig, hell, dunkel, stürmisch, nass, klar, trüb, trocken.
It is hot, cold, windy, foggy, bright, dark,   stormy,   wet, clear, dull, dry.

THE WEATHER

scene. When you have finished the test you will have acquired a stock of phrases which should enable you to cope easily with all normal occasions concerning the weather—a useful conversational accomplishment in any language!

Above: **der Schnee,** *snow;* **die Schneeflocke, -n,** *snowflake;* **der Schneesturm, ··-e,** *snowstorm;* **die Schneewehe, -n,** *snowdrift;* **die Kälte,** *cold;* **das Eis,** *ice;* **der Bergstock, ··-e,** *alpenstock;* **es schneit,** *it is snowing.*

Below: **der Mond,** *moon;* **das Mondlicht,** *moonlight;* **der Stern, -e,** *star;* **der Förster, -,** *gamekeeper;* **die Jagdtasche, -n,** *game-bag;* **das Gewehr, -e,** *gun;* **der Teich, -e,** *pond;* **das Bauernhaus, ··-er,** *farm-house.*

Schönes, schlechtes, feuchtes, heisses, herrliches, veränderliches, stürmisches Wetter.
Beautiful,   bad,   damp,   hot,   glorious,   changeable,   stormy   weather.

Am Morgen geht   **Am Mittag steht**   **Am Abend geht**
die Sonne auf   **die Sonne im Süden**   **die Sonne unter**

Am Morgen geht die Sonne auf, und am Abend geht sie unter. Im Sommer geht
am mor'-gĕn gayt dee zo'-nĕ ouf ŏŏnt am ah'-bĕnt gayt zee ŏŏn'-tĕr. im zo'-mĕr gayt
In the morning the sun rises and in the evening it sets.   In the summer

die Sonne früh auf, um drei Uhr oder um vier Uhr, und die Tage sind lang. Im
dee zo'-nĕ frēę ouf, ŏŏm drī ōōr oh'-dĕr ŏŏm feer ōōr, ŏŏnt dee tah'-gĕ zint lang. im
the sun rises early, at three o'clock or at four o'clock, and the days are long.   In the

Winter geht die Sonne spät auf, um sieben oder acht Uhr, und die Tage sind
vin'-tĕr gayt dee zo'-nĕ shpayt ouf, ŏŏm zee'-bĕn oh'-dĕr acht ōōr, ŏŏnt dee tah'-gĕ zint
winter the sun rises late, at seven or eight o'clock, and the days are

kurz. Um wieviel Uhr wird die Sonne heute Abend untergehen? Gegen acht,
kŏŏrts. ŏŏm vee'-feel ōōr wirt dee zo'-nĕ hoy'-tĕ ah'-bĕnt ŏŏn'-tĕr-gay-ĕn? gay'-gĕn acht,
short.   At what time will the sun set to-night?   At about eight

oder vielleicht sogar später. Wir sind jetzt im Frühling, und die Tage
oh'-dĕr fee-līcht' zoh-gahr' shpay'-tĕr. veer zint yetst im frēę'-ling, ŏŏnt dee tah'-gĕ
or perhaps even later.   It is now spring, and the days

werden länger. Im Winter sind die Tage kurz, weil die Sonne spät aufgeht
vayr'-dĕn leng'-ĕr. im vin'-tĕr zint dee tah'-gĕ kŏŏrts, vil dee zo'-nĕ shpayt ouf'-gayt
are getting longer.   In the winter the days are short because the sun rises late

und früh untergeht. Die Sonne geht im Osten auf, und im Westen geht sie unter.
ŏŏnt frēę ŏŏn'-tĕr-gayt. dee zo'-nĕ gayt im os'-tĕn ouf ŏŏnt im ves'-tĕn gayt zee ŏŏn'-tĕr.
and sets early.   The sun rises in the east and it sets in the west.

der Vollmond   **der Halbmond**   **die Mondsichel**

Am Mittag steht die Sonne im Süden. Gegenüber dem Süden ist der Norden,
am mi'-tak shtayt dee zo'-ně im zĕ̂'-děn. gay-gěn-ĕ̂'-běr daym zĕ̂-děn ist dayr nor'-děn,
At mid-day the sun is in the south. Opposite the south is the north,

aber die Sonne steht nie im Norden, wenn man in der nördlichen Erdhälfte lebt.
ah'-běr dee zo'-ně shtayt nee im nor'-děn, ven man in dayr nĕrt'-li-chěn ayrt'-helf-tě
but the sun is never in the north, if one lives in the northern hemisphere. [laypt.

Der Norden, der Süden, der Osten und der
dayr nor'-děn, dayr zĕ̂'-děn, dayr os'-těn ōōnt dayr
The north, the south, the east and the

Westen sind die vier Himmelsrichtungen.[1] Die
ves'-těn zint dee feer hi'-měls-rich-tōong-ěn. dee
west are the four points of the compass. The

Magnetnadel zeigt immer nach Norden.
mag-nayt'-nah-děl tsīkt i'-měr nach nor'-děn.
magnetic needle always points to the north.

Ein zuverlässiger Kompass ist sehr nützlich.
in tsōō'-fer-less-si-gěr kom'-pas ist zayr nĭts'-lich.
A reliable compass is very useful.

Dies ist ein Kompass

der Regenschirm

Dies ist ein Regenschirm. **Wenn es regnet oder wenn**
dees ist in ray'-gěn-shirm. ven es rayg'-ně̌t oh'-děr ven
This is an umbrella. If it is raining or if there

dunkle Wolken am Himmel sind, gehe ich nie ohne
dōōng'-klě vol'-kěn am hi'-měl zint, gay'-ě ich nee oh'-ně
are dark clouds in the sky I never go out without an

Regenschirm aus. Wenn es zu regnen beginnt, mache ich
ray'-gěn-shirm ous. ven es tsōō rayg'-něn bě-gint', ma'-chě ich
umbrella. When it begins to rain, I open

meinen Regenschirm auf. Wenn ich im Regen ohne Regenschirm ausgehe,
mī'-něn ray'-gěn-shirm ouf. ven ich im ray'-gěn oh'-ně ray'-gěn-shirm ous-gay'-ě,
my umbrella. If I go out in the rain without my umbrella

werden meine Kleider nass. Ich ziehe die nassen Kleider aus und trockne an. Ich
vayr'-děn mī'-ně klī'-děr nas. ich tsee'-ě dee na'-sěn klī'-děr ous ōōnt trok'-ně an. ich
my clothes get wet. I take off my wet clothes and put on dry ones. I

hänge die nassen Kleider an den Ofen, um sie zu
heng'-ě dee na'-sěn klī'-děr an dayn oh'-fěn, ōōm zee tsōō
hang my wet clothes by the stove in order to

trocknen. Im Sommer tragen wir dünne Kleider und
trok'-něn. im zo'-měr trah'-gěn veer dĭ'-ně klī'-děr ōōnt
dry them. In summer we wear thin clothes and

im Winter dicke. Wenn ich im Winter zu dünne
im vin'-těr di'-kě. ven ich im vin'-těr tsōō dĭ'-ně
in winter thick ones. If I wear too thin

der Sonnenschirm

---
[1] lit.: *directions of the sky.*

AUF DER EISBAHN BEI GARMISCH-PARTENKIRCHEN

Garmisch-Partenkirchen, in Oberbayern, sind Nachbarorte am Fusse der Zugspitze (2,963 m.), des höchsten Berges in Deutschland. Beide Orte sind beliebt als Sommerfrischen und als Wintersportplätze. Schlittschuhlaufen, Rodeln und Skilaufen sind die beliebtesten Arten des Wintersports.

(*Translation on page* 376)

die Eisbahn, -en	der Nachbar, -n	der Ort, -e	beliebt	die Sommerfrische, -n
skating rink	*neighbour*	*place, resort*	*popular*	*summer resort*
das Schlittschuhlaufen		das Rodeln	das Skilaufen	die Art, -en
skating		*tobogganing*	*ski-ing*	*kind*

K¹eider trage, ist mir kalt. **Ist Ihnen kalt?** Mir ist ein wenig kalt. **Wenn Sie nasse**
klī'-děr trah'-gě, ist meer kalt. ist ee'-něn kalt? meer ist in vay'-nich kalt. ven zee na'-sě
clothes in the winter I feel cold. Do you feel cold? *I feel a little cold.*

If you have wet
Füsse haben, ziehen Sie Ihre Schuhe aus und stellen Sie Ihre Füsse an den
f<u>ee</u>'-sě hah'-běn, tsee'-ěn zee ee'-rě sh<del>oo</del>'-ě aus <del>oo</del>nt shte'-lěn zee ee'-rě f<u>ee</u>'-sě an dayn
feet, take off your shoes and put your feet near the

Ofen. Sie müssen sich an den Ofen setzen, wenn Ihnen kalt ist. **Es ist nicht gut,**
oh'-fěn. zee m<u>i</u>'-sěn sich an dayn oh'-fěn ze'-tsěn, ven ee'-něn kalt ist. es ist nicht g<del>oo</del>t,
stove. You must sit by the stove if you are cold. It is not good

nasse Füsse zu haben. **Ist Ihnen noch kalt?** Danke, mir ist jetzt warm genug.
na'-sě f<u>ee</u>'-sě ts<del>oo</del> hah'-běn. ist ee'-něn noch kalt? dang'-kě, meer ist yetst vahrm gě'-n<del>oo</del>ch.
to have wet feet. Are you still cold? Thank you, *I am warm enough now.*

SEPARABLE VERBS
Er steht um a'cht Uhr auf.
He gets up at eight o'clock.

Die Sonne geht spät unter.
The sun sets late.

Schalten Sie das Licht ein!
Switch on the light!

Warum ziehen Sie sich nicht aus?
Why don't you undress?

Ziehen Sie sich nicht an?
Aren't you getting dressed?

Verbs like **aufstehen**=*to get up;* **einschal-**
ten=*to switch on;* **anzichen**=*to put on*
(*clothes*), etc., are called separable verbs,
because the first part is usually separated
from the rest and put at the end.

Er will noch nicht aufstehen.
He does not want to get up yet.

Sie müssen sich jetzt anziehen.
You must get dressed now.

Ich nehme meinen Regenschirm mit, wenn
ich ausgehe.
I take my umbrella with me when I go out.

Sie steht vor dem Spiegel, wenn sie den Hut
aufsetzt.
She stands in front of the mirror when she
puts on her hat.

The separable prefixes precede infinitives¹,
and verbs in dependent clauses which,
according to the rules given in Lesson 12
(p.105), are always at the end of the sentence.

FUTURE TENSE
Ich werde morgen nicht kommen.
I shan't come to-morrow.

Was werden Sie morgen tun?
What will you do to-morrow?

Die Gäste werden bald ankommen.
The guests will soon arrive.

Mein Bruder wird nächste Woche nach Paris
fahren.
My brother will go to Paris next week.

Ich	{ werde { schreiben	I	{ will { write
wir Sie sie	werden schreiben	we you they	will write
er sie es	wird schreiben	he she it	will write

Werden has two different meanings in
German. As a verb it means *to become,* but
it is also used as an auxiliary verb to form
the future tense (in the same way as English
shall and *will* are used for this purpose
with the infinitive of a verb).

Note that the auxiliary verb, just like any
finite verb, takes the second place, while
the infinitive is put at the end of the sentence. *I shall see you to-morrow morning*
at eight o'clock before breakfast=**Ich**
werde Sie morgen um acht Uhr vor dem
Frühstück sehen.

¹ The infinitive is that form of the verb that just names the verb, not limited by person or
number (e.g. *to see, to be, to take*).

Nach Regen kommt
Sonnenschein (Sprichwort)

ORDER OF WORDS (IV)

Wenn es regnet, bleibe ich zu Hause.
When it rains I stay at home.

Wenn die Sonne scheint, gehen wir spazieren.
When the sun shines we go for a walk.

Während wir spazieren gehen, arbeitet er im Garten.
While we go for a walk, he works in the garden.

Dass er nicht kommen kann, ist sehr schade.
That he can't come is a great pity.

In the sentences given above, the dependent clause precedes the main clause.

According to Rule II (see Lesson 12, p. 105) the verb comes at the end in a dependent clause. Now, if the whole sentence starts with a dependent clause, the verb of the main clause immediately follows in accordance with the rule that the verb must take second place, the dependent clause, considered as a unit, taking the first place.

1	2
Wenn es regnet,	bleibe ich zu Hause

IDIOMS

Mir ist warm	= *I am warm*
Mir ist kalt	= *I am cold*
Ist Ihnen kalt?	= *Are you cold?*
Ihm ist heiss	= *He is hot*
Mir ist schlecht	= *I feel sick*
Ihr ist schlecht	= *She feels sick*

HOW TO TRANSLATE *LIGHT*

(1) **Das Licht ist hier schlecht.**
   The light is bad here.

(2) **Das andere Zimmer ist heller.**
   The other room is lighter.

(3) **Wir müssen eine Kerze anzünden.**
   We must light a candle.

Whereas in English *light* is used (1) as a noun; (2) as an adjective; (3) as a verb, German has three different words for these uses: (1) **das Licht** = *the light;* (2) **hell** = *light* (i.e., *not dark*); (3) **anzünden** = *to light.*

IM SEE

Heute ist das Wasser warm,
heute kann's nicht schaden,
schnell hinunter an den See,
heute gehn wir baden!

Eins, zwei, drei—die Hosen aus,
Stiefel, Wams und Wäsche!
Und dann—plumps ins Wasser rein!
Grade wie die Frösche!

Und der schönste Sonnenschein
brennt uns nach dem Bade
Brust und Buckel knusperbraun,
braun wie Schokolade!

Adolf Holst

Schaden, *to harm;* **der Stiefel**, -, *boot;* **das Wams**, ⋯-er, *jersey;* **die Wäsche**, *underclothes;* **plumps**, *flop;* **rein**, *into ;* **g(e)rade wie**, *just like;* **der Frosch**, ⋯-e, *frog;* **die Brust**, ⋯-e, *chest;* **der Buckel**, -, *back;* **knusperbraun**, *crisp brown.*

NEW NOUNS

DER	Regen, -	rain
	Sonnenschein	sunshine
	Himmel, -	sky, heaven
	Schalter, -	electric light switch
	Morgen, -	morning
	Abend, -e	evening
	Mittag, -e	midday
	Osten	east
	Westen	west
	Süden	south
	Norden	north
DIE	Küche, -n	kitchen, cooking
	Kerze, -n	candle
	Wärme	warmth
	Kohle, -n	coal
	Heizung	heating, fuel
	Wolke, -n	cloud
	Strasse, -n	street
	Richtung, -en	direction
	Sichel, -n	crescent, sickle
	Nadel, -n	needle
DAS	Licht, -e	candle
	Licht, -er	light
	Wetter	weather

EXERCISES

I Read and Translate

1. Sehen Sie! Es beginnt zu regnen. Sie können jetzt nicht ausgehen. 2. Ich muss aber ausgehen. Man erwartet (erwarten = *to expect*) mich bei meinen Freunden. 3. Warten Sie noch einige (= *some*) Minuten. Bald wird der Regen aufhören (= *stop*) 4. Wollen Sie sich nicht setzen? Setzen Sie sich ans Feuer. 5. Es sind nicht genug Kohlen auf dem Feuer. Ich werde noch einige Kohlen auflegen. 6. Ist Ihnen warm genug? Danke, mir ist sehr warm, aber jetzt muss ich wirklich (= *really*) gehen. 7. Sie können aber nicht ohne Regenschirm gehen. 8. Haben Sie einen? Ich habe keinen. 9. Wenn Sie wirklich gehen müssen, nehmen Sie meinen Regenschirm. 10. Ich danke Ihnen sehr. Ich werde ihn morgen zurückbringen. 11. Es regnet schon weniger. Bald wird der Regen ganz aufhören.

II Answer in German

1. Ist es jetzt hell? 2. Was sehen wir in der Nacht am Himmel? 3. Scheint die Sonne in der Nacht? 4. Wann scheint die Sonne? 5. Wann steht die Sonne im Süden? 6. Um wieviel Uhr geht die Sonne im Juni auf? 7. Wann geht die Sonne früher auf, im April oder im Mai? 8. Können wir in der Nacht gut sehen? 9. Was müssen wir tun, wenn wir in der Nacht sehen wollen? 10. Was tun wir im Winter, um uns zu wärmen? 11. Tragen wir im Winter dünne Kleider? 12. Warum nicht? 13. Wie ist das Wetter heute? 14. Schneit es? 15. Welche Farbe hat der Schnee? 16. Was nehmen wir mit, wenn wir im Regen ausgehen müssen?

III Translate into German

1. What is the weather like to-day? 2. It is rather cold. 3. It is raining. 4. I am cold. 5. Are you cold? 6. I shall put on my overcoat. 7. What is the weather like here in the summer? 8. It is usually hot. Sometimes it rains. 9. In winter it is windy, sometimes stormy. 10. It is getting dark. We must switch on the light. 11. Switch it on, please. The switch is by the door. 12. I am going for a walk. Will you come with me? 13. I shall come with you, but only for half an hour. 14. I shall work in the garden in the afternoon. 15. The sun sets early now; it will be dark at five o'clock.

(*Answers on page* 360)

GESCHWINDIGKEIT!

Neugebackener Autobesitzer: "Ich werde Sie als Fahrer für meinen neuen Wagen anstellen; ich mache jedoch zur Bedingung, dass Sie nie schneller als dreissig Kilometer die Stunde fahren."

"Aber, mein Herr, dazu brauchen Sie doch kein Auto. Da genügt ja ein Kinderwagen."

Die Geschwindigkeit, *speed;* **neugebacken,** *recently become;* **der Besitzer,-,** *owner;* **der Fahrer, -,** *driver;* **der Wagen, -,** *car;* **anstellen,** *to engage;* **jedoch,** *however;* **die Bedingung, -en,** *condition;* **dazu,** *for that;* **brauchen,** *to need;* **genügen,** *to be sufficient;* **der Kinderwagen, -,** *pram.*

WIEN: KÄRNTNERSTRASSE MIT STEPHANSDOM

Die Kärntnerstrasse ist eine der vornehmsten Strassen von Wien. Vorn rechts ist das vornehme Hotel Bristol und im Hintergrund die Stephanskirche mit dem berühmten Turm. Die Kirche wurde im 14ten und 15ten Jahrhundert erbaut und ist 108 Meter lang. Der 137 Meter hohe Turm trägt eine 22 626 Kilogramm ($= 22\frac{1}{4}$ *tons*) schwere Glocke.

(*Translation on page* 376)

der Dom, -e	**vornehm**	**vorn**	**die Kirche, -n**	**erbauen**	**die Glocke, -n**
cathedral	*fashionable*	*in front*	*church*	*to build*	*bell*

PRONUNCIATION AT SIGHT

W E HAVE now reached a stage in this course where we no longer consider it necessary to provide phonetic transcriptions. We feel sure that by now every one of our readers will be able to pronounce German words at sight. As explained on pages 8-11, every letter and every combination of letters can—with very few exceptions—be pronounced in one way only. It is the object of this Section to enlarge on the details already given.

CONSONANTS

With the exceptions which are explained below, consonants in German are pronounced in the same way as in English.

b	as in English, if at end of syllable like **p**	die **Erbse**	= *pea*
d	as in English, if at end of syllable like **t**	das **Land**	= *country*
c {	like **k** like **ts** before e, ä or i	**Columbus** **Cäcilie** (tsay-tseel´-yĕ)	
ch {	like an exaggerated **h** in *huge* after **a, o, u, au** as in Scottish *loch* Exceptions: **Christ** (krist), **Charakter** (ka-rak´-tĕr), and other words of non-German origin	die **Milch** das **Buch** **auch** die **Nacht**	= *milk* = *book* = *also* = *night*
chs	like **x**	**sechs**	= *six*
g {	as in *get* in the ending -**ig** like the **h** in *huge*	**gut** **wenig**	= *good* = *little*
j	like **y** in *young*	**ja**	= *yes*
l	as in *low;* never as in *hill* or *milk*	das **Lied**	= *song*
ng	as in *singer*	der **Sänger**	= *singer*
qu	as English **kv**	die **Quelle**	= *well*
r	is distinctly sounded wherever it occurs (a trill or a gargling sound)	der **Herr**	= *gentle-man*
s {	like English **z**, before and between vowels like **s** in *so* before consonants or when final like **sh** before **p** or **t** at the beginning of a word or syllable	der **Soldat** die **Rose** **ist** das **Gas** das **Spiel** der **Stock**	= *soldier* = *rose* = *is* = *gas* = *play* = *stick*
sch	like English **sh**	das **Schaf**	= *sheep*
ti	in -**tion** is like English **tsee**	die **Nation**	= *nation*
tz	like English **ts**	die **Katze**	= *cat*
v {	usually like **f** like **v** in non-German words	der **Vater** die **Violine;** die **Vase**	= *father*
w	like English **v**	der **Wald**	= *forest*
z	like **ts** in *its*	die **Zeit**	= *time*

Double consonants are pronounced as single ones, but in compound words they are sounded separately: **abbrechen** (ap´-bre-chĕn)= *to break off;* **annehmen** (an´-nay-mĕn)= *to accept;* **aussehen** (ous´-zayn)= *to look like.*

VOWELS

a ah } long aa	like **ah**	der Vater	=*father*
		der Zahn	=*tooth*
		der Saal	=*hall*
a short	the **ah** cut short	der Mann	=*man*
e eh } long ee	like **a** in *gate*	der Regen	=*rain*
		sehr	=*very*
		die See	=*sea*
e short	as in *get*	das Geld	=*money*
i ie ih } long ieh	like **ee** in *bee*	der Tiger	=*tiger*
		das Tier	=*animal*
		ihr	=*her*
		er sieht	=*he sees*
i short	as in *tin*	das Kind	=*child*
o oh } long oo	as in *home*, but it must be pronounced as a pure vowel	wo	=*where*
		der Sohn	=*son*
		das Boot	=*boat*
o short	like **aw** in *lawyer*	der Zorn	=*anger*
u } long uh	like **oo** in *boot*	gut	=*good*
		der Stuhl	=*chair*
u short	like **oo** in *hood*	die Mutter	=*mother*

MODIFIED VOWELS

ä } long äh	like **a** in *gate*	spät	=*late*
		wählen	=*to choose*
ä short	like **e** in *get*	Hände	=*hands*
ö } long öh	has no English equivalent; it is like French **eu** in *deux* (say *day* with rounded lips)	hören	=*to hear*
		Söhne	=*sons*
ö short	like **er** in *herd*	Götter	=*gods*
ü } long üh	like French **u** in *tu* (say *tea* with rounded lips)	die Güte	=*kindness*
		die Bühne	=*stage*
ü short	same as above, only shorter	die Hütte	=*hut*

DIPHTHONGS

au	like **ou** in *house*	die Maus	=*mouse*
eu } äu	like **oy** in *boy*	heute	=*to-day*
		Bäume	=*trees*
ei ai } ey ay	like **ei** in *height*	die Zeit	=*time*
		der Mai	=*May*
		Meyer,	a surname
		Bayern	=*Bavaria*

STRESS

With the following exceptions, German words are usually stressed on the first syllable:

(1) Words beginning with **be-, ge-, er-, ver-, zer-, ent-** take the stress on the second syllable.

(2) Compound adverbs formed with **her, hin, da** or **wo** as the first part have the stress on the second part: **hin-aus', her-ein', da-mit', wo-hin'.**

(3) Many foreign words, especially proper names, retain their original pronunciation, e.g. **die Na-tion'; das Ho-tel'.** As verbs ending in **-ieren** are of foreign origin, the stress is on the **ie,** e.g. **stud-ie'-ren** = *to study.*

Note.—In compound words the stress is on the first part of the compound, e.g. **Hand'-tasche** = *handbag;* **auf'-stehen** = *to get up.*

LENGTH OF VOWELS

A vowel is short (1) when it is followed by two or more consonants: **Schwester; Gärtner;** (2) in some monosyllabic words: **es; in; das; von; mit; an;** (3) e at the end of a word and in the endings **-el, -en, -er: Nase; Gabel; Garten; Vater.**

A vowel is long (1) when final: **ja; da; Sofa;** (2) when followed by one consonant only: **rot; Tal; Öl; gut;** (3) when it comes before a single consonant followed by a vowel: **Frage; hören; Schule;** (4) when doubled: **Aal; See; Boot;** (5) when followed by an **h: Sohn; Uhr; fahren.**

LEBENDES SCHACH

Dieses lebende Schachspiel wurde auf dem Marktplatz zu Villingen in Baden gespielt. Die Schachfiguren wurden von Schwarzwäldern in ihrer Nationaltracht dargestellt.

(Translation on page 376)

das Schach	**lebend**	**die Schachfigur, -en**	**der Schwarzwälder, -**	**darstellen**
chess	*living*	*chess-man*	*inhabitant of Black Forest*	*to represent*

DAS GEPÄCK—LUGGAGE
(English key on page 368)

der Reisekoffer, -

der Handkoffer, -

der Stadtkoffer, -

die Reisetasche, -n

der Griff, -e

das Reise-Necessaire, .

die Handtasche, -n

die Thermosflasche, -n

das Reisekissen, -

die Reisedecke, -n

der Rucksack, ¨-e

der Bergstock, ¨-e

der Hutkoffer, -

das Luftkissen, -

die Wärmflasche, -n

der Regenschirm, -e

der Plaidriemen, -

die Kamera, -s

der Golfschläger, -

der Behälter, -

der Feldstecher, -

der Kofferzettel, -

SECHZEHNTE LEKTION: *SIXTEENTH LESSON*

TRAVEL TEST

Using the map on pages 22 and 23, select your own starting-points and destinations for the aeroplane (das **Flugzeug**), the ship (**das Schiff**) and the train (**der Zug**) and describe the scene in German as fully as you can. *To fly* is **fliegen**, *to travel* **fahren**.

VORBEREITUNGEN ZUR REISE

Wie wir schon erwähnt haben, ist die Familie Schulz mit der Familie Lessing verwandt. Lessings haben ihre hamburger Verwandten eingeladen, sie zu besuchen. Die Familie Schulz hat die Einladung angenommen. Sie werden eine Woche in Berlin bleiben und dann für vierzehn Tage an die See fahren.

Zwei Tage vor der Abreise hat Frau Schulz zu packen begonnen. Sie hat die meisten Sachen in einen grossen Reisekoffer gepackt. Für ihren Mann hat sie zwei Anzüge, drei Paar Schuhe, sechs Hemden, ebenso viele Unterhosen, ein Dutzend Kragen und ein halbes Dutzend Taschentücher eingepackt.

Für sich selbst hat sie Kleider, Wäsche und Schuhe eingepackt. Sie nimmt zwei Kostüme mit, hat aber nur eins eingepackt. Das andere wird sie auf der Reise tragen. Auch die

PREPARATIONS FOR THE JOURNEY

As we have already mentioned, the Schulz family is related to the Lessing family. The Lessings have invited their Hamburg relatives to visit them. The Schulz family have accepted the invitation. They will stay in Berlin for one week and then go to the seaside for a fortnight.

Two days before the departure Mrs. Schulz began to pack. She packed most of the things in a big trunk. For her husband she packed two suits, three pairs of shoes, six shirts, the same number of underdrawers, a dozen collars and half a dozen handkerchiefs.

For herself she packed dresses, underwear and shoes. She is taking two suits with her but has only packed one. She will wear the other on the journey. She also

143

DIE UNTERKLEIDUNG (WÄSCHE)—UNDERCLOTHING
(English key on page 368)

das Hemd, -en

das Nachthemd, -en

der Schlafrock, ˮ-e

das Unterkleid, -er

der Schlüpfer, -

der Büstenhalter, -

die Jacke, -n

der Strumpf, ˮ-e

der Strumpfhalter, -

das Korsett, -s

das Taschentuch, ˮ-er

der Unterrock, ˮ-e

die Hose, -n

der Schlafanzug, ˮ-e
(der Pyjama, -s)

der Kragen, -

der Manschettenknopf, ˮ-e

der Kragenknopf, ˮ-e

die Manschette, -n

das Oberhemd, -en

das Nachthemd, -en

der Hosenträger, -

die Socke, -n

die Unterhose, -n

das Unterhemd, -en

der Gürtel, -

der Sockenhalter, -

Sachen für die Kinder hat sie in den Reise-koffer gepackt. Die Toilettenartikel(Bürsten, Kämme, Seife, u.s.w.) hat sie in einen Handkoffer gelegt.

Während seine Frau mit Packen beschäftigt war, hat Herr Schulz das Kursbuch studiert. Das ist ein Buch, in dem man sehen kann, wann die Züge abfahren und wann sie ankommen. Ein Zug fährt um acht Uhr zehn von Hamburg ab, aber das ist etwas zu früh für sie. Der nächste Zug fährt um halb zehn, ist aber ein Personenzug, der sehr langsam fährt und auf allen kleinen Stationen hält. Sie haben sich entschlossen, den zehn Uhr Zug zu nehmen. Es ist ein Schnellzug.

Jetzt ist die Familie reisefertig. Hans hat ein Auto geholt, der Chauffeur hat den Koffer die Treppe hinuntergetragen und neben seinen Sitz gestellt. Das kleine Gepäck hat die Familie mit in den Wagen genommen. Die Nachbarn haben ihnen "Auf Wiedersehen" gesagt und "Gute Reise" gewünscht. Nun fährt das Auto ab.

packed the things for the children in the trunk. The toilet articles (brushes, combs, soap, etc.) she put into a suitcase.

While his wife was busy packing, Mr. Schulz has studied the time-table. This is a book in which one can see when the trains leave and when they arrive. One train leaves Hamburg at ten past eight, but that is rather too early for them. The next train leaves at half past nine, but it is a stopping-train, which is very slow and stops at all the small stations. They decided to take the ten o'clock train. It is a fast train.

Now the family is ready for the journey. Hans has fetched a car, the driver has taken the trunk downstairs and put it next to his seat. The family have taken the small luggage with them into the car. The neighbours have said " Good-bye " to them and wished them " Bon voyage". Now the car is setting off.

TRÖDELMARKT IN NÜRNBERG

Hier kann man seine alten Sachen verkaufen und gebrauchte Kleidungsstücke und Möbel billig kaufen.

(*Translation on page* 376)

der Trödel, -	**die Sache, -n**	**gebraucht**	**die Möbel** (plural)
second-hand goods	*thing*	*used, worn*	*furniture*

Sie sind im Kino

Sie gehen ins Kino   Sie kommen aus dem Kino

HOW TO TRANSLATE *GOING TO*

Wir fahren nach Berlin.
We are going to Berlin.

Sie fahren nach Amerika.
They are going to America.

Das Flugzeug fliegt nach Spanien.
The aeroplane is going to Spain.

Wir gehen zu meinem Onkel.
We are going to my uncle.

Die Kinder gehen zur Schule.
The children go to school.

Ich gehe zum Schneider.
I am going to the tailor.

Sie geht zur Schneiderin.
She is going to the dressmaker.

Wir gehen heute Abend ins Theater.
We are going to the theatre tonight.

Nach is *to* a country, town or village; zu is *to* a person, shop or place.

Use **in**, followed by the accusative case, to express going *into* a place, e.g. theatre, concert, etc.

Note that **zum** is a contraction of **zu dem** = *to the*. Similarly, **zur** = **zu der**, and **ins** = **in das.**

Sie ist beim Frisör

Sie geht zum Frisör   Sie kommt vom Frisör

PAST PARTICIPLE

The forms *forbidden, taken, seen*, etc., are the past participles of the verbs *to forbid, to take, to see*, etc. In German the past participle is formed by placing **ge-** in front and **-t** at the end of the stem of the verb, e.g. **geöffnet**=*opened;* **gesagt**=*said;* **gearbeitet**=*worked*, etc.

Bis zwei Uhr nachts geöffnet

A number of verbs, as in English, form their past participles irregularly by changing the vowel of the stem of the verb, and by having **-en** at the end instead of **-t**. Compare the English *break, broken*.

The chief use of the past participle is to form the perfect tense in conjunction with the auxiliary **haben**; some verbs take **sein** instead of **haben** (see Lesson 17).

Rauchen verboten

Frisch gestrichen

The following two groups of verbs do not take the prefix **ge-** in the past participle:

(1) Verbs with inseparable prefixes (**er-, ver-, zer-**, etc.; see Lesson 19); (2) Verbs ending in **-ieren**, like **studieren**=*to study;* **regieren**=*to reign*, etc. Their past participles are: **studiert, regiert.**
The past participles of separable verbs are dealt with on page 216.

Wegen Uberfüllung geschlossen

GEHEN, FAHREN, REISEN

Gehen is used only in the sense of *to walk*.

Fahren means *to go* (*by bus, train, ship*, etc.). **Die Fahrkarte, -n**=*ticket*.

Reisen means *to travel*. **Die Reise, -n**=*journey;* **der** or **die Reisende, -n**=*traveller*. (**Reisende** is an adjectival noun and changes its ending accordingly–see page 304.)

AUS DER GUTEN, ALTEN ZEIT

Während heute unsere Möbel in Massenproduktion fabriziert werden, wurden diese früher von Handwerkern hergestellt, die bemüht waren, auch das zum täglichen Gebrauch bestimmte, schön zu gestalten. Oben ein Esszimmer im Berner Oberland mit schön geschnitzten Möbeln; unten eine altfränkische Bauernstube. (*Translation on page* 376)

herstellen	**der Handwerker, -**	**bemüht sein**	**bestimmen**	**gestalten**	**fränkisch**
to produce	*craftsman*	*to endeavour*	*to destine*	*to create*	*Franconian*

PERFECT TENSE (I)

Present Tense	Perfect Tense
Wir hören Radio.	Wir haben Radio gehört.
Ich arbeite im Garten.	Ich habe im Garten gearbeitet.
Er öffnet das Fenster.	Er hat das Fenster geöffnet.
Sie hat eine deutsche Stunde.	Sie hat eine deutsche Stunde gehabt.
Sie rauchen Zigaretten.	Sie haben Zigaretten geraucht.
Ich esse ein Butterbrot.	Ich habe ein Butterbrot gegessen.
Trinken Sie Tee?	Haben Sie Tee getrunken?
Sie schreibt einen Brief.	Sie hat einen Brief geschrieben.
Liest er die Zeitung?	Hat er die Zeitung gelesen?
Wir sprechen Deutsch.	Wir haben Deutsch gesprochen.
Der Lehrer gibt uns eine Stunde.	Der Lehrer hat uns eine Stunde gegeben.
Wir nehmen deutsche Stunden.	Wir haben deutsche Stunden genommen.

Sie packen die Koffer   Sie haben die Koffer gepackt

Was tun Sie?	Was haben Sie getan?
Ich frühstücke um 8 Uhr.	Ich habe um 8 Uhr gefrühstückt.
Ich esse zu Mittag im Restaurant.	Ich habe im Restaurant zu Mittag gegessen.
Ich mache einen Spaziergang.	Ich habe einen Spaziergang gemacht.
Ich spiele Klavier.	Ich habe Klavier gespielt.
Wir singen und tanzen.	Wir haben gesungen und getanzt.
Wir laden ihn ein.	Wir haben ihn eingeladen.
Sie packt die Sachen ein.	Sie hat die Sachen eingepackt.
Sie nehmen die Einladung an.	Sie haben die Einladung angenommen.

The past tense most frequently used in German is the perfect. It corresponds not only to the English perfect (*I have taken*), but also in many cases to the English past tense (*I took*). Note that the past participle is placed at the end of the sentence.

HERBSTLIED

Bunt sind schon die Wälder,
gelb die Stoppelfelder,
und der Herbst beginnt.

Rote Blätter fallen,
graue Nebel wallen,
kühler weht der Wind.

J. G. v. Salis-Seewis

Das Herbstlied, -er, *autumn song;* **bunt,** *gay-coloured;* **schon,** *already;* **das Stoppelfeld, -er,** *stubble-field;* **das Blatt, ·-er,** *leaf;* **wallen,** *to drift, surge;* **kühl,** *cool;* **wehen,** *to blow.*

Die Kunst der Selbstverteidigung

SELF

Ich wasche mich vor dem Essen.
I wash before meals.

Sie haben sich schnell angekleidet.
They got dressed quickly.

Er hat sich in den Finger geschnitten.
He cut his finger.

Ich habe es selbst getan.
I did it myself.

Haben Sie das selbst gemacht?
Did you make that yourself?

Sie hat den Pullover selbst gestrickt.
She knitted the pullover herself.

Haben Sie diesen Kuchen selbst gebacken?
Did you bake this cake yourself?

The emphatic pronoun in German is **selbst**; it stands for *myself, himself, herself, itself, ourselves, yourselves* and *themselves*.

If *myself, yourself,* etc., are not used in an emphatic way (often they are not expressed in English), reflexive verbs are used as explained in Lesson 8.

Selbst is employed with the reflexive pronoun only if the latter is stressed, as in the examples: **Sie brauchen ihm nicht zu helfen. Er kann sich selbst verteidigen** = *You need not help him. He can defend himself.* **Sie ist gross genug, sich selbst anzuziehen** = *She is big enough to dress herself.*

NEW NOUNS

DER
Zug, ⸬-e	*train*
Koffer, -	*trunk*
Artikel, -	*article*
Kamm, ⸬-e	*comb*
Chauffeur, -e	*chauffeur*
Wagen, -	*car, carriage*
Nachbar, -n	*neighbour*
Bahnhof, ⸬-e	*railway station*
Friseur, -e	*hairdresser*
Schneider, -	*tailor*
Spaziergang, ⸬-e	*walk*
Pullover, -s	*pullover*

DIE
Vorbereitung, -en	*preparation*
Reise, -n	*journey*
Einladung, -en	*invitation*
See, -n	*sea*
(Note that **der See** = *the lake*)	
Sache, -n	*thing*
Unterhose, -n	*pants*
Bürste, -n	*brush*
Station, -en	*station, stop*
Treppe, -n	*staircase*

DAS
Flugzeug, -e	*aeroplane*
Schiff, -e	*ship*
Hemd, -en	*shirt*
Taschentuch, ⸬-er	*handkerchief*

Note.—**Der** or **die Verwandte, -n** (*relative*) is a further example of an adjectival noun —see page 304.

EXERCISES

I   Read and Translate

1. Um wieviel Uhr haben Sie gefrühstückt? Ich habe um acht Uhr gefrühstückt. 2. Ich habe Kaffee getrunken und Brötchen mit Marmelade gegessen. 3. Was haben Sie dann getan? Ich habe die Zeitung gelesen und Briefe geschrieben. Dann habe ich bis eins im Garten gearbeitet. 4. Um ein Uhr habe ich zu Mittag gegessen. Nachmittags habe ich Besuch gehabt. 5. Ein Freund, der gut Deutsch spricht, hat mich besucht, und wir haben zusammen Deutsch gesprochen. 6. Um vier Uhr haben wir Tee getrunken. Nach dem Tee haben wir einen Spaziergang gemacht. 7. Abends hat mein Freund Klavier gespielt, und wir haben deutsche Lieder gesungen.

II Answer in German

1. Spielen Sie Tennis? 2. Haben Sie heute Tennis gespielt? 3. Was haben Sie heute zum Frühstück gegessen? 4. Schreiben Sie viele Briefe? 5. Wie viele Briefe haben Sie diese Woche geschrieben? 6. Lesen Sie jeden Tag die Zeitung? 7. Welche Zeitung haben Sie heute gelesen? 8. Tanzen Sie gern? 9. Haben Sie gestern getanzt? 10. Wer hat die Familie Schulz eingeladen? 11. Haben sie die Einladung angenommen? 12. Wann hat Frau Schulz zu packen begonnen? 13. Was hat sie für ihren Mann eingepackt? 14. Was hat sie in den Handkoffer gelegt? 15. Um wieviel Uhr werden sie abfahren?

III Translate into German

1. Did you open the windows in the sitting room? 2. Did you have a German lesson last night? 3. Did you read the newspaper this morning? 4. Has your sister written to you? 5. She said in her letter: The train leaves at 9.30 and arrives at 5 in the afternoon. 6. Have you packed your handkerchiefs? 7. The train comes from Cologne and goes to Munich. 8. Is she at the hairdresser's? 9. I worked in the garden. 10. We accepted the invitation. 11. We got up early, had breakfast and packed our luggage. 12. I did it myself.

(*Answers on page* 361)

AUTOBAHN OHNE GESCHWINDIGKEITSGRENZE

Auf den Autobahnen, die wichtige Städte miteinander verbinden, ist keine Geschwindigkeitsgrenze zu beachten. Fussgänger dürfen die Autobahnen nicht betreten, sondern müssen Überführungen benutzen.   (*Translation on page* 376)

die Geschwindigkeitsgrenze, -n	verbinden	beachten	die Überführung, -en
speed limit	*to connect*	*to observe*	*overhead crossing*

DER BAHNHOF—
(English key

1. die Eingangshalle, -n	8. der Briefkasten, ···-	14. die Zeitung, -en
2. der Gepäckzettel, -	9. die Handgepäckauf-	15. der Bahnsteig, -e
3. der Gepäckträger, -	bewahrung, -en	16. der Zug, ···-e
4. die Gepäckannahme, -n	10. der Rolladen, -	17. die Sperre, -n
5. der Gepäckschein, -e	11. Ankunftszeiten	18. die Bahnhofsuhr, -en
6. Frauen	12. der Zeitungskiosk, -e	19. die Bahnhofswirtschaft,
7. das Plakat, -e	13. der Verkäufer, -	20. die Drehtür, -en [-en

THE RAILWAY STATION
on page 368)

21. der Bahnsteigschaffner, -	28. der Automat für Bahnsteig-	35. die Reisende, -n
22. der Abfall, ¨-e	29. der Fernsprecher, - [karten	36. der Reisende, -n
23. der Fahrplan, ¨-e	30. Männer	37. der Fahrkartenschalter, -
24. das Kursbuch, ¨-er	31. der Rucksack, ¨-e	38. der Handkoffer, -
25. der Wartesaal, -säle	32. der Feldstecher, -	39. der Gepäckkarren, -
26. die Auskunft, ¨-e	33. die Fahrkartenausgabe, -n	40. der Kinderwagen, -
27. die Gepäckbank, ¨-e	34. der Beamte, -n	41. das Gepäck

SIEBZEHNTE LEKTION: *SEVENTEENTH LESSON*

AT THE BOOKING OFFICE

This man is asking for two third-class return tickets to Berlin (**zwei Rückfahrkarten dritter Klasse nach Berlin**). Try to describe the scene in German, with the help of the picture vocabulary which is given on the preceding pages.

DIE ABREISE

Wie wir in Lektion 16 gelesen haben, ist die Familie Schulz in einem Taxi zum Bahnhof gefahren. Sie fuhren um neun Uhr von ihrem Hause ab und kamen zwanzig Minuten später am Bahnhof an.

Herr Schulz rief sofort einen Gepäckträger, der das grosse Gepäck in den Gepäckraum trug, um es dort aufzugeben. Frau Schulz ging mit ihm, um für die Gepäckaufgabe zu bezahlen.

Inzwischen ist ihr Mann zum Schalter gegangen, um die Fahrkarten zu kaufen. Die Kinder blieben in der Bahnhofshalle, um auf das Handgepäck aufzupassen.

Nach fünf Minuten war Frau Schulz mit der Gepäckaufgabe fertig und ging zu ihren Kindern zurück. Den Gepäckschein hat sie in ihre Handtasche gesteckt. Kurz darauf kam auch Herr Schulz mit den Fahrkarten. Dann ist die Familie zusammen durch die

THE DEPARTURE

As we read in Lesson 16, the Schulz family went in a taxi to the station. They left their house at nine o'clock and arrived at the station twenty minutes later.

Mr. Schulz at once called a porter, who carried the big luggage into the luggage room to have it registered there. Mrs. Schulz went with him to pay for the luggage registration.

Meanwhile her husband went to the booking-office to buy the tickets. The children remained in the station hall to keep an eye on the hand-luggage.

Five minutes later Mrs. Schulz finished with the luggage registration and went back to her children. She put the luggage receipt in her handbag. Soon afterwards Mr. Schulz also came back with the tickets. Then the family went together through the

Sperre gegangen, wo ein Beamter die Fahrkarten gelocht hat.

Auf dem Bahnsteig standen einige hundert Reisende und ihre Freunde, die gekommen waren, ihnen "Auf Wiedersehen" zu sagen. Der Zug war schon da, und unsere Reisenden sind in ein Abteil dritter Klasse eingestiegen.

In dem Abteil war Platz für sechs Personen. Zwei Plätze waren schon besetzt. Herr Schulz hat das Gepäck in das Gepäcknetz

barrier, where an official punched the tickets.

Several hundred travellers were standing on the platform with their friends who had come to say "Good-bye" to them. The train was already there and our travellers got into a third class compartment.

In the compartment there was room for six persons. Two seats were already occupied. Mr. Schulz put the luggage on the

Der Beamte rief:
Bitte, einsteigen!

Zu spät! Der Zug ist eben abgefahren

gelegt, und die Familie hat die freien Plätze genommen. Leider sind die Fensterplätze schon besetzt gewesen.

Kurz vor zehn hat ein Eisenbahnbeamter "Bitte, einsteigen" gerufen und die Türen geschlossen. Punkt zehn Uhr hat der Stationsvorsteher das Zeichen zur Abfahrt gegeben, und der Zug ist langsam, aber mit zunehmender Geschwindigkeit, aus der Bahnhofshalle hinausgefahren.

luggage rack and the family took the vacant seats. Unfortunately, the window seats were already taken.

Shortly before ten a railway official called out "Please board the train" and closed the doors. At ten o'clock sharp the stationmaster gave the sign for the departure and the train left the station slowly, but with increasing speed.

USE OF FERTIG

Fertig means both *ready* and *finished*, as shown in the following examples.

Ich bin mit Packen fertig.
I have finished packing.

Sind Sie mit der Arbeit fertig?
Have you finished your work?

Sie ist fertig auszugehen.
She is ready to go out.

Reisefertig.
Ready for the journey.

TRAVELLING EXPRESSIONS

Wo ist der Fahrkartenschalter?
Where is the booking office?

Eine Fahrkarte zweiter Klasse nach Berlin.
One second class ticket to Berlin.

Zwei dritter Leipzig und zurück.
Two third returns to Leipzig.

Eine Rückfahrkarte erster Klasse.
One first class return ticket.

Einen Platz belegen.
To reserve a seat.

Ein Oberbett (Unterbett) im Schlafwagen.
An upper berth (lower berth) in the sleeping car.

Wann fährt der nächste Zug nach ...?
What time does the next train leave for...?

Von welchem Bahnsteig fährt der Zug nach...?
From which platform does the train leave for...?

Wann kommt der Zug in ... an?
When does the train arrive at ...?

Habe ich direkte Verbindung oder muss ich umsteigen?
Have I a direct connection or do I have to change?

Ist dies der Zug nach Berlin?
Is this the train for Berlin?

Ist der Zug nach Leipzig schon da?
Has the train for Leipzig arrived?

Bitte, belegen Sie einen Platz für mich.
Please reserve a seat for me.

Ist dies ein Raucher- (Nichtraucher-) Abteil?
Is this a smoking (non-smoking) compartment?

Ist dieser Platz frei?
Is this seat vacant?

Bitte, legen Sie das ins Gepäcknetz.
Please put this on the luggage rack.

Träger, sind Sie frei?
Porter, are you free?

Bitte, geben Sie diese Koffer für mich auf.
Please register these trunks for me.

Bringen Sie das Handgepäck zum Zug.
Take the hand-luggage to the train.

IMPERFECT TENSE

ich er sie es	rauchte		rauchten	= smoked
	sagte	wir	sagten	= said
	liebte	Sie	liebten	= loved
	fragte	sie	fragten	= asked
	hatte		hatten	= had

ich er sie es	war		waren	= were
	kam		kamen	= came
	ging	wir	gingen	= went
	las	Sie	lasen	= read
	schrieb	sie	schrieben	= wrote
	gab		gaben	= gave
	nahm		nahmen	= took

In English the regular way of forming the past tense is by adding -ed. In German -te is added in singular, -ten in the plural. As in English, many verbs are irregular; they have no ending at all in the 1st and 3rd person singular, and their plural ending is -en.

Ich kam, ich sah, ich siegte

EIN IRISCHES GESCHICHTCHEN

Der Reisende stieg auf einer kleinen irischen Station aus. Auf dem Bahnhof befanden sich zwei Uhren, die eine verschiedene Zeit anzeigten. Erstaunt wandte sich der Fremde an den Stationsvorsteher: "Warum in aller Welt haben Sie hier zwei Uhren, die noch nicht einmal übereinstimmen?" Der Beamte schüttelte verwundert den Kopf: "Und warum sollten wir hier zwei Uhren haben, wenn sie beide die gleiche Zeit anzeigen?"

Stieg . . aus, *got out;* befanden sich, *there were;* verschieden, *different;* erstaunt, *astonished;* sich wenden, *to turn;* warum in aller Welt? *why on earth;* noch nicht einmal, *not even;* übereinstimmen, *to agree;* schütteln, *to shake;* verwundert, *surprised;* sollten, *should;* beide, *both;* gleich, *same.*

PERFECT TENSE (II)

Present	Perfect
Ich komme um acht Uhr.	Ich bin um acht Uhr gekommen.
Er geht in den Garten.	Er ist in den Garten gegangen.
Wir sind in Berlin.	Wir sind in Berlin gewesen.
Sie bleiben dort.	Sie sind dort geblieben.
Der Zug kommt an.	Der Zug ist angekommen.
Das Schiff fährt ab.	Das Schiff ist abgefahren.
Die Reisenden steigen ein.	Die Reisenden sind eingestiegen.
Sie steht früh auf.	Sie ist früh aufgestanden.
Ich bin krank.	Ich bin krank gewesen.
Er wird krank. (*He is becoming ill*).	Er ist krank geworden. (*He has become ill*).
Er stirbt. (*He is dying*).	Er ist gestorben. (*He has died*).

In English we can say both *he is gone* and *he has gone;* in German the only correct form is **er ist gegangen**. Verbs denoting either change of place or change of condition form their perfect with **sein** instead of **haben**, unless they are reflexive, in which case they take **haben**.

Note that **sein** (*to be*), **bleiben** (*to stay*) and **werden** (*to become*) also form their perfect with sein.

A simple test will enable you to decide whether **haben** or **sein** should be used. If the action of the verb is followed by a corresponding state use **sein**; if it is not, use **haben**. If you have come, travelled, gone, climbed, fallen, etc., you are somewhere, so we have to say in German **ich bin gekommen (gefahren, gegangen, geklettert, gefallen,** etc.). If someone has died, he is dead: **er ist gestorben.** If he has remained somewhere, he is somewhere: **er ist geblieben.** If he has become something, he is something: **er ist geworden.**

Er ist auf den Apfelbaum geklettert

Er klettert auf den Apfelbaum

Er fällt vom Apfelbaum

Er ist vom Apfelbaum gefallen

BAHNHOF FRIEDRICHSTRASSE, BERLIN

Der auf Bahnsteig A einfahrende Zug ist ein Triebwagenzug, der ehemals auf der Strecke Berlin-Köln verkehrte und eine Durchschnittsgeschwindigkeit von 130 Kilometern (=81 *miles*) pro Stunde hatte. Der Wagen wurde Diesel elektrisch betrieben und erreichte auf einer Probefahrt eine Geschwindigkeit von 186 Kilometern (=116 *miles*) pro Stunde.

(*Translation on page* 377)

einfahren	der Triebwagenzug, ···-e	ehemals	die Strecke, -n	verkehren
to run into	*electric train*	*formerly*	*stretch of line*	*to operate*
der Durchschnitt, -e	betreiben	erreichen	die Probefahrt, -en	
average	*to drive*	*to reach*	*trial run*	

158

COMPARISON BETWEEN ENGLISH AND GERMAN VERBS

Many German verbs are very much like their English counterparts. Most verbs which are regular in English are also regular in German, and even the change of vowel, which occurs with many irregular verbs, is frequently similar or even the same. Compare the following:

German				English
Present	Imperfect	Past Participle		
höre	hörte	gehört	=	*hear, heard, heard*
singe	sang	gesungen	=	*sing, sang, sung*
trinke	trank	getrunken	=	*drink, drank, drunk*
bringe	brachte	gebracht	=	*bring, brought, brought*
komme	kam	gekommen	=	*come, came, come*

Many other similarities can be discovered if you consult the list of irregular verbs on pages, 321-323.

In spite of frequent similarities in form, however, it would be wrong to assume that the German present tense corresponds in every case to the English present tense, and the German imperfect to the English past tense, or that the perfect forms are interchangeable. Compare the following:

Wie lange sind Sie schon hier?
How long have you been here?

Ich wohne seit drei Jahren in diesem Haus.
I have lived in this house for three years.

Wie lange sind Sie in Berlin geblieben?
How long did you stay in Berlin?

Wir haben vor Jahren in diesem Haus gewohnt.
We lived in this house years ago.

Als wir auf den Bahnsteig kamen, standen schon viele Leute da.
When we came on the platform many people were already standing there.

Er las die Abendzeitung, als ich in das Zimmer kam.
He was reading the evening paper when I came into the room.

Note.—(1) The present in German often corresponds to an English perfect, for an action beginning in the past and continuing up to the present time.

(2) Whereas the English perfect expresses what started in the past and is continuing up to the present, the German perfect belongs entirely to the past; it often cor-responds to the English past tense, especially in colloquial language.

(3) The German imperfect is used for narrative and description. In the colloquial language it is used to express continuous action in the past, and therefore often corresponds to the English form of the past expressed by *was* (*were*), with the verb ending in *-ing* (*was going, were playing*, etc.).

(4) **Als** is a special word for *when* used in connection with the past. **Wenn** is used in connection with the present and the future. Used with the past tense, **wenn** has the meaning of *whenever*.

NEW NOUNS

	Raum, ···-e	*room, space*
	Schalter, -	*booking-office*
	Schein, -e	*receipt, certificate*
DER	Beamte, -n	*official*
	Bahnsteig, -e	*platform*
	Freund, -e	*friend*
	Platz, ···-e	*place, seat*
	Fahrkarte, -n	*ticket*
	Halle, -n	*hall*
	Sperre, -n	*barrier*
DIE	Klasse, -n	*class*
	Abfahrt, -en	*departure*
	Geschwindigkeit, -en	*speed, velocity*
	Abteil, -e	*compartment*
	Netz, -e	*net*
DAS	Gepäcknetz, -e	*luggage rack*
	Zeichen, -	*sign, signal*

Er ist auf den
Berg gestiegen

Er steigt
auf den Berg

EXERCISES

I   Read and Translate

1. Wann sind Sie aufgestanden? Ich bin um halb acht aufgestanden. 2. Um viertel neun bin ich von Hause fortgegangen. Ich bin mit der Elektrischen zum Bahnhof gefahren. 3. Um neun bin ich am Bahnhof angekommen. Ich habe eine Fahrkarte gekauft und bin auf den Bahnsteig gegangen. 4. Der Zug war pünktlich da. Ich bin eingestiegen und habe mich in die Ecke ans Fenster gesetzt. 5. Auf der nächsten Station sind mehrere Personen eingestiegen. 6. Eine alte Dame hat keinen Platz gefunden. Ich bin aufgestanden und habe ihr meinen Platz angeboten (anbieten = *to offer*). 7. Um halb zehn sind wir angekommen. Ich bin ausgestiegen und zu Fuss in die Fabrik (*factory*) gegangen. 8. Dort habe ich bis eins gearbeitet. Um ein Uhr bin ich zu Mittag gegangen. 9. Um zwei bin ich wieder im Büro gewesen und habe noch dreieinhalb Stunden gearbeitet. 10. Abends bin ich ins Kino gegangen. 11. Um zehn bin ich nach Hause gekommen und gleich (*at once*) zu Bett gegangen. 12. Ich bin gleich eingeschlafen und habe viel geträumt. Ich bin auf einen hohen Berg gestiegen. Dort bin ich hingefallen und den Berg heruntergerollt.

II   Answer in German

1. Welcher Tag war gestern? 2. Sind Sie gestern im Theater gewesen? 3. Wann sind Sie heute aufgestanden? 4. Um wieviel Uhr sind Sie von Hause fortgegangen? 5. Sind Sie gegangen oder gefahren? 6. Haben Sie zu Hause zu Mittag gegessen oder in einem Restaurant? 7. Gehen Sie früh zu Bett? 8. Wann sind Sie gestern zu Bett gegangen? 9. Wann ist die Familie Schulz am Bahnhof angekommen? 10. Wer hat die Fahrkarten gekauft? 11. Sind Fensterplätze frei gewesen? 12. Wer hat das Zeichen zur Abfahrt gegeben?

III   Put the following sentences (a) into the Imperfect; (b) into the Perfect

1. Sie packt die Koffer. 2. Er legt den Anzug in den Koffer. 3. Der Zug ist voll. 4. Fritz holt ein Auto. 5. Wir gehen zu Fuss. 6. Sie fahren mit dem Taxi zum Bahnhof. 7. Der Zug kommt und sie steigen ein. 8. Der Stationsvorsteher gibt das Zeichen zur Abfahrt und der Zug fährt ab. 9. Wir singen und tanzen. 10. Die Kinder spielen im Garten und klettern auf Bäume. 11. Ich setze mich gern ans offene Fenster. 12. Er findet keinen Platz. Alle Plätze sind besetzt.

**Sein oder nicht sein,
das ist die Frage**

(*Answers on page* 357)

ACHTZEHNTE LEKTION: *EIGHTEENTH LESSON*

IN THE TRAIN

Here are the Schulzes and their travelling companions. When you have studied the German text, cover it over and reconstruct it as far as you can with the aid of the picture.

AUF DER REISE	ON THE JOURNEY
Auf diesem Bild sehen wir die Familie Schulz im D-Zug[1] auf der Reise von Hamburg nach Berlin. Sie reisen in einem Abteil zweiter Klasse. Auf der rechten Seite in der Ecke an der Tür sitzt Frau Schulz und neben ihr der kleine Hans. Herr Schulz sitzt gegenüber seiner Frau und Grete gegenüber[2] ihrem Bruder.	In this picture we see the Schulz family in the express train on the journey from Hamburg to Berlin. They are travelling in a second class compartment. On the right side, in the corner by the door, sits Mrs. Schulz, and next to her little Hans. Mr. Schulz sits opposite his wife and Grete opposite her brother.
Links in der Ecke am Fenster sitzt ein Herr vor dem kleinen Tisch. Er ist ein Engländer, der mit dem Schiff von London nach Hamburg gefahren ist und jetzt nach Berlin weiterfährt.	In the left hand corner by the window sits a gentleman, in front of the little table. He is an Englishman who has travelled by boat from London to Hamburg and is now going on to Berlin.

[1] **Durchgangszug** (*through train*). A specially fast train is a **Blitzzug** (*lightning train*)

[2] The preposition **gegenüber** (*opposite*) can either precede or follow its object, which must be in the dative case: **Ich sass der Dame gegenüber** or **Ich sass gegenüber der Dame.**

DER ZUG (AUSSEN)—
(*English key*)

1. der Triebwagen, -	7. der Puffer, -	13. der Rauch
2. der Führerstand, ˙˙-e	8. der Stationsvorsteher, -	14. das Sicherheitsventil, -e
3. die Oberleitung, -en	9. der Befehlstab, ˙˙-e	15. die Handstange, -n
4. der Reisende, -n	10. die Lokomotive, -n	16. der Dampfkessel, -
5. das Gleis, -e	11. die Laterne, -n	17. der Gepäckträger, -
6. die Schwelle, -n	12. der Schornstein, -e	18. das Gepäck

Ihm gegenüber sitzt eine ältere Dame. Sie fährt nach Dresden, um dort ihre Verwandten zu besuchen. Auf dem Tischchen vor ihr liegen ihre Handtasche und eine illustrierte Zeitung. In der Hand hat sie ein Strickzeug.

Auf dem Tischchen vor dem Engländer liegen eine Zeitung, seine Pfeife und seine Brille in einem Futteral.

Das Gepäck der Reisenden liegt in den Gepäcknetzen über den beiden Bänken. Der Überzieher des Herrn Schulz und der Mantel der Frau Schulz hängen rechts und links an Haken in den Ecken. Die Hüte der Damen und Herren sowie die Hüte und Mäntel der Kinder liegen auf den Koffern.

Opposite him sits an elderly lady. She is going to Dresden to visit her relatives there. On the little table in front of her lie her handbag and an illustrated newspaper. She has some knitting in her hand.

On the little table in front of the Englishman lie a newspaper, his pipe and his spectacles in a case.

The luggage of the travellers lies on the luggage racks over the two seats. Mr. Schulz's overcoat and Mrs. Schulz's coat hang at the right and left on hooks in the corners. The hats of the ladies and gentlemen as well as the hats and coats of the children lie on top of the suitcases.

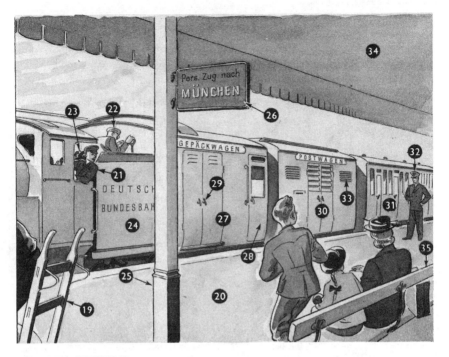

THE TRAIN (OUTSIDE)
on page 368)

19. der Gepäckkarren, -	25. der Pfosten, -	30. der Postwagen, -
20. der Bahnsteig, -e	26. der Richtungsanzeiger, -	31. der Eisenbahnwagen, -
21. der Lokomotivführer, -	(Personen Zug nach München)	32. der Eisenbahnschaffner,
22. der Heizer, -	27. der Gepäckwagen, -	33. das Ventil, -e
23. die Kohle, -n	28. die Tür, -en	34. das Dach, "-er
24. der Tender, -	29. der Türgriff, -e	35. die Bank, "-e

Es ist ziemlich heiss im Abteil, und Frau Schulz möchte das Fenster öffnen. Zuerst fragt sie, ob die Dame nichts dagegen hat.

Frau Schulz: Die Luft ist sehr stickig hier, finden Sie nicht auch?

Die Dame: Ja, die Luft ist hier schlecht.

Frau S.: Wenn Sie nichts dagegen haben, können wir das Fenster öffnen.

Dame: Es wäre mir sehr angenehm.

Der Herr: Gestatten Sie, dass ich es öffne.

Frau S.: Das ist sehr liebenswürdig von Ihnen.

Herr Schulz [zu der Dame]: Haben Sie etwas dagegen, wenn ich rauche?

It is rather hot in the compartment and Mrs. Schulz would like to open the window. First she asks if the lady minds.

Mrs. Schulz: The air is very stuffy in here, don't you think so?

The Lady: Yes, the air is bad here.

Mrs. S.: If you don't mind, we can open the window.

Lady: I would be very pleased if you would.

The Gentleman: Allow me to open it.

Mrs. S.: That is very kind of you.

Mr. Schulz (to the lady): Do you mind if I smoke?

163

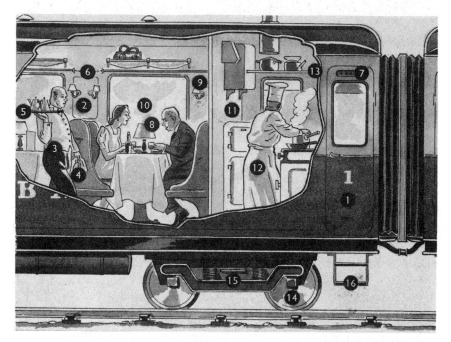

DER ZUG (INNEN)—
(*English key*)

1. die Erste Klasse	6. die Notbremse, -n	11. die Küche, -n 12. der Koch, ̈-e
2. der Speisewagen, -	7. die Ventilation, -en	13. das Regal, -e
3. der Kellner, -	8. die Tischlampe, -n	14. das Rad, ̈-er
4. die Serviette, -n	9. die Wandlampe, -n	15. das Radgestell, -e
5. das Tablett, -e	10. das Fenster, -	16. die Stufe, -n

Dame: Aber gewiss nicht. Ich rauche selbst.	Lady: Certainly not. I myself smoke.
Herr S.: Darf ich Ihnen eine Zigarette anbieten?	Mr. S.: May I offer you a cigarette?
Dame: Vielen Dank. Ich rauche nur meine eignen, eine sehr leichte Sorte. Aber vielleicht können Sie mir Feuer geben?	Lady: Many thanks. I smoke only my own, a very mild brand. But perhaps you can give me a light?
Herr S.: Mit Vergnügen.	Mr. S.: With pleasure.
Herr Schulz nimmt ein Feuerzeug aus der Tasche und gibt der Dame Feuer. Dann bietet er dem Herrn eine Zigarette an.	Mr. Schulz takes a lighter out of his pocket and gives the lady a light. Then he offers the gentleman a cigarette.
Herr: Sehr liebenswürdig von Ihnen. Ich ziehe aber meine Pfeife vor.	Gentleman: It's very kind of you. But I prefer my pipe.
Frau S. [zu der Dame]: Fahren Sie auch nach Berlin?	Mrs. S. (to the lady): Are you going to Berlin, too?

164

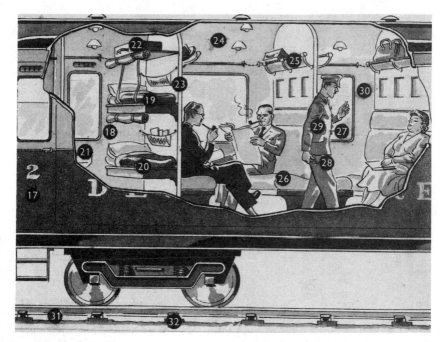

THE TRAIN (INSIDE)
on page 369)

17. die Dritte Klasse	22. der Koffer, -	27. der Fahrkartenkontrollör, -e
18. der Schlafwagen, -	23. die Wand, ¨-e	28. der Fahrkartenlocher, -
19. das Oberbett, -en	24. das Raucherabteil, -e	29. die Uniform, -en
20. das Unterbett, -en	25. das Gepäcknetz, -e	30. das Nichtraucherabteil, -e
21. das Waschbecken, -	26. der Platz, ¨-e	31. das Gleis, -e 32. die Schwelle, -n

Dame: Ich bleibe nur zwei Stunden in Berlin. Dann fahre ich nach Dresden weiter. Meine Tochter lebt dort. Ich besuche sie jedes Jahr. Wir fahren zusammen ins Gebirge.	Lady: I am staying only two hours in Berlin. Then I go on to Dresden. My daughter lives there. I go to see her every year. We go to the mountains together.
Frau S.: Wir besuchen auch Verwandte, aber in Berlin. Wir bleiben nur acht bis zehn Tage dort. Dann fahren wir an die See.	Mrs. S.: We, too, are visiting relatives, but in Berlin. We are staying there from eight to ten days only; then we go to the seaside.
Dame : Was für reizende kleine Häuser! Schauen Sie!	Lady: What charming little houses! Look!
Frau S.: Ja, sie sind hübsch.	Mrs. S.: Yes, they are pretty.
Grete [die in einem Buch gelesen hat]: Wo, Mama?	Grete [who has been reading a book]: Where, mother?

Erster Herr: Mein Herr,
dies ist ein Nichtraucher-
abteil.

Zweiter Herr: Ich bin
Nichtraucher.

Erster Herr: Sie rauchen
aber.

Zweiter Herr: Ja, aber nur
ausnahmsweise
(exceptionally).

Frau S.: Wir sind schon vorbei.	Mrs. S.: We have passed them already.
Grete: Wie schade!	Grete: What a pity!
Hans: Vater, wie heisst dieser Ort?	Hans: Father, what's the name of this place?
Herr S.: Kläden. Wir sind nicht weit von Stendal. Bald fahren wir über die Elbe.	Mr. S.: Kläden. We are not far from Stendal. Soon we shall cross the Elbe.
Hans: Wie spät ist es?	Hans: What time is it?
Herr S.: Es ist fünf Minuten vor zwölf. Wir haben noch über eine Stunde zu fahren.	Mr. S.: It is five minutes to twelve. We still have to travel for over an hour.
Herr: Können Sie mir bitte sagen, um wieviel Uhr wir in Berlin ankommen?	Gentleman: Can you tell me, please, at what time we arrive in Berlin?
Herr S.: Um ein Uhr fünf, wenn wir keine Verspätung haben.	Mr. S.: At five past one, if we have no delay.
Herr: Ich habe meine Uhr noch nicht vor-gestellt.	Gentleman: I have not put my watch forward yet.
Herr S.: Sie meinen, Sie haben noch nicht die mitteleuropäische Zeit?	Mr. S.: You mean you have not got Central European time yet?

Westeuropäische (Greenwich) Zeit   Mitteleuropäische Zeit   Osteuropäische Zeit

Herr: Ich komme von England und habe noch die westeuropäische Zeit.	Gentleman: I have come from England and still have Greenwich time.
Herr S.: Dann müssen Sie Ihre Uhr eine Stunde vorstellen.	Mr. S.: Then you must put your watch forward by one hour.
Herr: Können Sie mir bitte sagen, ob dieser Zug irgendwo längere Zeit hält?	Gentleman: Can you tell me, please, if this train stops anywhere for any length of time?
Herr S.: Ich glaube, dies ist ein durchgehender Zug, der nirgends hält.	Mr. S.: I believe this is a through train that stops nowhere.

DIE SCHWEBEBAHN IN WUPPERTAL

Um den Verkehr auf den Hauptstrassen zu entlasten, hat die Wuppertaler Stadtverwaltung eine Schwebebahn gebaut. Das Bild zeigt die Schwebebahn über einem gewöhnlichen Strassenbahnwagen in der Sonneborner Strasse. *(Translation on page 377)*

die Schwebebahn, -en	**der Verkehr**	**entlasten**	**die Stadtverwaltung, -en**	**gewöhnlich**
suspension railway	*traffic*	*to ease*	*municipality*	*ordinary*

GENITIVE (POSSESSIVE) CASE

Das Haus des Lehrers.
The teacher's house.

Die Farbe der Bluse.
The colour of the blouse.

Die Wände des Zimmers.
The walls of the room.

Das Geschenk der Grosseltern.
The grand-parents' present.

The possessive (genitive) case in German is expressed by a change in the endings of the article. Masculine and neuter articles end in **-es;** feminine and plural in **-er.** Masculine and neuter nouns add **-s** or **-es** to the noun. Feminine nouns have no ending, nor is there any special ending for the genitive case in the plural.

**Der Bräutigam (Verlobte)
meiner Schwester**

	Masc.	Neut.		Fem. and Pl.
Genitive:	**des**	**——(e)s**		**der ——**

Masculine and neuter nouns of one syllable add **-es;** those of more syllables **-s** only. The genitive of **der Vater** is **des Vaters,** but the genitive of **der Hut** is **des Hutes.** Masculine nouns of two syllables ending in **-e,** and a few others, add **-n** instead of **-s** in the genitive singular, e.g. **der Knabe** becomes **des Knaben, der Herr** becomes **des Herrn.**

His master's voice must be turned into *the voice of his master ; my father's house* into *the house of my father,* etc. ; i.e. the genitive follows the noun on which it depends.

Die Stimme seines Herrn

Der Kopf eines Hundes.
A dog's head.

Die Schwester meines Vaters.
My father's sister.

Der Schwanz einer Kuh.
A cow's tail.

Die Mutter meiner Frau.
My wife's mother.

Der Schirm dieses Herrn.
This gentleman's umbrella.

Die Handtasche jener Dame.
That lady's handbag.

Der Preis ihres neuen Kleides.
The price of her new dress.

Eine Seite des deutschen Buches.
A page of the German book.

Das Zimmer unserer kleinen Kinder.
The room of our little children.

Die Photographie seiner Braut (Verlobten)

Sie trägt den Mantel ihrer Schwester.
She wears her sister's coat.

Der Verfasser dieses kleinen Buches.
The author of this little book.

Der Komponist unseres schönen Liedes.
The composer of our beautiful song.

Note.—(1) Words like **ein(e), mein(e), sein(e), diese(r), jene(r)** also take **-(e)s** or **-er** in the genitive case.

(2) Adjectives preceded by a declinable word take the termination **-en** in the genitive case.

USE OF THE INFINITIVE

(1) **Rauchen verboten**=*Smoking forbidden.*
Lachen ist gesund=*Laughing is healthy.*
Das Pflücken von Blumen ist verboten=
The picking of flowers is forbidden.

Ich sehe ihn kommen=*I see him coming.*
Hören Sie sie singen?=*Do you hear her singing?*

The English present participle ending in
-*ing* and used as a verbal noun is rendered
in German by the infinitive. Every infinitive
can be used as a noun. Such nouns are neuter.

(2) **Ich hoffe, Sie morgen zu sehen**=*I hope
to see you tomorrow.*

**Ich freue mich, Ihre Bekanntschaft zu
machen**=*I am glad to make your
acquaintance.*

Sie brauchen Sonntag nicht zu kommen
=*You need not come on Sunday.*

**An kalten Wintertagen ist es gut, ein
warmes Zimmer zu haben**=*On cold
winter days it is good to have a warm
room.*

To in front of the infinitive is rendered by
zu. In most cases where *to* is omitted in
English, **zu** is also left out in German.
Compare the following:

Was kann ich für Sie tun?=*What can I do
for you?*

Sie müssen[1] **an die Tür klopfen**=*You must
knock at the door.*

Man darf[1] **im Theater nicht rauchen**=*One
must not smoke in the theatre.*

But: **Ich möchte etwas trinken**=*I should
like to drink something.*

Sie will nach Paris fahren=*She wants to go
to Paris.*

Er möchte die Wurst haben

(3) **Sie fahren nach Berlin, um ihre Verwandten zu besuchen**=*They go to
Berlin in order to visit their relatives.*

**Sie essen früher Abendbrot, um zur Zeit
ins Konzert zu kommen**=*They have
their evening meal earlier in order to
get to the concert in time.*

**Sie gehen ins Konzert, um den berühm-
ten Sänger zu hören**=*They go to the
concert in order to hear the famous
singer.*

Where in English we say *in order to*,
German uses the expression **um ... zu.**

**An heissen Tagen macht
das Baden viel Vergnügen**

---

[1] **ich (er, sie, es) muss ; wir (Sie, sie) müssen** = *must* in the sense of *have to.*
ich (er, sie, es) darf ; wir (Sie, sie) dürfen = *must* in the sense of *be allowed to.*

THERE IS, THERE ARE

(1) **Es gibt Flugzeuge, die über 900 Kilometer per Stunde fliegen** = *There are aeroplanes which fly over 900 kilometres per hour.*

Es gibt einen guten Film im Kino = *There is a good film on in the cinema.*

Was gibt es zu essen? = *What is there to eat.*

(2) **Es ist ein Mann an der Tür, der Sie sprechen will** = *There is a man at the door who wants to speak to you.*

Sind Zigaretten in dem Kasten? = *Are there any cigarettes in the box?*

Es sind einige darin = *There are some in it.*

Es gibt = *there is, there are,* in the sense of *there exists* or *there is to be had.*

Es ist (sind) = *there is (are)* with reference to some definite limited place.

Note that **es** is dropped in questions with **ist** and **sind,** but not with **gibt;** also that the object of **es gibt** is in the accusative case.

COLLOQUIAL USE OF *DER, DIE, DAS*

In colloquial language **der, die** and **das** frequently stand for *this* or *that* or *the one* *(those) who.* This meaning is made clear by special emphasis:

Meinen Sie diese Tür? Nein, die am Ende des Korridors = *Do you mean this door? No, the one at the end of the corridor.*

Welcher Herr ist der Lehrer? Der mit dem steifen Hut = *Which gentleman is the teacher? The one with the bowler hat.*

Welche Dame ist Ihre Tante? Die mit dem Sonnenschirm = *Which lady is your aunt? The one with the sunshade.*

Welches sind Ihre Handschuhe? Die auf dem Tische = *Which are your gloves? Those on the table.*

IM HAFEN

In Norddeutschland ist die Fischerei von besonderer Bedeutung. Der Fang des soeben eingelaufenen Bootes wird von Kennern besichtigt.   (*Translation on page 377*)

die Fischerei	die Bedeutung, -en	der Fang, ··-e	soeben	besichtigen
fishing	*importance*	*catch*	*just now*	*to examine*

NEW NOUNS

DER
Ort, -e or ··-er	place, spot
Bräutigam, -e	fiancé
Verlobte, -n[1]	fiancé
Kopf, ··-e	head
Schwanz, ···-e	tail
Film, -e	film

DIE
Pfeife, -n	pipe
Bank, ···-e	seat, bench
Luft, ···-e	air
Verspätung, -en	delay
Zeit, -en	time
Stimme, -n	voice
Photographie, -n	photograph
Braut, ···-e	fiancée
Verlobte, -n[1]	fiancée

DAS
Strickzeug, -e	piece of knitting
Futteral, -e	case
Vergnügen, -[2]	pleasure, enjoyment
Gebirge, -	mountain range

VERBS

Hängen=*to hang;* **fragen**=*to ask;* **öffnen**
=*to open;* **besuchen**=*to visit;* **vorstellen**=*to
put forward;* **nachstellen**=*to put back,*
are all regular verbs (**hängte, gehängt;
fragte, gefragt,** etc.).

The following verbs are irregular:

sitzen, sass, gesessen=*to sit.*

liegen, lag, gelegen=*to lie.*

fahren, fuhr, gefahren[3]=*to travel.*

anbieten (bietet an), bot an, angeboten=*to
offer.*

vorziehen (zieht vor), zog vor, vorgezogen=
to prefer.

MORE EASY PROVERBS

Eine Schwalbe macht keinen Sommer.
One swallow does not make a summer

Ende gut, alles gut.
All's well that ends well!

Neue Besen kehren gut.
New brooms sweep clean.

Bei den Blinden ist der Einäugige König.
Among the blind the one-eyed man is king.

EXERCISES

I   Read and Translate

1. Wir haben unsere Koffer gepackt und
sind fertig. 2. Ich hole ein Taxi und wir
fahren zum Bahnhof. 3. Ein Gepäckträger
nimmt die Koffer und gibt sie auf. 4. Wir
gehen zum Schalter, um die Fahrkarten zu
kaufen. Dann gehen wir auf den Bahnsteig.
Der Zug ist noch nicht da. 5. Wir gehen in
den Wartesaal, um eine Tasse Kaffee zu
trinken. 6. Bald ist es Zeit einzusteigen.
7. Wir finden zwei Fensterplätze. Der
Stationsvorsteher ruft "Einsteigen!" Der
Zug fährt ab.

II   Translate into German

1. We went to the station in a taxi. 2. The
train leaves at 4.15 p.m. and arrives at
6.35 a.m. 3. I said to the porter: "Please
take my luggage to the train. I want this
trunk registered[4]." 4. In Germany all big
luggage must be registered[5]. 5. I went to the
booking office to buy the tickets. Many
people waited in front of the booking
office. 6 I said: "Two third class returns to
Vienna[6]." 7. Then we followed the porter
to the platform. There were many people
on the platform. 8. The train arrived and
we got in. 9. The compartment was full.
There was one seat in a corner by the door.
My sister sat down and I had to stand. 10.
Opposite her sat a young Englishwoman.
She has come to Germany to learn the
language.

III   Insert the appropriate endings (-er or -es)

1. Der Vater d- Kindes ist der
Schwager mein- Schwester. 2. Welches ist
die Nummer Ihr- Hauses? 3. Die Farbe
dies- Tür ist nicht schön. 4. Das ist die Uhr
jen- Dame. 5. Dies ist das Zimmer mein-
Kinder. 6. Die Füllfeder mein- Bruders
ist besser als die mein- Schwester. 7. Ist
dies das Haus Ihr- Grosseltern? 8. Die
Handtasche sein- Frau ist nicht hier.

(Answers on page 362)

---

[1] Adjectival noun—see page 304.   [2] This word is an example of an infinitive used as a neuter
noun, as described in this lesson.   [3] Conjugated with sein.   [4] say : register.   [5] say : one must
register.   [6] Wien.

NEUNZEHNTE LEKTION: *NINETEENTH LESSON*

JOURNEY'S END

Here our characters are being met in Berlin by Mr. Lessing. In your own words, try to describe the busy scene of their arrival, after having studied the text below.

DIE ANKUNFT

Pünktlich fünf Minuten nach eins ist der Zug auf dem Lehrter Bahnhof in Berlin angekommen. Herr und Frau Schulz sowie die Kinder sind zuerst ausgestiegen, dann sind Herr Brown (der Engländer) und die ältere Dame gefolgt. Herr Schulz rief sofort einen Gepäckträger, der auf dem Bahnsteig stand, und sagte zu ihm: "Bitte, holen Sie unseren Koffer und bringen Sie ihn zu einem Wagen. Hier ist der Gepäckschein."

In diesem Augenblick sahen sie Herrn Lessing, der zum Bahnhof gekommen war, um seine Verwandten in Berlin zu begrüssen.

Herr Lessing: Ah, da seid ihr![1] Guten Tag, meine Lieben. Willkommen in Berlin!

Frau Schulz: Wie geht's dir,[1] Kurt?

Herr L.: Danke, gut. Und dir?

Frau S.: Auch nicht schlecht. Du[1] siehst gut aus.

THE ARRIVAL

Punctually at five minutes past one the train arrived at Lehrter Station in Berlin. Mr. and Mrs. Schulz as well as the children got out first, then Mr. Brown (the Englishman) and the elderly lady followed. Mr. Schulz at once called a porter, who was standing on the platform, and said to him: "Please fetch our trunk and take it to a taxi. Here is the receipt."

At this moment they saw Mr. Lessing, who had come to the station to welcome his relatives to Berlin.

Mr. Lessing: Ah, there you are! Hallo, my dears. Welcome to Berlin!

Mrs. Schulz: How are you, Kurt?

Mr. L.: Fine, thanks, and you?

Mrs. S.: Not bad either. You look fine.

[1] For an explanation of the familiar form of address see Lesson 21.

Herr L. [zu Herrn S.]: Du bist dicker geworden, Wilhelm. Das macht wohl das gute hamburger Bier. [Zu Hans] Hans, dich habe ich fast gar nicht erkannt. Ist der Schlingel gross geworden! Wie alt bist du denn jetzt?

Hans: Neun Jahre und drei Monate. Im April bin ich neun geworden. Ich danke auch schön für das schöne Geschenk, das ihr mir zum Geburtstag geschickt habt.

Herr S.: Darf ich vorstellen? Mein Schwager Herr Lessing—Herr Brown, ein Engländer, der nach Berlin gekommen ist, um unsere Sprache zu studieren. Er spricht aber schon ganz gut.

Herr L.: Es freut mich, Ihre Bekanntschaft zu machen. Wenn ich Ihnen irgendwie behilflich sein kann, stehe ich gern zu Diensten.

Herr Brown: Das ist sehr freundlich von Ihnen. Können Sie mir vielleicht ein Hotel empfehlen, das gut aber nicht zu teuer ist?

Mr. L. [to Mr. S.]: You have become stouter, Wilhelm. I suppose the good Hamburg beer does that. [To Hans] Hans, I hardly recognised you at all. How the young scamp has grown! How old are you now?

Hans: Nine years and three months. I was nine in April. Thank you very much for the nice present you sent me for my birthday.

Mr. S.: May I introduce? My brother-in-law, Mr. Lessing—Mr. Brown, an Englishman who has come to Berlin to study our language. But he speaks quite well already.

Mr. L.: Pleased to make your acquaintance. If I can be of any assistance to you I shall be pleased to do so (*lit.*, stand gladly at your services).

Mr. Brown: That is very kind of you. Can you perhaps recommend me an hotel that is good but not too expensive?

BERLIN: STRASSENBILD

Vor vielbesuchten Geschäften haben sich Fahrradwachen etabliert, die auf Fahrräder, Kinderwagen und dergleichen aufpassen. (*Translation on page 377*)

vielbesucht	die Wache, -n	der Kinderwagen, -	dergleichen	aufpassen
much-visited	*watch, guard*	*pram*	*the like*	*to keep watch*

CAFÉ IN BERLIN

Wie auf einem Pariser Boulevard reiht sich auf dem Kurfürstendamm Café an Café. Bei
schönem Wetter sitzt man auf der Terrasse.

(*Translation on page* 377)

sich anreihen	**Café an Café**	**bei schönem Wetter**
to link	*one cafe after another*	*in fine weather*

Herr L.: Lassen Sie mich einen Moment
nachdenken. Richtig! Das Hotel Walhalla.
Ich kann es Ihnen empfehlen. Es ist nicht
sehr weit von hier.

Herr B.: Vielen Dank. Ich werde gleich
hinfahren.

Herr L.: Wenn Sie sich in Berlin einsam
fühlen, besuchen Sie uns. Wir werden uns
sehr freuen.

Herr B.: Das ist sehr liebenswürdig. Ich
werde gern kommen.

Herr S. Ich glaube, der Gepäckträger wird
inzwischen den Koffer geholt haben.

Herr L.: Dann können wir gehen, nicht
wahr?

Sie gehen zusammen durch die Sperre, wo
die Reisenden ihre Fahrkarten abgeben.
Dann gehen sie durch die Bahnhofshalle zum
Bahnhofsvorplatz. Der Gepäckträger wartet

Mr. L.: Let me think for a moment. Right!
The Walhalla Hotel. I can recommend it
to you. It is not very far from here.

Mr. B.: Many thanks. I shall go there at
once.

Mr. L.: If you feel lonely in Berlin (come
and) visit us. We shall be very glad.

Mr. B.: That is very kind. I shall be pleased
to come.

Mr. S.: I believe the porter will have fetched
the trunk in the meantime.

Mr. L.: Then we can go, can't we?

They go together through the barrier,
where the travellers give up their tickets.
Then they go through the booking-hall to
the station square. The porter is already

dort schon mit einem Taxi, in das er das Gepäck gelegt hat. Herr Schulz bezahlt den Gepäckträger, während die anderen in das Taxi steigen und Herr Lessing dem Chauffeur seine Adresse sagt. Sobald sie alle eingestiegen sind und sich von Herrn Brown verabschiedet haben, fährt der Wagen ab.

Herr Brown nimmt sich auch ein Taxi und bittet den Chauffeur, ihn nach dem Hotel Walhalla zu fahren. Schon nach wenigen Minuten hält der Wagen vor dem Hotel. Herr Brown steigt aus, fragt den Chauffeur, was er ihm schuldig ist, und zahlt.

Inzwischen hat der Portier, der vor dem Hotel stand, ihm das Gepäck abgenommen und jetzt führt er Herrn Brown durch die Eingangshalle des Hotels zum Empfangsbüro.

waiting there with a taxi, in which he has put the luggage, Mr. Schulz pays the porter while the others get into the taxi, and Mr. Lessing tells the driver his address. As soon as they have all got in and said good-bye to Mr. Brown, the car sets off.

Mr. Brown also takes a taxi and asks the driver to take him to the Walhalla Hotel. After only a few minutes the car stops in front of the hotel. Mr. Brown gets out, asks the driver what he owes him, and pays.

Meanwhile, the porter, who was standing in front of the hotel, has taken the luggage and led Mr. Brown through the entrance hall of the hotel to the reception office.

Darf ich vorstellen?

Haben Sie ein Zimmer frei?

Herr B. [zum Empfangschef]: Haben Sie ein Zimmer frei?

Empfangschef: Wir sind zur Zeit sehr voll. Es ist nur ein kleines Hinterzimmer im fünften Stock frei. Am Ende der Woche wird ein grösseres Vorderzimmer frei.

Herr B.: Wie teuer sind die Zimmer?

Empfangschef: Das kleine Zimmer 8.50 Mark pro Tag, das grössere 9.50 Mark.

Herr B.: Was rechnen Sie pro Woche? Ich denke einige Zeit zu bleiben.

Mr. B. [to the reception clerk]: Have you a room vacant?

Reception Clerk: At the moment we are very full. Only a small back room on the fifth floor is vacant. At the end of the week a larger front room becomes vacant.

Mr. B.: How much are the rooms?

Clerk: The smaller room 8 marks 50 pfennigs per day, the larger one 9 marks 50 pfennigs.

Mr. B.: What do you charge per week? I am thinking of staying for some time.

Empfangschef: Wir gewähren Ermässigung bei längerem Aufenthalt. 65 Mark für das kleine Hinterzimmer und 70 Mark für das grössere Vorderzimmer.

Herr B.: Ist Frühstück einbegriffen?

Empfangschef: Das ist extra, 2.50 Mark pro Tag. Sie können aber auch volle Pension (pang-zyohn') für 18 Mark pro Tag oder 95 Mark die Woche haben.

Herr B.: Kann ich mir das Zimmer bitte ansehen?

Empfangschef: Mit Vergnügen. Ich bringe Sie im Fahrstuhl hinauf.

Sie fahren in den fünften Stock hinauf und gehen in das Zimmer Nr. 28.

Herr B.: Das Zimmer ist wirklich sehr klein und auch ziemlich dunkel.

Empfangschef: Es ist leider das einzige, das wir zur Zeit frei haben. Wenn Sie sich einige Tage mit diesem Zimmer begnügen, können Sie von Sonntag ab das grosse, helle Vorderzimmer haben.

Herr B.: Gut, ich nehme dieses Zimmer vorläufig und werde in das andere Zimmer ziehen, sobald es frei wird.

Empfangschef: Ich werde Ihnen Ihr Gepäck sofort heraufschicken. Darf ich Sie bitten, später zum Empfangsbüro zu kommen und sich ins Hotelbuch einzutragen?

Herr B.: Ich werde bald hinunterkommen.

Empfangschef: Es hat keine Eile.

Der Empfangschef verlässt das Zimmer. Herr Brown hängt seinen Mantel in den Kleiderschrank und legt seine Jacke ab, um sich die Hände zu waschen. Er geht zum Waschbecken, dreht den Wasserhahn auf und lässt das Waschbecken vollaufen, nimmt die Seife aus dem Seifenschälchen und wäscht sich die Hände.

Dann nimmt er das Handtuch, das an einer Stange neben dem Waschbecken hängt, und trocknet sich die Hände ab. Während er sich noch die Hände abtrocknet, klopft es an der Tür. Herr Brown sagt: "Herein"; und der Hausdiener bringt das Gepäck. Nun kann Herr Brown seine Sachen auspacken und sich für einen Spaziergang fertigmachen.

Clerk: We grant a reduction for a longer stay. 65 marks for the small back room and 70 marks for the larger front room.

Mr. B.: Is breakfast included?

Clerk: That is extra, 2.50 marks per day. But you can also have full board for 18 marks per day or 95 marks per week.

Mr. B.: May I see the room, please?

Clerk: With pleasure. I'll take you up in the lift.

They go up to the fifth floor and enter room No. 28.

Mr. B.: The room is really very small and also rather dark.

Clerk: Unfortunately it is the only one we have free at the moment. If you would put up with this room for a few days you could have the large bright front room from Sunday on.

Mr. B.: All right, I'll take this room for the time being, and move into the other as soon as it becomes vacant.

Clerk: I'll send your luggage up to you at once. May I ask you to come to the reception office later on to enter your name in the hotel register?

Mr. B.: I shall come down soon.

Clerk: There is no hurry.

The reception clerk leaves the room. Mr. Smith hangs his overcoat in the wardrobe and takes off his jacket to wash his hands. He goes to the wash-basin, turns on the tap and fills the basin (lit., lets the basin run full), takes the soap out of the soap dish and washes his hands.

Then he takes the towel which hangs on a rail near the wash-basin, and dries his hands. While he is still drying his hands, there is a knock at the door. Mr. Brown says: "Come in"; and the bellboy brings in the luggage. Now Mr. Brown can unpack his things and get ready for a walk.

DIE SPREE ZUGEFROREN

Während des Winters erreicht die Kälte in Berlin zuweilen Temperaturen, die viele Grade unter dem Gefrierpunkt liegen. Dann ist die Spree, wie die meisten Flüsse Norddeutschlands, zugefroren. Auf dem Bild sieht man eingefrorene Schiffe im Hafen der deutschen Hauptstadt. *(Translation on page 377)*

zufrieren	**während**	**erreichen**	**die Kälte**	**zuweilen**	**der Grad, -e**
to freeze over	*during*	*to reach*	*cold*	*sometimes*	*degree*

der Gefrierpunkt, -e	**der Fluss, ⋯-e**	**eingefroren**	**die Hauptstadt, ⋯-e**
freezing point	*river*	*frozen-in, ice-bound*	*capital*

1. die Eingangshalle, -n
2. das Empfangsbüro, -s
3. der Schalter, -
4. der Fernsprecher, -
5. das Tintenfass, ···-er
6. das Fremdenbuch, ···-er
7. der Empfangschef, -s

8. das Fach, ···-er
9. die Post der Hotelgäste
10. das Schlüsselbrett, -er
11. der Ventilator, -en
12. der Gast, ···-e
13. die Wanduhr, -en
14. der Lüster, -

15. der Vorhang, ···-e
16. der Portier, -s
17. der Hoteldiener, -
18. die Schürze, -n
19. die Klingel, -n
20. der Koffer, -
21. die Matte, -n

178

THE HOTEL
on page 369)

22. der Fahrstuhl, ···-e
23. der Fahrstuhljunge, -n
24. die Fahrstuhltür, -en
25. der Pfeiler, -
26. die Bekanntmachung,-en
27. der Schirmständer, -
28. der Schirm, -e

29. der Tisch, -e
30. der Aschenbecher, -
31. der Blumentopf, ···-e
32. die Palme, -n
33. der Kleiderständer, -
34. das Bild, -er
35. die Hoteldiele, -n

36. das Sofa, -s
37. der Teppich, -e
38. der Sessel, -
39. der Page, -n
40. die Bar, -s
41. der Bartender, -
42. der Hocker, -

INSEPARABLE VERBS

besuchen
to visit

> **Er besucht uns oft.**
> *He often visits us.*
>
> **Er hat uns gestern besucht.**
> *He visited us yesterday.*

gehören
to belong

> **Das Buch gehört mir.**
> *The book belongs to me*
>
> **Das Haus hat uns gehört.**
> *The house belonged to us.*

erzählen
to tell

> **Erzählen Sie uns eine Geschichte** = *Tell us a story.*
>
> **Was hat er Ihnen erzählt?**
> *What did he tell you?*

zerbrechen
to break

> **Das Glas zerbrach.**
> *The glass broke.*
>
> **Der Junge hat die Fensterscheibe zerbrochen** = *The boy broke the window pane.*

verlieren
to lose

> **Er hat seinen Regenschirm verloren** = *He lost his umbrella.*

be-, ent-, ge-, ver- and **zer-** are not separate words, as are the prefixes of separable verbs (compare Lesson 15). The inseparable prefixes (1) are never separated from the verb, e.g. **ich besuche**; (2) are unstressed in pronunciation, e.g. **besu′chen Sie ihn!**

The past participles of verbs compounded with inseparable prefixes are formed without adding **ge-**; e.g. **besucht, vergessen, erzählt, zerbrochen.**

Er hat das Glas zerbrochen

CASES WITH VERBS

Nominative:

Er ist Lehrer an einer Mädchenschule.
He is a teacher at a girls' school.

Er ist ein grosser Junge geworden.
He has become a big boy.

Accusative:

Sie schreibt einen Brief.
She is writing a letter.

Ich sah meinen Freund.
I saw my friend.

Er kauft einen Regenschirm.
He buys an umbrella.

Dative:

Antworten Sie mir.
Answer me.

Ich kann Ihnen nicht helfen.
I cannot help you.

Er dankte ihr vielmals.
He thanked her many times.

Sie folgte ihm.
She followed him.

Glauben Sie ihnen nicht.
Don't believe them.

Er gehorcht seiner Mutter nicht.
He does not obey his mother.

Sie erlaubt ihrer Tochter nicht, abends auszugehen.
She does not allow her daughter to go out at night.

Most German verbs govern their object in the accusative case, but **sein** and **werden** are followed by the nominative case, and the following verbs require the dative case:

antworten = *to answer*　**erlauben** = *to allow*
befehlen = *to command*　**folgen** = *to follow*
begegnen = *to meet*　**gehorchen** = *to obey*
danken = *to thank*　**glauben** = *to believe*
drohen = *to threaten*　**helfen** = *to help*
raten = *to advise*

The verbs listed above have this in

common, that they can govern a personal object only; it is obvious that we can answer, thank, advise, etc., only a person, not a thing. If the object may be either a person or a thing the accusative case is used.

If a verb has two objects, one a person, the other a thing, the person stands in the dative, the thing in the accusative case, e.g.: **Können Sie mir** (dative) **ein Buch** (accusative) **leihen?** = *Can you lend me a book?*

EACH OTHER

sich sehen
  to see each other
sich lieben
  to love each other
sich zanken
  to quarrel (with each other)
sich trennen
  to separate one from the other

Note that reflexive verbs are used in German when in English we use *each other*, either expressed or understood.

NEW NOUNS

DER	Schlingel, -	*scamp, rascal,*
	Geburtstag, -e	*birthday*
	Dienst, -e	*service*
	Bahnhofsvor-	*station square*
	platz, ···-e	
	Portier, -s	*hall porter*
	Chef, -s	*chief, head*
	Stock, ···-e	*storey, stick*
	Fahrstuhl, ···-e	*lift*
	Wasserhahn, ···-e	*water-tap*
	Diener, -	*servant*
DIE	Sprache, -n	*language*
	Bekanntschaft, -en	*acquaintance*
	Ermässigung, -en	*reduction*
	Pension, -en	*boarding house*
	Eile	*hurry*
	Stange, -n	*rail, bar*
	Eingangshalle, -n	*entrance hall*
DAS	Hotel, -s	*hotel*
	Waschbecken, -	*wash-basin*
	Schälchen, -	*small dish, bowl*
	Handtuch, ···-er	*hand towel*

Sie sehen sich

Sie lieben sich

Sie zanken sich

Sie trennen sich

LIEBE AUF DEN ERSTEN BLICK—LOVE AT FIRST SIGHT

VERBS

folgen=*to follow* is a regular verb (**folgte, gefolgt**) conjugated with **sein**. The person whom you follow is expressed in the dative case: **Er ist ihr gefolgt**=*He followed her.*

begrüssen=*to greet*, is a regular verb (**begrüsste, begrüsst**) conjugated with **haben**. The person whom you greet is expressed in the accusative case: **Er hat sie begrüsst**=*He greeted her.* There is also a verb **grüssen** (**grüsste, gegrüsst**) which means either *to salute* or *to send greetings, to give one's regards*. **Bitte grüssen Sie Ihren Vater von mir**=*Please give my regards to your father.*

Der Herr grüsst die Dame
(Sie grüssen sich)

aussehen (conjugated like **sehen**) is *to look like, to appear*. **Er sieht gut aus**=*He looks well.* **Es sieht so aus, als ob es regnen wird**=*It looks as if it will rain.*

werden=*to become* (**wurde, geworden**) is conjugated with **sein**. **Was ist aus ihm geworden?**=*What has become of him?*

erkennen=*to recognise* (**erkannte, erkannt**) is conjugated like **kennen**. **Sie hat uns nicht erkannt**=*She did not recognise us.*

danken=*to thank*, is a regular verb (**dankte, gedankt**). The person you thank is expressed in the dative case. **Er dankte mir** =*He thanked me.* **Ich danke Ihnen**=*I thank you.*

vorstellen=*to introduce*, is a regular verb with a separable prefix. **Er stellte mich ihm vor**=*He introduced me to him.*

Der Herr begrüsst die Dame
(Sie begrüssen sich)

sich freuen=*to be glad*, is a regular verb, but reflexive. **Ich freue mich, Sie kennen zu lernen**=*I am glad to make your acquaintance.*

empfehlen=*to recommend* (**empfahl, empfohlen**). **Können Sie es mir empfehlen?**= *Can you recommend it to me?*

nachdenken=*to think over, to consider* (**dachte nach, hat nachgedacht**). **Er dachte lange nach**=*He thought for a long while.* **Lassen Sie mich einen Augenblick nachdenken**=*Let me think for a moment.*

fühlen=*to feel*, is regular (**fühlte, gefühlt**), but is also reflexive (**sich fühlen**) when referring to a person's wellbeing. **Sie hat sich nicht ganz wohl gefühlt**=*She did not feel quite well.*

abgeben=*to deliver*, is conjugated like **geben**, with **ab** as a separable prefix (**gab ab, hat abgegeben**).

sich verabschieden=*to take leave* or *to say good-bye*, is a regular verb, but **ver-** is not a separable prefix. **Er hat sich nicht von uns verabschiedet**=*He did not say good-bye to us.*

ansehen=*to (have a) look at*, is conjugated like **sehen**, with **an** as a separable prefix.

rechnen=*to reckon* or *to charge;* **gewähren** =*to grant;* and **sich begnügen**=*to content oneself*, are regular verbs.

verlassen (**verlässt**), **verliess, verlassen**= *to leave.*

laufen (**läuft**), **lief, gelaufen**=*to run.*

EXERCISES

I Answer in German

1. Um wieviel Uhr ist der Zug in Berlin angekommen? 2. Wer ist zuerst ausgetiegen? 3. Warum ist Herr Lessing zum Bahnhof gekommen? 4, Warum hat er Hans nicht erkannt? 5. Wen stellt Herr Schulz seinem Schwager vor? 6. Wo geben die Reisenden die Fahrkarten ab? 7. Wer nimmt Herrn Brown die Koffer ab? 8. Sind viele Zimmer im Hotel frei? 9. Wie lange will Herr Brown in Berlin bleiben? 10. Was tut er, nachdem er sich die Hände gewaschen hat?

II Translate into German

1. Will the train arrive punctually? 2. Get out first. I shall follow with the suit-cases. 3. You don't look well. You have become thinner. 4. I did not recognise you at first. 5. I have come to Germany to study the language. 6. Can you recommend a restaurant where one can eat well but not too dearly? 7. Please stop in front of the station. 8. I shall be down in five minutes. 9. Won't you take off your overcoat? 10. May I ask you to come up?

III Give the following verbal forms (a) in the imperfect, (b) in the perfect

1. Er zerbricht viele Gläser. 2. Sie lieben sich. 3. Ich stelle ihm meinen Freund vor. 4. Sie dankt ihm. 5. Wir steigen aus. 6. Ich freue mich. 7. Sie sieht gut aus.

(Answers on page 362)

IDIOMS

Es klopft = *Someone is knocking.*

Es ist eilig $\Big\}$ = *It is urgent.*
Es hat Eile

Es hat keine Eile = *There is no hurry.*

HOLZSAMMELN IM WALDE

Diese Frauen suchen ihren Brennstoff im Walde, um sich für den Winter vorzubereiten.

(Translation on page 378)

| **sammeln** | **suchen** | **der Brennstoff, -e** | **vorbereiten** |
| *to gather* | *to seek* | *fuel* | *to prepare* |

HÄUSER—HOUSES
(English key on page 369)

das Bauernhaus, ¨-er

das Einfamilienhaus, ¨-er

das Doppelhaus, ¨-er

Reihenhäuser

das einstöckige Haus, ¨-er

das Mietshaus, ¨-er

die Laube, -n

das Bürohaus, ¨-er

ZWANZIGSTE LEKTION : *TWENTIETH LESSON*

THE LESSINGS' HALL

This picture illustrates the description on pages 187 and 189. Return to it when you have finished the text and see how successfully you can describe the scene yourself.

DAS HAUS DER FAMILIE LESSING

Die Familie Lessing wohnt in einer Villa in einem Vorort von Berlin. Die Villa hat zwei Stockwerke über dem Erdgeschoss. Im Erdgeschoss befinden sich das Wohnzimmer, das Esszimmer, der Salon und die Küche. Im ersten Stock sind mehrere Schlafzimmer, ein Badezimmer und das Arbeitszimmer des Hausherrn. Die Kinderzimmer und die Zimmer der erwachsenen Kinder sind im zweiten Stock.

Jedes Stockwerk hat einen Balkon. Das Erdgeschoss hat hinten (nach dem Garten zu) eine grosse Veranda, wo die Familie sich im Sommer aufhält. In jedem Stockwerk befindet sich ein Klosett (eine Toilette; twah-let'-tĕ).

Über dem zweiten Stock ist ein grosser Bodenraum mit mehreren Dachkammern. Eine der Dachkammern dient als Mädchenzimmer. Die übrigen stehen leer. In dem

THE LESSING FAMILY'S HOUSE

The Lessing family lives in a villa in a suburb of Berlin. The villa has two storeys above the ground floor. On the ground floor are the sitting-room, the dining-room, the drawing-room and the kitchen. On the first floor are several bedrooms, a bathroom and the study of the master of the house. The nurseries and the rooms of the grown-up children are on the second floor.

Every storey has a balcony. The ground floor has at the back (towards the garden) a big veranda where the family stays in summer. On each storey there is a lavatory.

Over the second floor is a big loft with several attics. One of the attics serves as the maid's room. The others are empty. In the big loft there are trunks, old broken furni-

185

DAS HAUS (AUSSEN)—THE HOUSE (OUTSIDE)
(*English key on page* 369)

1. der Schornstein, -e
2. der Rauch
3. der Blitzableiter, -
4. das Dach, ̈-er
5. der Boden, ̈-
6. die Antenne, -n
7. die Dachrinne, -n
8. das Abflussrohr, -e

9. das Obergeschoss, -e
10. das Erdgeschoss, -e
11. der Keller, -
12. das Fenster, -
13. der Fensterladen, ̈-
14. der Balkon, -e
15. das Portal, -e
16. die Haustür, -en

17. der Pfeiler, -
18. die Treppe, -n
19. der Gartenweg, -e
20. die Gartentür, -en
21. der Gartenzaun, ̈-e
22. der Garten, ̈-
23. die Seitentür, -en
24. das Spalier, -e

IN THE LOFT

Here is another opportunity to test the knowledge you have gained from this lesson. Cover over the text and see if you can make a convincing description of the picture.

grossen Bodenraum stehen Koffer, alte zerbrochene Möbel und eine Leiter. Kreuz und quer durch den Bodenraum ist eine Leine gespannt, auf die man die Wäsche zum Trocknen hängt.

Über dem Boden ist das Dach. Es ist mit Schiefer gedeckt und spitz (nicht flach). Auf dem Dach sind mehrere Schornstein, aus denen der Rauch aufsteigt.

Unter dem Erdgeschoss ist der Keller, in dem man Kohlen, Kartoffeln und Wein aufbewahrt. Vom Erdgeschoss führen Treppen hinab in den Keller und hinauf zu den oberen Stockwerken.

Die Haustür ist fast immer geschlossen; nachts ist sie zugeschlossen. Wer in das Haus will, muss klingeln. Die Klingel befindet sich rechts von der Haustür. Herr und Frau Lessing und die beiden älteren Kinder haben jeder einen Hausschlüssel und können hinein ohne zu klingeln.

Wenn man in das Haus eintritt, kommt man zuerst in den Hausflur. Links ist ein Kleiderständer, an dem Mäntel und Hüte hängen. Neben dem Kleiderständer ist ein

ture and a ladder. Criss-cross through the loft a line is stretched on which one hangs the washing to dry.

Over the loft is the roof. It is covered with slates and is pointed (not flat). On the roof are several chimneys, out of which smoke rises.

Beneath the ground floor is the cellar, in which one stores coal, potatoes and wine. From the ground floor, stairs lead down to the cellar, and up to the upper floors.

The front door is nearly always closed; at night it is locked. Whoever wants to get into the house must ring the bell. The bell is to be found to the right of the front door. Mr. and Mrs. Lessing and the two older children each have a front door key and can get in without ringing the bell.

When one enters the house one first comes into the hall. On the left is a clothes-stand on which coats and hats hang. Next to the clothes-stand is a big mirror. On the

DAS HAUS (INNEN) — THE HOUSE (INSIDE)
(*English key on page* 369)

1. die Dachkammer, -n
2. der Dachsparren, -
3. der Wasserbehälter, -
4. die Falltür, -en
5. der Boden, ··-
6. die Holztreppe, -n
7. das Badezimmer, -
8. das Schlafzimmer, -

9. das Herrenzimmer, -
10. der Schreibtisch, -e
11. das Kinderzimmer, -
12. das Kinderbett, -en
13. das Schaukelpferd, -e
14. das Wohnzimmer, -
15. der Radioapparat, -e
16. der Hausflur, -e

17. der Kleiderständer, ·
18. die Treppe, -n
19. das Treppengeländer, -
20. das Esszimmer, -
21. die Küche, -n
22. der Keller, -
23. der Kohlenkasten, ··-
24. die Feuerung, -en

188

In dem Keller

grosser Spiegel. Rechts steht ein Tischchen, auf dem das Telefon steht. Neben dem Tischchen steht ein Korbsessel. Links und rechts sind Türen, die in die verschiedenen Wohnräume führen.

In dem Hausflur sind zwei Personen: ein Besucher, der seinen Mantel abnimmt, und eine Dame, die ihren Hut aufsetzt. Sie ist eine Engländerin, die zweimal in der Woche ins Haus kommt, um den Kindern englische Stunden zu geben.

right is a little table, on which the telephone stands. Beside the little table is a wicker chair. To the left and right are doors which lead to the different living rooms.

There are two persons in the hall: a visitor taking off his overcoat and a lady putting on her hat. She is an Englishwoman who comes to the house twice a week to give English lessons to the children.

Note.—There are two German words for *room;* der Raum and das Zimmer. Raum is the more general term, as it also means *space* or *capacity.* Das Zimmer is a room for human habitation, like Wohnzimmer, Schlafzimmer, etc.

VERBS—REGULAR

dienen = *to serve* klopfen = *to knock* decken = *to cover*

aufbewahren = *to store* klingeln = *to ring* führen = *to lead*

hinaufführen = *to take* (or *lead*) *up* (führt. .hinauf, führte. .hinauf, hat . . hinaufgeführt)

hinabführen = *to take* (or *lead*) *down*

VERBS—IRREGULAR

sich befinden = *to find itself (oneself), to be situated,* and is conjugated like finden = *to find.*

Er klopft

schliessen = *to shut* (schloss, geschlossen).
zuschliessen = *to lock* (schliesst ... zu, schloss ... zu, hat ... zugeschlossen).
eintreten = *to enter* (tritt .. ein, trat .. ein, ist .. eingetreten).
sich aufhalten = *to stay* (hielt .. auf, hat .. aufgehalten).

Sie klingelt

DIE KÜCHE—
(English key

1. der Küchentisch, -e
2. die Scheuerbürste, -n
3. die Waschseife, -n
4. das Becken, -
5. der Küchenstuhl, ¨-e
6. der Küchenschrank, ¨-e
7. die Sanduhr, -en
8. die Kaffeemühle, -n

9. die Waage, -n
10. das Geschirrbrett, -er
11. das Salzfass, ¨-er
12. der Krug, ¨-e
13. der Teigstecher, -
14. der Teig, -e
15. das Nudelholz, ¨-er
16. das Hackbrett, -er

17. die Rührschüssel, -n
18. die Köchin, -nen
19. die Fleischmaschine, -n
20. das Küchenhandtuch, ¨-er
21. der Ausguss, ¨-e
22. das Fensterbrett, -er
23. der Wasserhahn, ¨-e
24. der Eimer, -

THE KITCHEN
on page 369)

25. der Abwaschtisch, -e
26. das Küchenhandtuch, ··-er
27. der Mülleimer, -
28. der Eisschrank, ···-e
29. der Griff, -e
30. die Wanduhr, -en
31. die Speisekammer, -n
32. die Brotbüchse, -n

33. die Mehlbüchse, -n
34. der Speck
35. die Wurst, ···-e
36. der Schinken, -
37. der Gaskocher, -
38. der Teekessel, -
39. der Gasring, -e
40. die Fliese, -n

41. der Küchenherd, -e
42. der Backofen (Bratofen),
43. der Feuerhaken, -   [··-
44. die Bratpfanne, -n
45. der Kochtopf, ···-e
46. der Schöpflöffel, -
47. die Ofenröhre, -n
48. der Topfdeckel, -

191

RELATIVE PRONOUNS

Masculine

Kennen Sie
den Mann,
Do you know
the man
{
der dort steht?
who is standing there?
den ich grüsste?
whom I saluted?
dessen Haus abgebrannt ist?
whose house is burnt down?
dem ich geschrieben habe?
to whom I have written?
}

Dies ist der
Garten,
This is the
garden
{
der mir so gefällt.
which I like so much (lit.,
pleases me so).
den ich kaufen will.
which I want to buy.
dessen Obstbäume schon
blühen.
*of which the fruit trees are
already in blossom.*
in dem wir als Kinder
gespielt haben.
*in which we played as
children.*
}

Feminine

Die Frau,
The woman
{
die es gesagt hat.
who said it.
die er liebt.
whom he loves.
deren Bruder Sie kennen.
whose brother you know.
der wir das Geld schulden.
*to whom we owe the
money.*
}

(*continued at top of next column*)

Die Küche,
The kitchen
{
die zu klein ist.
which is too small.
deren Wände weiss sind.
*the walls of which are
white.*
in der wir sassen.
in which we sat.
}

Neuter

Das Haus,
The house
{
das er gekauft hat.
which he bought.
dessen Eigentümer er ist.
of which he is the owner.
in dem wir gewohnt haben.
in which we lived.
}

Plural (all genders)

Die Männer
(Frauen,
Kinder),
The men
(*women,
children*)
{
die hier sind.
who are here.
die wir kennen.
whom we know.
deren Geld ich habe.
whose money I have.
denen ich Geld schulde.
to whom I owe money.
}

Die Gärten
(Häuser,
Schulen),
The gardens
(*houses,
schools*)
{
die wir sahen.
which we saw.
deren Eigentümer Sie ken-
nen.
*of which you know the
owner.*
von denen wir sprachen.
*we spoke about (of which
we spoke).*
}

The relative pronouns are:

	Masc.	Fem.	Neut.	Pl.		
Nominative:	... der	die	das	die	=	who; which; that
Accusative:	... den	die	das	die	=	whom; which; that
Genitive:	... dessen	deren	dessen	deren	=	whose; of which
Dative:	... dem	der	dem	denen	=	to whom; to which

Note.—Whereas, in English, different forms of relative pronouns are used when they refer to either persons (*who, whom, whose*) or things (*which, that*), in German no such distinction is made.

The relative pronoun is the same as the definite article, except in the genitive and in the dative plural, as shown above.

Relative pronouns cannot be omitted in German, as they often are in English: *The watch I bought*=Die Uhr, die ich gekauft habe. *The man you see there*=Der Mann, den Sie dort sehen.

Care must be taken when translating the English word *who*. As a question word (interrogative pronoun) it is **wer** (Wer ist

Halt! Wer geht da?

da? = *Who is there?*); as a relative pronoun
it is **der, die, das.** Similarly, *whom* as an
interrogative pronoun is **wen;** as a relative
pronoun it is **den, die** or **das,** according to
the gender or number of the noun or nouns
referred to.   *Whose* as an interrogative
pronoun is **wessen;** as a relative pronoun
it is **dessen** or **deren.** *To whom* as an interrogative pronoun is **wem;** as a relative pronoun
it is **dem, der,** or **denen.**

Der junge Mann ist drinnen
Die junge Dame ist draussen
Der junge Mann sagt: "Kommen Sie herein"
Die junge Dame sagt: "Kommen Sie heraus"

Er kommt zu Fuss (hier)her.
He comes here on foot.

Sie war gestern nicht hier.
She was not here yesterday.

Bleiben Sie hier.
Stay here.

Der Knabe ist oben
Das Mädel (=Mädchen) ist unten
Der Knabe sagt: "Komm herauf"
Das Mädel sagt: "Komm herunter"

Ich gehe heute Abend (dort)hin.
I am going there to-night.

Sie fährt mit der Strassenbahn (dort)hin.
She is going there by tram.

Er war nicht dort.
He was not there.

Er will nicht herkommen.
He does not want to come here.

Sie kann nicht hingehen.
She cannot go there.

There are two German words for *here*
and two for *there.* In former times in Eng-

lish a distinction was made between *here* and *hither*, *there* and *thither*. In German this distinction still holds good: **hierher** is *hither*; **dorthin** is *thither*. **Her** and **hin** are often used as abbreviations for **hierher** and **dorthin**, especially if attached to other words. **Her** denotes a motion towards the speaker, **hin** away from the speaker. **Da** is often used instead of **dort**, which is the more emphatic of the two. **Ah, da ist mein Regenschirm**=*Oh, there is my umbrella.* **Wo ist er? Dort!**=*Where is it? There!*

NEW NOUNS

DER	Vorort, -e	*suburb*
	Salon, -s	*drawing-room*
	Balkon, -s	*balcony*
	Boden, ¨-	*loft*
	Schiefer, -	*slate*
	Schornstein, -e	*chimney*
	Rauch	*smoke*
	Kleiderständer, -	*hall stand*
	Besucher, -	*visitor*
	Keller, -	*cellar*

DIE	Villa, Villen	*villa*
	Veranda, Veranden	*veranda*
	Kammer, -n	*small room*
	Leiter, -n	*ladder*
	Leine, -n	*line*
	Treppe, -n	*stair*
	Klingel, -n	*bell*
	Stunde, -n	*lesson*

DAS	Erdgeschoss, -e	*ground floor*
	Stockwerk, -e	*storey*
	Klosett, -s	*lavatory*
	Dach, ¨-er	*roof*

EXERCISE

I Answer in German

1. Wie viele Stockwerke hat das Haus? 2. In welchem Stockwerk ist das Wohnzimmer? 3. In welchem Zimmer isst man? 4. Was tut man in der Küche? 5. Wo bewahrt man die Kohlen auf? 6. Wo ist der Boden? 7. In welchem Raum ist das Tischchen, auf dem das Telefon steht? 8.

Er ist hier
Sie ist dort
Die Katze kommt hierher
Der Hund geht dorthin
Die Frau sagt: "Komm her"
Der Mann sagt: "Geh hin"

Wer ist die Dame, die gerade ihren Hut aufsetzt? 9. Was muss man tun, um die Haustür zu öffnen? 10. Was tut ein Besucher, wenn er in das Haus hinein will?

II Translate into German

1. Where do you live? 2. Is it far from here? 3. How many rooms has your house? 4. Is there a bathroom in his house? 5. On what floor is the nursery? 6. It is on the second floor. 7. Your trunks are in the loft. 8. You have beautiful flower beds in your garden, haven't you? 9. Have you got vegetables in your garden? 10. We have only a few flowers. 11. Is this child asleep? 12. The kitchen is near the dining room. 13. The study is on the left. 14. The telephone is on the right by the side of the hall stand. 15. The first door on the right leads to the sitting room, the second to the dining room and the third to the kitchen.

III Insert one of the following: der, die, das, den, dem, dessen, denen, deren

1. Das Buch, ... auf dem Tisch liegt, ist ein interessanter, englischer Roman. 2. Der Mann, ... das Buch geschrieben hat, ist tot. 3. Ich habe den Mann gesprochen, ... Sie den Brief geschrieben haben. 4. Der Bleistift,...auf dem Tisch liegt, ist gelb, aber der, ... Sie in der Hand haben, ist rot. 5. Die Lampe, ... dort steht, ist nicht sehr hell. 6. Das Kätzchen, ... Sie die Milch gegeben haben, gehört mir. 7. Die Füllfeder, ... ich in der Hand habe, gehört mir, aber die, ... dort liegt, können Sie haben. 8. Ist das Buch, ... Sie lesen, interessant? 9. Der Junge, ... Eltern Sie kennen, heisst Hans. 10. Das Öl, ... man dort findet, ist nicht sehr gut. 11. Der erste Mensch, ... flog[1], war Lilienthal. 12. Die Frau, ... dort sitzt, ist meine Grossmutter. 13. Das Kind, ... dort spielt, ist meine Kusine. 14. Die Personen, ... dort stehen, sind meine Verwandten. 15. Der Herr, ... Sie gestern getroffen[2] haben, ist mein Bruder. 16. Das Kind, ... Eltern Sie kennen, ist krank. 17. Die Leute, ... Kinder hier spielen, sind reich. 18. Das Kind, ... Sie Schokolade gegeben haben, ist der Sohn der Dame, ... Sie die Blumen gegeben haben.

(*Answers on page* 363)

EIN SONNTAGMORGENRITT IN GRUNEWALD

Diese Berliner sind in der glücklichen Lage, einen Sonntagmorgenritt unternehmen zu können. Sie reiten durch Grunewald, den vornehmen Villenvorort im Westen von Berlin.

(*Translation on page* 378)

glücklich	die Lage, -n	unternehmen	vornehm	der Vorort, -e
fortunate	*position*	*to undertake*	*fashionable*	*suburb*

---

[1] from **fliegen (flog, geflogen)** = *to fly*. [2] from **treffen (traf, getroffen)** = *to meet*.

SCHULE IM FREIEN

Das obere Bild zeigt Berliner Schulkinder beim "Ringelreihen". Das untere zeigt eine Klasse beim Englischunterricht in einer "Schule im Freien" im Grunewald bei Berlin. Einer der Schüler schreibt an die Tafel, während der Lehrer an die anderen Fragen stellt.

(Translation on page 378)

das Freie	**"Ringelreihen"**	**der Unterricht,**	**die Tafel, -n**	**Fragen stellen**
open air	*"Ring o' Roses"*	*lessons, instruction*	*blackboard*	*to ask questions*

196

EINUNDZWANZIGSTE LEKTION

Lass mich schlafen. Ich will noch nicht aufstehen

AM MORGEN

Im Hause der Familie Lessing hat man für die Gäste Platz gemacht. Herr und Frau Schulz schlafen im Fremdenzimmer, Grete schläft im Zimmer ihrer Kusine Hilde und Hans bei seinem Vetter Fritz.

Während die beiden Vettern noch fest schlafen, klopft jemand an die Tür.

Hans: Hörst du, Fritz?

Fritz: Was?

Hans: Jemand klopft an die Tür.

Fritz: Es ist mein Vater.

Hans: Warum klopft er?

Fritz: Um mich aufzuwecken.

Hans: Wieviel Uhr ist es?

Fritz: Halb acht. Hast du gut geschlafen?

Hans: Danke, ich habe sehr gut geschlafen.

Fritz: Willst du nicht aufstehen?

Hans: Noch nicht. Ich brauche mich nicht zu beeilen. Ich habe Ferien.

Fritz: Hast du nicht gestern gesagt, dass du heute früh aufstehen willst?

Hans: Ich habe inzwischen meine Meinung geändert. Es ist so schön im Bett zu liegen, und ich brauche noch nicht aufzustehen.

IN THE MORNING

In the house of the Lessing family room has been made for the guests. Mr. and Mrs. Schulz are sleeping in the guest room, Grete is sleeping in her cousin Hilde's room, and Hans with his cousin Fritz.

While the two (boy) cousins are still fast asleep someone knocks at their door.

Hans: Do you hear, Fritz?

Fritz: What?

Hans: Someone is knocking at the door.

Fritz: It's my father.

Hans: Why is he knocking?

Fritz: To wake me up.

Hans: What time is it?

Fritz: Half-past seven. Did you sleep well?

Hans: Thank you, I slept very well.

Fritz: Don't you want to get up?

Hans: Not yet. I needn't hurry. I am on holiday.

Fritz: Didn't you say yesterday that you wanted to get up early to-day?

Hans: I have changed my mind in the meantime. It is so lovely to lie in bed, and I needn't get up yet.

197

DAS BADEZIMMER—THE BATHROOM
(*English key on page* 369)

1. der Badeofen, ̈-	9. der Wäschekorb, ̈-e	17. die Nagelbürste, -n
2. der Bademantel, ̈-	10. der Rasierapparat, -e	18. der Wasserhahn, ̈-e
3. die Badewanne, -n	11. das Wasserglas, ̈-er	19. das Handtuch, ̈-er
4. die Seife, -n	12. das Mundwasser, -	20. die Zahnpaste, -n
5. der Schwamm, ̈-e	13. das Rasiermesser, -	21. die Zahnbürste, -n
6. das Badesalz, -e	14. die Seifenschale, -n	22. der Rasierpinsel, -
7. die Dusche, -n	15. der Waschlappen, -	23. die Rasierseife, -n
8. das Badehandtuch. ̈-er	16. das Waschbecken, -	24. der Spiegel, -

198

Fritz: Glücklicher Mensch![1] Ich muss jetzt aufstehen. Sonst komme ich zu spät ... Das ist aber komisch!

Hans: Was ist los?

Fritz: Ich kann mein Hemd nicht finden.

Hans: Da ist es, auf dem Bett.

Fritz: Schönen Dank. Kannst du vielleicht auch meine Unterhose[2] finden?

Hans: Da ist sie, unter dem Tisch.

Fritz: Du bist ein richtiger Detektiv.

Hans: Vielleicht werde ich mal[3] einer.

Fritz: Dann hilf mir auch meine Krawatte finden.

Fritz: Lucky man! I must get up now. Otherwise I'll be late. ... That's funny!

Hans: What's the matter?

Fritz: I can't find my shirt.

Hans: There it is, on the bed.

Fritz: Many thanks! Perhaps you can also find my underdrawers?

Hans: There they are, under the table.

Fritz: You are a real detective.

Hans: Perhaps some day I'll be one.

Fritz: Then help me to find my tie as well.

Die Kommode

die obere Schublade ———>

die mittlere Schublade ———>

die untere Schublade ———>

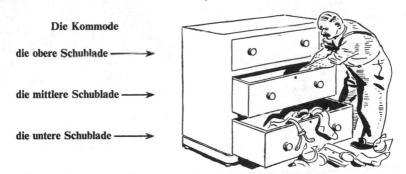

Hans: Da ist sie auf der Kommode, direkt vor deinen Augen.

Fritz: Unglaublich!

Hans: Vielleicht ist dein Kragen auch da?

Fritz: Tatsächlich, du hast recht. Nun habe ich meine Hose,[2] meine Weste, und meine Schuhe. Ich gehe ins Badezimmer mich waschen und ankleiden. Ich hoffe, du wirst angekleidet sein, wenn ich zurück bin.

Hans: Das ist nicht sehr wahrscheinlich.

Hans bleibt im Bett, bis sein Vetter zurückkommt. Dann steht auch er auf und geht ins Badezimmer. Er wäscht sich die Hände und

Hans: There it is, on the chest-of-drawers, right in front of your eyes.

Fritz: Unbelievable!

Hans: Perhaps your collar is also there.

Fritz: Indeed, you are right. Now I have got my trousers, my waistcoat, and my shoes. I am going to the bathroom to wash and dress. I hope you will be dressed when I come back.

Hans: That is not very likely.

Hans stays in bed until his cousin returns. Then he also gets up and goes to the bathroom. He washes his hands and his face, his

---

[1] Der Mann is *man*, as distinct from *woman*. Der Mensch is a more general term and includes both sexes, e.g., der Mensch ist sterblich=*man is mortal.*

[2] Note that die Hose (*trousers*) and die Unterhose (*underdrawers*) are singular in German, though plural in English. The same applies to die Brille (*spectacles*).

[3] Short form for einmal=*once, one (some) day.*

MISS LESSING'S BEDROOM

When you have finished the Lesson, use this picture to test your bedroom vocabulary. See how fully you can describe the scene without reference to the printed text.

das Gesicht, den Hals und die Ohren. Dann trocknet er sich mit einem Handtuch ab. Er putzt sich die Zähne mit einer Zahnbürste.

Dann kleidet er sich an. Zuerst zieht er die Strümpfe an, dann das Hemd, die Unterhose, die Hose und den Hosenträger. Vor dem Spiegel kämmt er sich die Haare mit einem Kamm und bürstet sie mit einer Haarbürste. Dann zieht er seine Jacke an und zuletzt die Schuhe. Er beeilt sich nicht. Er nimmt sich Zeit.

Um viertel zehn ist er fertig und geht ins Esszimmer hinunter, wo die Familie fast mit dem Frühstück fertig ist. Er sagt "Guten Morgen" und entschuldigt sich, dass er so spät kommt.

Das Bild auf dieser Seite zeigt uns das Schlafzimmer von Fräulein Lessing. Links in der Ecke steht der Toilettentisch mit einem grossen Spiegel, vor dem sie jeden Tag viel Zeit verbringt. Der Toilettentisch hat drei

neck and his ears. Then he dries himself with a towel. He cleans his teeth with a tooth brush.

Then he gets dressed. First he puts on his stockings, then his shirt, underdrawers, trousers and braces. In front of the mirror he combs his hair with a comb and brushes it with a hairbrush. Then he puts on his jacket and finally his shoes. He does not hurry. He takes his time.

At a quarter past nine he is ready and goes down to the dining-room, where the family have almost finished breakfast. He says "Good morning" and apologizes for being so late.

The picture on this page shows us Miss Lessing's bedroom. On the left in the corner stands the dressing table, with a large mirror, in front of which she spends much time every day. The dressing table has three

Schubladen. In der oberen sind ihre Toiletten-artikel: ihre Bürsten, Kämme, Puderdosen, Lippenstifte und ihr Parfüm. In der mittleren Schublade bewahrt sie ihre Juwelen auf: ihre Ringe, Armbänder und Broschen. Die untere Schublade enthält ihre Taschentücher und Schale, sowie ihr Nähzeug.

Rechts sicht man einen Schrank, der aus zwei Teilen besteht: dem Kleiderschrank, der ihre Kleider und Mäntel enthält, und dem Wäscheschrank mit vielen Fächern, in denen sie ihre Wäsche aufbewahrt.

Neben dem Bett steht ein Nachttischchen, auf dem sich ein Buch, ein Kasten Konfekt, ein Aschenbecher und eine Weckuhr befinden. Fräulein Lessing liebt es, im Bett zu lesen und dabei Konfekt zu essen oder Zigaretten zu rauchen.

drawers. In the top one are her toilet articles: her brushes, combs, boxes of powder, lipstick and her scent. In the middle drawer she keeps her jewels: her rings, bracelets and brooches. The lower drawer contains her handkerchiefs and her scarfs, as well as her sewing material.

On the right, one sees a cupboard consisting of two parts: the wardrobe, which contains her dresses and coats, and the linen cupboard with many shelves, in which she keeps her underwear.

Beside the bed stands a little bed-side table, on which there are a book, a box of sweets, an ash-tray and an alarm clock. Miss Lessing likes to read in bed while eating sweets or smoking cigarettes.

* * * * *

HOW TO APOLOGIZE

Es tut ihm leid

Entschuldigen Sie = Excuse me.
Ich bitte um Entschuldigung = I apologize.
Es tut mir leid = I am sorry.
Verzeihen Sie = Forgive me.
Ich bitte um Verzeihung = I beg your pardon.
Verzeihung! or Pardon! = Sorry!
Verzeihen Sie, bitte, dass ich Sie störe (dass ich so spät komme).
Please forgive me for disturbing you (for being so late).

CLEAN

When used as an adjective, *clean* is sauber. As a verb it can be translated in three ways:

(1) **Sauber machen,** used particularly of rooms.

(2) **Reinigen,** used of articles of clothing, etc.

(3) **Putzen,** which actually means *to polish* but is also used in connection with teeth: **die Zähne putzen**=*to clean one's teeth.*

NICHT SEHR SCHWER

Wenn eine Waage am Wege steht, wiegt man sich. Dies tat auch Wanda, die Wohlbeleibte. Wanda stieg auf die Waage. Die Waage schlug kräftig aus.

Die boshafte Freundin staunte: "Was, Wanda? Hundertzehn Kilo wiegst du?"

Meinte Wanda: "Ja, aber mit Hut und Handschuhen!"

Die Waage, -n, *weighing machine;* **der Weg, -e,** *way;* **wiegen,** *to weigh;* **wohlbeleibt,** *stout, well covered;* **ausschlagen,** *to incline, weigh down;* **kräftig,** *heavily;* **boshaft,** *malicious;* **staunen,** *to say in amazement;* **110 Kilo,** *approx. 240 lb.*

1. der Toilettentisch, -e
2. der Pantoffel, -
3. der Morgenrock, ··-e
4. der Handspiegel, -
5. die Haarbürste, -n
6. der Kamm, ··-e
7. die Gesichtskreme

8. der Spiegel, -
9. die Puderquaste, -n
10. die Puderdose, -n
11. der Zerstäuber, -
12. der Lippenstift, -e
13. die Blumenvase, -n
14. der Vorhang, ··-e

15. die Schnur, ··-e
16. der Lampenschirm, -e
17. der Wandschirm, -e
18. die Steckdose, -n
19. der Nachttisch, -e
20. die Nachttischlampe, -n
21. der Kalender, -

THE BEDROOM
on page 370)

22. der Wecker, -
23. der Bettvorleger, -
24. der Läufer, -
25. das Bett, -en
26. die Steppdecke, -n
27. die Bettdecke, -n
28. das Laken, -

29. die Matratze, -n
30. das Keilkissen, -
31. das Kissen, -
32. das Mädchen, -
33. die Schürze, -n
34. die Kommode, -n
35. die Photographie, -n

36. die Nippsfigur, -en
37. die Schublade, -n
38. der Kleiderschrank, ···-e
39. der Divan, -s or -e
40. das Kissen, -
41. die Decke, -n
42. der Puff, -e

FAMILIAR FORM

While in English the familiar form—*thou, thine, thee, ye*—is almost extinct, it is used in German when talking to children, near relations and intimate friends. There are different forms for singular and plural.

(1) *THOU, YE*

Ordinary Form	Familiar Form	
	Singular	*Plural*
Sie gehen	du gehst	ihr geht
kommen Sie?	kommst du?	kommt ihr?
Sie lesen	du liest	ihr lest
Sie sehen	du siehst	ihr seht
Sie geben	du gibst	ihr gebt
Sie nehmen	du nimmst	ihr nehmt
schlafen Sie?	schläfst du?	schlaft ihr?
haben Sie es?	hast du es?	habt ihr es?
Sie haben geschlafen	du hast geschlafen	ihr habt geschlafen
sind Sie müde?	bist du müde?	seid ihr müde?
werden Sie kommen?	wirst du kommen?	werdet ihr kommen?

The verb ends in -st in connection with du (*thou*) and in -t with ihr (*ye*).

Schlaf, Kindchen, schlaf!

The change of the root vowel in the third person singular of certain verbs (see page 86) also applies to the form with du, but not to the form with ihr, e.g.

ich lese,	du liest,	er liest;
wir lesen,	ihr lest,	sie lesen
ich gebe,	du gibst,	er gibt;
wir geben,	ihr gebt,	sie geben.

(2) *IMPERATIVE*

Ordinary Form	Familiar Form	
	Singular	*Plural*
hören Sie!	höre!	hört!
gehen Sie!	geh!	geht!
kommen Sie!	komm!	kommt!
stehen Sie auf!	steh auf!	steht auf!
lesen Sie!	lies!	lest!
sehen Sie!	sieh!	seht!
nehmen Sie!	nimm!	nehmt!
schlafen Sie!	schlaf!	schlaft!
seien Sie so gut![1]	sei so gut!	seid so gut!
haben Sie Geduld![2]	habe Geduld!	habt Geduld!

The familiar imperative singular of regular verbs is the same as the infinitive, but without the final n.   In the case of irregular verbs it is the same form of the verb as used

---

[1] *Be so kind.*   [2] *Have patience.*

with **du,** omitting the final -st. Note that verbs with **a** as their root vowel do not take an umlaut in the imperative. In the plural the same form is used as with **ihr** (for both regular and irregular verbs).

(3) YOUR

	Ordinary Form	Familiar Form	
		Singular	*Plural*
	Ihr Garten	dein Garten	euer Garten
	Ihre Wohnung	deine Wohnung	eure Wohnung
	Ihr Haus	dein Haus	euer Haus
	Ihre Brüder	deine Brüder	eure Brüder

Dein, and its plural **euer,** are used with masculines and neuters in the singular. **Deine** and **eure** are the corresponding forms for the feminine and plural (all genders).

(4) THEE

er liebt Sie	er liebt dich	er liebt euch
ich höre Sie	ich höre dich	ich höre euch
ich danke Ihnen	ich danke dir	ich danke euch
schreibt er Ihnen?	schreibt er dir?	schreibt er euch?

Dich is the accusative of **du** (compare **ich** and **mich).** The dative form is **dir.** The plural of both **dir** and **dich** is **euch.**

(5) REFLEXIVE

setzen Sie sich!	setze dich!	setzt euch!
haben Sie sich gewaschen?	hast du dich gewaschen?	habt ihr euch gewaschen?
wollen Sie sich hinlegen?	willst du dich hinlegen?	wollt ihr euch hinlegen?

Reflexive verbs use **dich** in the singular and **euch** in the plural.

ONE AND NONE

Hier ist ein Stuhl und da ist noch einer, aber für mich ist keiner da.
Here is a chair and there is another, but there is none for me.

Hier ist eine Tasse und da ist noch eine, aber für Sie ist keine da.
Here is a cup and there is another, but there is none for you.

Hier ist ein Messer und da ist noch eins, aber für ihn ist keins da.
Here is a knife and there is another, but there is none for him.

Ich habe einen Stuhl und Sie haben einen, aber mein Bruder hat keinen.
I have a chair and you have one, but my brother has none.

If *one* is used like *a* or *an*, i.e. followed by a noun or adjective, its German equivalent is **ein** with masculine and neuter, **eine** with feminine nouns. The same applies to **kein, keine.**

If no noun or adjective follows, different forms are used for masculine and neuter:

masc.	fem.	neut.	plur.
einer	eine	eins	—
keiner	keine	keins	keine

These are the forms for the nominative case. The accusative is like the nominative except for the masculine singular, which always takes the ending -en (see example 4 above). The forms for genitive and dative are the same as those of the indefinite article, i.e. **eines, einer, einem, einer,** etc.

NEW NOUNS

DER
Gast, ⋯-e	guest
Detektiv, -e	detective
Apparat, -e	apparatus
Hosenträger, -	braces
Teil, -e	part
Aschenbecher, -	ash-tray

DIE
Meinung, -en	mind, opinion
Kommode, -n	chest of drawers
Wäsche	underwear, linen, washing
Schublade, -n	drawer
Brosche, -n	brooch

DAS
Armband, ⋯-er	bracelet
Fach, ⋯-er	shelf, compartment
Regal, -e	book-shelf
Konfekt, -e	sweets

VERBS—REGULAR

glauben	=	to believe
rasieren	=	to shave
sich beeilen	=	to hurry
sich bürsten	=	to brush (oneself)
sich entschuldigen	=	to excuse oneself
aufwecken	=	to waken, arouse
ankleiden	=	to dress
sich kämmen	=	to comb (oneself)

VERBS—IRREGULAR

schlafen (schläft), schlief, geschlafen } *to sleep*

helfen (hilft), half, geholfen } *to help*

finden (findet), fand, gefunden } *to find*

anziehen (zieht ... an), zog ... an, angezogen } *to put on (clothes)*

IDIOMS

Sie haben recht	=	You are right
Er hat recht	=	He is right
Was ist los?	=	What is the matter?
Das ist aber komisch	=	That's funny
Schönen Dank	=	Many thanks

EXERCISES

I Answer in German

1. Wo schläft Hans? 2. Warum klopft Fritz's Vater an die Tür? 3. Warum will Hans nicht aufstehen? 4. Warum muss Fritz aufstehen? 5. Wie lange bleibt Hans im Bett? 6. Was zieht er zuletzt an? 7. Um wieviel Uhr ist er fertig? 8. Was bewahrt Fräulein Lessing in der oberen Schublade ihrer Kommode auf? 9. Wo bewahrt sie ihre Taschentücher auf? 10. Was steht neben ihrem Bett?

II Translate, using (a) the ordinary form; (b) the familiar form singular; (c) the familiar form plural

1. Please come in. 2. Do you play tennis? 3. Did you sleep well? 4. Give me your book. 5. Are you ill? 6. Will you come? 7. How are you? 8. I saw you yesterday.

III Translate into German

1. We get up at six o'clock. 2. Don't you go to bed early? 3. They don't wash in the bedroom. 4. I am going to lie down at eight o'clock. 5. Are there any chairs in the bedroom? 6. Don't forget to wake me up. 7. Everybody was asleep. 8. He did not want to wash before breakfast. 9. She put her jewellery into the third drawer of her dressing table. 10. He liked to read in bed.

(Answers on page 363)

WIEGENLIED

Singet leise, leise, leise,
singt ein flüsternd Wiegenlied,
von dem Monde lernt die Weise,
der so still am Himmel zieht.
   Singt ein Lied so süss gelinde,
wie die Quellen auf den Kieseln,
wie die Bienen um die Linde
summen, murmeln, flüstern, rieseln.

Clemens Brentano

Das Wiegenlied, -er, *cradle song;* **flüstern,** *to whisper;* **die Weise, -n,** *melody, manner, way;* **gelind, gelinde, -n,** *gentle;* **die Quelle, -n,** *fountain;* **der Kiesel,-,** *pebble;* **die Biene, -n,** *bee;* **die Linde, -n,** *lime tree;* **summen,** *to hum;* **rieseln,** *to ripple,*

ZWEIUNDZWANZIGSTE LEKTION

HERR BROWN IN BERLIN

Herr Brown hat kein deutsches Geld und geht deshalb zu einer Bank, um sein englisches Geld in deutsches umzuwechseln.

Herr B. [zu einem Bankbeamten]: Wollen Sie mir bitte englisches Geld in deutsches umwechseln?

Bankbeamter: Gewiss. Wieviel wünschen Sie zu wechseln?

Herr B.: Acht Pfund, bitte. Wie ist der Kurs heute?

Bankbeamter: Zwölf Mark für ein Pfund Sterling. Das macht sechsundneunzig Mark für acht Pfund. Wie möchten Sie das Geld haben, Scheine oder Hartgeld?

Herr B.: Achtzig Mark in Scheinen und den Rest in Hartgeld.

Bankbeamter [ihm das Geld reichend]: Ein Fünfzigmarkschein, ein Zwanzigmarkschein, ein Zehnmarkschein, zwei Fünfmarkstücke, ein Zweimarkstück und vier Markstücke.

Herr B. [nachdem er das Geld gezählt hat]: Stimmt. Vielen Dank. Guten Morgen.

Seine Taschen voll Geld, betritt Herr Brown den nächsten Zigarrenladen.

Herr B.: Eine Schachtel Zigaretten, bitte.

Verkäuferin: Welche Sorte wünschen Sie?

Herr B.: Geben Sie mir ... ich kenne die deutschen Sorten nicht.

Verkäuferin: Wünschen Sie milde oder starke?

Herr B.: Sie haben nicht zufällig englische Zigaretten?

Verkäuferin: Aber gewiss. Wir haben alle bekannten Sorten.

Herr B.: Dann geben Sie mir, bitte, zwanzig Player's und, um sie zu probieren, ein Päckchen deutsche Zigaretten. Wie heisst die Sorte, für die so viel Reklame in der Untergrundbahn gemacht wird?

Verkäuferin: Reemtsma? Manoli?

Herr B.: Richtig. Manoli. Geben Sie mir bitte ein Päckchen. Was macht das?

MR. BROWN IN BERLIN

Mr. Brown has no German money and therefore goes to a bank to change his English money into German.

Mr. B. [to a bank clerk]: Would you please change English money into German for me?

Bank Clerk: Certainly. How much do you wish to change?

Mr. B.: Eight pounds, please. What is the rate of exchange today?

Bank Clerk: Twelve marks for one pound sterling. That makes ninety-six marks for eight pounds. How would you like to have the money, in notes or coins?

Mr. B.: Eighty marks in notes and the remainder in coins.

Bank Clerk [handing him the money]: One fifty-mark note, one twenty-mark note, one ten-mark note, two five-mark pieces, one two-mark piece and four one-mark pieces.

Mr. B. [after having counted the money]: Right. Many thanks. Good morning.

His pockets full of money, Mr. Brown enters the nearest tobacconist's shop.

Mr. B.: A packet of cigarettes, please.

Shopgirl: What kind would you like?

Mr. B.: Give me ... I don't know the German makes.

Shopgirl: Do you want mild or strong?

Mr. B.: You haven't any English cigarettes by any chance?

Shopgirl: Certainly. We have all the well-known brands.

Mr. B.: Then give me twenty Player's, please, and, in order to try them, a packet of German cigarettes. What is the kind called, for which so much advertising is done in the subway?

Shopgirl: Reemtsma? Manoli?

Mr. B.: Right. Manoli. Please give me a packet. How much is that?

DER TABAKHÄNDLER—THE TOBACCONIST
(English key on page 370)

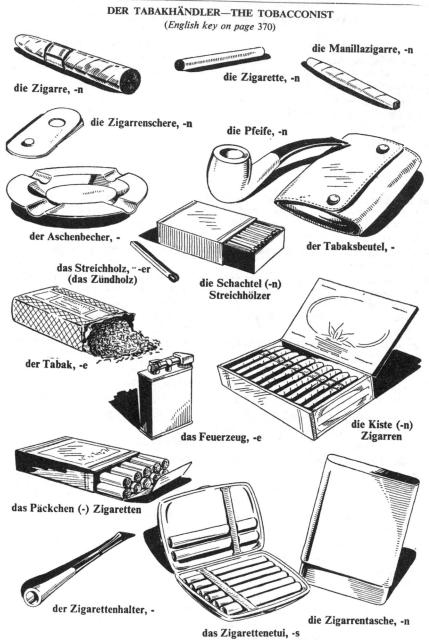

die Zigarre, -n

die Zigarette, -n

die Manillazigarre, -n

die Zigarrenschere, -n

die Pfeife, -n

der Aschenbecher, -

der Tabaksbeutel, -

das Streichholz, " -er
(das Zündholz)

die Schachtel (-n)
Streichhölzer

der Tabak, -e

das Feuerzeug, -e

die Kiste (-n)
Zigarren

das Päckchen (-) Zigaretten

der Zigarettenhalter, -

das Zigarettenetui, -s

die Zigarrentasche, -n

Verkäuferin: Sechzig Pfennig das Päckchen mit zehn, und eine Mark sechzig die englischen.

Herr B.: Ich habe ganz vergessen—geben Sie mir bitte auch eine Kiste Zigarren, ein Geschenk für meine Freunde, und eine Schachtel Streichhölzer. Das ist aber wirklich alles für heute.

Er bezahlt, zündet sich eine Zigarette an und ist wieder auf der Strasse. Er bemerkt ein Papiergeschäft auf der anderen Seite der Strasse und erinnert sich, dass er viele Briefe schreiben muss, aber kein Schreibmaterial hat. Deshalb überquert er die Strasse und betritt das Papiergeschäft, um die nötigen Einkäufe zu machen.

Verkäufer: Womit kann ich Ihnen dienen?

Herr B.: Ich möchte etwas Briefpapier.

Verkäufer: In welcher Farbe wünschen Sie es, mein Herr?

Herr B.: Zeigen Sie mir weisses, aber von guter Qualität, bitte.

Verkäufer: Wünschen Sie auch Umschläge?

Herr B.: Jawohl, und auch Tinte.

Verkäufer: Gewöhnliche Tinte oder Füllfedertinte?

Herr B.: Schwarze Füllfedertinte, bitte. Verkaufen Sie auch Ansichtskarten?

Verkäufer: Jawohl, wir haben eine grosse Auswahl: Ansichten der Stadt, Photographien von Filmstars, Reproduktionen der Meisterwerke aus den Berliner Museen. Bitte, wählen Sie.

Herr B.: Was kosten diese?

Verkäufer: 15 Pfennig das Stück. Wir haben auch Mappen mit einem Dutzend zu 1.50 Mark.

Herr B.: Bitte, zeigen Sie mir einige.

Verkäufer: Mit grösstem Vergnügen.

Er bringt einen grossen Kasten, stellt ihn auf den Ladentisch und nimmt einige Mappen mit Ansichtskarten heraus, die er Herrn Brown vorlegt.

Herr B.: Ich nehme diese. Nun habe ich alles, was ich brauche. Können Sie mir auf zwanzig Mark herausgeben?

Shopgirl: Sixty pfennigs the packet of ten and one mark sixty the English ones.

Mr. B.: I quite forgot—please give me also a box of cigars, a present for my friends, and a box of matches. But that is really all for to-day.

He pays, lights a cigarette and is back in the street. He notices a stationer's on the other side of the road and remembers that he has to write many letters but has no writing materials. So he crosses the street and enters the paper shop to make the necessary purchases.

Assistant: What can I do for you?

Mr. B.: I should like some notepaper.

Assistant: What colour do you want (it), sir?

Mr. B.: Show me some white, but of good quality, please.

Assistant: Do you want envelopes also?

Mr. B.: Yes, and ink as well.

Assistant: Ordinary ink or fountain-pen ink?

Mr. B.: Black fountain-pen ink, please. Do you also sell picture-postcards?

Assistant: Yes, we have a large selection: views of the city, photos of film stars, reproductions of the masterpieces from the Berlin museums. Please take your choice.

Mr. B.: How much are these?

Assistant: 15 pfennigs each. We also have folders with one dozen at one mark fifty.

Mr. B.: Please show me some.

Assistant: With the greatest of pleasure.

He brings a big box, puts it on the counter and takes out some folders with picture-postcards, which he puts in front of Mr. Brown.

Mr. B.: I'll have these. Now I have got everything I want. Can you give me change for twenty marks?

PAPIERWAREN—STATIONERY
(*English key on page* 370)

der Kalender, -

die Schreibblock, "-e

das Heft, -e

das Lineal, -e

der Federhalter, -

der Füllbleistift, -e

der Bleistift, -e

der Bleistiftanspitzer, -

der Füllfederhalter, -

die Schreibfeder, -n

der Kugelschreiber,-

das Tintenfass, "-er

der Radiergummi, -s

die Heftklammer, -n

das Notizbuch, "-er

die Tintenflasche, -n

der Brieföffner, -

der Siegellack

das Siegel, -

das Briefpapier, -e

der Aufklebezettel,

der Briefbogen, -

die Briefwaage, -n

die Postkarte, -n

der Briefumschlag, "-e

die Ansichtskarte, -n

Verkäufer: Haben Sie kein Kleingeld?

Herr B.: Leider nicht.

Wir wissen natürlich, dass Herr Brown zwei Fünfmarkstücke in der Tasche hat. Er will aber kleines Geld haben, weil er sich in einem Zeitungskiosk eine englische Zeitung kaufen will. Der Verkäufer gibt ihm auf zwanzig Mark heraus. Herr Brown steckt das Kleingeld in die Tasche, kauft seine Zeitung und geht ins Hotel zurück, um seine Briefe zu schreiben.

Mit den Briefen, die er geschrieben hat, in der Tasche und einem Paket unter dem Arm verlässt Herr Brown zwei Stunden später das Hotel. Nachdem er sich mehrmals erkundigt hat, wo sich das nächste Postamt befindet, findet er endlich eins am Ende der Strasse.

Herr B. [zu einer Postbeamtin am Schalter]: Eine Zehnpfennigmarke, bitte, und . . .

Beamtin: Schalter Nummer drei, bitte.

Herr B. (zu der Beamtin am Schalter Nr. 3): Können Sie mir bitte sagen, wieviel das Porto nach England beträgt? Ich habe drei Briefe. Diesen möchte ich einschreiben lassen, diesen als gewöhnlichen Brief senden und diesen als Drucksache.

Beamtin: Ich sehe, Sie sind Ausländer. Ich werd die Briefe für Sie frankieren. Für den Einschreibebrief müssen Sie dieses Formular ausfüllen. Hier schreiben Sie den Namen und die Adresse des Empfängers und dort die des Absenders, das heisst Ihren Namen und Ihre Adresse. So, das ist richtig, hier ist die Quittung.

Herr B.: Das ist sehr liebenswürdig von Ihnen. Noch eine Frage. Wo befindet sich die Paketannahme?

Beamtin: Ganz hinten links. Ich fürchte, Sie werden anstehen müssen.

Herr Brown stellt sich ans Ende der "Schlange" und wartet, bis er an die Reihe kommt. Der Beamte legt das Paket auf eine Waage. Es wiegt drei Pfund und fünfzig Gramm, und Herr B. muss dafür neunzig Pfennig bezahlen.

Assistant: Have you no small change?

Mr. B.: Unfortunately not.

Of course we know that Mr. Brown has two five-mark pieces in his pocket. However, he wants to have smaller change because he wants to buy an English newspaper from a newspaper kiosk. The assistant gives him change for twenty marks. Mr. Brown puts the change in his pocket, buys his newspaper and goes back to the hotel to write his letters.

With the letters which he has written in his pocket, and a parcel under his arm, Mr. Brown leaves the hotel two hours later. After having inquired several times where the nearest post office is, he finally finds one at the end of the street.

Mr. B [to a woman assistant at the counter]: A ten-pfennig stamp, please, and . . .

Assisant: Counter number three, please.

Mr. B. (to assistant at counter No. 3): Please, can you tell me how much the postage is to England? I've three letters. This one I would like to have registered, this one to be sent as an ordinary letter, and this one as printed matter.

Assistant: I see you are a foreigner. I'll stamp the letters for you. For the registered letter you'll have to fill in this form. Here you write the name and address of the addressee and there that of the sender, i.e. your name and address. Yes, that's right, here is the receipt.

Mr. B.: That is very kind of you. Yet another question. Where is the parcel counter?

Assistant: Right at the back on the left. I'm afraid you'll have to queue up.

Mr. Brown joins the end of the queue and waits until his turn comes. The official puts the parcel on the scales. It weighs three pounds and fifty grammes and Mr. B. has to pay ninety pfennigs for it.

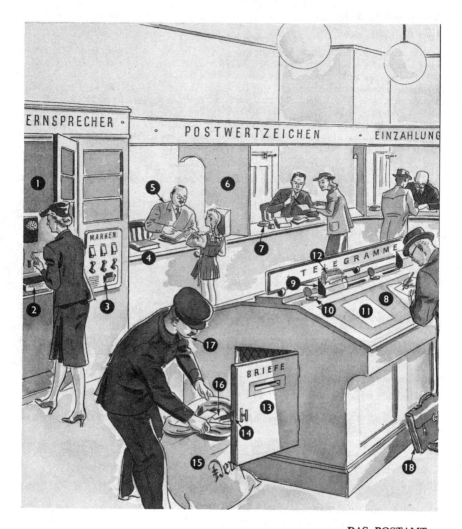

ERNSPRECHER · POSTWERTZEICHEN · EINZAHLUNG

MARKEN

BRIEFE

TELEGRAMME

1. die Telefonkabine, -n
2. das Telefonbuch, ···-er
3. der Briefmarkenautomat, -en
4. der Schalter, -
5. der Beamte, -n
6. die Scheidewand, ···-e

7. der Schwamm, ···-e
8. das Schreibpult, -e
9. der Formularhalter, -
10. das Tintenfass, ···-er
11. das Löschpapier, -e
12. das Telegrammformular, -e

13. der Briefkasten, ···-
14. das Schloss, ···-er
15. der Postsack, ···-e
16. der Brief, -e
17. der Briefträger, -
18. die Aktentasche, -n

Here are the English equivalents of some of the signs shown in the picture : **Postwertzeichen,** *Postage Stamps;* **Einzahlungen,** *Postal Orders;* **Postsparkasse,** *Savings Bank;*

212

THE POST OFFICE
on page 371)

19. die Beleuchtung, -en	25. das Fach, ··-er	31. das Paket, -e
20. die Decke, -n	26. die Tür, -en	32. der Zettel, -
21. die Wand, ··-e	27. die Paketwaage, -n	33. die Schürze, -n
22. die Wanduhr, -en	28. das Formular, -e	34. das eingeschriebene
23. der Flugpostkasten, ··	29. die Leimtopf, ··-e	35. der Bindfaden, ··- [Paket
24. das Scharnier, -e	30. der Pinsel, -	36. das Siegel, -

Gebührentafel, *Postal Rates ;* Postlagernde Sendungen, *Poste Restante ;* Paket-Annahme, *Parcels.* Note that postage stamps may be called either Briefmarken or Postwertzeichen.

213

AUF DEM POSTAMT—AT THE POST OFFICE

Wie hoch ist das Porto, bitte?
What is the postage, please?

Zwei Zehnpfennig Marken, bitte.
Two ten-pfennig stamps, please.

Ich möchte diesen Brief einschreiben lassen.
I want to have this letter registered.

Sind Briefe für mich da?
Are there any letters for me?

Bitte senden Sie meine Briefe an diese Adresse.
Please forward my letters to this address.

Ich möchte mit London sprechen.
I wish to telephone to London.

die Briefmarke, -n	= *postage stamp*
die Postkarte, -n	= *postcard*
die Luftpost	= *air-mail*
der Briefkasten, ¨ -	= *letter box*
das Telegramm, -e	= *telegram*
die Postanweisung, -en	= *money order*
das Paket, -e	= *parcel*
der Einschreibebrief, -e	= *registered letter*
das Telefon, -e	} = *telephone*
der Fernsprecher, -	
telefonieren	= *to telephone*
die Telefonnummer, -n	= *telephone number*
das Telefonbuch, ¨-er	= *telephone directory*
die Telefonzelle, -n	= *telephone box*

Er wechselt einen Hundertmarkschein

Er steigt von dem Omnibus in die Strassenbahn um

Er kleidet sich um (Er zieht sich um)

TO CHANGE

Können Sie einen Hundertmarkschein wechseln?
Can you change a hundred-mark note?

Deutsches Geld in englisches umwechseln.
To change German into English money.

Die Schuhe sind zu eng. Es ist besser, Sie tauschen sie um.
The shoes are too narrow. You had better change them.

Müssen wir uns zum Abendessen umziehen?
Do we have to change for dinner?

Sie müssen zweimal umsteigen.
You have to change (trains) twice.

Ich habe meine Meinung geändert.
I have changed my mind.

The foregoing sentences illustrate the various ways in which the verb *to change* can be translated. Note the special and limited meaning of each of the German expressions:

wechseln = *to change money, seats, partners, etc.*

umwechseln = *to change into the currency of another country.*

umtauschen = *to change an article bought from a shop.*

umziehen (or **umkleiden**)= *to change clothes.*

umsteigen = *to change trains or buses, etc.*

ändern = *to change in the sense of to alter.*

Note.—*Small change* is **das Kleingeld**.

TO KNOW

Ich kenne diesen Herrn nicht.
I do not know this gentleman.

Ich weiss, wer er ist.
I know who he is.

Er kennt Berlin gut.
He knows Berlin well.

Wissen Sie, ob Ihr Bruder ihn kennt?
Do you know if your brother knows him?

Haben Sie ihn gekannt?
Did you know him?

Haben Sie das gewusst?
Did you know that?

Kennen and **wissen** both mean *to know.* **Kennen** is *to be acquainted with, to know a person* or *to be familiar with something.* **Wissen** is *to know about them, to have knowledge of.* They are conjugated as follows:

kennen: Present, **ich kenne;** imperfect, **ich kannte;** perfect, **ich habe gekannt.**

wissen: Present, **ich (er, sie, es) weiss, wir (Sie, sie) wissen;** imperfect, **ich wusste;** perfect, **ich habe gewusst.**

HOW TO TRANSLATE *RIGHT*

Das ist nicht richtig=*That is not right.*

Richtig is *right,* as opposed to *wrong.*

Nehmen Sie die erste Strasse rechts.
Take the first street on the right.

Rechts is *on* (or *to*) *the right.* **Der rechte Arm**=*the right arm;* **die rechte Hand**=*the right hand.* (*On the left* is **links; der linke Arm**=the left arm, etc.)

Die Rechnung stimmt=*The bill is right.*

Das stimmt=*That's right.*

Stimmt is used in connection with sums of money or to express agreement.

AUF DEM WEIHNACHTSMARKT

Spruchherzen, d.h. Lebkuchen mit einem Spruch in Zuckeraufguss, sind eine altherkömmliche Ware des deutschen Weihnachtsmarkts.   (*Translation on page 378*)

die Weihnachten   **der Spruch, ·· -c**   **d.h. (das heisst)**   **der Lebkuchen,-**   **altherkömmlich**
Christmas   *motto*   *that is*   *gingerbread*   *traditional*

SEPARABLE VERBS

Present Tense

Sie fahren um 8 Uhr ab.
Der Zug kommt in Berlin an.
Wir gehen fort.
Ich komme mit.
Sie setzt sich hin.
Er steht auf.
Sie machen die Tür auf.

Imperative

Fahren Sie um 8 Uhr ab!
Gehen Sie fort!
Kommen Sie mit!
Setzen Sie sich hin!
Stehen Sie auf!
Machen Sie die Tür auf!
Gehen Sie bitte nicht fort!

Imperfect

Sie fuhren um 8 Uhr ab.
Der Zug kam in Berlin an.
Wir gingen fort.
Ich kam mit.
Sie setzte sich hin.
Er stand auf.

Past Participle

Sie sind um 8 Uhr ab*ge*fahren.
Der Zug ist in Berlin an*ge*kommen.
Wir sind fort*ge*gangen.
Ich bin mit*ge*kommen.
Sie hat sich hin*ge*setzt.
Er ist auf*ge*standen.

Ich steige ein

Ich steige

Ich steige aus

Ich steige auf

Ich steige ab

Infinitive

(a) without **zu**

Sie werden um 8 Uhr abfahren.
Der Zug wird in Berlin ankommen.
Wir wollen fortgehen.
Ich kann nicht mitkommen.
Sie müssen sich hinsetzen.

(b) with **zu**

Sie hoffen, um 8 Uhr abzufahren.
Wir brauchen nicht fortzugehen.
Sie haben Zeit sich hinzusetzen.
Der Kranke hofft, bald aufzustehen.
Sie brauchen nicht mitzukommen.
Er wünscht die Tür aufzumachen.
Es ist zu spät, dort hinzugehen.
Es ist nicht möglich, auf den Turm
hinaufzusteigen.

The commonest separable prefixes are: **ab, an, auf, aus, ein, fort, hin, her, mit, nach, vor** and **zu**. In the present and imperfect (in principal clauses), and in the imperative, they are separated from the verb and placed at the end of the sentence.

In the past participle the prefix is attached to the verb and precedes the **ge-**. The prefix also precedes an infinitive, and if the infinitive requires **zu,** the **zu** is placed between the prefix and the verb.

In dependent clauses the prefix is attached to the verb:

Er schreibt, dass er abends ankommt.
Sie war traurig, weil ich fortging.
Kennen Sie den Herrn, der heute abend herkommt?

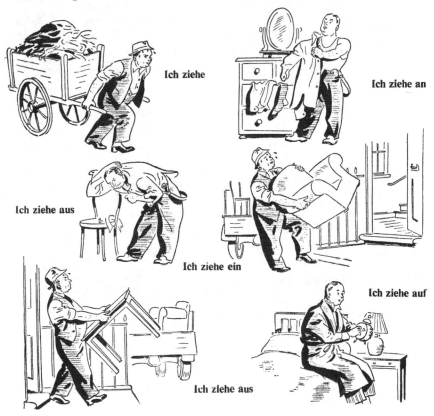

Ich ziehe

Ich ziehe an

Ich ziehe aus

Ich ziehe ein

Ich ziehe auf

Ich ziehe aus

NEW NOUNS

DER
Laden, ··-	shop
Kurs, -e	rate of exchange
Kasten, ···-	box, case
Schein, -e	note (of money), receipt
Einkauf, ···-e	purchase
Ausländer, -	foreigner

DIE
Bank, -en	bank
Reklame, -n	advertisement
Mappe, -n	folder, cover
Sorte, -n	make, variety
Tinte, -n	ink
Karte, -n	card, map
Schlange, -n	snake, queue
Reihe, -n	turn
Waage, -n	scales, weighing machine

DAS
Paket, -e	} packet
Päckchen, -	

VERBS—REGULAR

wechseln	=	to change
reichen	=	to hand, reach
anzünden (sep.)	=	to light
verkaufen	=	to sell
zeigen	=	to show
wünschen	=	to wish
zählen	=	to count
bemerken	=	to notice
wählen	=	to choose
brauchen	=	to require
sich erkundigen	=	to enquire

VERBS—IRREGULAR

betreten (betritt),
betrat, betreten } = to enter

vergessen (vergisst),
vergass, vergessen } = to forget

betragen (beträgt),
betrug, betragen } = to amount

senden (sendet),
sandte, gesandt } = to send

anstehen (steht ... an),
stand...an, angestanden } = to queue up

EXERCISES

I Answer in German

1. Wo kann man Geld umwechseln? 2. Wo kauft man Zigaretten? 3. Kennt Herr Brown die deutschen Sorten? 4. Was hat er vergessen? 5. Was kauft er in dem Papiergeschäft? 6. Wo schreibt er seine Briefe? 7. Was tut er, nachdem er seine Briefe geschrieben hat? 8. Was muss man tun, wenn man einen Brief einschreiben lassen will? 9. Warum muss Herr Brown anstehen? 10. Wie sendet man durch die Post (a) einen wichtigen Brief; (b) eine Zeitung; (c) Geld?

II Give the third person singular of (a) Present Tense; (b) Past Tense; (c) Perfect, of the following verbs:

1. aufstehen. 2. fortgehen. 3. mitkommen. 4. abfahren. 5. ankommen. 6. sich ankleiden.

III Translate into German

1. My cigars are better than your cigarettes. 2. The best tobacco is very dear. 3. German cigarettes are cheaper. 4. They are 5 pfennigs each. 5. How much is a packet of ten? 6. He has to write many letters. 7. Will you change your English banknotes? 8. I shall not forget to buy a box of matches and some ink. 9. Is there a stationer's near here? 10. I should like some picture-postcards.

(*Answers on page 363*)

DER ERSTE MAI

Der erste Tag im Monat Mai
ist mir der glücklichste von allen.
Dich sah ich und gestand dir frei,
den ersten Tag im Monat Mai,
dass dir mein Herz ergeben sei.
Wenn mein Geständnis dir gefallen,
so ist der erste Tag im Mai
für mich der glücklichste von allen.

Friedrich von Hagedorn

Glücklich, *lucky;* gestehen, *to confess;* ergeben, *devoted;* das Geständnis, *confession;* gefallen, *to please.*

DREIUNDZWANZIGSTE LEKTION

IM KAUFHAUS

Herr und Frau Schulz gehen mit ihren Kindern Einkäufe machen. Zuerst gehen sie in ein Einheitspreisgeschäft.

Herr Schulz [wendet sich an eine Verkäuferin]: Bitte, wo ist die Abteilung für Toilettenartikel?

Verkäuferin: Gehen Sie geradeaus bis in die Mitte und dann nach rechts.

Hans: Mama, du hast doch nicht vergessen, was du uns versprochen hast?

Frau S.: Du wirst dein Eis schon bekommen. Sei nicht so ungeduldig.

Herr S.: Da sind wir. [Zu einer Verkäuferin] Bedienen Sie hier?

Verk.: Gewiss, mein Herr, was steht zu Diensten?

Frau S.: Geben Sie mir ein Stück von dieser Seife.

Verk.: Bitte schön. Sonst noch etwas?

Frau S.: Nein, danke. Oh doch, Eine Tube Zahnpaste.

Verk.: Bitte schön. Eine Mark die Tube.

Frau S.: Ist sie auch gut?

Verk.: Es ist die beste Zahnpaste. Eine sehr bekannte Marke.

Frau S.: Das ist alles für heute. Was macht das zusammen?

Verk.: Eine Mark fünfzig, bitte.

[Herr Schulz bezahlt.]

Frau S.: Ich möchte lieber in ein Kaufhaus gehen. Ich glaube nicht, dass ich hier alles bekomme, was ich brauche.

Herr S.: Wie du willst.

Hans: Aber, Mama, dann kann ich doch nicht haben, was du uns versprochen hast.

Frau S.: Mein Sohn, du fällst mir wirklich auf die Nerven.

Sie verlassen das Einheitspreisgeschäft und gehen in ein Kaufhaus.

Ein Empfangsherr: Kann ich Ihnen behilflich sein?

IN THE STORE

Mr. and Mrs. Schulz go shopping with their children. First they go to a one-price store.

Mr. Schulz (addressing a salesgirl): Where is the department for toilet articles, please?

Salesgirl: Go straight ahead up to the middle, and then to the right.

Hans: Mother, you have not forgotten what you promised us?

Mr. S.: You will get your ice-cream in good time. Don't be so impatient.

Mr. S.: There we are [To the salesgirl] Are you serving here?

Salesgirl: Certainly, sir, what can I do for you?

Mrs. S.: Give me a piece of this soap.

Salesgirl: There. Anything else?

Mrs. S.: No, thank you. Oh yes. A tube of toothpaste.

Salesgirl: There. One mark the tube.

Mrs. S.: Is it good?

Salesgirl: It is the best toothpaste. A well-known brand.

Mrs. S.: That is all for to-day. How much is that altogether?

Salesgirl: One mark fifty, please.

[Mr. Schulz pays.]

Mrs. S.: I would rather go to a department store. I don't think I shall get all I need here.

Mr. S.: As you like.

Hans: But, Mummy, then I can't have what you promised us.

Mrs. S.: My son, you are really getting on my nerves.

They leave the one-price store and go to a department store.

Floorwalker: Can I help you?

Frau S.: Ich möchte ein Paar Handschuhe.

Empfangsherr: Die Handschuhabteilung ist im ersten Stock. Wenn Sie den Fahrstuhl nehmen wollen . . .

Frau S.: Das lohnt sich kaum. Wir können die Treppe hinaufgehen. Ich danke Ihnen.

Sie gehen in den ersten Stock hinauf und wenden sich an eine Verkäuferin in der Handschuhabteilung.

Frau S.: Ich möchte ein Paar gute Glacé Handschuhe, Grösse sechseinhalb.

Verk.: Welche Farbe, bitte?

Frau S.: Dunkelblau, zu meiner Handtasche passend.

Die Verkäuferin bringt verschiedene Paare und legt sie der Dame vor.

Verk.: Dies ist eine ausgezeichnete Qualität. Die neuste Mode . . . sehr elegant.

Frau S.: Das ist keine gute Qualität. Haben Sie nichts besseres?—Die Farbe gefällt mir nicht.—Das ist nicht die richtige Grösse.—Das ist viel zu teuer.

Nachdem sie sich viele Handschuhe angesehen und mehrere anprobiert hat, findet sie endlich ein Paar, das ihr gefällt und nicht zu teuer ist.

Verk.: Bitte an der Kasse zu zahlen. Hier ist der Kassenzettel.

Nachdem Herr S. bezahlt hat und sie die Handschuhe von der Warenausgabe abgeholt haben, besuchen sie noch andere Abteilungen. Sie kaufen Strümpfe, Socken, Wäsche und sogar ein Kleid für Grete.

Herr S.: Du musst sehr müde sein. Ich schlage vor, dass ihr euch in den Erfrischungsraum setzt und etwas trinkt. Hans kann das versprochene Eis essen. Ich gehe inzwischen in den Frisiersalon, mir die Haare schneiden zu lassen. In einer Viertelstunde bin ich zurück.

Frau S.: Du hast recht. Ich kann nicht weiter. Wir werden dich im Erfrischungsraum erwarten, aber ich bitte dich, bleibe nicht zu lange.

Während seine Frau und seine Kinder sich in den Erfrischungsraum setzen, geht Herr

Mrs. S.: I want a pair of gloves.

Floorwalker: The glove department is on the first floor. If you wish to take the lift . . .

Mrs. S.: That is hardly worth while. We can walk up the stairs. Thank you.

They walk up to the first floor and address a salesgirl in the glove department.

Mrs. S.: I want a pair of good kid gloves, size $6\frac{1}{2}$.

Salesgirl: What colour, please?

Mrs. S.: Dark blue, to match my handbag.

The salesgirl brings various pairs and puts them in front of the lady.

Salesgirl: This is an excellent quality. The latest fashion . . . very smart.

Mrs. S.: This is not a good quality. Haven't you got anything better?—I don't like the colour.—That is not the right size.—That is much too expensive.

After having looked at many gloves and tried on several, she at last finds a pair which she likes and which is not too dear.

Salesgirl: Please pay at the desk. Here is the check.

After Mr. S. has paid and they have collected the gloves from the packing counter, they visit other departments. They buy stockings, socks, underwear and even a frock for Grete.

Mr. S.: You must be very tired. I suggest that you sit down in the refreshment room and have something to drink. Hans can eat the promised ice-cream. Meanwhile I'll go to the hairdresser's to have a haircut. I'll be back in a quarter-of-an-hour.

Mrs. S.: You are right. I can't walk any further. We shall wait for you in the refreshment room, but please don't stay too long.

While his wife and his children are sitting down in the refreshment room, Mr.

Schulz in den Frisiersalon, der sich im Kaufhaus befindet. Er muss zehn Minuten warten, bis er an die Reihe kommt.

Friseur: Der nächste Herr, bitte.

Herr S.: Bitte, Haarschneiden und Rasieren.

Friseur: Wie möchten Sie das Haar geschnitten haben?

Herr S.: Ziemlich kurz an den Seiten, nicht zu kurz vorn.

Nachdem der Frisör ihn rasiert und ihm die Haare geschnitten hat, fragt er, ob er ihm auch den Kopf waschen soll. Herr Schulz, der schon ungeduldig ist, weil seine Frau auf ihn wartet, sagt: "Nein, danke, ein andermal", bezahlt und eilt zurück zu seiner Familie.

Schulz goes to the barber's shop which is in the store. He has to wait ten minutes until his turn comes.

Barber: The next gentleman, please.

Mr. S.: Haircut and shave, please.

Barber: How would you like yóur hair cut?

Mr. S.: Rather short at the sides, not too short at the front.

After having shaved him and cut his hair, the hairdresser asks him whether he wishes to have a shampoo as well. Mr. Schulz, who is already impatient because his wife is waiting for him, says: "No, thanks, another time", pays and hurries back to his family.

KISTEN, KÄSTEN UND GEFÄSSE—CHESTS, BOXES AND CONTAINERS

der Koffer, -   die Schachtel, -n   der Kasten, ‥-   die Flasche, -n

die Tüte, -n   das Paket, -e   der Ballen, -   das Fass, ‥-er

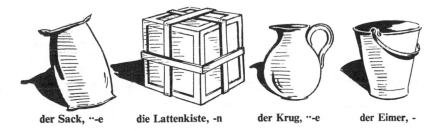

der Sack, ‥-e   die Lattenkiste, -n   der Krug, ‥-e   der Eimer, -

1. die Herrenkleidung, -en
2. die Schublade, -n
3. der Schrank, ··-e
4. die Kleiderpuppe, -n
5. der Auslagenständer, -
6. der Toilettenartikel, -
7. das Regal, -e

8. die Zahnbürste, -n
9. die Seife, -n
10. der Preiszettel, -
11. der Topf, ···-e
12. die Schaufel, -n
13. das Badesalz, -e
14. die Schere, -n

15. die Verkäuferin, -nen
16. das Packpapier, -e
17. der Bindfaden, ···-
18. die Waage, -n
19. der Ladentisch, -e
20. der Kunde, -n
21. das Fahrstuhlfräulein, -

THE STORE
on page 371)

22. der Fahrstuhl, ···-e
23. der Pullover, -
24. die Kassierin, -nen
25. die Kasse, -n
26. die Registrierkasse, -n
27. die Damenabteilung, -en
28. der Stoff, -e

29. der Verkäufer, -
30. das Metermass, -e
31. der Vorhang, ···-e
32. die Kundin, -nen
33. die Pendeltür, -en
34. der Türgriff, -e
35. der Türsteher, -

36. das Schaufenster, -
37. der Kleiderstoff, -e
38. die Kleiderbürste, -n
39. das Reklameschild, -er
40. der Schwamm, ···-e
41. die Kopfbürste, -n
42. der Rasierapparat, -e

SCHUHE UND STIEFEL—SHOES AND BOOTS
(English key on page 371)

1. der Absatz, ¨-e
2. der Rist, -e
3. die Sohle, -n
4. der Rahmen, -
5. die Kappe, -n
6. der Schnürsenkel,
7. die Zunge, -n
   (die Lasche, -n)

der Halbschuh, -e

der Schnürstiefel, -

die Gamasche, -n

der Reitstiefel, -

der Lackschuh, -e

der Spangenschuh, -e

die Pumps

die Sandale, -n

der Tennisschuh, -e

der Bergstiefel, -

der Langschäfter, -

der Überschuh, -e

die Gamasche, -n

der Gummischuh, -e

der Pantoffel, -n

der Schneeschuh, -e

EINKÄUFE—SHOPPING

das Geschäft, -e	=business (of any size, wholesale or retail)
der Laden, ··-	=shop
das Kaufhaus, ··-er	=department store
der Markt, ··-e	=market
kaufen	=to buy
verkaufen	=to sell
bezahlen (bezahlt)	=to pay (paid)
Einkäufe machen gehen	=to go shopping
Ich möchte etwas Seife	=I'd like some soap

Haben Sie Rasierklingen?
Have you got any razor blades?

Wie viele möchten Sie haben?
How many do you want?

ein Dutzend; ein Paar.
a dozen; a pair.

ein Pfund; ein halbes Pfund.
a pound; half a pound.

Wieviel kostet das?
How much is that?

Was kosten diese?
How much are these?

Was kostet der Meter (das Pfund)?
How much a yard (a pound) is it?

Können Sie mir etwas anderes zeigen?
Can you show me something different?

Ich nehme das (diese).
I'll take that (these).

Das ist That is Diese sind These are	zu too	gross = big klein = small dick = thick dünn = thin lang = long kurz = short breit = wide schmal = narrow teuer = dear

Die Bäckerei, -en = baker's shop

der Bäcker, -	baker
das Brot, -e	bread
ein Brot	a loaf
das Brötchen, -	roll
der Kuchen, -	cake

Das Fischgeschäft, -e = fishmonger's
(see page 236)

Die Buchhandlung, -en = book shop

der Buchhändler, -	bookseller
antiquarisch	second-hand
das Buch, ··-er	book
das Wörterbuch, ··-er	dictionary
der Reiseführer, -	guide book
der Sprachführer, -	phrase book
das Lehrbuch, ··-er	textbook
der Roman, -e	novel

Der Schuhmacher, - = bootmaker
(see page 224)

reparieren	to mend
die Schuhcreme	boot polish
putzen	to polish
der Schnürsenkel, -	bootlace, shoelace
der Schuhriemen, -	shoe strap

Die Fleischerei, -en = butcher's shop
(see page 230)

der Fleischer, -	butcher

Die Drogerie, -n = drug store, druggist's

die Apotheke, -n	dispensing chemist's
die Seife, -n	soap
das Rasiermesser, -	razor
der Rasierapparat, -e	safety-razor
die Rasierklinge, -n	razor blade
die Rasierseife, -n	shaving soap
der Rasierpinsel, -	shaving brush
der Lippenstift, -e	lipstick
der Puder, -	powder
das Parfüm, -s	scent, perfume
die Creme, -s	cream
die Zahnbürste, -n	tooth brush
die Zahnpaste, -n	tooth paste
das Aspirin	aspirin
das Vaselin	Vaseline
das Jod	iodine
die Watte	cotton wool

Das Milchgeschäft, -e = dairy

die Milch	milk
die Butter	butter
das Ei, -er	egg
der Käse, -	cheese

Das Obstgeschäft, -e = fruiterer's
(see page 60)

Die Tuchhandlung, -en = *draper's*

das Tuch, -e	*cloth*
der Stoff, -e	*textile material*
die Wolle, -n	*wool*
die Baumwolle, -n	*cotton*
die Seide, -n	*silk*
die Kunstseide, -n	*artificial silk*

Das Lebensmittelgeschäft, -e
= *provision store*

der Zucker	*sugar*
das Salz	*salt*
der Speck	*bacon*
der Schinken, -	*ham*

Das Kurzwarengeschäft = *haberdashery*

der Zwirn, -e	*sewing cotton*
die Nadel, -n	*needle*
die Stecknadel, -n	*pin*
die Sicherheitsnadel, -n	*safety-pin*
der Knopf, ¨-e	*button*

Das Hutgeschäft, -e = *hat shop*
(*see below*)

Süssigkeiten = *sweetmeats*

die Schokolade, -n	*chocolate*
Bonbons (m. pl.)	*sweets*
ein Kasten Konfekt	*a box of sweets*

Der Frisör, -e = *hairdresser*

Bitte, Rasieren!	*Shave, please!*
Bitte, Haarschneiden!	*Haircut, please!*
Kopfwaschen	*shampoo*
nicht zu kurz	*not too short*
ziemlich kurz	*rather short*
die Ondulation, -en	*marcel wave*
die Dauerwelle, -n	*permanent wave*

Eisenwaren = *ironmongery*

der Nagel, ¨-	*nail*
der Hammer, ¨-	*hammer*
die Zange, -n	*tongs, pincers*

Der Juwelier, -e = *jeweller*
(*see page 92*)

Die Modistin, -nen = *milliner*

Die Wäscherei, -en = *laundry*
(*see page 144*)

die Wäsche	*washing*
die Wäscheliste, -n	*laundry list*

Der Optiker, - = *optician*

Das Papierwarengeschäft, -e = *stationer's*
(*see page 210*)

Der Zigarettenladen, - = *tobacconist's*
(*see page 208*)

HÜTE—HATS

der weiche Hut

der steife Hut

der Strohhut

der Zylinder, -

der Panama Hut

die Mütze, -n

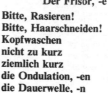

EIN WURSTSTAND IN FRANKFURT

Die Deutschen sind als Wurstesser bekannt. In grossen Städten sieht man unzählige solcher Läden und Verkaufsstände, wo es Würste aller Art zu kaufen gibt, und man warme Würstchen an Ort und Stelle essen kann. Frankfurter Würstchen sind besonders beliebt.

(*Translation on page* 378)

der Wurststand, ˮ-e	**bekannt**	**unzählig**	**an Ort und Stelle**	**besonders**
sausage stall	*known*	*innumerable*	*on the spot*	*especially*

227

**Komm
hier herein!**

**Geh
dort hinein!**

**Komm
hier heraus!**

**Geh
dort hinaus!**

Komm herauf!

**Geh
hinauf!**

**Komm
herunter!**

**Geh
hinunter!**

IN AND *OUT*—*UP* AND *DOWN*

Kann er heraufkommen?
May he come up?

Sie will nicht hereinkommen.
She does not want to come in.

Sie können dort nicht hineingehen.
You can't go in there.

Sie müssen dort hinaufgehen.
You have to go up there.

Wollen Sie nicht herüberkommen?
Won't you come over?

Herein, heraus, herauf, herunter; hinein, hinauf, hinaus, hinunter, etc., are separable parts of compound verbs and are placed at the end of the sentence if the verb is in a principal clause, or are joined to the verb when it comes at the end of a dependent clause. When used with the infinitive it is always attached to it in front, sometimes with **zu** in between, eg. **um herüberzukommen** = *in order to come over.*

WHERE, WHITHER, WHENCE

Wo sind Sie?
Where are you?

Wohin gehen Sie?
Where are you going?

Woher kommen Sie?
Where are you coming from?

Womit schreiben Sie?
What are you writing with?

Worüber sprechen Sie?
What are you talking about?

In former times a distinction was made in English between *where* and *whither*. In German this distinction still holds good and you have to distinguish carefully between **wo** and **wohin**. *From where* is **woher.**

There are also English words like *wherein, whereof, wherewith,* etc., which are not used in modern colloquial English and we say instead *in what, of what, with what.* In German **was** cannot be used with prepositions and is replaced by **wo** (**wor** before a vowel), with the preposition added. **Womit** = *with what,* **worauf** = *on what,* **woraus** = *out of what,* etc.

DOCH

Er ist doch noch krank = *But he is still ill.*

Kommen Sie doch = *Do come.*

Ich kann nicht kommen. Doch, Sie müssen.
I can't come. Yes, you must.

There is no single English equivalent of the German **doch**. **Doch** is mainly used for emphasis and often corresponds to the English emphatic *do,* e.g. **Setzen Sie sich doch** = *Do sit down;* **Nehmen Sie doch eine Zigarette** = *Do take a cigarette.* In expressing contradiction **doch** is more emphatic than a mere **ja** (compare French *si*).

EXERCISES

I Answer in German

1. Was haben die Eltern den Kindern versprochen? 2. Wo haben sie das Eis gegessen? 3. Essen Sie gern Eis? 4. Warum kaufen sie nicht alles im ersten Geschäft? 5. Hat ein grosses Kaufhaus viele Abteilungen? 6. Wo kauft man Handschuhe? 7. Was tut Herr Schulz, während (*while*) seine Familie im Erfrischungsraum ist? 8. Wo ist der Frisiersalon? 9. Lässt Herr Schulz sich den Kopf waschen? 10. Warum ist er ungeduldig?

II Translate into German

1. Come in. 2. You cannot go in there. 3. Tell her to come up. 4. She doesn't want to come up. 5. Don't come in now. 6. Won't you come down? 7. Bring up your gramophone (das Grammophon). 8. I would like to buy an umbrella. 9. I don't like the colour. 10. That's too expensive. 11. I'll have this one. 12. Where can I have my laundry done?

III Insert hin or her

1. Ich bin oben. Kommen Sie auch -auf. 2. Gehen Sie die Treppe -auf. 3. Kommen Sie bitte -unter. 4. Gehen Sie dort -unter. 5. Ich gehe in dieses Café. Kommen Sie mit -ein? 6. Wir sind bei unserem Onkel. Kommen Sie auch .... 7. Geht sie -aus? 8. Wo- gehen Sie? 9. Nehmen Sie das Geld -aus!

(*Answers on page 364*)

DAS FLEISCH—MEAT
(English key on page 371)

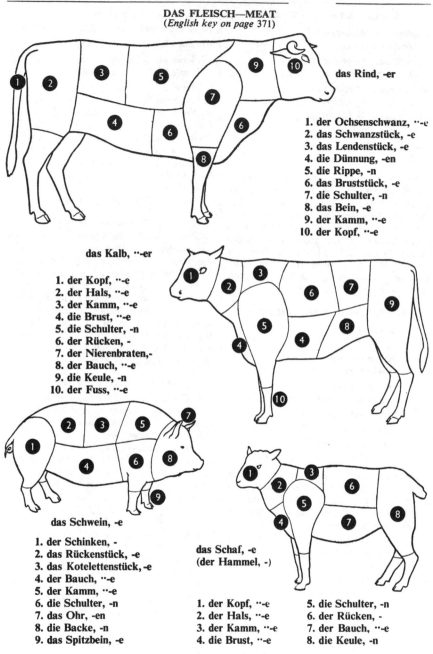

das Rind, -er

1. der Ochsenschwanz, ̈-e
2. das Schwanzstück, -e
3. das Lendenstück, -e
4. die Dünnung, -en
5. die Rippe, -n
6. das Bruststück, -e
7. die Schulter, -n
8. das Bein, -e
9. der Kamm, ̈-e
10. der Kopf, ̈-e

das Kalb, ̈-er

1. der Kopf, ̈-e
2. der Hals, ̈-e
3. der Kamm, ̈-e
4. die Brust, ̈-e
5. die Schulter, -n
6. der Rücken, -
7. der Nierenbraten,-
8. der Bauch, ̈-e
9. die Keule, -n
10. der Fuss, ̈-e

das Schwein, -e

1. der Schinken, -
2. das Rückenstück, -e
3. das Kotelettenstück, -e
4. der Bauch, ̈-e
5. der Kamm, ̈-e
6. die Schulter, -n
7. das Ohr, -en
8. die Backe, -n
9. das Spitzbein, -e

das Schaf, -e
(der Hammel, -)

1. der Kopf, ̈-e
2. der Hals, ̈-e
3. der Kamm, ̈-e
4. die Brust, ̈-e
5. die Schulter, -n
6. der Rücken, -
7. der Bauch, ̈-e
8. die Keule, -n

VIERUNDZWANZIGSTE LEKTION

GOOD HEALTH !

Mr. Lessing plays host at a luncheon party. After mastering the Lesson, imagine that you are in his place in the scene above and try your hand at ordering a meal.

MITTAGESSEN IM RESTAURANT

Herr Lessing hat Herrn und Frau Schulz zum Mittagessen in einem Restaurant eingeladen, das sich in der Nähe seines Büros befindet. Da er sehr beschäftigt ist, ist es ihm nicht möglich, zu Mittag nach Hause zu gehen. Um ein Uhr hat er seine Verwandten am Ausgang der Untergrundbahn getroffen; von dort gingen sie zu Fuss zum Restaurant. Der Oberkellner führte sie an einen Tisch und legte ihnen die Speisekarte vor.

Herr Lessing [zu Frau Schulz]: Was nimmst du als Vorspeise? Ich nehme Heringssalat.

Herr Schulz: Dasselbe für mich, bitte.

Frau Schulz: Ich nehme keine Vorspeise. Bringen Sie mir lieber eine Suppe.

LUNCH IN A RESTAURANT

Mr. Lessing has invited Mr. and Mrs. Schulz for lunch in a restaurant which is situated near his office. As he is very busy it is not possible for him to go home for lunch. At one o'clock he met his relations at the exit of the subway; from there they walked to the restaurant. The head waiter took them to a table and placed the menu before them.

Mr. Lessing [to Mrs. Schulz]: What hors d'œuvre will you have? I'll have herring salad.

Mr. Schulz: The same for me, please.

Mrs. Schulz: I won't have any hors d'œuvre. Bring me rather a soup.

231

DAS GEMÜSE—VEGETABLES
(*English key on page* 371)

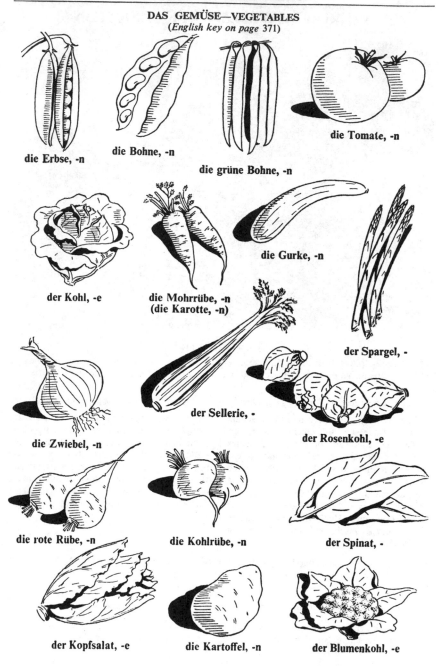

die Erbse, -n

die Bohne, -n

die grüne Bohne, -n

die Tomate, -n

der Kohl, -e

die Mohrrübe, -n
(die Karotte, -n)

die Gurke, -n

der Spargel, -

die Zwiebel, -n

der Sellerie, -

der Spargel, -

der Rosenkohl, -e

die rote Rübe, -n

die Kohlrübe, -n

der Spinat, -

der Kopfsalat, -e

die Kartoffel, -n

der Blumenkohl, -e

Der Ober: Tomatensuppe oder Ochsenschwanzsuppe?

The Waiter: Tomato or oxtail?

Frau S.: Tomatensuppe, bitte.

Mrs. S.: Tomato, please.

Herr L.: Also zweimal Heringssalat und eine Tomatensuppe. Vergessen Sie das Brot nicht.

Mr. L.: So it's herring salad for two and tomato soup for one. Don't forget the bread.

Ober: Es steht bereits auf dem Tisch.

Waiter: It is already on the table.

Herr L.: Verzeihung, ich hatte es nicht gesehen.

Mr. L.: Sorry, I hadn't seen it.

Ober: Was nehmen Sie als nächsten Gang?

Waiter: What will you have for the next course?

Herr L.: Schweinebraten mit Rotkohl und Kartoffeln.

Mr. L.: Roast pork with red cabbage and potatoes.

Frau S.: Für mich ein Kalbskotelett mit Blumenkohl.

Mrs. S.: For me a veal cutlet with cauliflower.

Herr S.: Können Sie den Hasenbraten empfehlen?

Mr. S.: Can you recommend the roast hare?

Ober: Ich kann ihn sehr empfehlen. Wir servieren ihn in Weisswein.

Waiter: I can recommend it very much. We serve it in white wine.

Herr S.: Gut, bringen Sie ihn mir.

Mr. S.: Good. Let's have it.

Ober: Und was für Gemüse?

Waiter: And what kind of vegetable?

Herr S.: Erbsen, bitte.

Mr. S.: Peas, please.

Ober: Als Wein empfehle ich Hochheimer 1931. Er ist ausgezeichnet.

Waiter: For wine I recommend Hochheimer 1931. It is excellent.

Herr L.: Bringen Sie uns lieber eine gute Flasche Burgunder.

Mr. L.: Bring us rather a good bottle of Burgundy.

Ober: Sehr wohl, mein Herr. Und als Nachspeise?

Waiter : Very well, sir. And for dessert?

Frau S.: Erdbeereis für mich, bitte.

Mrs. S.: Strawberry ice for me, please.

Herr S.: Gemischtes Kompott.

Mr. S.: Mixed stewed fruit.

Herr L.: Für mich Käse, bitte.

Mr. L.: Cheese for me, please.

Der Oberkellner entfernt sich, und einige Minuten darauf bringt ein Kellner die Vorspeisen für die beiden Herren und die Suppe für die Dame.

The head waiter goes off (" removes himself ") and some minutes later a waiter brings the hors d'œuvre for the two gentlemen and the soup for the lady.

Frau S.: Die Suppe ist ausgezeichnet.

Mrs. S.: The soup is excellent.

Herr S.: Ist eigentlich das Friedrichmuseum weit von hier?

Mr. S.: I was wondering if the Friedrich Museum is far from here?

Herr L.: Es ist ganz in der Nähe. Habt Ihr die Absicht nach dem Essen hinzugehen?

Mr. L.: It is quite near. Do you intend to go there after the meal?

DAS WILD UND DAS GEFLÜGEL—GAME AND POULTRY
(English key on page 371)

die Ente, -n

der Hahn, ¨-e

das Huhn, ¨-er

die Gans, ¨-e

die Pute, -n

die Taube, -n

das Kaninchen, -

der Hase, -n

der Hirsch, -e

der Fasan, -en

das Reh, -e

das Rebhuhn, ¨-er

die Waldschnepfe, -n

das Wald-
huhn, ¨-er

die Schnepfe, -n

Frau S.: Da wir in der Nähe sind, können wir die Gelegenheit ausnutzen.	Mrs. S.: Since we are in the neighbourhood we could take the opportunity.
Herr L.: Ich kann leider nicht mitkommen, da ich um drei Uhr eine Besprechung habe. Ich werde euch aber hinbringen. Wir könnten uns nachher zu einer Tasse Kaffee treffen; sagen wir um halb fünf.	Mr. L.: Unfortunately, I cannot come with you, as I have a conference at three o'clock. But I'll take you there. We could meet afterwards for a cup of coffee, say at half-past four.
Frau S.: Mit Vergnügen. Wir haben nichts weiter vor. Die Kinder haben einen Ausflug in den Grunewald gemacht. Da kommt der Kellner.	Mrs. S.: With pleasure. We have no further plans. The children have gone on an excursion to the Grunewald (forest). There comes the waiter.
Ober: Entschuldigen Sie, gnädige Frau, es sind keine Kalbskoteletts mehr da. Mein Kollege hat eben die letzten serviert.	Waiter: Excuse me, madam, there are no more veal cutlets. My fellow-waiter has just served the last ones.
Frau S.: Das ist schade. Bringen Sie mir stattdessen Rinderbraten.	Mrs. S.: That's a pity. Bring me roast beef instead.
Herr L.: Lassen Sie uns bitte nicht länger warten.	Mr. L.: Please don't keep us waiting any longer.
Ober: Es ist heute ungewöhnlich voll hier. Ich werde mein Möglichstes tun.	Waiter: It is unusually crowded here to-day. I'll see what I can do.
Er entfernt sich und kommt nach kurzer Zeit mit den Bratenplatten, den Gemüse- und den Kartoffelschüsseln zurück, die er zuerst auf einen Seitentisch stellt und dann herumreicht. Inzwischen hat der Weinkellner den Burgunder gebracht und eingeschenkt.	He goes off and comes back after a short while with the meat dishes, the vegetable and potato dishes, which he first puts on a side table and then hands round. Meanwhile the wine waiter has brought the Burgundy and poured it out.
Herr L.: [sein Glas hebend]: Zum Wohl.	Mr. L. [raising his glass]: Your health.
Herr und Frau S. [ihre Gläser hebend]: Zum Wohl.	Mr. and Mrs. S. [raising their glasses]: Your health.
Herr S.: Der Wein ist ausgezeichnet.	Mr. S.: The wine is excellent.
Frau S.: Die Küche ist auch nicht schlecht. Mir schmeckt es sehr gut.	Mrs. S.: The cooking is not bad either. I like it very much.
Nachdem der Ober die Fleischteller abgeräumt hat, bringt er den Nachtisch und den Kaffee. Danach bezahlt Herr Lessing die Rechnung, die ein Trinkgeld von zehn Prozent einschliesst. Dann verlassen sie das Restaurant.	After the waiter has cleared the meat plates away he brings the dessert and the coffee. Afterwards Mr. Lessing pays the bill, which includes a ten per cent tip. Then they leave the restaurant.
Auf der Strasse kauft Herr Lessing eine Mittagszeitung, und liest die Hauptüberschriften.	In the street Mr. Lessing buys a midday paper and reads the main headlines.

FISCHE—FISH
(English key on page 371)

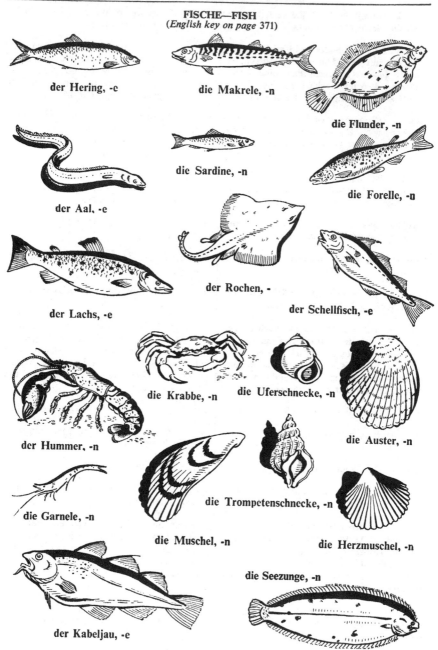

der Hering, -e

die Makrele, -n

die Flunder, -n

der Aal, -e

die Sardine, -n

die Forelle, -n

der Lachs, -e

der Rochen, -

der Schellfisch, -e

die Krabbe, -n

die Uferschnecke, -n

der Hummer, -n

die Auster, -n

die Garnele, -n

die Trompetenschnecke, -n

die Muschel, -n

die Herzmuschel, -n

die Seezunge, -n

der Kabeljau, -e

WHAT'S IN THE NEWS?

When you have read the accompanying text carefully, you should be able without difficulty to describe in German what is happening in this picture and to reconstruct (with your own variations) the ensuing conversation about the newspaper headlines.

Herr S.: Gibt's was (=etwas) Neues?	Mr. S.: Is there any news?
Herr L.: Nichts besonderes. **Donnerwetter!** Der Spandauer Mörder ist verhaftet worden.	Mr. L.: Nothing special. I say! The Spandau murderer has been arrested.
Frau S.: Ich wusste nicht, dass du dich für Mordfälle interessierst.	Mrs. S.: I didn't know you took an interest in murder cases.
Herr L.: Es ist ein ganz aussergewöhnlicher Fall. Habt Ihr denn nichts davon gehört? Ganz Berlin spricht davon. Ein Glück, dass die Polizei ihn verhaftet hat. Unsere Polizei arbeitet nicht schlecht. Ich will aber von vorn beginnen.	Mr. L.: This is quite an extraordinary case. Haven't you heard about it? The whole of Berlin is talking of it. A good thing ("luck") the police have caught him. Our police don't work badly. But I'll start from the beginning.
Also, vor vier oder fünf Tagen . . .	Well, four or five days ago. . . .
Auf dem Wege zum Museum erzählt Herr Lessing den ausserordentlichen Fall von dem Mord in der Morgenstrasse.	On the way to the museum Mr. Lessing tells the extraordinary case of the murder in the Morgenstrasse.

Note.—**Die Küche** can mean *kitchen* or *cooking;* **französische Küche**=*French cooking.*

DAS EI—EGG

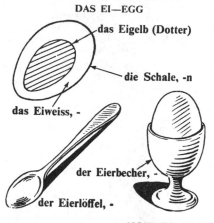

das Eigelb (Dotter)

die Schale, -n

das Eiweiss, -

der Eierbecher, -

der Eierlöffel, -

IDIOMS

Was gibt's zu essen?
What is there to eat?

Was gibt's Neues?
What's the news?

Was gibt's im Theater?
What is on at the theatre?

Was haben Sie heute Abend vor?
What are you doing to-night?

Ich habe vor, ins Kino zu gehen.
I intend going to the cinema.

Es kommt alles auf das Wetter an.
It all depends upon the weather.

HOW TO TRANSLATE *TO LIKE*

Er (sie) gefällt mir.
I like him (her).

Sie gefallen mir.
I like them.

Er (sie, es) gefällt mir.
I like it (according to gender).

Wie gefällt Ihnen das?
How do you like that?

Wie hat Ihnen der Film gefallen?
How did you like the film?

Er gefiel mir nicht.
I did not like it.

Gefallen, gefiel, gefallen, is *to like somebody* or *something*. It is constructed like the English verb *to please; I like it* = *It pleases me* (**Es gefällt mir**).

Essen Sie gern Kirschen?
Do you like eating cherries?

Gehen Sie gern ins Theater?
Do you like going to the theatre?

Gern essen (trinken, sehen, hören, etc.) is *to like eating, drinking,* etc., i.e., to do it *gladly*. The comparative of **gern** is **lieber,** its superlative **am liebsten.**

Ich habe ihn (sie) gern.
I am fond of him (her).

Haben Sie Katzen gern?
Do you like cats?

Ich habe Hunde lieber als Katzen.
I prefer dogs to cats.

Use **gern haben** for *to be fond of.*

Wie schmeckt Ihnen der Kuchen?
How do you like the cake?

Er hat sehr gut geschmeckt.
I liked it very much.

Schmecken means *to taste*. To say that you like something you eat (or ate) say that it *tastes* (or *tasted*) *good* = **Es schmeckt gut (es hat gut geschmeckt).**

Ich möchte etwas essen.
I should like to eat something.

Was möchten Sie zum Frühstück haben?
What would you like to have for breakfast?

Ich mag diese Suppe nicht.
I don't like this soup.

Mögen Sie Hunde?
Do you like dogs?

Er mochte keine Erdbeeren.
He did not like strawberries.

Ich habe ihn nie gemocht.
I never liked him.

Mögen (ich, er, sie, es mag; mochte; gemocht) can be used as an alternative to the forms given in the earlier examples.

BEI TISCH—AT TABLE

Würden Sie so gut sein, mir das Salz herüberzureichen?
Would you be so kind as to pass me the salt?

Kann ich Ihnen
Can I pass you

etwas reichen? Darf ich Ihnen noch etwas Fleisch auflegen?
anything? May I help you to some more meat?

Nein, danke.
No, thank you.

Nur ein wenig, bitte.   **Nein, ich will wirklich nicht mehr, danke schön.**
Just a little, please.   No, I really won't have any more, thank you.

Nein, danke. Es hat mir sehr gut geschmeckt, aber ich will wirklich nichts mehr.
No, thanks. I enjoyed it very much, but really I won't have any more.

Darf ich Ihnen ein Glas Wein eingiessen?   **Darf ich Ihnen noch ein Glas eingiessen?**
May I pour you out a glass of wine?   May I pour you out another glass?

Kann ich Ihnen eine Orange schälen?   **Nehmen Sie noch etwas Pudding, Herr Smith?**
May I peel an orange for you?   Have some more pudding, Mr. Smith?

Nehmen Sie sich doch etwas ...?   **Essen Sie gern ...?   Es ist meine Lieblingsspeise.**
Won't you help yourself to some ...?   Are you fond of ...? It is my favourite dish.

Wie hat Ihnen ... geschmeckt?   **Offen gestanden, nicht besonders.**
How did you like the ...?   If you will forgive my frankness, not very much.

Es war ausgezeichnet (or **Ganz hervorragend**).   It was excellent.

ZELL AM SEE

Zell am See ist ein als Sommerfrische beliebter Ort in der Gegend von Salzburg. Der Zeller
See liegt 753 Meter über dem Meeresspiegel.   *(Translation on page 378)*

der See, -n   **die Sommerfrische, -n**   **der Ort, -e**   **der Meeresspiegel, -**
lake   *summer resort*   *place*   *sea level*

NEW NOUNS

DER
Ausgang, ⸱⸱-e	exit, way out	
Salat, -e	salad	
Braten, -	roast meat	
Nachtisch, -e	sweet, dessert	
Gang, ⸱⸱-e	course, passage	
Kollege, -n	colleague	
Ausflug, ⸱⸱-e	excursion	
Mörder, -	murderer	
Mord, -e	murder	
Fall, ⸱⸱-e	case, event	

DIE
Nähe	proximity
Vorspeise, -n	hors d'œuvre
Suppe, -n	soup
Speisekarte, -n	menu
Erbse, -n	green pea
Untergrund- bahn, -en	subway
Besprechung, -en	conference
Absicht, -en	intention
Überschrift, -en	headline
Polizei	police

DAS
Kotelett, -s	cutlet
Kompott, -e	stewed fruit
Museum, Museen	museum
Glück	(good) luck

VERBS—REGULAR

beschäftigen	to occupy, to be busy
sich entfernen	to remove oneself
ausnutzen	to make use of
servieren	to serve at table
reichen	to hand, to offer
einschenken	to pour out (drinks)
schmecken	to taste
erzählen	to tell
verhaften	to arrest

VERBS—IRREGULAR

einladen (ladet . . . ein), lud . . . ein, hat . . . eingeladen	to invite
treffen (trifft), traf, getroffen	to meet
empfehlen (empfiehlt), empfahl, empfohlen	to recommend
heben, hob, gehoben	to lift, to raise
einschliessen (schliesst . . . ein), schloss . . . ein, hat . . . eingeschlossen	to lock in, to enclose, to include
sich befinden, befand sich, hat sich . . . befunden	to find oneself, to be situated

* * * * *

EXERCISES

I Read and Translate

Ich möchte gern etwas essen. Ich habe heute ziemlich früh gefrühstückt. Kennen Sie ein gutes Restaurant hier in der Nähe? Es ist ein recht[1] gutes hier um die Ecke. Wo wollen Sie lieber sitzen, oben oder hier unten? Ich glaube, oben ist's netter.[2] Bitte nicht zu nahe bei der Musik. Was nehmen Sie als Vorspeise? Was nehmen Sie als nächsten Gang? Ein Messer (eine Gabel, ein Löffel) fehlt.[3] Wie schmeckt es Ihnen? Ober, bitte zahlen.

II Answer in German

1. Wo befindet sich das Restaurant? 2. Wer hat wen eingeladen? 3. Warum kann Herr Lessing nicht zu Mittag nach Hause kommen? 4. Wo hat er seine Verwandten getroffen? 5. Was nehmen die beiden Herren als Vorspeise? 6. Was nehmen sie als nächsten Gang? 7. Was kann der Ober- kellner empfehlen? 8. Bestellt Herr Lessing den Wein, den der Oberkellner empfiehlt? 9. Wie schmeckt Frau Schulz das Essen? 10. Wohin gehen sie nach dem Essen?

III Translate into German

1. Do you know my friend Charles? 2. Do you like him? 3. How do you like my new hat? 4. I went to the theatre last night but I did not like the play[4]. 5. Are you fond of dancing? 6. Would you like to dance? 7. Do you like this music? 8. Would you like something to eat? 9. I should like some ice-cream. 10. Did you like the ice-cream? (*Answers on page 364*).

[1] quite.   [2] nicer.   [3] is missing.   [4] das Stück.

ARBEITERWOHNUNGEN IN SIEMENSSTADT BEI BERLIN

Die Siemenswerke beschäftigten viele tausende Arbeiter und Angestellte. Um diese in der Nähe der Fabrik unterzubringen, wurden hunderte von riesigen Häuserblocks mit modern eingerichteten Arbeiterwohnungen errichtet. So enstand ein neuer Vorort im Norden Berlins: die Siemensstadt.

(*Translation on page* 378)

die Wohnung, -en	**beschäftigen**	**der Angestellte, -n**	**unterbringen**	**riesig**
flat	*to employ*	*clerical worker*	*to accommodate*	*huge*
einrichten	**errichten**	**entstehen (entstand, entstanden)**		**der Vorort, -e**
to equip	*to erect*	*to arise*		*suburb*

241

1. die Hauptstrasse, -n
2. die Strassenbahnschiene, -n
3. der Übergang, ̈-e
4. die Bordkante, -n
5. der Bürgersteig, -e
6. der Fahrdamm, ̈-e
7. die Fussgängerin, -nen
8. der Bettler, -

9. die Krücke, -n
10. das Ladenschild, -er
11. der Karren, -
12. der Strassenhändler, -
13. die Hausfrau, -en (beim
    Einkäufe machen)
14. die Einholtasche, -n
15. der Kinderwagen, -

16. der Strassenbahnwagen, -
17. der Fahrer, -
18. das Fahrziel, -e
19. der Stromabnehmer, -
20. der Leitungsdraht, ̈-e
21. der Radfahrer, -
22. der Schutzmann, Schutz-
    leute; der Polizist, -en

THE STREET
on page 372)

23. die Strassenkreuzung, -en
24. der Autobus, -se
25. der Schaffner, -
26. der untere Teil
27. der obere Teil; das Verdeck,
28. die Plakatsäule, -n   [-e
29. die Markise, -n
30. das Dach, "-er

31. die Laterne, -n
32. der Laternenpfahl, "e
33. die Seitenstrasse, -n; die
    Querstrasse, -n
34. der Lastwagen, -
35. die Strassenecke, -n
36. der Fussgänger, -
37. der Briefkasten, "-

38. das Schaufenster, -
39. der Laden, "-
40. der Fensterladen, -
41. das Verkehrszeichen, -
42. der Ladeneingang, "-e
43. das Auto, -s
44. die Schutzinsel, -n
45. der Abfallkasten, "-

FÜNFUNDZWANZIGSTE LEKTION

HERR BROWN NIMMT DEUTSCHE STUNDEN

Im Hotel hat Herr Brown einen Landsmann kennen gelernt, einen Herrn Adams, der aus Birmingham stammt.

Herr A.: Sprechen Sie Deutsch?

Herr B.: Leider nur wenig. Aber ich muss es lernen. Ich brauche es fürs Geschäft.

Herr A.: Nehmen Sie deutsche Stunden?

Herr B.: Noch nicht. Aber ich möchte Stunden haben. Ich suche einen Lehrer. Können Sie mir einen empfehlen?

Herr A.: Gern. Ich kenne einen sehr guten Lehrer. Ich habe bei ihm sechs Monate Stunden gehabt und sehr viel gelernt.

Herr B.: Das ist sehr nett von Ihnen. Wie heisst der Herr?

Herr A.: Walter Müller.

Herr B.: Wo wohnt er?

Herr A.: Karlstrasse achtundzwanzig.

Herr B.: Vielen Dank. Ich will mir die Adresse notieren.

Her A.: Ich schreibe es Ihnen auf. Haben Sie ein Stück Papier?

Herr B.: Bitte, schreiben Sie es hier in mein Notizbuch. Hier bitte, auf diese Seite. Hier ist ein Bleistift. Übrigens, was nimmt der Herr für die Stunde?

Herr A.: Ich habe ihm fünf Mark pro Stunde bezahlt. Das ist sein gewöhnliches Honorar.

Herr B.: Ich finde das etwas viel.

Herr A.: Vielleicht. Er ist aber ein sehr guter Lehrer, und ich glaube, Sie können bei ihm mehr lernen als bei anderen, die weniger nehmen.

Herr B.: Ich glaube, Sie haben recht. Um welche Zeit treffe ich ihn am besten zu Hause?

Herr A.: Sie treffen ihn am besten abends.

Herr B.: Vielen Dank. Ich will noch heute hingehen.

MR. BROWN TAKES GERMAN LESSONS

In the hotel Mr. Brown has made the acquaintance of a compatriot, a Mr. Adams who comes from Birmingham.

Mr. A.: Do you speak German?

Mr. B.: Unfortunately, only a little. But I have to learn it. I need it for business.

Mr. A.: Do you take German lessons?

Mr. B.: Not yet. But I want to have lessons. I am looking for a teacher. Can you recommend me one?

Mr. A.: Gladly. I know a very good teacher. I had lessons with him for six months and learnt a great deal.

Mr. B.: That is very kind of you. What is the man's name?

Mr. A.: Walter Müller.

Mr. B.: Where does he live?

Mr. A.: Karlstrasse twenty-eight.

Mr. B.: Many thanks. I'll make a note of the address.

Mr. A.: I'll write it down for you. Have you a piece of paper?

Mr. B.: Please write it here in my note-book. There, please, on this page. Here is a pencil. By the way, what does the man charge for a lesson?

Mr. A.: I paid him five marks a lesson. That is his usual fee.

Mr. B.: I find that rather a lot.

Mr. A.: Perhaps. But he is a very good teacher and I believe you can learn more from him than from others who charge less.

Mr. B.: I believe you are right. What is the best time to find him at home?

Mr. A.: The best time to find him would be in the evening.

Mr. B.: Many thanks. I'll go there to-day.

* * *

Herr B. [zu einem Schutzmann]: Verzeihung! Können Sie mir bitte sagen, wo die Karlstrasse ist?

Mr. B. [to a policeman]: Excuse me! Can you tell me, please, where Karlstrasse is?

Schutzman: Im Norden der Stadt.

Policeman: In the northern part of the city.

Herr B.: Ist das hier in der Nähe?

Mr. B.: Is that near here?

Schutzmann: Nein, es ist ziemlich weit von hier.

Policeman: No, it is rather far from here.

Herr B.: Wie kann ich am besten hinkommen?

Mr. B.: How can I best get there?

Schutzmann: Wollen Sie zu Fuss gehen oder fahren?

Policeman: Do you want to walk or to ride?

Herr B.: Wie lange geht man zu Fuss?

Mr. B.: How long does it take to walk?

Schutzmann: Eine Stunde, wenn Sie schnell gehen.

Policeman: One hour, if you go quickly.

Herr B.: Dann will ich lieber fahren. Wie fahre ich am besten?

Mr. B.: Then I would rather ride. What is the best way of travelling?

Schutzmann: Mit der Untergrundbahn bis Friedrichstrasse. Aber Sie können auch mit dem Omnibus fahren.

Policeman: By subway to the Friedrichstrasse, but you can also go by bus.

POLIZIST UND ZIVILIST

Der Mann mit dem Rucksack, sowie der Polizist mit seinem Helm, sind eine häufige Erscheinung im Strassenleben Berlins. (Translation on page 378)

der Polizist, -en	der Zivilist, -en	sowie	häufig	die Erscheinung, -en
policeman	*civilian*	*as well as*	*frequent*	*sight, occurrence*

Herr B.: Was geht schneller?

Schutzmann: Beides dauert etwa zwanzig Minuten. Mit dem Omnibus können Sie bis zur Karlstrasse fahren, aber Sie müssen einmal umsteigen. Mit der Untergrundbahn brauchen Sie nicht umzusteigen. Sie können von hier direkt nach der Friedrichstrasse fahren. Vom Bahnhof Friedrichstrasse müssen Sie aber zehn Minuten zu Fuss gehen.

Herr B.: Dann fahre ich lieber mit der Untergrundbahn. Wo ist die nächste Untergrundbahnstation?

Schutzmann: Nicht weit von hier. Gehen Sie geradeaus, dann die zweite Strasse links, dort sehen Sie schon die Station.

Herr B.: Vielen Dank, Herr Wachtmeister. Guten Abend.

Er überquert die Strasse und wird beinahe überfahren. Im letzten Augenblick reisst ihn

Mr. B.: Which is the quicker?

Policeman: Each takes about twenty minutes. You can go up to Karlstrasse by bus, but you have to change once. Going by subway you need not change. You can go from here direct to the Friedrichstrasse. From the Friedrichstrasse station you'll have to walk for ten minutes.

Mr. B.: Then I'd rather go by subway. Where is the nearest station?

Policeman: Not far from here. Go straight on, then take the second street to the left; there you can already see the station.

Mr. B.: Many thanks, officer. Good evening.

He crosses the road and is nearly run over (by a car). At the last moment a passer-

MODERNER HÄUSERBLOCK IN BERLIN

In deutschen Grosstädten sind Einfamilienhäuser nicht sehr häufig, und die grosse Masse der Bevölkerung lebt in Mietswohnungen. Dieser Häuserblock enthält hunderte von Wohnungen.

(Translation on page 378)

das Einfamilienhaus, ···-er
one-family house

die Bevölkerung, -en
population

enthalten (enthielt, enthalten)
to contain

ein Vorübergehender zurück und ruft: "Passen Sie auf! Sie wären beinahe überfahren worden".

Herr B. [am Schalter der Untergrundbahnstation]: Eine Rückfahrkarte dritter Klasse nach Friedrichstrasse.

Beamter: Dreissig Pfennig, bitte.

Beamter an der Sperre: Die Fahrkarte, bitte.

Herr Brown zeigt die Fahrkarte, die der Beamte locht.

Herr B.: Von welchem Bahnsteig fahren die Züge nach Friedrichstrasse?

Beamter: Bahnsteig B, rechts.

Herr B.: Wann kommt der nächste Zug?

Beamter: In zwei Minuten.

Herr B.: Danke.

Herr Brown geht auf den Bahnsteig. Bald kommt der Zug; er steigt ein und setzt sich auf einen freien Platz. Auf der nächsten Station steigen viele Leute ein. Der Wagen ist nun überfüllt und viele müssen stehen. Herr Brown ist ein Kavalier und bietet einer Dame seinen Platz an. Er sagt: "Bitte, setzen Sie sich". Die Dame erwidert: "Danke sehr". Herr Brown steigt in Friedrichstrasse aus.

Herr B. [zu einem Schutzmann]: Verzeihung! Wie komme ich von hier zur Karlstrasse?

Schutzmann: Gehen Sie diese Strasse entlang, dann die zweite Querstrasse rechts und die führt in die Karlstrasse. Welche Hausnummer suchen Sie?

Herr B.: Nummer achtundzwanzig.

Schutzmann: Ich glaube, das ist auf der rechten Seite. Ich bin aber nicht ganz sicher.

Herr B.: Ich werde es schon finden. Vielen Dank, Herr Wachtmeister.

Herr B. [zum Portier des Hauses Karlstrasse 28]: Wo wohnt hier Herr Walter Müller?

Portier: Im vierten Stock. Hier ist der Fahrstuhl, bitte. Ich bringe Sie hinauf.

by pulls him back, shouting: "Look out! You were nearly run over".

Mr. B. [at the subway booking office]: A third-class return to Friedrichstrasse.

Booking Clerk: Thirty pfennigs, please.

Ticket Collector at the barrier: Ticket, please.

Mr. Brown shows his ticket, which the ticket collector punches.

Mr. B.: From which platform do the trains for the Friedrichstrasse leave?

Ticket Collector: Platform B, on the right.

Mr. B.: When is the next train?

Ticket Collector: In two minutes.

Mr. B.: Thank you.

Mr. Brown goes on to the platform. Soon the train comes; he gets in and sits down on a vacant seat. Many people get in at the next station. The carriage is now crowded and many have to stand. Mr. Brown is a gentleman and offers his seat to a lady. He says: "Please, sit down". The lady replies: "Thank you very much". Mr. Brown gets out at Friedrichstrasse.

Mr. B. [to a policeman]: Excuse me! How do I get from here to Karlstrasse?

Policeman: Go along this street, then take the second turning to the right and that leads to Karlstrasse. What number are you looking for?

Mr. B.: Number twenty-eight.

Policeman: I think that is on the right-hand side, but I am not quite sure.

Mr. B.: I shall find it all right. Many thanks, officer.

Mr. B. [to the porter of 28 Karlstrasse]: Where does Mr. Walter Müller live here?

Porter: On the fourth floor. Here is the lift. I'll take you up.

Der Portier bringt ihn hinauf. Herr Brown klingelt, ein Dienstmädchen öffnet.

Herr B.: Ist Herr Müller zu Hause?

Dienstmädchen: Ja, bitte treten Sie näher. Wen darf ich bitte melden?

Herr B.: Hier ist meine Karte.

Dienstmädchen [Herrn B. in den Salon führend]: Wollen Sie bitte hier Platz nehmen. [Nach kurzer Zeit] Herr Müller ist im Moment beschäftigt. Er gibt eine Stunde. Er bittet Sie, zehn Minuten zu warten.

Herr B.: Gut, ich warte.

Dienstmädchen: Hier ist die heutige Zeitung. Dort auf dem Tisch finden Sie einige illustrierte Zeitungen.

Nach etwa einer Viertelstunde kommt Herr Müller herein.

Herr M.: Mein Name ist Müller. Es tut mir leid, dass ich Sie warten liess. Ich war beschäftigt. Womit kann ich Ihnen dienen?

Herr B.: Ich komme auf Empfehlung von Herrn Adams. Ich möchte gern bei Ihnen deutsche Stunden nehmen. Herr Adams hat mir gesagt, dass er gute Fortschritte bei Ihnen gemacht hat.

Herr M.: Ich bin zur Zeit sehr beschäftigt, habe nur einige Stunden am späten Nachmittag frei. Würde Ihnen Dienstag und Freitag von fünf bis sechs passen?

Herr B.: Ich kann mich mit der Zeit ganz nach Ihnen richten. Ich bin nach Berlin gekommen, um Deutsch zu lernen und habe den ganzen Tag nichts anderes zu tun. Ich würde gern täglich Stunden haben, oder wenigstens viermal die Woche.

Herr M.: Leider kann ich Ihnen zur Zeit nur zweimal die Woche zur Verfügung stehen. Vom ersten April an werde ich mehr Zeit haben. Dann wird es mir möglich sein, Ihnen fünf oder sechs Stunden pro Woche zu geben.

Herr B.: Ich hätte gern mehr Stunden gehabt, aber wenn es nicht anders geht, fangen wir mit zwei Stunden pro Woche an. Was nehmen Sie für die Stunde?

Herr M.: Fünf Mark pro Stunde.

The porter takes him up. Mr. Brown rings the bell, a maid opens.

Mr. B.: Is Mr. Müller at home?

Maid: Yes, please step in. What name, please? (Whom may I announce, please?)

Mr. B.: Here is my card.

Maid [conducting Mr. B. into the drawing room]: Will you please take a seat here. [After a short while] Mr. Müller is busy at the moment. He is giving a lesson. He asks you to wait for ten minutes.

Mr. B.: Very well, I'll wait.

Maid: Here is to-day's paper. On that table you'll find some illustrated papers.

After about a quarter of an hour, Mr. Müller enters.

Mr. M.: My name is Müller. I am sorry I kept you waiting. I was busy. What can I do for you?

Mr. B.: I have come on the recommendation of Mr. Adams. I should like to have German lessons with you. Mr. Adams told me he made good progress with you.

Mr. M.: I am very busy at the moment. I have only a few hours free in the late afternoon. Would Tuesday and Friday from five to six suit you?

Mr. B.: I can fit in my time to suit you. I came to Berlin to learn German, and have nothing else to do all day. I would like to have daily lessons or at least four times a week.

Mr. M.: Unfortunately, at the moment I can be at your disposal only twice a week. From the first of April onwards I shall have more time. Then it will be possible for me to give you five or six lessons a week.

Mr. B.: I should have liked more lessons, but if it can't be done let us start with two lessons a week. What do you charge per lesson?

Mr. M.: Five marks per lesson.

DAS ZEUGHAUS IN BERLIN

Dieses stattliche Gebäude, das früher ein Museum von Ausrüstungen des Heeres enthielt, steht in der berühmten Strasse Unter den Linden.   *(Translation on page 378)*

das Zeughaus, ···-er	stattlich	das Gebäude, -	die Ausrüstung, -en	das Heer, -e
arsenal	*stately*	*building*	*equipment*	*army*

Herr B.: Gut. Morgen ist Dienstag. Können wir dann anfangen?

Herr M.: Mit grösstem Vergnügen.

Herr B.: Was für Bücher soll ich mir besorgen?

Herr M.: Sind Sie Anfänger oder fortgeschritten?

Herr B.: Mein Deutsch ist noch sehr lückenhaft. Ich kann einigermassen lesen, aber spreche noch sehr wenig, und meine Aussprache ist sehr schlecht. Ich glaube, Sie fangen am besten ganz von Anfang an.

Herr M.: Das werden wir morgen sehen. Nach der ersten Stunde kann ich besser entscheiden, was für Bücher für Sie geeignet sind.

Herr B.: Gut. Ich komme dann morgen um fünf. Auf Wiedersehen, Herr Müller.

Herr M.: Auf Wiedersehen, Herr Brown.

Mr. B.: All right. To-morrow is Tuesday. Can we start then?

Mr. M.: With the greatest of pleasure.

Mr. B.: What sort of books shall I get (myself)?

Mr. M.: Are you a beginner or advanced?

Mr. B.: My German is rather elementary at present. I can read fairly well, but I can speak very little yet and my pronunciation is very bad. I think you'd best start right from the beginning.

Mr. M.: Well, we'll see to-morrow. After the first lesson I can decide better what books are suitable for you.

Mr. B.: Very well. Then I'll come to-morrow at five o'clock. Good-bye, Mr. Müller.

Mr. M.: Good-bye, Mr. Brown.

1. der Kanal, ···-e
2. der Lastkahn, ···-e
3. der Zaun, ···-e
4. die Schule, -n
5. der Spielplatz, ···-e
6. das Wetterdach, ···-er
7. der Markt, ···-e
8. die Plakatsäule, -n

9. die Strassenlaterne, -n
10. der Platz, ···-e
11. das Standbild, -er
12. die Hauptstrasse, -n
13. die Seitenstrasse, -n
14. das Rathaus, ···-er
15. die Vortreppe, -n
16. das Türmchen, -

17. der Glockenturm, ···-e
18. das Stadttor, -e
19. die Feuerwehr, -en
20. die Motorspritze, -n
21. das flache Dach, ···-er
22. der Park, -e
23. der See, -n
24. der Häuserblock, -s

THE TOWN
on page 372)

25. die Kirche, -n	33. die Parkstelle, -n	41. das Café, -s
26. der Kirchturm, ⁏-e	34. das Flussufer, -	42. der Bahnhof, ⁏-e
27. der Strebebogen, ⁏-	35. der Fluss, ⁏-e	43. das Warnungszeichen,
28. der Kirchhof, ⁏-e	36. das Schloss, ⁏-er	44. die Eisenbahnschiene, -n
29. der Grabstein, -e	37. der Schlossturm, ⁏-e	45. die Fabrik, -en
30. der Pfad, -e	38. die Brücke, -n	46. der Fabrikschornstein, -e
31. das Tor, -e	39. der Bogen, ⁏-	47. der Wasserbehälter, -
32. das Blumenbeet, -e	40. das Geländer, -	48. der Vorort, -e

251

Ich stelle die Flasche auf den Tisch

Die Flasche steht
auf dem Tisch

PREPOSITIONS WITH ACCUSATIVE OR DATIVE

Wohin?	Wo?
Er geht an das Fenster.	Er steht an dem Fenster.
Ich stelle die Tasse auf den Tisch.	Die Tasse steht auf dem Tisch.
Die Katze kriecht (*crawls*) unter das Bett.	Die Katze liegt unter dem Bett.
Ich stelle die Milchflasche vor die Tür.	Sie steht vor der Tür.
Ich gehe hinter das Haus.	Der Garten ist hinter dem Haus.
Er steckt die Hände in die Taschen.	Er hat die Hände in den Taschen.
Stellen Sie den Stuhl neben den Ofen.	Er sitzt neben dem Ofen.
Wir hängen die Lampe über den Tisch.	Die Lampe hängt über dem Tisch.
Ich setze mich zwischen meinen Freund und seine Frau.	Ich sitze zwischen meinem Freund und seiner Frau.

The following prepositions are followed by either the accusative or the dative case:

an	= *at, to, by*
auf	= *on, upon*
hinter	= *behind*
in	= *in, into*
neben	= *beside, by the side of*

über	= *over, above, across*
unter	= *under, below*
vor	= *before, in front of*
zwischen	= *between*

They require the accusative in answer to the question **Wohin?** to indicate movement. They are used with the dative in answer to the question **Wo?** to indicate position.

Ich hänge den
Mantel in den
Schrank

Der Mantel ist
in dem Schrank

**Er hängt das Bild
an die Wand**

**Das Bild hängt
an der Wand**

Note the difference between **legen (legte, gelegt),** *to lay, to place;* and **liegen (lag, gelegen),** *to lie, to be situated.* When one of the above prepositions is used with **legen,** indicating movement, it is followed by the accusative case (apart from a few exceptions of an idiomatic character); whereas with **liegen,** indicating position, the preposition is normally followed by the dative case.

ASKING FOR HELP WITH THE LANGUAGE

Ich verstehe Sie leider nicht.
I'm afraid I don't understand you.

Ich verstehe nicht gut Deutsch.
I don't understand German well.

Ich verstehe Sie leider nicht ganz.
I'm sorry, I don't quite understand you.

Ich kann ein wenig Deutsch, aber nicht viel.
I know a little German, but not much.

Ich kann mich gerade verständlich machen.
I can just make myself understood.

Ich verstehe einigermassen, wenn man langsam spricht.
I understand fairly well when people speak slowly.

Es fällt mir schwer zu verstehen, wenn man schnell spricht.
It's difficult for me to understand when people speak quickly.

Bitte, sprechen Sie nicht so schnell.
Please don't speak so quickly.

Bitte, sagen Sie es noch einmal.
Please say it again.

Könnten Sie etwas langsamer sprechen?
Could you speak a little more slowly?

Das Lesen fällt mir nicht schwer.
I don't find it difficult to read.

Ich kann fast alles verstehen.
I can understand almost everything.

Ich habe nicht genug Übung im Sprechen.
I don't get enough practice in speaking.

Er liegt auf dem Bett

**Er legt sich aufs
(= auf das) Bett**

Würden Sie so gut sein, mir zu helfen?
Would you be good enough to help me?

Was bedeutet dieses Wort?
What does this word mean?

Was heisst ... auf Englisch?
What is ... in English?

Wie schreibt man es?
How do you spell it?

Wie spricht man es aus?
How do you pronounce it?

Wollen Sie es bitte wiederholen?
Will you please repeat it?

Ist es ein gebräuchliches Wort?
Is it a word in common use?

Ist dieser Ausdruck gebräuchlich?
Is this expression often used?

Ist es in der Umgangssprache gebräuchlich oder nur in der Schriftsprache?
Is it used in every-day language or only in the literary language?

Ist dieser Ausdruck richtig?
Is this expression correct?

Kann man es irgendwie anders sagen?
Is there any other way of saying it?

TO ASK

Er fragt ihn, wie alt er ist.
He asks him how old he is.

Sie bat um noch eine Tasse Tee.
She asked for another cup of tea.

Fragen is to ask a question; **bitten (bat, gebeten)** to make a request. **Die Frage** = *the question;* **die Bitte** = *the request.*

NEW NOUNS

DER
{ Schutzmann, pl. Schutzleute } *policeman*
Omnibus, -se — *omnibus*
Fortschritt, -e — *progress*
Moment, -e — *moment*

DIE
{ Zeit, -en — *time*
Nummer, -n — *number*
Aussprache, -n — *pronunciation*
Empfehlung, -en — *recommendation* }

DAS
{ Honorar, -e — *fee*
Monument, -e — *monument* }

VERBS—REGULAR

suchen	= *to seek*
brauchen	= *to need*
notieren	= *to take note of*
überqueren	= *to cross (a road)*
melden	= *to report, announce*
passen	= *to suit*

VERBS—IRREGULAR

umsteigen (steigt ... um), stieg ... um, ist umgestiegen } *to change (trains)*

anfangen (fängt ... an), fing ... an, angefangen } *to start*

entscheiden (entscheidet), entschied, entschieden } *to decide*

EXERCISES

I Answer in German

(a) Der Omnibus, der vom Bahnhof nach dem Vorort fährt, hält vor dem Museum.
1. Woher kommt der Omnibus? 2. Wohin fährt er? 3. Wo hält er?

(b) Ich nehme den Stuhl, der an dem Tisch stand, und stelle ihn an das Fenster.
1. Wo stand der Stuhl? 2. Woher nehme ich ihn? 3. Wohin stelle ich ihn? 4. Wo steht er jetzt?

(c) Die Mutter kommt aus der Küche in das Esszimmer. Sie trägt ein Tablett (*tray*) mit Gläsern, die sie auf den Tisch stellen wird.
1. Wo war die Mutter? 2. Woher kommt sie? 3. Wohin geht sie? 4. Wo sind die Gläser? 5. Wohin wird sie sie stellen?

II Translate into German

1. Can you recommend an hotel to me? 2. Is this the way to the station? 3. How long does it take to walk? 4. I would rather go by bus. 5. Where do I have to change? 6. Where do you want to go? 7. She is not at home. 8. I'll come back later. 9. I cannot understand you. 10. Please speak more slowly.

(*Answers on page* 364)

SECHSUNDZWANZIGSTE LEKTION

Sie hat starke Zahnschmerzen

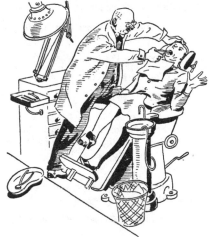

Er hat eine leichte Hand

FRAU SCHULZ GEHT ZUM ZAHNARZT

Frau Schulz: Ich habe seit ein paar Tagen starke Zahnschmerzen. Habt Ihr einen guten Zahnarzt?

Frau Lessing: Ja, ich kann dir meinen Zahnarzt sehr empfehlen. Er wohnt ganz in der Nähe. Wir waren mit ihm immer sehr zufrieden. Er hat eine leichte Hand, und es tut überhaupt nicht weh.

Frau S.: Ist er teuer?

Frau L.: Nein, er ist nicht sehr teuer. Eine gewöhnliche Füllung kostet ungefähr fünf Mark, und dasselbe rechnet er für Zahnziehen mit lokaler Betäubung.

Frau S.: Ich will mir die Adresse aufschreiben. Wie heisst er?

Frau L.: Er heisst Dr. Selz, Ahornallee 28. Am besten rufst du ihn an und machst eine Verabredung.

Frau S.: Das werde ich sofort tun. Hast du seine Telefonnummer?

Frau L.: Sehen wir im Telefonbuch nach.— Westend 7586.

MRS. SCHULZ GOES TO THE DENTIST

Mrs. Schulz: I have had bad toothache for a few days. Have you a good dentist?

Mrs. Lessing: Yes, I can recommend my dentist. He lives quite near. We were always very satisfied with him. He has a light touch and it doesn't hurt at all.

Mrs. S.: Is he expensive?

Mrs. L.: No, he is not very expensive. An ordinary filling costs about five marks, and he charges the same for a tooth extraction with local anæsthetic.

Mrs. S.: I'll write down his address. What is his name?

Mrs. L.: His name is Dr. Selz, Ahornallee 28. It would be best if you were to ring him up and make an appointment.

Mrs. S.: I'll do so at once. Have you got his 'phone number?

Mrs. L.: Let's look it up in the directory.— Westend 7586.

Frau S. geht zum Telefon und nimmt den Hörer ab. Das Amt meldet sich.

Mrs. S. goes to the telephone and lifts the receiver. The exchange replies.

Telefonistin: Hier Amt.

Operator: Exchange speaking.

Frau S.: Bitte, Westend fünfundsiebzig sechsundachtzig.

Mrs. S.: Westend 75 86, please.

Tel. [wiederholt]: Westend 7586.

Operator [repeating]: Westend 7586.

Frau S.: Ja, bitte.

Mrs. S.: Yes, please.

Eine Stimme: Hier bei Dr. Selz.

Voice: This is Dr. Selz's house.

Frau S.: Hier Frau Schulz. Meine Schwägerin, Frau Lessing, hat mir Herrn Doktor empfohlen. Ich habe starke Zahnschmerzen und möchte gern Herrn Doktor besuchen.

Mrs. S.: This is Mrs. Schulz speaking. My sister-in-law, Mrs. Lessing, has recommended Dr. Selz to me. I have acute toothache and would like to see the dentist.

Die Stimme: Passt es Ihnen morgen, Mittwoch, um 11 Uhr?

Voice: Would to-morrow, Wednesday, at 11 o'clock, be convenient?

Frau S.: Ja, danke, das passt mir sehr gut.

Mrs. S.: Yes, thank you, that suits me very well.

Die Stimme: Danke sehr, also morgen um elf.

Voice: Thank you, all right then, to-morrow at eleven.

Frau S.: Danke. Auf Wiedersehen. [Hängt ab].

Mrs. S.: Thank you. Good-bye. [Puts back the receiver.]

* * *

* * *

Frau S. klingelt an der Tür von Dr. Selz. Fräulein Werner, die Sprechstundenhilfe, öffnet.

Mrs. S. rings the bell at Dr. Selz's door. Miss Werner, the receptionist, opens the door.

Frau S.: Guten Tag. Ich bin auf 11 Uhr bestellt.

Mrs. S.: Good morning. I have an appointment for 11 o'clock.

Frl. W.: Wie heissen Sie, bitte?

Miss W.: What name, please?

Frau S.: Frau Schulz, Wielandstr. 26.

Mrs. S.: Mrs. Schulz, Wielandstrasse 26.

Frl. W. [öffnet die Tür zum Wartezimmer]: Bitte, nehmen Sie einen Augenblick Platz.

Miss W. [opens the door of the waiting-room]: Please sit down for a moment.

Dr. S. [öffnet nach ein paar Minuten die Tür seines Sprechzimmers]: Darf ich bitten?

Dr. S. [after a few minutes, opening the door of his surgery]: Will you come in, please? (lit. May I request?)

Frau S.: Guten Tag, Herr Doktor. Meine Schwägerin, Frau Lessing, hat Sie mir empfohlen. Ich habe seit ein paar Tagen starke Zahnschmerzen.

Mrs. S.: Good morning, doctor. My sister-in-law, Mrs. Lessing, has recommended you to me. For a few days I have had acute toothache.

Dr. S.: Wir wollen gleich sehen. Bitte, nehmen Sie hier Platz. [Untersucht die Zähne]. Hier rechts ist alles in Ordnung.

Dr. S.: We'll look at it at once. Please sit down. [He examines the teeth]. Here on the right everything seems all right.

Aha! Hier links oben ist ein kleines Loch. Haben Sie dort die Schmerzen?

Frau S.: Ja.

Dr. S.: Wir wollen es gleich füllen. Bitte, machen Sie den Mund weit auf.—So, danke.—Es tut nicht weh.—Bitte spülen Sie. Danke.—Frl. Werner, die Füllung, bitte.

Frl. W.: Hier, Herr Doktor.

Dr. S.: Danke, noch ein wenig, bitte.— Danke. Bitte, beissen Sie die Zähne fest aufeinander. Ist es gut?

Ah! Here at the top on the left is a little hole. Is it painful there?

Mrs. S.: Yes.

Dr. S.: We'll fill it at once. Please open your mouth very wide.—So, thank you. —It won't hurt.—Rinse, please. Thank you.—Miss Werner, the filling, please.

Miss W.: Here, doctor.

Dr. S.: Thank you, a little more, please. — Thank you. Please bite hard. Is it all right?

" Bitte weit aufmachen "

Frau Schulz zahlt

Frau S.: Ja, sehr schön, danke. Ist sonst alles in Ordnung?

Dr. S.: Ja, Sie haben sehr gute Zähne.

Frau S.: Darf ich gleich zahlen?

Dr. S.: Fünf Mark, bitte. [Frau Schulz zahlt.]

Dr. S.: Danke sehr.

Frau S.: Auf Wiedersehen. Vielen Dank.

Dr. S.: Auf Wiedersehen.

Frau Schulz verliess den Zahnarzt, froh darüber, dass er es nicht für nötig gefunden hatte, den Zahn zu ziehen.

Mrs. S.: Yes, quite all right, thank you. Is everything else in order?

Dr. S.: Yes, you have very good teeth.

Mrs. S.: May I pay you now?

Dr. S.: Five marks, please. [Mrs. Schulz pays.]

Dr. S.: Thank you very much.

Mrs. S.: Good-bye. Many thanks.

Dr. S.: Good-bye.

Mrs. Schulz left the dentist, pleased because he had not found it necessary to extract the tooth.

DER MENSCHLICHE KÖRPER—THE HUMAN BODY

der	Kopf, ¨-e	head		das	Bein, -e	leg
das	Haar, -e	hair		der	Oberschenkel, -	thigh
die	Stirn, -en	forehead		das	Knie, -e	knee
das	Auge, -n	eye		die	Wade, -n	calf
das	Ohr, -en	ear		das	Schienenbein, -e	shin
die	Backe, -n			der	Fuss, ¨-e	foot
	(Wange, -n)	cheek		die	Zehe, -n	toe
der	Mund, ¨-er	mouth		die	Hacke, -n	heel
die	Lippe, -n	lip		der	Arm, -e	arm
der	Zahn, ¨-e	tooth		die	Hand, ¨-e	hand
die	Nase, -n	nose		der	Ellbogen, -	elbow
der	Hals, ¨-e	neck		die	Kehle, -n	throat
der	Rumpf, ¨-e	trunk		die	Lunge, -n	lung(s)
die	Schulter, -n	shoulder		das	Herz, -en	heart
die	Brust, ¨-e	chest, breast		der	Magen, -	stomach

DIE HAND—THE HAND

der	Daumen, -	thumb		das	Handgelenk, -e	wrist
der	Zeigefinger, -	index finger		der	Puls, -e	pulse
der	Mittelfinger	middle finger		der	Fingernagel, ¨-	finger-nail
der	Ringfinger	ring finger		der	Ring, -e	ring
der	kleine Finger	little finger		der	Knöchel, -	knuckle

Im Wartezimmer des Arztes

Die junge Dame hat Kopfschmerzen.	Das Mädel hat Halsschmerzen.
Der alte Mann hat Rückenschmerzen.	Der junge Mann hat sich den Arm verletzt.
Der Junge hat Magenschmerzen.	Der Hund hat sich das Bein verletzt.

Sie setzt den Hut auf

Sie nimmt ihn ab

USE OF DEFINITE ARTICLE IN PLACE OF POSSESSIVE ADJECTIVE

When there can be no doubt as to the possessor, German uses the definite article where English uses the possessive adjective, especially with parts of the body and articles of clothing.

Der Kopf tut mir weh = *My head aches.*
Er zieht die Hose an = *He puts on his trousers.*
Sie setzt den Hut auf = *She puts on her hat.*
Nimm den Hut ab! = *Take off your hat.*

Note.—As **ziehen** means *to pull, to draw,* you cannot use **anziehen** or **ausziehen** for putting on your hat, for no pulling is involved. *To put on one's hat* = **den Hut aufsetzen;** *to take it off* = **ihn abnehmen.**

MORE PROVERBS

Keine Rose ohne Dorn.
No rose without a thorn.
Zeit ist Geld.
Time is money.
Wer zuerst kommt, mahlt zuerst.
First come, first served.

NUMERAL ADVERBS

There is a group of very useful endings employed in connection with numbers.

-mal means *so many times:* **einmal** = *once;* **zweimal** = *twice;* **dreimal** = *three times;* **viermal** = *four times;* **hundertmal** = *a hundred times,* etc.

-fach means *so many fold:* **einfach** = *onefold* (it also means *simple*); **zweifach** = *twofold;* (**doppelt** = *double*); **dreifach** = *threefold;* **tausendfach** = *a thousand-fold.*

-tens when added to the ordinal numbers gives meanings corresponding to English *-ly:* **erstens** = *firstly;* **zweitens** = *secondly;* **drittens** = *thirdly;* **viertens** = *fourthly;* **fünftens** = *fifthly;* and so on.

-tel
-stel when added to a number forms the fractions: **ein Drittel** = *one third;* **ein Viertel** = *one quarter;* **zwei Fünftel** = *two fifths.* Above nineteen the ending is -stel: **drei zwanzigstel** = 3/20; **ein hundertstel** = 1/100.

Halb = *half* and **ganz** = *whole* are adjectives and follow the article, e.g.:
eine halbe Stunde = *half an hour*
ein ganzer Kürbis = *a whole pumpkin*
den ganzen Tag = *all day long*

Er zieht den Mantel an

Er zieht ihn aus

THE PASSIVE VOICE

The passive voice in German is formed by using the past participle with the auxiliary verb **werden** (*to become*).

Present

Ich werde ans Telefon gerufen.
I am called to the phone.

Imperfect

Ich wurde gebeten, nicht so laut zu sprechen.
I was asked not to speak so loudly.

Perfect

Bist du geschlagen worden?
Have you been beaten?

Pluperfect

Sie waren getötet worden.
They had been killed.

Future

Sie werden besiegt werden.
They will be vanquished.

Note that the past participle of **werden**,

which for the full verb is **geworden,** takes the form **worden** when used as an auxiliary. The passive voice in German is less frequent than its corresponding English form. Many sentences which in English are in the passive voice are rendered in German in the active voice by means of one of the indefinite pronouns like **man** (*one*), **jemand** (*someone*), **niemand** (*no one*), i.e., by saying that someone does something instead of saying that something is done.

Hier spricht man Englisch.
English is spoken here.

All the sentences given above in the passive voice could be expressed in the active voice, e.g.:

1. **Man ruft mich ans Telefon.**
2. **Jemand bat mich, nicht so laut zu sprechen.**
3. **Hat jemand dich geschlagen?**
4. **Man hatte sie getötet.**
5. **Man wird sie besiegen.**

* * * * *

NEW NOUNS

DER
Schmerz, -en	*pain*
Arzt, ···-e	*doctor*
Zahnarzt, ···-e	*dentist*

DIE
Füllung, -en	*filling*
Betäubung, -en	*anæsthetic*
Verabredung, -en	*appointment*

DAS
Amt, ···-er	*exchange*
Loch, ···-er	*hole*

VERBS — REGULAR

klingeln	= *to ring* (*a bell*)
bestellen	= *to order; to give* (*a message*)
bestellt sein	= *to be told to call*
füllen	= *to fill*

VERBS — IRREGULAR

anrufen (sep.) like **rufen** = *to ring up*
nachsehen (sep.) like **sehen** = *to look up* (*in a book, etc.*)
beissen, biss, gebissen = *to bite*

EXERCISES

1 Read and Translate

Der Körper besteht aus[1] dem Kopf, dem Rumpf und den Gliedern[2]. Der vordere Teil des Kopfes heisst das Gesicht. In der Mitte des Gesichts ist die Nase. Wir riechen mit der Nase. Über der Nase sind die Augen, mit denen wir sehen. Unter der Nase ist der Mund, in dem sich die Zähne und die Zunge[3] befinden. Wir beissen mit den Zähnen und schmecken mit der Zunge. Rechts und links am Kopf sind die Ohren, mit denen wir hören.

Der Hals verbindet[4] den Kopf mit dem Rumpf. In dem Rumpf befinden sich die Lunge, mit der wir atmen,[5] das Herz, durch das das Blut zirkuliert, und der Magen, das Organ der Verdauung.[6] Wenn alle Organe gut funktionieren, ist der Mensch gesund. Wenn ein Organ nicht in Ordnung ist, ist der Mensch krank und muss zum Arzt gehen.

---

[1] **besteht aus** = *consists of.*   [2] **das Glied,-er,** = *limb.*   [3] *tongue.*   [4] *joins.*   [5] *breathe.*   [6] *digestion.*

II   Answer in German

1. Aus welchen Teilen besteht der Körper des Menschen? 2. Wie heisst der vordere Teil des Kopfes? 3. Was tun wir mit den Augen? 4. Womit riecht man? 5. Was tun wir mit den Ohren? 6. Durch welches Organ zirkuliert das Blut? 7. Wie heisst das Organ der Verdauung? 8. Zu wem geht man, wenn man Zahnschmerzen hat? 9. Wer hat Frau Schulz den Zahnarzt empfohlen? 10. Zieht er ihr den Zahn? 11. Warum ist Frau Schulz froh? 12. Was tun wir mit den Zähnen?

IIIa   Put into the passive voice

1. Er nimmt die Medizin dreimal täglich. 2. Sie müssen das nicht wieder tun. 3. Ich habe die Briefmarken verkauft. 4. Man ruft mich ans Telefon. 5. Seine Mutter begleitete[1] ihn.

IIIb   Put into the active voice

6. Die Kinder werden von ihren Eltern oft geschlagen. 7. Sie wurde von ihrer Lehrerin begleitet.[1] 8. Er wird getötet werden. 9. Der Arzt wurde zu dem Kranken gerufen.

(Answers on page 365)

IM SPREEWALD

Der Spreewald ist ein ausgedehntes Waldgebiet südöstlich von Berlin. Er wird von der Spree durchschnitten, die sich in viele Arme aufteilt.   *(Translation on page 378)*

ausgedehnt	das Gebiet, -e	durchschneiden	der Arm, -e	aufteilen
extensive	*region*	*to cut through*	*branch*	*to divide*

[1] **begleiten** = *to accompany*

SCHWARZWALDBILD : GLOTTERTAL

Der Schwarzwald ist ein dunkles Waldgebirge in Südwestdeutschland. Er ist stark ge-
gliedert und wird durch das Kinzigtal in den nördlichen und südlichen Schwarzwald getrennt.
Im südlichen Schwarzwald liegen die höchsten Berge: der Feldberg (1493 m.), das
(*Translation*

das Tal, ···**-er**	**dunkel**	**das Waldgebirge, -**	**gliedern**	**trennen**	**enthalten**
valley	*dark*	*wooded mountains*	*to divide*	*to separate*	*to contain*

262

MIT GLOTTERBAD

Herzogenhorn (1417 m.), der Belchen (1414 m.) und andere. Beide Teile enthalten Seen und zahlreiche Mineralquellen. Das Bild zeigt das im Glottertal gelegene Glotterbad. Vorn rechts sehen wir Schwarzwälderinnen in ihrer charakteristischen Tracht.

on page 378)

der See, -n	**zahlreich**	**die Quelle, -n**	**vorn**	**die Tracht, -en**
lake	*numerous*	*spring*	*in front*	*costume*

DER SPORT—SPORT

(English key on page 372)

das Schwimmen

das Fischen

das Segeln

das Tennis

das Rudern

das Fussballspiel

das Boxen

das Ringen

das Fechten

das Golfspiel

das Schlittschuhlaufen

das Skilaufen

das Schiessen

die Jagd

das Wettlaufen

das Springen

SIEBENUNDZWANZIGSTE LEKTION

<table>
<tr>
<td>

SPORT

Georg Lessing, der Bruder von Fritz, ist ein begeisterter Sportsmann. Er ist Mitglied einer Fussballmannschaft, die zu den besten des Landes gehört. Gewöhnlich spielt er als linker Läufer, doch manchmal auch als Mittelstürmer. Seine Mannschaft hat einen sehr guten Ruf und hat bedeutende Wettspiele gegen andere Mannschaften gewonnen.

Er ist auch Mitglied eines Sportvereins, der einen grossen Sportplatz besitzt. Auf dem Sportplatz sind mehrere Fussballfelder, Tennisplätze und sogar ein Schwimmbad.

Neulich hat Georg seine hamburger Verwandten zu einem Sportfest eingeladen. Es gab Wettlaufen, Diskuswerfen, Speerwerfen, Hoch- und Weitsprung, Stabhochsprung, Ringen, Boxen, Fechten und andere Wettbewerbe. Unter den Teilnehmern befanden sich die besten deutschen Leichtathleten, darunter mehrere Weltmeister.

Fussball ist nicht der einzige Sport, für den sich Georg interessiert. Er boxt auch. Neulich wurde er in der fünften Runde k.o. geschlagen. "Ich war nicht gut trainiert", hat er nachher gesagt.

Fräulein Lessing spielt Tennis. Sie ist eine gute Tennisspielerin und gewinnt viele Spiele. Sie nimmt auch an grossen Wettspielen gegen andere Tennisklubs teil.

Der Sport, der Herrn Lessing hauptsächlich interessiert, ist Pferderennen. Mit seinem Schwager und seiner Schwester hat er den Rennplatz "Ruhleben" besucht, einen der beliebtesten in der Umgebung von Berlin.

Herr Lessing setzte zehn Mark auf ein Pferd, für das er einen guten Tip hatte. Frau Schulz machte keinen Gebrauch von den Tips, die man ihr gegeben hatte. Sie setzte fünf Mark auf ein Pferd, das ihr gefiel. Sie hatte Glück und gewann. Es muss ihr Glückstag gewesen sein.

Hildes Ehrgeiz ist es, eine gute Schlittschuhläuferin zu werden. Mit ihrer Kusine geht sie dreimal in der Woche Schlittschuhlaufen. In dem Bezirk, in dem sie wohnt, ist eine künstliche Eisbahn eröffnet worden.

</td>
<td>

SPORT

Georg Lessing, the brother of Fritz, is an enthusiastic sportsman. He is a member of a football team which is one of the best in the country. He usually plays as left halfback, but sometimes also as centre forward. His team has a very good reputation and has won important matches against other teams.

He is also a member of a sports club which possesses a big sports ground. In the sports ground are several football fields, tennis courts and even a swimming pool.

Recently Georg invited his Hamburg relatives to a sports meeting. There was running, discus-throwing, javelin-throwing, high and long jump, pole-jump, wrestling, boxing, fencing and other competitions. Among those taking part were some of the best German athletes, among whom were several world champions.

Football is not the only sport in which Georg is interested. He also boxes. The other day he was knocked out in the fifth round. "I was not in good training", he said afterwards.

Miss Lessing plays tennis. She is a good player and wins many sets. She also takes part in big tournaments against tennis clubs.

The sport which chiefly interests Mr. Lessing is horse-racing. With his brother-in-law and his sister he visited the "Ruhleben" race course, one of the most popular in the neighbourhood of Berlin.

Mr. Lessing put ten marks on a horse for which he had a good tip. Mrs. Schulz did not make use of the tips she had been given. She put five marks on a horse she liked. She was lucky and won. It must have been her lucky day.

It is Hilde's ambition to become a good skater. With her cousin she goes skating three times a week. In the district where she lives an artificial ice-rink has been opened.

</td>
</tr>
</table>

FUSSBALL—FOOTBALL
(*English key on page* 372)

1. der Zuschauer, -
2. das Spielfeld, -er
3. die Eckstange, -n
4. die Torlinie, -n
5. das Tor, -e
6. der Torwart, -e
7. der Torpfosten, -
8. der Torraum, ¨-e

9. der Strafraum, ¨-e
10. der linke Verteidiger, -
11. der rechte Verteidiger, -
12. der linke Läufer, -
13. der Mittelläufer, -
14. der rechte Läufer, -
15. der Linksaussen, -
16. der Halblinks, -

17. der Mittelstürmer, -
18. der Halbrechts, -
19. der Rechtsaussen, -
20. der Linienrichter, -
21. der Schiedsrichter, ·
22. der Ball, ¨-e
23. die Seitenlinie, -n
24. die Tribüne, -n

Der Lieblingssport von Fritz und Hans ist Radfahren. Neulich hatte Fritz sich verirrt, als er von einem Ausflug in die Umgebung Berlins zurückkehrte. Ausserdem war einer seiner Reifen geplatzt. Glücklicherweise traf er einen Herrn, den er nach dem Weg fragen konnte.

Fritz: Verzeihung, mein Herr, könnten Sie mir bitte sagen, wo ich mich befinde. Ich habe mich verirrt.

Herr: Du bist nicht weit von Babelsberg. Wo willst du hin?

Fritz: Nach Berlin.

Herr: Geh geradeaus, bis du an eine Strassenkreuzung kommst, wo du einen Wegweiser findest, der dir die Richtung nach Berlin angibt.

Fritz: Werde ich meinen Reifen in Babelsberg reparieren lassen können?

Herr: Sicherlich. Du findest dort mehrere Garagen und möglicherweise auch ein Fahrradgeschäft.

Fritz: Vielen Dank, mein Herr.

Er folgt den Anweisungen des Herrn, sein Fahrrad vor sich herschiebend, als ein Polizist ihn plötzlich anhält.

Polizist: Halt, kleiner Schlingel, du musst deine Lampe anzünden.

Fritz: Schon? Wieviel Uhr ist es denn?

Polizist: Es ist zehn vor sieben.

Fritz: Muss ich denn auch anzünden, wenn ich nicht auf dem Rade sitze?

Polizist: Gewiss, mein Kleiner.

Fritz: Dann muss ich wohl anzünden. Ich kannte die Bestimmung nicht.

The favourite sport of Fritz and Hans is cycling. The other day Fritz lost his way when he came back from an excursion in the neighbourhood of Berlin. Moreover, one of his tyres had burst. Fortunately he met a gentleman of whom he could ask the way.

Fritz: Excuse me, sir, could you please tell me where I am. I have lost my way.

Gentleman: You are not far from Babelsberg. Where do you want to go?

Fritz: To Berlin.

Gentleman: Go straight ahead until you come to a crossroads, where you'll find a signpost which gives the direction to Berlin.

Fritz: Shall I be able to have my tyre mended at Babelsberg?

Gentleman: Certainly. You'll find several garages and possibly also a cycle shop there.

Fritz: Many thanks, sir.

He follows the gentleman's instructions, pushing his bicycle in front, when suddenly he is stopped by a policeman.

Policeman: Stop, little rascal, you must light your lamp.

Fritz: Already? What time is it?

Policeman: It is ten to seven.

Fritz: Do I have to light up even if I'm not on the bicycle?

Policeman: Certainly, little man.

Fritz: Then I suppose I must light up. I did not know the regulation.

ADVERBS

Ihre Stimme ist schön.
Her voice is beautiful.

Sie singt schön.
She sings beautifully.

Er ist ein guter Fussballspieler. Er spielt gut.
He is a good football player. He plays well.

In German any adjective can be used as an adverb without change of form. A few adverbs are formed from nouns or adjec-

tives by means of suffixes, e.g.: teilweise == *partly*, glücklicherweise=*fortunately*, blindlings=*blindly*, hoffentlich=*it is to be hoped*, bekanntlich=*as it is well known*, etc.

English *well* is usually rendered by gut, but there is also an adverb, wohl, which is used in certain set phrases, such as Schlafen Sie wohl (*sleep well*). Another meaning of wohl is *presumably, I suppose*, e.g.: Er ist wohl krank=*I suppose he is ill.*

ein langer Weg   eine lange Zunge   ein langes Kleid

ENDINGS OF ADJECTIVES

Adjectives in German, as you will have discovered, have a confusing habit of changing their endings.

das Deutsche	= (the) German (language)
im Deutschen	= in German
ein deutscher Fluss	= a German river
eine deutsche Stadt	= a German town
deutsches Bier	= German beer
deutsche Städte und Flüsse	= German towns and rivers
auf deutschen Flüssen	= on German rivers
in deutschen Städten	= in German towns
der neue Mantel	= the new overcoat
mein neuer Hut	= my new hat

Is there any guiding principle here, any short cut to an understanding of the various endings of German adjectives? Well, there is. Compare the following:

Singular

der grosse Fluss	(*k*)*ein* grosser Fluss
die grosse Stadt	(*k*)*eine* grosse Stadt
das grosse Land	(*k*)*ein* grosses Land

Plural

die grossen Flüsse	*keine* grossen Flüsse
die grossen Städte	*keine* grossen Städte
die grossen Länder	*keine* grossen Länder

I. When preceded by **der, die, das,** and certain similar words, namely **dieser, jener, jeder, mancher, solcher, welcher,** the adjective always ends in **-e** in the nominative case.

II. When the adjective is preceded by **ein, eine, ein,** and certain similar words, namely **mein, dein, sein, ihr, unser, euer,** and **kein,** the terminations vary according to the gender: **-er** for masculine, **-e** for feminine and **-es** for neuter, if in the nominative case.

In the first case the word preceding the adjective clearly indicates the gender, but in the case of **ein,** which can be either masculine or neuter, the characteristic masculine or neuter ending (**-r** or **-s**) is added to the adjective. **Eine, keine,** etc., clearly show by their **-e** that they are feminine, so there is no necessity to have a different ending here.

The whole matter can be expressed in a nutshell in the following way:

The characteristic endings (**-r, -s,** or **-e**) appear either in the adjective or in the word preceding it, never in both.

The above rule applies to the nominative case only. In the singular of the dative and genitive cases, as well as in all plural cases, the ending of the adjective is **-en,** no matter whether a word of group I or group II precedes it.

With regard to the accusative case, the golden rule applies that the accusative is always like the nominative, with the exception of the masculine singular, which is as follows:

I

Ich sehe *den* grossen Fluss

II

Ich sehe *einen* grossen Fluss

As you see, the adjective ends in **-en** when used in connection with the accusative masculine, and it does not matter whether a word from group I or group II precedes.

SUMMARY

We can summarise like this:

I. When preceded by **der, die, das,** and similar words, the terminations are:

	Masc.	Fem.	Neuter
Nominative	-e	-e	-e
Accusative	-en	-e	-e

In all other cases and in the plural: **-en.**

II. When preceded by **ein, eine, ein,** and similar words, the terminations are:

	Masc.	Fem.	Neuter
Nominative	-er	-e	-es
Accusative	-en	-e	-es

In all other cases and in the plural : **-en**

Now, there are cases when words neither of group I nor of group II precede the adjectives. In such cases adjectives are declined like **dieser, diese, dieses,** i.e.: **guter Wein, gute Milch, gutes Wasser;** plural: **gute Weine,** etc.

In the genitive singular, masculine or neuter, the adjectives end either in **-es** or **-en,** the latter form being preferred in modern German, e.g.: **der Geschmack guten Weines** = *the taste of good wine,* is generally preferred in the modern language, whereas **gutes Weines** is obsolete, but may still be used in poetry.

ORDER OF WORDS
(POSITION OF *NICHT*)

(a) **Die Eier sind nicht zerbrochen.**
The eggs are not broken.

(b) **Wir gehen heute nicht ins Kino.**
We are not going to the cinema to-day.

(c) **Wir gingen nicht gestern, sondern vorgestern.**
We did not go yesterday, but the day before yesterday.

(d) **Sie kommen heute nicht.**
They are not coming to-day.

(e) **Ich habe das Geld nicht.**
I haven't got the money.

(f) **Wir werden morgen nicht kommen.**
We won't come to-morrow.

(g) **Wir haben noch nicht gefrühstückt.**
We haven't had breakfast yet.

Nicht precedes the word it negatives (examples *a, b, c*). If the whole sentence is negatived, **nicht** is at the end (examples *d* and *e*), but it precedes an infinitive (example *f*) or a past participle (example *g*).

KOPFWEH

"Auf meiner letzten Fahrt mit dem Motorrad bekam ich auf einmal heftiges Kopfweh, so dass mir weiter nichts übrigblieb, als vor einer Apotheke zu halten und mir Tabletten geben zu lassen. Als ich dann die Apotheke verliess, war es weg!"

"Grossartig! Wie heisst das Mittel?"

"Ich meine ja nicht das Kopfweh, sondern das Motorrad!"

Bekam ich (from **bekommen**), *I got;* **auf einmal,** *all of a sudden;* **heftig,** *violent;* **das Kopfweh,** *headache;* **so dass mir weiter nichts übrigblieb,** *so that I had no other choice* (lit. *so that nothing further remained over for me);* **die Apotheke, -n,** *chemist's shop;* **mir Tabletten geben zu lassen,** *to have tablets given to me;* **verliess** (from **verlassen**), *left;* **weg,** *gone away;* **grossartig,** *magnificent;* **das Mittel,** *remedy;* **sondern,** *but.*

TENNIS
(English key on page 372)

1. der Tennisplatz, ···-e
2. der Tennisspieler, -
3. der Tennisschläger, -
4. der Tennisball, ···-e
5. die Aufschlaglinie, -n
6. die Tennishose, -n
7. die Mittellinie, -n
8. das Netz, -e

9. der Pfosten, -
10. der Balljunge, -n
11. das Aufschlagfeld, -er
12. die Grundlinie, -n
13. der Linienrichter, -
14. die Walze, -n
15. die Seitenlinie, -n
16. die Tribüne, -n

17. der Zuschauer, -
18. der Schiedsrichter, -
19. die Zählkarte, -n
20. das Tischtennis
21. der Schläger, -
22. der Ball, ···-e
23. das Scharnier, -e
24. das Gestell, -e

NEW NOUNS

DER
Sport, -s	*sport*
Fussball, ···-e	*football*
Verein, -e	*club*
Teilnehmer, -	*participant*
Tip, -s	*racing tip*
Bezirk, -e	*district*
Läufer, -	*runner*
Tennisplatz, ···-e	*tennis court*
Athlet, -en	*athlete*
Schlittschuh, -e	*ice-skate*
Ausflug, ···-e	*excursion*
Weg, -e	*way, route*
Wegweiser, -	*signpost*
Stürmer, -	*attacker, forward*
Sprung. ···-e	*jump*
Weltmeister, -	*world champion*
Ruf, -e	*reputation*
Kampf, ···-e	*fight, contest*
Ehrgeiz	*ambition*
Reifen, -	*tyre*

DIE
Mannschaft, -en	*team*
Eisbahn, -en	*ice-rink*
Bestimmung, -en	*regulation*
Runde, -n	*round (of boxing)*
Garage, -n	*garage*
Umgebung, -en	*surroundings*
Anweisung, -en	*instruction*

DAS
Mitglied, -er	*member*
Fest, -e	*meeting, festival*
Wettspiel, -e	*match, contest*
Rennen, -	*racing*
Schwimmbad, ···-er	*swimming pool*

VERBS—REGULAR

gehören	— *to belong*
sich interessieren (für)	= *to be interested (in)*
boxen	= *to box*
sich verirren	= *to lose one's way*
platzen	= *to burst*

VERBS—IRREGULAR

gewinnen, gewann, gewonnen	= *to win*
besitzen, besass, besessen	= *to possess*
einladen (ladet ... ein), lud ... ein, hat ... eingeladen	= *to invite*
laufen (läuft), lief, gelaufen	= *to run*
werfen (wirft), warf, geworfen	= *to throw*

schlagen (schlägt), schlug, geschlagen	= *to beat*
teilnehmen (nimmt ... teil) nahm ... teil, hat ... teilgenommen	= *to take part*

EXERCISES

I Answer in German

1. Für welchen Sport hat Georg Interesse? 2. Wozu hat er seine Verwandten eingeladen? 3. Wer befand sich unter den Teilnehmern? 4. Was sagte Georg, als er k.o. geschlagen wurde? 5. Welchen Ehrgeiz hat Hilde? 6. Wie oft geht sie Schlittschuhlaufen? 7. Welches ist der Lieblingssport von Hans und Fritz? 8. Wohin macht Fritz gern Ausflüge? 9. Was tut man, wenn man sich verirrt? 10. Was muss ein Autofahrer tun, wenn es dunkel wird?

II Translate into German

1. This is (I know) a beautiful picture. 2. This is (I know) an enthusiastic sportsman. 3. This is (I know) a Berlin newspaper. 4. This is (I know) a French skater. 5. This is (I know) my American aunt. 6. This is (I know) his new car. 7. This is (I know) their old (male) teacher.

III Insert the missing endings:
-er, -es, -en, -e

1. Dieser arm- Mann hat ein sehr klein- Haus. 2. Haben Sie ein interessant- Buch für mich? 3. Nehmen Sie diesen lang- Bleistift. Der kurz- schreibt nicht gut. 4. Dieses neu-, blau- Kleid ist nicht sehr schön. 5. Hier sind meine neu- Schuhe und da sind meine alt-. 6. Diese reich- Leute wohnen in einem gross- Haus. 7. Dies ist das Häuschen des alt- Mannes. 8. Dies ist ein gut- Apfel. 9. Dies ist gut- Obst. 10. Hier sind schön- Blumen. 11. Dies ist eine gut- Birne. 12. Wir fahren mit einem gross- Wagen. 13. Dies ist der neu- Tisch, die neu- Uhr, das neu- Klavier. 14. Dies sind die neu- Stühle. 15. Ich habe einen neu- Hut. 16. Er hat eine neu- Krawatte. 17. Sie hat ein neu- Kleid. 18. Sie haben neu- Hüte und neu- Kleider.

(*Answers on page* 365)

1. die Bühne, -n
2. der Vorhang, ···-e
3. die Requisiten
4. die Schauspielerin, -nen
5. der Schauspieler, -
6. der Statist, -en
7. die Scenerie

8. die Kulisse, -n
9. der Bühnenarbeiter, -
10. die Vorbühne, -n
11. das Fusslicht
12. der Souffleurkasten, ···-
13. das Orchester, -
14. der Dirigent, -en

15. das Dirigentenpult,- e
16. der Violinist, -en
17. der Flötenspieler, -
18. der Klarinettenbläser, -
19. der Saxophonbläser, -
20. der Trompeter, -
21. der Trommler, -

THE THEATRE
on page 372)

22. der Notenständer, -
23. das Notenblatt, ···-er
24. der Bühnenmeister, -
25. der Notausgang, ···-e
26. die Loge, -n
27. die vordere Reihe, -n
28. der Orchestersessel, -

29. das Parkett
30. die Absperrung, -en
31. der Gang, ···-e
32. das Parterre
33. das Programm, -e
34. das Opernglas, ···-er
35. die Platzanweiserin, -nen

36. der erste Rang, ···-e
37. der Feuerlöschapparat, -e
38. Schokoladenverkäuferin,
39. der Ausgang, ···-e [-nen
40. der zweite Rang, ···-e
41. die Gallerie, -n
42. die Beleuchtung, -en

273

ACHTUNDZWANZIGSTE LEKTION

AN EVENING AT HOME

In this picture the Lessings and the Schulzes are enjoying various forms of indoor amusement. Try to describe in German what each of them is doing.

VERGNÜGUNGEN	ENTERTAINMENTS
In Berlin gibt es Theater und Vergnügungsstätten für jeden Geschmack.	In Berlin there are theatres and places of entertainment to suit every taste.
Frau Schulz ist sehr musikalisch, und für sie bedeutet der Besuch eines klassischen Sinfonie-Konzerts höchsten Genuss. Ihr Mann hat einen weniger künstlerischen Geschmack und zieht es vor, ein Varieté zu besuchen.	Mrs. Schulz is very musical, and to her a visit to a classical symphony concert means the highest enjoyment. Her husband has a less artistic taste and prefers to visit a variety theatre.
Bei den Kindern ist das Kino überaus beliebt. Den grössten Spass macht ihnen aber der Zirkus, wo sie sich über die drolligen Streiche der Clowns amüsieren.	With the children the cinema is extremely popular. But the greatest fun they have is at the circus, where they enjoy the comic tricks of the clowns.
Herr Lessing hat nicht die Geduld, stundenlang stillzusitzen. Sein liebster Zeitvertreib ist Billardspielen.	Mr. Lessing has not the patience to sit still for hours. His favourite pastime is playing billiards.

Einmal in der Woche geht er kegeln. Auch sein älterer Sohn, der als Student den ganzen Tag lang über seinen Büchern sitzt, zieht einen Zeitvertreib vor, bei dem er sich bewegen und körperlich beschäftigen kann. Bei gutem Wetter macht er abends längere Spaziergänge in der schönen, wald- und seenreichen Umgebung Berlins.

An Sonntagen, an denen er nicht Fussball spielt, macht er ganz- oder halbtägige Wanderungen, und in seinen Ferien fährt er ins Gebirge, um auf die Berge zu klettern. Jeden Morgen treibt er zehn Minuten Gymnastik in seinem Schlafzimmer, und zweimal in der Woche geht er abends in eine Turnhalle, um am Reck und am Barren zu turnen.

Fräulein Lessing findet ihre grösste Freude an geistiger Betätigung, am Lesen guter Bücher und an der Betrachtung der Werke der grossen Maler und Bildhauer. In ihrer freien Zeit malt und zeichnet sie, und manche ihrer Ölmalereien und Zeichnungen sind von Kennern bewundert worden.

Once a week he goes to play skittles. His elder son also, who as a student sits all day long over his books, prefers a pastime at which he can move about and be physically active. In good weather he goes for long walks in the evening in the beautiful surroundings of Berlin, with their many woods and lakes.

On Sundays, when he does not play football, he makes whole-day or half-day excursions, and in his holidays he goes to the mountains to do some climbing. Every morning he does ten minutes' exercise in his bedroom and twice a week he goes in the evening to a gymnasium to practise on the horizontal bar and on the parallel bars.

Miss Lessing finds her greatest joy in mental activity, in the reading of good books and in studying the works of the great painters and sculptors. In her spare time she paints and draws, and some of her oil paintings and drawings have been admired by connoisseurs.

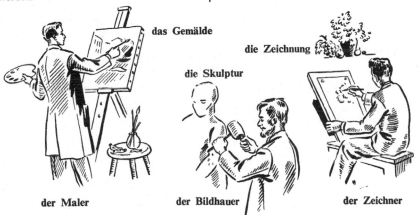

das Gemälde

die Zeichnung

die Skulptur

der Maler   der Bildhauer   der Zeichner

Ihre Interessen sind vielseitig. Wir haben schon erwähnt, dass sie eine gute Tennisspielerin ist, und wollen noch hinzufügen, dass sie auch gern tanzt, sei es auf einer kleinen Familiengesellschaft oder in einem der geräumigen Tanzsäle der Stadt.

Frau Lessing geht selten ins Theater und nie ins Kino. Sie beschäftigt sich lieber mit

Her interests are many-sided. We have already mentioned that she is a good tennis player and would add that she also likes to dance, be it at a small family party or in one of the city's spacious dance halls.

Mrs. Lessing rarely goes to a theatre and never to a cinema. She prefers to occupy

◆ Karo   ♠ Pik

♥ Herz   ♣ Kreuz (Treff)

SPIELKARTEN

1. Herz Ass	3. Karo König	5. Kreuz Dame	7. Pik Bube
2. Herz Zehn	4. Karo Neun	6. Kreuz Acht	8. Pik Sieben

Handarbeiten oder Strickerei. Ihr Sohn Fritz zerreisst die Strümpfe schneller als seine Mutter sie stopfen kann. Auch strickt sie für die ganze Familie Strümpfe, Handschuhe, Pullover, Wolljäckchen, usw. Auch wenn sie ihre Freunde und Verwandten besucht, nimmt sie eine Strickarbeit mit, um sich nützlich zu beschäftigen, während die anderen Karten oder Domino spielen.

herself with needlework or knitting. Her son Fritz tears stockings quicker than his mother can mend them. She also knits, for the entire family, stockings, gloves, pullovers, cardigans, etc. Even when she visits her friends and relations she takes some knitting along with her, with which to occupy herself usefully while the others play cards or dominoes.

EIN BESUCH IM ZOO

Am vorletzten Tag ihres Berliner Aufenthalts gehen die Kinder in den Zoologischen Garten. Georg und Lotte begleiten sie. Der Autobus Nr. 2 bringt sie fast bis zum Eingang. So viele Leute wollen hinein, dass sie sich am Schalter anstellen müssen. Über dem Schalter hängt ein Plakat:

A VISIT TO THE ZOO

On the last day but one of their stay in Berlin the children go to the Zoological Gardens. Georg and Lotte accompany them. Bus No. 2 takes them almost to the entrance. So many people want to get in that they have to queue up in front of the pay-desk. Above the desk hangs a notice:

KINDER 0.50 M.

ERWACHSENE 1.00 M.

Halbe Preise am Montag.

CHILDREN 50 PFENNIGS

ADULTS I MARK

Half price on Mondays.

Georg [am Schalter]: Bis zu welchem Alter wird man als Kind betrachtet?

Kassiererin: Bis zu sieben Jahren.

Georg [at booking desk]: Up to what age is one considered a child?

Cashier: Up to seven years.

Georg: Dann geben Sie mir bitte sechs Karten für Erwachsene. Hier sind zehn Mark.

Die Kassiererin gibt ihm vier Mark heraus und Georg erhält die Eintrittskarten.

Hans: In Hamburg wird man bis zu vierzehn Jahren als Kind betrachtet. Wenn Grete und ich in den Zoo gehen, bezahlen wir nur den halben Preis.

Grete: Ich möchte gern die Affen sehen. Sie sind wohl dort drüben auf dem grossen Felsen.

Lotte: Gehen wir hin.

Tatsächlich tummeln sich auf dem Felsen die Affen. Die einen sitzen gleichgültig da; andere jagen einander unter wilden Schreien; wieder andere stehen am Rande des Grabens, der sie vom Publikum trennt, und fangen die Nüsse auf, die die Kinder ihnen zuwerfen. Georg, Lotte und die Kinder bleiben lange stehen und beobachten dieses amüsante Schauspiel. Dann bemerken sie einen Wärter, der zwei Eimer voll Fische vorbeiträgt.

Georg: Er geht sicher die Seehunde füttern. Gehen wir uns das ansehen!

Sie eilen dem Wärter nach, der tatsächlich die Seehunde füttern geht. Er wirft ihnen die Fische zu, die sie auffangen und sofort verschlucken. Nicht weit von den Seehunden sind die Löwen und Tiger. Man kann sie schon von weitem brüllen hören.

So gehen sie von einem Käfig zum anderen und schauen sich alle Tiere der Schöpfung an. Sie verbringen einen angenehmen und lehrreichen Nachmittag und fahren gegen Abend wieder mit dem Autobus nach Hause zurück.

Georg: Then give me six tickets for adults, please. Here are ten marks.

The cashier gives him four marks change and Georg receives the tickets.

Hans: In Hamburg one is considered a child up to fourteen years. When Grete and I go to the Zoo we only pay half price.

Grete: I should like to see the monkeys. I suppose they are over there on the big rock.

Lotte: Let's go there.

Monkeys are in fact frolicking about on the rock. Some are sitting down looking indifferent; others are chasing each other with wild cries; others again are standing at the edge of the ditch which separates them from the public, catching the nuts which the children are throwing to them. Georg, Lotte and the children stay for a long time watching this amusing spectacle. Then they notice a keeper carrying two pails full of fish.

Georg: He is certainly going to feed the seals. Let's go and watch.

They hurry after the keeper, who is in fact going to feed the seals. He throws them the fish, which they catch and swallow at once. Not far from the seals are the lions and tigers. They can be heard roaring from a distance.

In this way they go from one cage to another looking at all the animals in creation. They pass a pleasant and instructive afternoon and towards evening they take the bus again to go home.

HOW TO TRANSLATE *TO SPEND*

Er hat viel Geld ausgegeben.
He spent a lot of money.

Ich habe dort zwei Wochen verbracht.
I spent two weeks there.

Sie brauchen nicht zu bezahlen. Er spendiert für uns alle.
You needn't pay. He is treating us all.

The above examples show the uses of three

separate verbs meaning *to spend:*

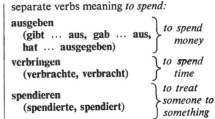

ausgeben (gibt ... aus, gab ... aus, hat ... ausgegeben)	to spend money
verbringen (verbrachte, verbracht)	to spend time
spendieren (spendierte, spendiert)	to treat someone to something

DER ZOOLOGISCHE GARTEN—
(English key

1. die Schlange, -n
2. der Ast, ···-e
3. das Palmenblatt, ···-er
4. das Krokodil, -e
5. der Schwanz, ···-e
6. die Klaue, -n
7. die Schildkröte, -n

8. der Schildkrötenpanzer,-
9. der Käfig, -e
10. der Menschenaffe, -n
11. der Affe, -n
12. der Leopard, -en
13. der Tiger, -
14. der Löwe, -n

15. die Mähne, -n
16. die Löwin, -nen
17. der Felsen, -
18. der braune Bär, -en
19. der Eisbär, -en
20. die Gemse, -n
21. der Wärter, -

THE ZOOLOGICAL GARDENS
on page 372)

22. der Elefant, -en
23. der Rüssel, -
24. die Giraffe, -n
25. der Büffel, -
26. das Horn, ···-er
27. die Einfriedung, -e
28. das Kamel, -e

29. der Höcker, -
30. der Vogelkäfig, -e
31. das Nilpferd, -e
32. das Känguruh, -e
33. der Storch, ···-e
34. der Schnabel, ···-
35. der Strauss, -e

36. der Seehund, -e
37. die Flosse, -n
38. der Teich, -e
39. der Pelikan, -e
40. der Flügel, -
41. der Pinguin, -e
42. der Pfau, -en

SHALL, WILL, MAY, CAN, MUST

Er wollte herauskommen, aber er konnte nicht.
He wanted to come out but he could not.

Er wird morgen kommen können.
He will be able to come to-morrow.

Mussten Sie es tun?
Did you have to do it?

Ich werde es tun müssen.
I shall have to do it.

Er durfte nicht ausgehen.
He was not allowed to go out.

Er wird nicht ausgehen dürfen.
He will not be allowed to go out.

Sie sollten sich schämen.
You ought to be ashamed.

Konnten Sie nicht früher aufstehen?
Couldn't you get up earlier?

The English verbs *shall, will, may, can, must* and *ought* are defective, i.e. the first four have present and past tenses only, while *must* and *ought* have only a present tense. The missing tenses have to be expressed with other words, e.g. *I shall be able; I had to; I was allowed to,* etc.

In German, the corresponding verbs can form all tenses. They also have infinitives which their English equivalents do not possess.

Er wollte herauskommen, aber er konnte nicht

Notes.—(1) These verbs are followed by the infinitive without **zu.** (2) They have two forms of past participle, one of which is identical with the infinitive. The latter is used after an infinitive, e.g.: **Ich habe nicht kommen können**=*I have not been able to come;* **Ich habe nicht gewollt**=*I did not want to;* **sie hat nicht schreiben wollen**=*she did not want to write;* **er hätte schreiben sollen**=*he ought to have written;* **er hätte es tun können**=*he could have done it.* (**Hätte** is the imperfect subjunctive of the auxiliary verb **haben.** A note on the subjunctive mood and the occasions on which it is used is given on page 304).

Infinitive		Present ich (er)	Imperfect ich (er)	Past Part.
können	= *to be able*	**kann**	**konnte**	**gekonnt** or **können**
wollen	= *to want, wish, intend*	**will**	**wollte**	**gewollt** or **wollen**
müssen	= *to be obliged to, have to*	**muss**	**musste**	**gemusst** or **müssen**
sollen	= *shall, should, ought to, to be said to, is (are) to*	**soll**	**sollte**	**gesollt** or **sollen**
dürfen	= *may, to be allowed to*	**darf**	**durfte**	**gedurft** or **dürfen**

PREPOSITIONS WITH GENITIVE CASE

Während der Nacht sind die Sterne am
Himmel.
During the night the stars are in the sky.

Wegen des schlechten Wetters blieben
wir zu Hause.
*On account of the bad weather we
stayed at home.*

Trotz des Regens gingen sie aus.
In spite of the rain they went out.

The prepositions **während**, *during;* **wegen**,
on account of; and **trotz**, *in spite of*, require
the genitive case as in the above examples.

Während also means *while*, e.g. **Während
wir spazieren gingen, beendete er seine
Arbeit** = *While we went for a walk he
finished his work.*

ORDER OF WORDS (V)

Adverbial Expressions.

Sie fahren nächste Woche mit dem Auto an
die See.
*They are going to the seaside by car next
week.*

Wir gehen heute Abend ins Theater.
We are going to the theatre to-night.

Er kam gestern nach Hause.
He came home yesterday.

These sentences illustrate the order in
which adverbial expressions are placed.
Note that such expressions appear in order
of : time (**nächste Woche**); manner (**mit dem
Auto**); place (**an die See**).

SPRUCH

Denke nicht immer an dich allein,
füge gefälligst dich dem Ganzen!
Es können eben nicht alle tanzen,
einer muss auch der Spielmann sein.

Johannes Trojan

Der Spruch, ···-e, *saying, epigram;* **allein,**
alone; **fügen,** *to join, fit together;* **gefälligst,**
if you please; **der Spielmann,** pl. **die Spiel-
leute,** *musician.*

NEW NOUNS

DER	Geschmack	*taste*
	Besuch, -e	*visit*
	Genuss, ···-e	*enjoyment*
	Spass, ···-c	*fun*
	Zirkus, -se	*circus*
	Streich, -e	*trick, prank*
	Clown, -s	*clown*
	Zeitvertreib, -e	*pastime*
	Barren, -	*parallel bars*
	Maler, -	*painter*
	Bildhauer, -	*sculptor*
	Kenner, -	*connoisseur*
	Saal, Säle	*hall*
	Aufenthalt, -e	*stay*
	Eingang, ···-e	*entrance*
	Felsen, -	*rock*
	Schrei, -c	*cry*
	Wärter, -	*keeper, attendant*
	Graben, ···	*ditch*
	Eimer, -	*bucket, pail*

DIE	Vergnügung, -en	*pleasure, entertainment*
	Stätte, -n	*place*
	Geduld	*patience*
	Wanderung, -en	*walking tour*
	Ferien (pl. only)	*holidays*
	Gymnastik	*gymnastics*
	Turnhalle, -n	*gymnasium*
	Freude, -n	*joy*
	Betätigung, -en	*activity*
	Betrachtung, -en	*consideration*
	Malerei, -en	*painting*
	Zeichnung, -en	*drawing*
	Gesellschaft, -en	*company, gathering, party*
	Handarbeit, -en	*handicraft, usually needlework*
	Strickerei	*knitting*
	Schöpfung, -en	*creation*
	Nuss, ···-e	*nut*

DAS	Varieté, -s	*variety theatre*
	Billard	*billiards*
	Reck, -e	*horizontal bar*
	Interesse, -n	*interest*
	Plakat, -e	*notice*
	Publikum	*public*
	Schauspiel, -e	*spectacle*
	Tier, -e	*animal*

MUSIKINSTRUMENTE—MUSICAL INSTRUMENTS
(English key on page 373)

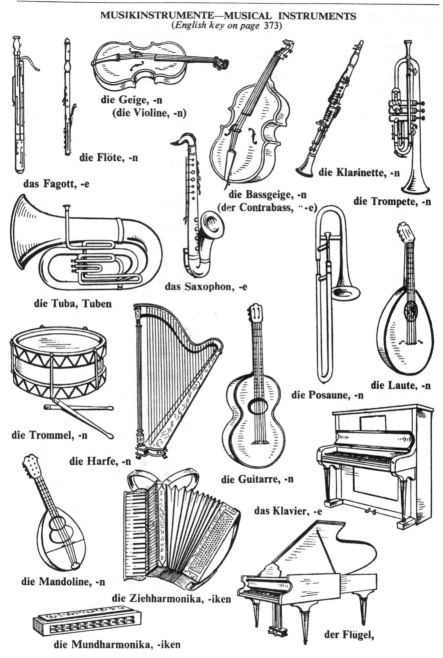

die Geige, -n
(die Violine, -n)

die Flöte, -n

das Fagott, -e

die Bassgeige, -n
(der Contrabass, ¨-e)

die Klarinette, -n

die Trompete, -n

die Tuba, Tuben

das Saxophon, -e

die Posaune, -n

die Laute, -n

die Trommel, -n

die Harfe, -n

die Guitarre, -n

das Klavier, -e

die Mandoline, -n

die Ziehharmonika, -iken

die Mundharmonika, -iken

der Flügel,

VERBS—REGULAR

bedeuten	= *to mean*
sich bewegen	= *to move*
malen	= *to paint*
bewundern	= *to admire*
hinzufügen (sep.)	= *to add*
anstrengen	= *to strain*
beobachten	= *to observe*
verschlucken	= *to swallow*
anschauen	= *to look at*
sich amüsieren	= *to enjoy oneself*
sich beschäftigen	= *to occupy oneself*
zeichnen	= *to draw*
erwähnen	= *to mention*
tanzen	= *to dance*
betrachten	= *to regard, consider*
füttern	= *to feed*
brüllen	= *to roar*

VERBS—IRREGULAR

vorziehen (like ziehen)(sep.)= *to prefer*
treiben, trieb, getrieben   = *to drive*
   (Sport treiben = *to go in for sports*)
zerreissen, zerriss, zerrissen= *to tear*
zuwerfen (like werfen) (sep.)= *to throw*
vorbeitragen (like tragen)
                 (sep.)= *to carry past*
auffangen (like fangen)(sep.)= *to catch*

EXERCISES

I   Answer in German

1. Wer besucht gern Sinfonie-Konzerte?
2. Was zieht Herr Schulz vor? 3. Was ist
bei den Kindern beliebt? 4. Worüber
amüsieren sie sich? 5. Warum geht Herr
Lessing nicht gern ins Theater? 6. Welches
ist sein liebster Zeitvertreib? 7. Was tut
Herr Lessing jun. an Sonntagen, an denen
er nicht Fussball spielt? 8. Was tut seine
ältere Schwester in ihrer freien Zeit? 9.
Womit beschäftigt sich Frau Lessing am
liebsten? 10. Wer begleitet die Kinder in
den Zoologischen Garten? 11. Was wirft
man den Affen zu? 12. Für welche Tiere
bringt der Wärter die Fische?

II   Translate into English

1. Er besitzt mehrere Häuser. 2. Sie hat
einen schlechten Geschmack. 3. Kegeln ist
bei den Deutschen sehr beliebt. 4. Welches
ist Ihr liebster Zeitvertreib? 5. Wenn Sie
dünner werden wollen, müssen Sie sich
körperlich mehr beschäftigen. 6. Sie findet
ihre grösste Freude an der Betrachtung der
Meisterwerke in den Museen. 7. Er malt,
zeichnet, turnt und tanzt. 8. Kann ich Sie
begleiten? 9. Es ist verboten, die Tiere zu
füttern! 10. Fangen Sie auf, was ich Ihnen
zuwerfe.

III   Translate into German

1. He had to do it. 2. Will you be able to
do it again? 3. I could not come yesterday.
4. I shall have to eat in a restaurant. 5. The
children were not allowed to go to the
cinema because of the bad weather. 6.
Which do you prefer, playing cards or going
to the concert? 7. I shall go to the mountains in my holidays. 8. I admire his
paintings. 9. You will have to queue up.
10. I should like to see the lions.

   (*Answers on page 365*)

ÜBERTÖNT

Führer am Niagara: "Meine Damen und
Herren, dies ist der stärkste Wasserfall des
Landes, und wenn die Damen einen
Augenblick schweigen würden, könnten Sie
das schreckliche Brüllen der tosenden
Wassermassen hören!"

   Übertönen, *to drown (a noise);* der
Führer, -, *guide;* stärkste, *strongest;* der
Augenblick, -e, *moment;* schweigen, *to keep
silent;* schrecklich, *terrific;* das Brüllen,
roaring; tosen, *to rage.*

GENAU

"Hast du denn den Pullover ganz allein
gestrickt, Gretchen?" fragte die freundliche
Tante.

"Ja, ganz allein .. nur das Loch nicht,
wo man den Kopf durchsteckt—das war
schon da, als ich mit Stricken anfing!"

   Genau, *precise;* ganz allein, *all alone;*
durchstecken, *to put through;* schon, *already;*
anfangen, *to begin.*

DAS AUTO—THE MOTOR CAR
(English key on page 373)

1. die Stosstange, -n
2. das Nummernschild, -er
3. das Stopplicht, -er
4. der Kofferraum, ···-e
5. das Verdeck, -e
6. der Kotflügel, -
7. das Hinterrad, ···-er
8. der Reifen, -
9. das Trittbrett, -er

10. das Ersatzrad, ···-er
11. die Handbremse, -n
12. der Schalthebel, -
13. der Kupplungshebel, -
14. die Fussbremse, -n
15. der Gashebel, -
16. das Lenkrad, ···-er
17. der Signalkopf, ···-e
18. das Schaltbrett, -er

19. der Anlasser, -
20. der Geschwindigkeits-
    messer, -
21. die Windschutzscheibe, -n
22. der Scheibenwischer, -
23. die Motorhaube, -n
24. der Winker, -
25. der Kühler, -
26. der Scheinwerfer, -
27. das Vorderrad, ···-er

NEUNUNDZWANZIGSTE LEKTION

GUTE REISE !

The younger contingent of our two families sets off by car for the seaside. Write as fully as you can, in German, an account of their departure as depicted above.

AUF DER LANDSTRASSE

Die beiden Familien haben beschlossen, die Ferien an der See zu verbringen. Sie fahren nach einem Seebad an der Ostsee. Die jüngeren Mitglieder der Familie fahren im Auto mit Georg am Steuer. Auch Frau Schulz fährt mit. Da im Auto nicht genug Platz für alle ist, fahren die übrigen Familienmitglieder mit dem Zug.

Es dauert fast eine Stunde, bis sie aus Berlin heraus sind. Zuerst fahren sie durch die Stadtmitte, wo sie den gewaltigen Schaden sehen, den der Krieg verursacht hat. Dann fahren sie durch die Vororte, bis sie endlich die offene Landstrasse erreichen.

Während er sich in der Stadt an die Geschwindigkeitsgrenze von 30 km. pro Stunde halten musste, fährt Georg jetzt schneller und schneller: 50, 60, 70, 90, 100

ON THE ROAD

The two families have decided to spend their holidays at the seaside. They are going to a seaside resort on the Baltic Sea. The younger members of the family are going by car, with Georg at the wheel. Mrs. Schulz is also going with them. As there is not enough room in the car for all of them, the rest of the family are going by train.

It takes almost an hour before they are out of Berlin. First they drive through the centre of the city, where they see the immense damage the war has caused. Then they drive through the suburbs until at last they reach the open road.

While in town he had to keep to the speed limit of 30 km. per hour, Georg now drives faster and faster: 50, 60, 70, 90, 100 km. an hour. Mrs. Schulz asks him not

IN THE FARMYARD

This scene is fully described below and on the following page. When you have read the description and are familiar with it, cover over the printed text and try your hand at reconstructing it as fully as you can by referring to the picture.

km. pro Stunde. **Frau Schulz bittet ihn, nicht so schnell zu fahren und erinnert ihn daran, dass er seiner Mutter versprochen hat, nicht schneller als 100 km. pro Stunde zu fahren. Georg, der gemerkt hat, dass seine Fahrgäste sich ungemütlich zu fühlen beginnen, verlangsamt das Tempo und die anderen sind froh darüber.**

Es ist ein herrlicher Tag. Sie haben das Verdeck zurückgeschlagen und die Fenster heruntergelassen. Sie lassen sich die Sonne ins Gesicht scheinen und können ungestört die Landschaft bewundern. Für einen Stadtbewohner sind Wiesen und Felder, Bäume und Wälder, Kühe und Pferde ein ungewöhnlicher Anblick. In den Dörfern und auf den Bauernhöfen sehen sie auch Ziegen, Hühner, Enten, Gänse und Tauben.

An einem Bauernhof machen sie für kurze Zeit Halt, um zu versuchen, frische Milch zu bekommen. Das Bild auf dieser Seite zeigt den Bauernhof und ein Feld, auf dem schwer

to drive so fast, and reminds him that he promised his mother not to drive faster than 100 km. an hour. Georg, who has realized that his passengers are beginning to feel uncomfortable, slows down and the others are glad about it.

It is a glorious day. They have pulled back the hood and let down the windows. They let the sun shine into their faces and can admire the landscape unhindered. For a town dweller, meadows and fields, trees and forests, cows and horses are an unusual sight. In the villages and in the farmyards they also see goats, hens, ducks, geese and pigeons.

Near a farmyard they stop for a short while to try and get some fresh milk. The picture on this page shows the farmyard and a field on which hard work is being

gearbeitet wird. Es ist Erntezeit. Zwei kräftige Pferde ziehen die Mähmaschine, die das Getreide schneidet (mäht) und gleichzeitig die Garben bindet.

In einem anderen Teil des Feldes, wo das Getreide schon gemäht ist, werden die Garben abgeladen und in die Dreschmaschine geworfen. Die Maschine macht einen ohrenbetäubenden Lärm. Vor der Dreschmaschine häufen sich die Getreidesäcke. Ein Arbeiter ist damit beschäftigt, die Säcke auf einen Wagen zu laden, um sie in die Scheune zu fahren.

In dem Bauernhof sieht man die Scheune mit weit geöffneten Toren. Daneben ist der Pferdestall, über dem sich der Heuboden befindet. Hinter dem Hof ist der Obstgarten mit Apfelbäumen, Birnbäumen, Kirschbäumen und Pflaumenbäumen. Die Äpfel, Birnen und Pflaumen sind noch nicht reif. Die Kirschen waren im Juni gepflückt worden.

Auf Einladung der Bauersfrau setzte die Reisegesellschaft sich in den Obstgarten, in den Schatten eines grossen Baumes. Frau Lessing hatte ihnen einen Korb voll mit belegten Broten und anderen guten Sachen mitgegeben. Dazu tranken sie frisch gemolkene Milch, die sie von der Bauersfrau gekauft hatten. Nach ihrem Imbiss gingen sie in den Hof und sahen zu, wie die Hühner gefüttert wurden. Die Kinder schauten auch in den Kuhstall hinein, wo die Kühe gemolken wurden. So verbrachten sie eine interessante halbe Stunde auf dem Bauernhof.

Dann stiegen sie wieder ins Auto und fuhren weiter. Als sie eine ziemlich steile

done. It is harvest time. Two strong horses pull the reaper and binder which cuts (mows) the corn and at the same time binds the sheaves.

In another part of the field, where the corn has already been mown, the sheaves are being unloaded and thrown into the threshing machine. The machine makes a deafening noise. In front of the threshing machine bags of corn are piling up. A labourer is busy loading the sacks on a cart in order to drive them into the barn.

In the farmyard you see the barn with wide open gates. Next to it is the stable, above which is the hay-loft. Behind the yard is the orchard with apple trees, pear trees, cherry trees and plum trees. The apples, pears and plums are not ripe yet. The cherries had been gathered in June.

At the invitation of the farmer's wife the travelling party sat down in the orchard in the shade of a big tree. Mrs. Lessing had given them a basket full of sandwiches and other good things. With it they drank the freshly-drawn milk which they had bought from the farmer's wife. After their snack they went into the farmyard and watched the hens being fed. The children also looked into the cowshed, where the cows were being milked. Thus they spent an interesting half hour in the farmyard.

Then they got back into the car and drove on. When they were climbing a

Eine Panne

DAS DORF—THE VILLAGE
(*English key on page* 373)

1. das Küken, -
2. der Trog, ⋯-e
3. der Hühnerstall, ⋯-e
4. die Leiter, -n
5. die Scheune, -n
6. der Teich, -e
7. der Meilenstein, -e
8. der Wegweiser, -

9. die Wiese, -n
10. die Schule, -n
11. die Kirche, -n
12. die Kirchturmspitze, -n
13. die Windmühle, -n
14. das Strohdach, ⋯-er
15. der Karren, -
16. der Pferdestall, ⋯-e

17. das Bauernhaus, ⋯-er
18. der Kuhstall, ⋯-e
19. die Kuh, ⋯-e
20. das Kalb, ⋯-er
21. die Pumpe, -n
22. der Wassertrog, ⋯-e
23. die Deichsel, -n
24. der Pfau, -en

Böschung hinauffuhren, hatten sie eine kleine Panne. Der Wagen blieb plötzlich stehen, und Georg konnte ihn nicht wieder in Bewegung bringen.

Er stieg aus, öffnete die Motorhaube und fand, dass der Vergaser schmutzig war. Er nahm einen Schraubenzieher aus seinem Werkzeugkasten und machte sich an die Arbeit. Die beiden Knaben halfen ihm, die Düsen zu säubern.

Dann prüfte Georg das Wasser im Kühler und versuchte, den Motor anzulassen. Es gelang ihm. Dann rief er Frau Schulz und die Mädels, die auf und abgingen, um sich die Beine zu strecken. Der Rest der Fahrt verlief ohne weitere Zwischenfälle, und sie kamen vor Einbruch der Nacht an ihrem Bestimmungsort an.

rather steep gradient they had a slight breakdown. The car stopped suddenly and Georg could not get it going again.

He got out, opened the bonnet and found that the carburettor was dirty. He took out a screwdriver from the tool box and set to work. The two boys helped him to clean the jets.

Then Georg tested the water in the radiator and tried to start the engine. He was successful. Then he called Mrs. Schulz and the girls, who were walking up and down to stretch their legs. The remainder of their drive passed without further incident and they arrived at their destination before nightfall.

VERKEHRSZEICHEN—ROAD SIGNS

 **Allgemeines Gefahrenschild** *General danger sign*

 Auf Vorfahrtrecht achten *Major road ahead*

 Parken verboten *No parking*

 Scharfe Kurve *sharp bend*

Für alle Fahrzeuge verboten *All vehicles forbidden*

 Höchstgeschwindigkeit *Speed limit*

 Kreuzung *cross-roads*

Für Kraftwagen verboten *Motor cars forbidden*

 Nur für Radfahrer *Cyclists only*

 Querrinne *Gully across road*

Für Krafträder verboten *Motor cycles forbidden*

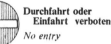 **Haltezeichen an Zollstellen** *Halt sign at Customs*

 Beschränkter Bahnübergang *Level crossing with gates*

 Durchfahrt oder Einfahrt verboten *No entry*

Parkplatz *Parking place*

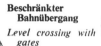 **Unbeschränkter Bahnübergang** *Level crossing without gates*

 Halten verboten *No halting*

Vorsicht! (z.B. nahe einer Schule) *Caution! (e.g. near a school)*

1. der Zweisitzer, -	8. der Wanderer, -	15. die Tankstelle, -n
2. das Fahrrad, ···-er	9. der Zaun, ···-e	16. die Garage, -n
3. die Lenkstange, -n	10. die Panne, -n	17. der Mechaniker, -
4. das Pedal, -e	11. das Dreirad, ···-er	18. der Lastkraftwagen, -
5. die Kette, -n	12. die Limousine, -n	19. der Rennwagen, -
6. das Verkehrszeichen, -	13. der Omnibus, -se	20. die Hecke, -n
7. der Hügel, -	14. die Zapfsäule, -n	21. die Burg, -en

ON THE ROAD
on page 373)

22. der Wald, ··-er
23. das Tandem, -s
24. das Kabriolett, -e
25. die Landstrasse, -n
26. die Strassenecke, -n
27. die Rettungsstelle, -n
28. das Motorrad, ··-er

29. der Bürgersteig, -e
30. das Rennrad, ···-er
31. der Wohnwagen, -
32. der Salonwagen, -
33. der Beiwagen, -
34. die Kurve, -n
35. das Feld, -er

36. der Fussweg, -e
37. die Mauer, -n
38. der Briefkasten, ··-
39. die Sperre, -n
40. der Bahnübergang, ··-e
41. der Bahnwärter, -
42. die Flagge, -n

FURTHER MOTORING WORDS AND PHRASES

der Führerschein, -e	driving licence	**Mein Wagen hat eine Panne.**	
die Achse, -n	axle	*My car has broken down.*	
die Batterie, -n	battery		
die Zündung, -en	ignition	**Bitte, lassen Sie ihn holen.**	
der Auspuff, -e	exhaust	*Please send someone to fetch it.*	
der Vergaser, -	carburettor		
die Düse, -n	jets (of carburet-	**Wechseln Sie bitte dieses Rad (diesen**	
die Bremse, -n	brakes [tor)	**Reifen).**	
bremsen	to put on the	*Please change this wheel (this tyre).*	
	brake		
die Laternen (f., pl.)	lamps	**Bitte, waschen Sie meinen Wagen.**	
		Please wash my car.	

die Geschwindigkeit, -en ⎫
das Tempo   ⎬ *speed*

der Werkzeugkasten, ··-	tool-box	**Wann kann ich ihn wiederhaben?**	
der Schraubenschlüssel, -	spanner	*When can I have it back?*	
der Wagenheber, -	jack		
das Benzin	gasoline	**Kann ich meinen Wagen hier stehen lassen?**	
die Strassenkarte, -n	road map	*Can I park my car here?*	
fahren	to drive		
den Motor anlassen	to start the	**Ich habe kein Benzin mehr.**	
	engine	*I have run out of gas.*	
anhalten	to stop		
zu schnell fahren	to drive too fast	**Wollen Sie bitte Benzin auffüllen.**	
langsamer fahren	to slow down	*Will you fill up with gas, please.*	
ölen, schmieren	to oil, grease		
		Ist eine Garage hier in der Nähe?	
		Is there a garage near here?	

LUCKY AND HAPPY

Sie haben Glück.
You are lucky.

Ich habe (kein) Glück gehabt.
I was (unlucky) lucky.

Sie sind sehr (un-) glücklich.
They are very (un-) happy.

das Glück	=	happiness, luck
das Unglück	=	unhappiness
glücklich	=	happy
unglücklich	=	unhappy
Glück haben	=	to be lucky
Unglück haben	=	to be unlucky

Glückliche Menschen

TO SUCCEED

Es gelingt mir nie, den ersten Preis zu gewinnen.
I never succeed in winning the first prize.

Ich hoffe, es wird Ihnen gelingen.
I hope you will succeed.

Es gelang ihm (ihr) nicht.
He (she) did not succeed.

Es ist uns (ihnen) gelungen.
We (they) have succeeded.

Gelingen (gelang, gelungen) is an impersonal verb, i.e. it can be used in the third person only. As shown in the foregoing examples, the person who succeeds is put in the dative case.

COMPOUNDS WITH *DA*

Ich kann damit nicht schreiben.
I cannot write with it.

Es sind keine Streichhölzer darin.
There are no matches in it.

Sprechen Sie nicht darüber.
Don't talk about it.

Wollen Sie etwas davon haben?
Do you want some of it?

Sie sitzen darauf.
You are sitting on it.

The pronoun of the third person is not used with a preposition in speaking of objects. Its place is taken by **da** (**dar** before a vowel) with the preposition appended. **Damit**=*with it* or *with them* (*therewith*); **dafür**=*for it* or *for them* (*therefor*); **darin**= *in it* or *in them* (*therein*), etc.

Note.—**Da** is also combined with **hin** and **her**. **Dahin** is *there* in the sense of *thither*, and **daher** means *from there* and also *therefore*, e.g.:

Wir fahren jedes Jahr dahin.
We go there every year.

Wir kommen gerade daher.
We are just coming from there.

Ich bin sehr beschäftigt und muss daher zu Hause bleiben.
I am very busy and must therefore stay at home.

PLUPERFECT TENSE

Sie hatten schon gegessen, als wir ankamen.
They had already eaten when we arrived.

Die Auskunft, die er mir gegeben hatte, war falsch.
The information which he had given me was wrong.

Er war ausgegangen.
He had gone out.

Wir waren verreist.
We had been away (on a journey).

The pluperfect tense (which expresses what *had* happened) is formed by means of the past participle with the imperfect of **haben** or **sein**.

NEW NOUNS

DER		
	Schaden, ··	damage
	Krieg, -e	war
	Fahrgast, ··-e	passenger
	Bewohner, -	inhabitant
	Wald, ··-er	forest
	Anblick, -e	sight, view
	Hof, ··-e	yard
	Lärm	noise
	Sack, ··-e	bag, sack
	Schatten, -	shadow
	Imbiss, -e	snack
	Zwischenfall, ··-e	incident
	Schraubenzieher, -	screwdriver
	Einbruch, ··-e	burglary
	Einbruch der Nacht	nightfall
	Bestimmungsort, -e	destination

DIE		
	Mitte, -n	centre
	Landschaft, -en	landscape
	Wiese, -n	meadow
	Ziege, -n	goat
	Ente, -n	duck
	Ernte, -n	harvest
	Garbe, -n	sheaf
	Gesellschaft, -en	company, gathering
	Böschung, -en	slope, gradient
	Grenze, -n	limit, frontier

DAS		
	Bad, ··-er	resort, bath
	Verdeck, -e	hood
	Getreide	corn
	Werkzeug, -e	tool

GEBESSERT

"Angeklagter, wurden Sie schon früher einmal bestraft?"

"Ja, vor zehn Jahren, Herr Richter!"

"Wofür?"

"Wegen Badens an verbotener Stelle."

"Und seitdem?"

"Seitdem habe ich nicht mehr gebadet."

Gebessert, *reformed;* **angeklagt,** *accused;* **bestrafen,** *to punish;* **der Richter,** -, *judge;* **wegen,** *on account of* (followed by the genitive case); **seitdem,** *since.*

VERBS—REGULAR

verursachen	=	*to cause*
bewundern	=	*to admire*
merken	=	*to notice, to realise*
verlangsamen	=	*to slow down*
säubern	=	*to clean*
erreichen	=	*to reach*
erinnern	=	*to remind*
pflücken	=	*to pick, to gather*
prüfen	=	*to test, to examine*

VERBS—IRREGULAR

beschliessen, beschloss,
beschlossen =*to decide*
halten (hält), hielt,
gehalten =*to hold, to keep*
bitten, bat,
gebeten =*to request*
lassen (lässt), liess,
gelassen =*to let*
scheinen, schien,
geschienen =*to shine, to seem*
helfen (hilft), half,
geholfen =*to help*
melken, molk,
gemolken =*to milk*

EXERCISES

I Compound Adverbs

Complete each sentence, using one of the following: damit, darin, dahinter, davor, daraus, davon, dazu, darüber. 1. Hier ist ein Tintenfass. Es ist genug Tinte ... 2. Diese Feder schreibt nicht gut. Ich kann ... nicht schreiben. 3. Bitte, stehen Sie nicht vor der Lampe. Ich kann nicht lesen, wenn Sie immer ... stehen. 4. Diese Tasse ist schmutzig. Man kann ... nicht trinken. 5. Der Tisch ist in der Mitte und der Kamin (*fireplace*) ist .... 6. Der Kuchen ist gut. Möchten Sie ein Stück ...? 7. Man kann hier nicht lesen. Das Licht ist nicht gut genug .... 8. Worüber sprechen Sie? Über Politik? Ich kann ... nicht sprechen. 9. Dieses Messer ist stumpf. Ich kann ... nicht schneiden. 10. Die Flasche ist leer. Es ist kein Tropfen mehr ...

II Das Gegenteil

Klein *ist das Gegenteil von* gross; kurz *ist das Gegenteil von* lang. *Was ist das Gegenteil von?* . . . 1. alt. 2. gut. 3. breit. 4. schön. 5. hell. 6. früh. 7. jung. 8. sich setzen. 9. hinausgehen. 10. oben. 11. sich ankleiden. 12. richtig. 13. stark. 14. voll. 15. rechts. 16. leicht. 17. dunkel. 18. spät.

III Translate into German

1. I decided to spend my holidays at the seaside. 2. They live in a suburb, half an hour by bus from the centre of the town. 3. What is the speed-limit in this village? 4. You are driving too fast. Please slow down. 5. Let's stop for a short while. 6. Let's try to get something to eat. 7. When we arrived they had already milked the cows. 8. How long will it take to have the car repaired (= to let the car repair)? 9. Our car broke down. 10. These tools are dirty. Can you help me to clean them?

(*Answers on page* 366)

AUF DER WOHNUNGSSUCHE

Hauswirt: "Ich muss Sie darauf aufmerksam machen, dass keine Kinder in dieser Wohnung gestattet sind."

Wohnungssuchender: "Wir haben keine Kinder."

Hauswirt: "Auch keine Haustiere oder Klaviere?"

Wohnungssuchender: "Wir haben keine Haustiere, und wir sind dabei, unser Klavier zu verkaufen."

Hauswirt: "Es ist auch nicht gestattet .."

Wohnungssuchender: "Moment, bitte. Haben Sie etwas dagegen, dass die neuen Schuhe meiner Frau ein wenig knarren?"

Die Wohnungssuche, -, *flat hunting;* **der Hauswirt, -,** *landlord;* **aufmerksam machen,** *draw attention, to allow;* **das Haustier, -e,** *pet;* **wir sind dabei,** *we are about;* **haben Sie etwas dagegen,** *do you mind;* **knarren,** *squeak.*

DAS STRANDBAD AM WANNSEE BEI BERLIN

Nur eine halbe Stunde Bahnfahrt von Berlin liegt der Wannsee. An seinem ausgedehnten Strandbad sonnen sich, baden und schwimmen unzählige Menschenmassen an schönen Sommersonntagen. Liegestühle und Strandkörbe sind knapp geworden. Die meisten liegen im Sande und lassen sich von der Sonne braun brennen.

(Translation on page 378)

das Strandbad, ···-er	ausgedehnt	sich sonnen	unzählig	die Menschenmasse, -n
bathing beach	*extensive*	*to sunbathe*	*innumerable*	*crowd of people*

der Liegestuhl, ···-e	der Strandkorb, ···-e	knapp	brennen
deck chair	*covered wicker beach chair*	*scarce*	*to burn*

295

1. das Zelt, -e
2. der Zeltpflock, ···-e
3. das Segelboot, -e
4. die Badende, -n
5. der Eimer, -
6. der Bademantel, ···-
7. die Badehose, -n

8. der Wasserball, ···-e
9. der Liegestuhl, ···-e
10. der Strand, -e
11. der Wellenbrecher, -
12. die Welle, -n
13. die See, -n
14. die Sandbank, ···-e

15. die Sandburg, -en
16. das Ruderboot, -e
17. die Landungsbrücke, -n
18. die Möwe, -n
19. der Ausflugsdampfer, -
20. der Pavillon, -s
21. der Seesteg, -e

AT THE SEASIDE
on page 373)

22. das Hotel, -s
23. das Bootshaus, ··-er
24. die Badekabine, -n
25. der Verkaufsstand, ··-e
26. der Musikpavillon, -s
27. die Uferpromenade, -n
28. der Felsen, -

29. das Felsgestein, -e
30. der Strandkorb, ··-e
31. die Rettungsstelle, -n
32. der Rettungsring, -e
33. die Schwimmweste, -n
34. der Sonnenschirm, -e
35. das Badetuch, ··-er

36. die Badekappe, -n
37. der Badeanzug, ··-e
38. der Badeschuh, -e
39. das Ruder, -
40. der Bootsmann, ··-er
41. der Anker, -
42. die Ruderklampe, -n

297

DREISSIGSTE LEKTION

AN DER SEE

Die beiden Familien hatten zusammen eine möblierte Wohnung in Heringsdorf, einem bekannten Seebad an der Ostsee[1], gemietet[2]. Das ist billiger als im Hotel zu wohnen.

Am ersten Tag, während Frau Schulz damit beschäftigt war auszupacken und alles einzuordnen, gingen die jungen Leute dem Strande zu.

Hilde: Wie schade, dass wir nicht unsere Badesachen mithaben! Wir hätten im Sand spielen und nachher baden können!

Lotte: Wir werden nachmittags baden gehen können.

Hans: Ist jetzt Ebbe oder Flut?

Georg: Weisst du denn nicht, dass es an der Ostsee kaum einen Unterschied zwischen Ebbe und Flut gibt?

Hans: Das habe ich nicht gewusst. Bei uns an der Nordsee ist das anders.

AT THE SEASIDE

The two families had together rented a furnished flat in Heringsdorf, a well-known seaside place on the Baltic Sea. This is cheaper than living in an hotel.

On the first day, while Mrs. Schulz was busy unpacking and arranging everything, the young people walked towards the beach.

Hilde: What a pity that we haven't our bathing things with us! We would have been able to play on the sand and bathe afterwards!

Lotte: We shall be able to go bathing in the afternoon.

Hans: Is the tide low or high now?

Georg: Don't you know that on the Baltic there is hardly any difference between low tide and high tide?

Hans: I didn't know that. It is different with us on the North Sea.

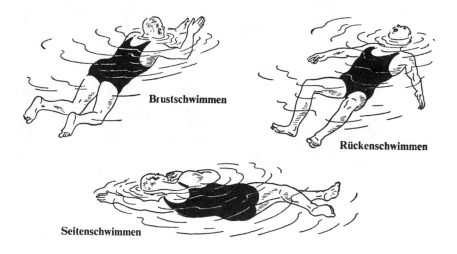

Brustschwimmen

Rückenschwimmen

Seitenschwimmen

---

[1] There are two German words for *sea* : **die See** and **das Meer**. **Die See** is especially used for **die Nordsee** and **die Ostsee,** and in the expression **an der See** (*at the seaside*). **Der See** is *the lake*.
[2] Past participle of **mieten,** *to rent*. Note that **vermieten** = *to let* and **die Miete** = *the rent*.

298

Georg: An der Ostsee beträgt der Unterschied nur einige Zentimeter und ist kaum bemerkbar.

Georg: On the Baltic the difference amounts to only a few inches and is hardly noticeable.

Lotte: Ah, die See! Was für ein herrlicher Anblick!

Lotte: Ah, the sea! What a magnificent sight!

Grete: Und der Strand besteht ganz aus Sand. Keine Steine, an denen man sich die Füsse verletzen kann. Wie schön!

Grete: And the beach is all sand. No stones on which one can hurt one's feet. How lovely!

Hans: Seht ihr den grossen Dampfer dort am Horizont? Wo mag der wohl hinfahren?

Hans: Do you see the big steamer there on the horizon? I wonder where she is going?

Georg: Es muss das Schiff sein, das nach Schweden fährt.

Georg: It must be the boat which goes to Sweden.

Hilde: Was für eine Menge Fischerboote! Was für Fische fängt man denn hier?

Hilde: What a lot of fishing boats! What kind of fish do they catch here?

Lotte: Meistens Flundern. Ich glaube, es gibt heute welche zum Mittagessen.

Lotte: Mostly flounders. I believe there are some for lunch to-day.

Georg: Da die anderen inzwischen angekommen sein werden, gehen wir lieber zurück, sonst werden sie noch alles aufessen.

Georg: As the others will have arrived meanwhile, we'd better go back, otherwise they'll eat up everything.

DIE HEIMREISE NACH ENGLAND

THE JOURNEY HOME TO ENGLAND

Während die beiden Familien ihre Ferien an der See hatten, erinnerte sich Mr. Brown, dass er Herrn Lessing versprochen hatte, ihn zu besuchen. Er ging in eine Telefonkabine, nahm den Hörer ab und sagte: Westend zweiunddreissig, siebenundsechzig.

While the two families were having their holidays at the seaside, Mr. Brown remembered that he had promised Mr. Lessing to call on him. He went into a telephone box, took off the receiver and said: Westend three-two, six-seven.

Das Mädchen [bei Lessing]: Hier bei Lessing.

The Maid [at the Lessing's]: This is Mr. Lessing's house.

Herr B.: Hier Brown. Kann ich bitte Herrn Lessing sprechen?

Mr. B.: Mr. Brown speaking. May I speak to Mr. Lessing please?

Mädchen: Er ist verreist.

Maid: He has gone away.

Herr B.: Ist Frau Lessing zu Hause?

Mr. B.: Is Mrs. Lessing at home?

Mädchen: Sie ist auch mitgefahren. Sie haben auch die Kinder mitgenommen.

Maid: She has also gone with him. They have taken the children, too.

Herr B.: Wohin sind sie gefahren?

Mr. B.: Where have they gone?

Mädchen: Sie sind an die See gefahren, nach Heringsdorf.

Maid: They have gone to the seaside, to Heringsdorf.

Herr B.: Wie lange werden sie dort bleiben?

Mr. B.: How long will they stay there?

Mädchen: Drei bis vier Wochen. Sie werden Ende August zurück sein. Kann ich etwas bestellen[1]?

Maid: Three to four weeks. They will be back at the end of August. Can I give them a message?

---

[1] Normally bestellen means *to order*, but its use here, in the sense of *to give a message*, should be noted.

der Gleitflug

der Abflug

die Landung

Herr B.: Bestellen Sie einen schönen Gruss von Herrn Brown aus London. Sagen Sie bitte, dass es mir leid tut, sie nicht angetroffen zu haben. Ich werde Ende August wieder anrufen.

Es war ihm aber nicht möglich, die Familie Lessing wiederzusehen, da er plötzlich nach London zurückmusste. Sein Vater war schwer erkrankt, und ein dringendes Telegramm hat ihn nach London zurückgerufen.

Um so schnell wie möglich an das Krankenbett seines Vaters zu gelangen, entschloss er sich zu fliegen. Eine Stunde nach Empfang des Telegramms war er bereits auf dem Flughafen. Glücklicherweise flog zwanzig Minuten später ein Flugzeug nach London ab.

Der Flug von Berlin nach London dauerte etwas über zwei Stunden. In London wurde er durch die Pass- und Zollrevision aufgehalten. Ein Zollbeamter fragte ihn, ob er etwas zu verzollen habe. Er musste seine Koffer aufmachen, und der Beamte untersuchte sein Gepäck, fand aber nichts zollpflichtiges.

Nachdem er auch durch die Passkontrolle gegangen war, stürzte er zu einem Taxi und

Mr. B.: Give them best regards from Mr. Brown from London. Please say that I am sorry not to have found them at home. I shall ring again at the end of August.

However, it was not possible for him to see the Lessing family again, as suddenly he had to go back to London. His father had fallen seriously ill and an urgent telegram recalled him to London.

In order to get to his father's sick-bed as quickly as possible, he decided to fly. One hour after having received the telegram he was already at the airport. Fortunately, twenty minutes later an aeroplane was leaving for London.

The flight from Berlin to London took just over two hours. At London he was held up by the passport and customs examinations. A customs official asked him if he had anything to declare. He had to open his trunks, and the official examined his luggage but did not find anything dutiable.

After he had also passed the passport examination, he rushed to a taxi and hur-

eilte nach dem Krankenhaus, wohin man seinen Vater gebracht hatte. Glücklicherweise ging es seinem Vater etwas besser, und bald erholte er sich völlig.

Auch Herr Adams, den Herr Brown in Berlin kennen gelernt hatte, blieb nicht mehr lange in Deutschland. Da er es nicht so eilig hatte und nicht gern fliegt, weil er immer luftkrank wird, fuhr er mit der Eisenbahn und mit dem Schiff.

Die Fahrt von Berlin nach London dauert etwa zwanzig Stunden. Man fährt zuerst mit der Eisenbahn nach Holland oder Belgien und von Vlissingen mit dem Schiff nach Harwich, oder von Ostende nach Dover. Man kann auch über Hamburg fahren, aber dann dauert die Seefahrt länger.

Da Herr Adams immer seekrank wird, wenn die See stürmisch ist, hat er keinen dieser üblichen Reisewege gewählt. Die kürzeste Seefahrt über den Ärmelkanal ist von Calais nach Dover. Obwohl es eine längere Eisenbahnfahrt bedeutete, hat er diese Route gewählt; denn Calais ist bekanntlich der von England nächste Ort auf dem europäischen Festland.

ried to the hospital to which his father had been taken. Fortunately, his father was a little better and he soon recovered completely.

Mr. Adams, whom Mr. Brown had met in Berlin, did not stay much longer in Germany either. As he was not in such a hurry and does not like flying, because he always gets air-sick, he went by train and boat.

The journey from Berlin to London takes about twenty hours. First one goes by train to Holland or Belgium and from Flushing by boat to Harwich, or from Ostend to Dover. One can also go via Hamburg, but then the sea voyage takes longer.

As Mr. Adams always gets sea-sick when the sea is rough, he chose neither of these usual travel routes. The shortest crossing across the English Channel is from Calais to Dover. Although it meant a longer train journey he chose this route, because Calais is, as is well known, the place nearest to England on the Continent of Europe.

* * *

HOW TO TRANSLATE *WHEN*

Wann wird das Schiff ankommen?
When will the ship arrive?

Ich fragte ihn, wann er mich besuchen würde.
I asked him when he would come to see me.

Als ich gestern Abend nach Hause kam, ging ich sofort zu Bett.
When I came home last night I went to bed at once.

Es war vier Uhr, als sie fortgingen.
It was four o'clock when they went away.

Es ist noch dunkel, wenn wir aufstehen.
It is still dark when we get up.

Wird es nicht zu spät sein, wenn Sie mit der Arbeit fertig sind?
Won't it be too late when you have finished your work?

Wann is used to introduce a question, either direct or indirect; **als** refers to a single

occurrence in the past; and **wenn** is used with verbs in the present or future tense, though it is also used with the past tense in the sense of *whenever*. Compare the following:

Als er kam, hatte er einen Blumenstrauss in der Hand.
When he came [single happening] *he had a bunch of flowers in his hand.*

Wenn er kam, brachte er immer Blumen mit.
When(ever) he came [repeated action] *he always brought flowers with him.*

Note that **wenn** also means *if*:

Wir werden um sieben ankommen, wenn der Zug keine Verspätung hat.
We shall arrive at seven if the train is not delayed.

But *if* in the sense of *whether* is **ob**.

1. der Raddampfer, -
2. das Fährschiff, -e
3. der Ventilator, -en
4. der Scheinwerfer, -
5. der Bootskran, ¨-e
6. die Persenning, -e
7. das Rettungsboot, -e
8. das Seil (Tau), -e

9. das (Steuer-) Ruder, -
10. der Schiffsoffizier, -e
11. der Kapitän, -e
12. der Feldstecher, -
13. die Kommandobrücke,- n
14. die Geländerstange, -n
15. der Schlepper, -
16. das Segelboot, -e

17. das Segel, -
18. der Frachtdampfer,
19. der Bug, -e
20. der Ladebaum, ¨-e
21. das Heck, -e
22. der Kran, ¨-e
23. das Fischerboot, -e
24. die Fähre, -n

THE HARBOUR
on page 373)

25. der Passagierdampfer, -
26. der Schornstein, -e
27. der Rumpf, ¨-e
28. das Schwimmdock, -s
29. der Kai, -e
30. der Schuppen, -
31. die Fabrik, -en
32. der Wagen, -

33. die Mole, -n
34. der Schleppkahn, ¨-e
35. das Motorboot, -e
36. das Kielwasser, -
37. der Poller, -
38. die Back, -en
39. das Bullauge, -n
40. der Laderaum, ¨-e

41. der Matrose, -n
42. der Mast, -e
43. das Krähennest, -er
44. das Promenadendeck, -e
45. das Bootsdeck, -e
46. der Passagier, -e
47. das Ruderboot, -c
48. das Ruder, -

"Was für
einen
schönen
Hut Sie
haben!"

WHAT A . . . . !

Was für grosse Zähne dieser Mann hat!
What big teeth this man has!

Was für einen schönen Hut Sie haben!
What a beautiful hat you have!

Was für eine grosse Tochter Sie haben!
What a big daughter you have!

Was für ein hässliches Gesicht der Junge hat!
What an ugly face that boy has!

Was für reizende Blumen!
What charming flowers!

The exclamation *What a ...!* is translated by **Was für** followed by **ein**, which is declined according to case and gender. In the plural **Was für** is used by itself, as in the first example above. It does not govern the case of the noun it precedes; this is dependent upon the relationship of the noun with the verb.

SUBJUNCTIVE MOOD

(1) **Er sagte, dass er müde sei.**
   He said that he was tired.

   Er fragte, ob er etwas zu verzollen habe.
   He asked if he had anything to declare.

(2) **Ich wünschte, er wäre hier.**
   I wished he were here.

   Er fürchtete, dass sie nicht kommen könnte.
   He was afraid that she could not come.

The subjunctive is used: (1) in indirect speech to express uncertainty; (2) in expressions of wishing, fearing, doubting, permission and ordering (when it is doubtful if the order will be obeyed).

A comparison of the forms given on page 319 shows that in the present tense the subjunctive retains the root vowel of the infinitive, and that the third person singular ends in -e; e.g. **er habe, er nehme, er sehe, er gebe**, etc. Note the irregular forms of the present subjunctive of **sein**.

The imperfect subjunctive of regular verbs is identical with the imperfect indicative. In the case of irregular verbs, the imperfect subjunctive takes the **Umlaut** and the ending -e in the first and third persons singular, e.g.:

Indicative	Subjunctive
ich (er) war	**ich (er) wäre**
ich (er) kam	**ich (er) käme**
ich (er) nahm	**ich (er) nähme**

ADJECTIVES USED AS NOUNS

der Fremde	=	*the stranger*
ein Fremder	=	*a stranger*
die Fremden	=	*the strangers*
Fremde	=	*strangers*

der Eingeborene	=	*the native*
ein Eingeborener	=	*a native*
die Eingeborenen	=	*the natives*
Eingeborene	=	*natives*

The following common nouns are declined like adjectives in the same way as the above examples:

der Deutsche	=	*the German*
der Beamte	=	*the official*
der Geistliche	=	*the clergyman*
der Reisende	=	*the traveller*
der Untergebene	=	*the subordinate*
der Angestellte	=	*the employee*
(die Angestellten	=	*the staff)*

You will have to be especially careful when meeting one of these, as they are nouns and yet have to be treated like adjectives, thus: **ein Deutscher**=*a German;* **die Deutschen**=*the Germans;* **diese Deutschen**=*these Germans;* **eine Deutsche**=*a German woman;* **das Haus des Deutschen**= *the German's house,* etc.

NEW NOUNS

DER		
	Sand, -e	sand
	Gruss, "-e	greeting
	Pass, "-e	passport
	Punkt, -e	point
	Flug, "-e	flight
	Zoll, "-e	Customs
	Unterschied, -e	difference
	Dampfer, -	steamer
	Hafen, "-	harbour

DIE		
	Ebbe, -n	low tide
	Flut, -en	high tide
	Flunder, -n	flounder
	Menge, -n	crowd
	Revision, -en	examination
	Kontrolle, -n	control

DAS		
	Ende, -n	end
	Schiff, -e	ship, boat

VERBS—REGULAR

mieten = *to rent, to hire*
einordnen (sep.) = *to put in its proper place*
erkranken = *to be taken ill*

VERBS—IRREGULAR

betragen (like tragen) = *to amount*
bestehen (aus) (like stehen) = *to consist (of)*
fangen (fängt), fing, gefangen = *to catch*
anrufen (sep.) (like rufen) = *to ring up*
antreffen (sep.) (like treffen) = *to find at home*

EXERCISES

I Read and Translate

1. Wann haben Sie dieses Jahr Ihre Ferien? 2. Werden Sie zu Hause bleiben, oder werden Sie verreisen? 3. Wohin fahren Sie, an die See oder ins Gebirge? 4. Wir fahren nach einem Seebad an der Südküste von England. 5. Wir haben Zimmer in einer Pension (*boarding-house*) gemietet. 6. Wir werden in der See baden und Ausflüge in die Umgebung machen. 7. Wir werden auch in einem Segelboot aufs Meer hinausfahren. 8. Haben Sie ein Zimmer zu vermieten? 9. Es ist leider keins frei. 10. Ich möchte eine möblierte Wohnung mieten. 11. Für wie lange? 12. Für ein halbes Jahr. 13. Wieviel beträgt die Miete? 14. Sind Licht und Heizung einbegriffen (*included*)?

15. Mit Frühstück oder mit voller Pension (*full board*)? 16. Das Badezimmer ist im ersten Stock. 17. Wollen Sie mich bitte um halb acht wecken.

II Translate into German

1. What a beautiful sight! 2. When will the boat leave? 3. He said that it would arrive to-morrow. 4. She asked him if he was ill. 5. When the teacher arrived the students sat down. 6. What a pity that he did not come with us! 7. Can you show me the way to the beach, please? 8. How long does it take to fly to Paris? 9. I ordered a room in a hotel. 10. We shall leave to-morrow. May I have my bill, please?

(*Answers on page 366*)

DIE RACHE

"Gott sei Dank! Ich bin endlich gerächt", sagte der Schuhhändler, nachdem eine Kundin seinen Laden verliess.

"Was meinen Sie damit?" fragte seine Angestellte.

"Haben Sie das Mädel gesehen, das eben herausging? Sie ist eine Telefonistin und ich habe ihr eine falsche Nummer gegeben."

Die Rache, *revenge;* rächen, *to revenge;* der Schuhhändler, -, *shoe dealer;* die Kundin, -nen, *customer;* verlassen, *to leave;* die Angestellte, -n, *employee;* falsch, *wrong.*

DER STAMMBAUM

"Hier ist ein ganz besonderer Hund mit einem allerersten Stammbaum", pries der Hundeverkäufer ein kleines unscheinbares Tierchen an.

"Kann ich den Stammbaum mal sehen?" meinte der Käufer.

"Den müssen Sie sich selbst aufstellen—er ist der allererste von seiner Zucht!"

Der Stammbaum, "-e, *pedigree;* besonder, *special;* allererst, *first class;* pries .. an (from anpreisen), *extolled;* der Verkäufer, -, *salesman;* unscheinbar, *inconspicuous;* der Käufer, -, *buyer, customer;* aufstellen, *to establish;* der allererste, *the very first;* die Zucht, -en, *breed.*

DER FLUGPLATZ (FLUGHAFEN)—
(English key

1. das Flugzeug, -e
2. der Propeller, -
3. der Motor, -en
4. das Fahrgestell, -e
5. das Laufrad, ‥-er
6. der Reifen, -
7. die Tragfläche, -n

8. der Führersitz, -e
9. die Kabine, -n
10. der Ortssucher, -
11. das Segelflugzeug, -e
12. der Geschwindigkeitsmesser, -
13. die Rumpfnase, -n
14. der Pilot, -en

15. der Helm, -e
16. die Fliegerbrille, -n
17. der Fliegeranzug, ‥-e
18. der Luftfahrgast, ‥-e
19. der Polizist, -en
20. das Flughafen-Gebäude,-
21. der Kontrollturm, ‥-e

THE AIRPORT
on page 373)

22. der Balkon, -e
23. der Windsack, ˮ-e
24. die Antenne, -n
25. der Funkmast, -en
26. der Doppeldecker, -
27. das Wasserflugzeug, -e
28. der Schwimmer, -

29, der Fallschirm, -e
30. der Fallschirmspringer, -
31. der Kran, ˮ-e
32. die Flugzeughalle, -n
33. der Benzintank, -s
34. der Elektrokarren, -
35. der Zollbeamte, -n

36. das Verkehrsflugzeug, -e
37. der Lastwagen, -
38. die Kiste, -n
39. der Rumpf, ˮ-e
40. die Kielflosse, -n
41. der Sauerstoffbehälter, -

WÜRZBURG : WEINLESE AM "STEIN" MIT BLICK ZUR STEINBURG

Die Weinlese findet in Deutschland meist Oktober bis November statt. Wein wird nur in Südwestdeutschland gebaut, am Rhein, an der Mosel, am Neckar und am mittleren Main. In diesen Gegenden ist Wein billig und wird mehr getrunken als Bier.

(*Translation on page* 379)

die Weinlese, -n	**der Blick, -e**	**meist**	**bauen**	**die Gegend, -en**
grape harvest	*view*	*mostly, usually*	*to grow*	*region*

SUMMARY OF GRAMMAR

This section provides a means of ready reference to the most important rules of German grammar, and contains a revision of earlier instruction as well as other features designed to clarify and facilitate study of the language.

THE GERMAN ALPHABET AND CHARACTERS

	Gothic		Written		Pronounced		Gothic		Written		Pronounced
A	𝔄	α			ah	N	𝔑	n			enn
B	𝔅	b			bay	O	𝔇	o			oh
C	ℭ	c			tsay	P	𝔓	p			pay
D	𝔇	d			day	Q	𝔔	q			koo
E	𝔈	e			ay	R	𝔑	r			airr
F	𝔉	f			eff	S	𝔖	ſs			ess
G	𝔊	g			gay	T	𝔗	t			tay
H	𝔥	h			hah	U	𝔘	u			oo
I	𝔍	i			ee	V	𝔙	v			fow
J		j			yot	W	𝔚	w			vay
K	𝔎	k			kah	X	𝔛	x			iks
L	𝔏	l			ell	Y	𝔜	y			ip'-see-lon
M	𝔐	m			emm	Z	ℨ	z			tset

In Germany to-day both the Roman (Latin) and the Gothic type are used. To make the beginner's path easier, this book is printed in Latin type. As to the German script, it is an unnecessary complication for students of German to learn it, since the Latin script is widely used. The forms of the Gothic and written characters are given here solely for reference in case of need.

The Gothic type has two forms for the letter *s*. The form ß is used at the end of a word or syllable; ſ is used in all other cases. *ss* is used between two short vowels only; ß is a special sign for double *s* to indicate that the preceding vowel is long; it also stands at the end of a word. These differences, however, do not apply when Latin characters are used.

SIMILARITY BETWEEN ENGLISH AND GERMAN WORDS

German is in many respects similar to English, especially in the realm of vocabulary.

Apart from those words which are identical or almost so (like **Arm, Finger, Hand, Butter, Fisch, Haus, lang, Mann, ist,** **kommen, bringen,** etc.), the meaning of many words can be ascertained without reference to a dictionary by knowing the following principles according to which English and German words frequently correspond.

ENGLISH		GERMAN	
d	*good, God, red*	t	**gut, Gott, rot**
th	*brother, bath, then, this*	d	**Bruder, Bad, dann, dies**
t	*tin, heart, water, nut*	z or ss	**Zinn, Herz, Wasser, Nuss**
v	*live, love, have, give*	b	**lebe, liebe, habe, gebe**
k	*cook, make, milk, cake*	ch	**Koch, mache, Milch, Kuchen**
p	*pipe, plant, ship, ripe*	pf,ff or f	**Pfeife, Pflanze, Schiff, reif**
gh	*daughter, through, night, light*	ch	**Tochter, durch, Nacht, Licht**
y	*day, say, way, lay*	g	**Tag, sage, Weg, lege**
ch	*cheese, chamber, chart*	k	**Käse, Kammer, Karte**
s and *consonant*	*snow, swan, sly, sledge*	sch and *consonant*	**Schnee, Schwan, schlau, Schlitten**

GENDER OF NOUNS

There are no rules by which the genders of all nouns can be readily ascertained, but the following guide will be found useful, though subject to numerous exceptions.

Masculine
1. Names of male beings (except **das Pferd,** and those ending in **-chen** and **-lein**): **der Mann, der Wolf**
2. Names of seasons, months, days: **der Winter, der Januar, der Montag**

Feminine
1. Names of female beings (except **das Weib** and those ending in **-chen** and **-lein**): **die Lehrerin, die Katze**
2. Most words ending in **-e**: **die Karte, die Lampe**
3. Words ending in **-heit** and **-keit**: **die Schönheit, die Freiheit**
4. Words ending in **-ei**: **die Bäckerei**
5. Words ending in **-ung**: **die Zeitung**
6. Words ending in **-schaft**: **die Freundschaft**
7. Words of foreign origin ending in **-ion**, **-ie, -ik, -tät**: **die Nation, die Familie, die Musik, die Universität**

Neuter
1. Diminutives in **-chen** and **-lein**: **das Mädchen, das Fräulein**
2. Infinitives when used as nouns: **das Essen, das Singen**
3. Most names of countries and places (except **die Schweiz, die Türkei, die Tschechoslowakei**): **das schöne Schottland**
4. Most metals (except **der Stahl**): **das Gold, das Silber**

PLURAL OF NOUNS

(1) **Nouns adding -e.** Most masculines and neuters, some feminines. Most of the masculines, all the feminines and none of the neuters take the Umlaut. Examples:

Masc.: **der Stuhl, die Stühle.** No Umlaut with **der Tag, die Tage; der Schuh, die Schuhe; der Hund, die Hunde.**

Fem.: **die Kuh, die Kühe; die Hand, die Hände; die Wand, die Wände; die Stadt, die Städte; die Nuss, die Nüsse; die Frucht, die Früchte.**

Neut.: **das Jahr, die Jahre; das Ding, die Dinge.**

(2) **Nouns adding -(e)n.** Most feminines; masculines ending in -e (and the word **Herr**); and a few neuters. Examples:

Masc.: **der Knabe, die Knaben; der Herr, die Herren.**

Fem.: **die Feder, die Federn; die Frau, die Frauen.**

Neut.: **das Bett, die Betten; das Hemd, die Hemden; das Auge, die Augen; das Ohr, die Ohren.**

(3) **Nouns adding -er.** Many neuters and a few masculines, all of one syllable. They modify **a, o, u** and **au.** Examples:

Masc.: **der Mann, die Männer; der Wald, die Wälder.**

Neut.: **das Ei, die Eier; das Haus, die Häuser; das Glas, die Gläser; das Kind, die Kinder; das Dorf, die Dörfer; das Wort, die Wörter.**

(4) **Nouns adding -s.** Many foreign words. They do not take the Umlaut. Examples:

das Auto, die Autos; das Hotel, die Hotels; das Kino, die Kinos.

(5) **Nouns with no ending.** Masculines and neuters ending in -en, -el, -er, -chen, -lein; and two feminines. Some of the masculines, and both the feminines, take the Umlaut. Examples:

Masc.: **der Garten, die Gärten; der Löffel, die Löffel.**

Fem.: **die Mutter, die Mütter; die Tochter, die Töchter.**

Neut.: **das Messer, die Messer; das Mädchen, die Mädchen; das Fräulein, die Fräulein.**

MEANINGS AND USES OF THE FOUR CASES

(1) The *nominative case* expresses the subject of the sentence.

(2) The *accusative case* denotes the direct object, i.e. the person or thing directly affected by an action.

(3) The *genitive case* expresses possession.

(4) The *dative case* is used to express the indirect object, i.e. the person to whom we speak, write, give, show, etc.; or the thing to which we apply something.

The following sentence illustrates the use of all four cases:

Die Freundin meiner Mutter sendet uns Blumen.

| | | | |
Nominative   *Genitive*   *Dative   Accusative*

Certain prepositions are followed automatically by the accusative, genitive or dative case. A full list is given on pages 313–314.

ORDER OF WORDS

GEBIRGSFEST IM BERNER OBERLAND

Ringkampf, Musik und Tanz sind die Hauptattraktionen bei diesem alljährlich stattfindenden Gebirgsfest im Berner Oberland. Oft muss man die Ringkämpfer vom Tanz-
boden holen, wenn sie für den nächsten Ringkampf an der Reihe sind.

(Translation on page 379)

das Gebirgsfest, -e	**der Ringkampf, ···-e**	**alljährlich**	**stattfinden**
mountain festival	*wrestling*	*annual*	*to take place*
der Ringkämpfer, -	**der Tanzboden, ···-**	**holen**	**wenn sie an der Reihe sind**
wrestler	*dance floor*	*to fetch*	*when their turn comes*

DECLENSION TABLES

Masculine

	the	*this*	*that*	*which*	*a*	*no*	*my*	
Nom.:	der	dieser	jener	welcher	ein	kein	mein	Vater
Acc.:	den	diesen	jenen	welchen	einen	keinen	meinen	Vater
Gen.:	des	dieses	jenes	welches	eines	keines	meines	Vaters
Dat.:	dem	diesem	jenem	welchem	einem	keinem	meinem	Vater

Feminine

Nom.:	die	diese	jene	welche	eine	keine	meine	Frau
Acc.:	die	diese	jene	welche	eine	keine	meine	Frau
Gen.:	der	dieser	jener	welcher	einer	keiner	meiner	Frau
Dat.:	der	dieser	jener	welcher	einer	keiner	meiner	Frau

Neuter

Nom.:	das	dieses	jenes	welches	ein	kein	mein	Kind
Acc.:	das	dieses	jenes	welches	ein	kein	mein	Kind
Gen.:	des	dieses	jenes	welches	eines	keines	meines	Kindes
Dat.:	dem	diesem	jenem	welchem	einem	keinem	meinem	Kind(e)

Plural (all Genders)

Nom.	die	diese	jene	welche	—	keine	meine	Bücher
Acc.:	die	diese	jene	welche	—	keine	meine	Bücher
Gen.:	der	dieser	jener	welcher	—	keiner	meiner	Bücher
Dat.:	den	diesen	jenen	welchen	—	keinen	meinen	Büchern

Notes on Ending of Nouns

(1) All neuter and most masculine nouns add -s in the genitive singular; those of one syllable add -es.

(2) Masculine nouns ending in -e, as well as the word **Herr** and many masculines of foreign origin, add -n or -en in all cases, singular and plural, except the nominative singular.

der Knabe, den Knaben, des Knaben, dem Knaben, die Knaben.

der Herr, den Herrn, des Herrn, dem Herrn, die Herren.

(3) Feminine nouns do not change in the singular.

(4) The dative plural always ends in -n.

(5) The accusative form of the noun is the same as the nominative, except for the singular of those masculines in (2) above.

(6) In the plural, the nominative, accusative and genitive forms are the same.

(7) Masculine and neuter nouns of one syllable sometimes add -e in the dative singular. This ending is optional and can be omitted.

PREPOSITIONS

Governing the accusative case — { durch, *through;* für, *for;* gegen, *against;* ohne, *without;* um, *round, at (of time).*

Governing the genitive case — { während, *during;* statt, *instead of;* trotz, *in spite of;* wegen, *on account of.*

Governing the dative case — { aus, *out of;* bei, *near, by;* mit, *with;* nach, *after, to;* seit, *since;* von, *of, from;* zu, *to, at.*

[*Continued overleaf*

PREPOSITIONS—*Continued*

Governing the accusative (in answer to the question *where to?*) or the dative (in answer to the question *where?*)

{ **an,** *on, at;* **auf,** *on;* **hinter,** *behind;* **in,** *in, into;* **neben,** *beside;* **über,** *over, across;* **unter,** *under;* **vor,** *before;* **zwischen,** *between.*

Several prepositions can be contracted with the dative or accusative of the definite article, masculine or neuter: **am**=**an dem; ans**=**an das; aufs**=**auf das; beim**=**bei dem; fürs**=**für das; im**=**in dem; ins**=**in das; zum**=**zu dem;** and others.

Only one contraction, **zur**=**zu der,** is formed with the feminine article.

PRONOUNS

(1) Personal

Singular

Nom.:	ich, *I*	du, *thou*	er, *he*	sie, *she*	es, *it*
Acc.:	mich, *me*	dich, *thee*	ihn, *him*	sie, *her*	es, *it*
Gen.:	meiner, *of me*	deiner, *of thee*	seiner, *of him*	ihrer, *of her*	seiner, *of it*
Dat.:	mir, *to me*	dir, *to thee*	ihm, *to him*	ihr, *to her*	ihm, *to it*

Plural

Nom.:	wir, *we*	Sie or ihr, *you*	sie, *they*
Acc.:	uns, *us*	Sie or euch, *you*	sie, *them*
Gen.:	unser, *of us*	Ihrer or euer, *of you*	ihrer, *of them*
Dat.:	uns, *to us*	Ihnen or euch, *to you*	ihnen, *to them*

The genitive case of the personal pronouns is rarely used, but is necessary with the prepositions **statt** (or **anstatt**) and **trotz**: **anstatt meiner**=*instead of me,* **trotz Ihrer**=*in spite of you.* **Wegen** (also governing the genitive case) contracts with the personal pronouns as follows: **meinetwegen**=*for my sake,* **unsertwegen**=*for our sake,* etc.

(2) Reflexive

Singular: **mich,** *myself*   **dich,** *thyself*   **sich,** *himself, herself, itself*

Plural: **uns,** *ourselves*   **euch** or **sich,** *yourself, yourselves*   **sich,** *themselves*

(3) Possessive

	mine	thine	his, its	hers	ours	yours	theirs
Masc. sing.:	meiner	deiner	seiner	ihrer	unserer	Ihrer, eurer	ihrer
Fem. sing.:	meine	deine	seine	ihre	unsere	Ihre, eure	ihre
Neut. sing.:	meines	deines	seines	ihres	unseres	Ihres, eures	ihres

They are all declined like **dieser, diese, dieses** (see page 313)

(4) Relative

	Masc.	Fem.	Neut.	Plural
Nom. (*who, which, that*):	der	die	das	die
Acc. (*whom, which, that*):	den	die	das	die
Gen. (*whose, of which*):	dessen	deren	dessen	deren
Dat. (*to whom, to which*):	dem	der	dem	denen

(5) Interrogative

Nom.: **wer,** *who?*   **was,** *what?*   Gen.: **wessen,** *whose? of whom, of what?*

Acc.: **wen,** *whom?*   **was,** *what?*   Dat.: **wem,** *to whom?*

When **was** is the object of a preposition, it is generally expressed by **wo-** (**wor-** before a vowel) + preposition: **Womit schreiben Sie?** = *with what are you writing?*

CONJUGATION OF AUXILIARY VERBS

HABEN (TO HAVE)

Tense	I	He, She, It	We, You, They	Familiar Form
Present	ich habe	er sie } hat es	wir Sie } haben sie	du hast ihr habt
Imperfect	ich hatte	er Sie } hatte es	wir Sie } hatten sie	du hattest ihr hattet
Perfect	ich habe ... gehabt	er sie } hat ... es } gehabt	wir Sie } haben ... sie } gehabt	du hast } ihr habt } gehabt
Future	ich werde ... haben	er sie } wird ... es } haben	wir Sie } werden ... sie } haben	du wirst } ihr werdet } haben
Imperative	—	—	haben Sie ...!	habe ...! habt ...!

SEIN (TO BE)

Tense	I	He, She, It	We, You, They	Familiar Form
Present	ich bin	er sie } ist es	wir Sie } sind sie	du bist ihr seid
Imperfect	ich war	er sie } war es	wir Sie } waren sie	du warst ihr wart
Perfect	ich bin ... gewesen	er sie } ist ... es } gewesen	wir Sie } sind ... sie } gewesen	du bist } ihr seid } ...gewesen
Future	ich werde ... sein	er sie } wird ... es } sein	wir Sie } werden ... sie } sein	du wirst } ihr werdet } ... sein
Imperative	—	—	seien Sie ...!	sei ...! seid ...!

IM MÜNCHENER ZOOLOGISCHEN GARTEN

Der Zoologische Garten in München ist einer der grössten und modernsten Europas und ist bei Kindern so wie bei Erwachsenen höchst beliebt. Wie überall ist der Elefant, mit seinem riesigen Körper, langen Rüssel und drolligen Streichen, eine der Haupt-attraktionen.

(Translation on page 379)

so wie	**der** (or **die**) **Erwachsene, -n**	**wie überall**	**riesig**	**der Körper,**
as well as	*adult*	*as everywhere*	*gigantic*	*body*

der Rüssel, -	**drollig**	**der Streich, -e**	**die Hauptattraktion, -en**
trunk	*amusing*	*trick*	*chief attraction*

316

CONJUGATION OF REGULAR VERBS
(Imperfect ending in -te, past participle in -t)
Example: sagen = to say

Tense	I	He, She, It	We, You, They	Familiar Form
Present	ich sage	er sie }sagt es	wir Sie }sagen sie	du sagst ihr sagt
Imperfect	ich sagte	er sie }sagte es	wir Sie }sagten sie	du sagtest ihr sagtet
Perfect	ich habe ... gesagt	er sie } hat ... es } gesagt	wir Sie } haben ... sie } gesagt	du hast } ihr habt } ... gesagt
Future	ich werde ... sagen	er sie } wird ... es } sagen	wir Sie } werden ... sie } sagen	du wirst } ihr werdet } ...sagen
Imperative	—	—	sagen Sie!	sag(e)! sagt!

COMPOUND VERBS

Verbs prefixed by another word (usually a preposition or an adverb) have the accent on the prefix. In principal clauses in the present and imperfect tenses the prefix is separated; in dependent clauses it is not.

aufmachen = to open

Present: **ich mache auf**   Perfect: **ich habe aufgemacht**

Imperfect: **ich machte auf**   Future: **ich werde aufmachen**

When I open (dependent clause) = **Wenn ich aufmache**

Note that in the past participle the ge is placed between the two components: **aufgemacht**. The same applies to **zu** used with the infinitive: **Sie brauchen die Tür nur aufzumachen** = *You need only to open the door.*

VERBS WITH INSEPARABLE PREFIXES

Verbs with the prefixes **be-, ent-, er-, ge-, ver-, zer-**, which are always unaccented, form their past participles without the additional ge, e.g.:

besuchen = *to visit*; **ich habe ihn besucht** = *I went to see him.*

entkommen = *to escape;* **der Gefangene ist entkommen** = *the prisoner has escaped.*

erfinden = *to invent;* **Edison hat viele nützliche Sachen erfunden** = *Edison invented many useful things.*

gehören = *to belong;* **die Uhr hatte meinem Vater gehört** = *the watch belonged to my father.*

verlieren = *to lose;* **ich habe meinen Schlüssel verloren** = *I lost my key.*

zerbrechen = *to break;* **die Tasse ist zerbrochen** = *the cup is broken.*

CONJUGATION OF IRREGULAR VERBS

(changing their root vowel in the imperfect, some also in the past participle)

Examples: lesen = *to read;* schlafen = *to sleep;* gehen = *to go*

Tense	I	He, She, It	We, You, They	Familiar Form
Present	ich ⎰ lese ⎱ schlafe ⎰ gehe	er ⎰ liest ⎱ schläft sie ⎰ geht es	wir ⎰ lesen Sie ⎰ schlafen sie ⎰ gehen	du liest, schläfst, gehst ihr lest, schlaft, geht
Imperfect	ich ⎰ las ⎱ schlief ⎰ ging	er ⎰ las sie ⎰ schlief es ⎰ ging	wir ⎰ lasen Sie ⎰ schliefen sie ⎰ gingen	du last, schliefst, gingst ihr last, schlieft, gingt
Perfect	ich ⎰ habe gelesen habe ge- schlafen bin gegangen	er ⎰ hat gelesen sie ⎰ hat ge- schlafen es ⎰ ist gegangen	wir ⎰ haben gelesen Sie ⎰ haben ge- schlafen sie ⎰ sind gegangen	du hast gelesen, bist gegangen, etc. ihr habt gelesen, seid gegangen, etc.
Future	ich werde lesen (schlafen, gehen), etc.			
Imperative	—	—	⎰ lesen Sie! schlafen Sie! gehen Sie!	lies! schlaf! geh! lest! schlaft! geht!

NOTES ON CONJUGATION OF VERBS

(1) When the root vowel is **a, au** or **e,** it is often changed to **ä, äu, i** or **ie** in the familiar form and third person of the present tense singular. This change does not, however, always occur: **ich gehe, du gehst, er geht.**

(2) Most verbs form their perfect tense with **haben.** Those expressing change of place or condition take **sein: ich bin gekommen** = *I have come;* **er ist gestorben** = *he has died.* **Sein** is also used with the perfect tenses of **sein, bleiben** and **werden: ich bin gewesen** = *I have been;* **ich bin geblieben** = *I have stayed;* **ich bin geworden** = *I have become.*

(3) The following verbs drop the final letter in the first and third persons singular of the present tense: **wissen** = *to know;* **können** = *to be able;* **müssen** = *to have to;* **wollen** = *to want;* **mögen** = *to like;* **sollen** = *ought;* **dürfen** = *to be allowed*

Present:	ich er sie es ⎰	weiss kann muss will mag soll darf	wir Sie sie ⎰	wissen können müssen wollen mögen sollen dürfen	du ⎰	weisst kannst musst willst magst sollst darfst	ihr ⎰	wisst könnt müsst wollt mögt sollt dürft

[Continued on next page

NOTES ON CONJUGATION OF VERBS—*Continued*

Imperfect:

| ich
er
sie
es | wusste
konnte
musste
wollte
mochte
sollte
durfte | wir
Sie
sie | wussten
konnten
mussten
wollten
mochten
sollten
durften | du | wusstest
konntest
musstest
wolltest
mochtest
solltest
durftest | ihr | wusstet
konntet
musstet
wolltet
mochtet
solltet
durftet |

Perfect: ich habe gewusst (gekonnt, gemusst, gewollt, gemocht, gesollt, gedurft)

Future: ich werde wissen (können, müssen, wollen, mögen, sollen, dürfen)

SUBJUNCTIVE MOOD

As already explained on page 304, the subjunctive mood is used in indirect speech to express uncertainty and in expressions of wishing, fearing, doubting, permission and ordering (when it is doubtful if the order will be obeyed).

It is also used after als wenn and als ob (*as if*), damit (*in order that*), and damit nicht (*lest*).

The tenses of the subjunctive are formed as follows :

Present Tense

The forms for the present tense are the same as for the indicative (given on pages 315-318) with the exception of the third person singular and the familiar form. Compare the following:

Indicative	Subjunctive
er hat	er habe
du hast	du habest
ihr habt	ihr habet
er sagt	er sage
du sagst	du sagest
ihr sagt	ihr saget
er sieht	er sehe
du siehst	du sehest
ihr seht	ihr sehet
er schläft	er schlafe
du schläfst	du schlafest
ihr schlaft	ihr schlafet

Entirely different from the indicative is the subjunctive of sein:

Indicative	Subjunctive
Ich bin	ich sei
du bist	du seiest
er ist	er sei
wir sind	wir seien
ihr seid	ihr seiet
sie sind	sie seien

Imperfect Tense

The imperfect subjunctive of regular verbs is identical with the imperfect indicative as given on page 317. With irregular verbs the imperfect subjunctive takes the Umlaut throughout and it ends in -e in the first and third persons singular.

Indicative	Subjunctive
ich hatte	ich hätte
du hattest	du hättest
er hatte, etc.	er hätte, etc
ich war	ich wäre
du warst	du wärest
er war, etc.	er wäre, etc.
ich sprach	ich spräche
du sprachst	du sprächest
er sprach	er spräche, etc.
ich ging	ich ginge
du gingst	du gingest
er ging, etc.	er ginge, etc.

HEUERNTE IM SCHWEIZER TIEFLAND

Während der Heuwagen geladen wird und alle Landarbeiter und Erntehelfer sich unter der heissen Sommersonne abmühen, kann sich der Ochs ausruhen. Er benutzt die Pause, um einen Imbiss zu sich zu nehmen.

(*Translation on page* 379)

die Heuernte, -n	**das Tiefland, ···-er**	**das Heu**	**der Landarbeiter, -**	**heiss**
haymaking	*plain*	*hay*	*farm worker*	*hot*
sich abmühen	**sich ausruhen**	**benutzen**	**der Imbiss, -e**	**zu sich nehmen**
to toil	*to rest*	*to use*	*snack*	*to partake of*

ALPHABETICAL LIST OF IRREGULAR VERBS

N.B.—Compound verbs are not given. They have the same forms as the corresponding simp'e verbs. Those with * take **sein** to form their compound tenses.

INFINITIVE	PRESENT (3rd sing.)	IMPERFECT (1st & 3rd sing.)	PAST PARTICIPLE	ENGLISH
backen	bäckt	buk	gebacken	*to bake*
befehlen	befiehlt	befahl	befohlen	*to command*
beginnen	beginnt	begann	begonnen	*to begin*
beissen	beisst	biss	gebissen	*to bite*
betrügen	betrügt	betrog	betrogen	*to deceive*
biegen	biegt	bog	gebogen	*to bend*
bieten	bietet	bot	geboten	*to offer*
binden	bindet	band	gebunden	*to bind*
bitten	bittet	bat	gebeten	*to ask*
blasen	bläst	blies	geblasen	*to blow*
*bleiben	bleibt	blieb	geblieben	*to remain*
brechen	bricht	brach	gebrochen	*to break*
brennen	brennt	brannte	gebrannt	*to burn*
bringen	bringt	brachte	gebracht	*to bring*
denken	denkt	dachte	gedacht	*to think*
empfehlen	empfiehlt	empfahl	empfohlen	*to recommend*
*erschrecken	erschrickt	erschrak	erschrocken	*to become frightened*
essen	isst	ass	gegessen	*to eat*
*fahren	fährt	fuhr	gefahren	*to go* (*in any conveyance*)
fallen	fällt	fiel	gefallen	*to fall*
fangen	fängt	fing	gefangen	*to catch*
finden	findet	fand	gefunden	*to find*
*fliegen	fliegt	flog	geflogen	*to fly*
*fliehen	flieht	floh	geflohen	*to flee*
*fliessen	fliesst	floss	geflossen	*to flow*
frieren	friert	fror	gefroren	*to freeze*
geben	gibt	gab	gegeben	*to give*
*gehen	geht	ging	gegangen	*to go*
*gelingen	gelingt	gelang	gelungen	*to succeed* (impers.)
*geschehen	geschieht	geschah	geschehen	*to happen*
gewinnen	gewinnt	gewann	gewonnen	*to win*
giessen	giesst	goss	gegossen	*to pour*
graben	gräbt	grub	gegraben	*to dig*
halten	hält	hielt	gehalten	*to hold*
heben	hebt	hob	gehoben	*to lift*
heissen	heiss	hiess	geheissen	*to be called*
helfen	hilft	half	geholfen	*to help*
kennen	kennt	kannte	gekannt	*to know, to be acquainted*
*kommen	kommt	kam	gekommen	*to come* [*with*
*kriechen	kriecht	kroch	gekrochen	*to creep*
laden	lädt	lud	geladen	*to load*
lassen	lässt	liess	gelassen	*to let, allow, permit*
*laufen	läuft	lief	gelaufen	*to run*

ALPHABETICAL LIST OF IRREGULAR VERBS—(Continued)

INFINITIVE	PRESENT (3rd sing.)	IMPERFECT (1st & 3rd sing.)	PAST PARTICIPLE	ENGLISH
leiden	leidet	litt	gelitten	to suffer
leihen	leiht	lieh	geliehen	to lend or borrow
lesen	liest	las	gelesen	to read
liegen	liegt	lag	gelegen	to lie
lügen	lügt	log	gelogen	to (tell a) lie
messen	misst	mass	gemessen	to measure
nehmen	nimmt	nahm	genommen	to take
nennen	nennt	nannte	genannt	to name
pfeifen	pfeift	pfiff	gepfiffen	to whistle
raten	rät	riet	geraten	to advise, guess
reissen	reisst	riss	gerissen	to tear
†reiten	reitet	ritt	geritten	to ride
*rennen	rennt	rannte	gerannt	to run
riechen	riecht	roch	gerochen	to smell
rufen	ruft	rief	gerufen	to call, shout
scheinen	scheint	schien	geschienen	to shine, seem
schieben	schiebt	schob	geschoben	to push
schiessen	schiesst	schoss	geschossen	to shoot
schlafen	schläft	schlief	geschlafen	to sleep
schlagen	schlägt	schlug	geschlagen	to beat
schliessen	schliesst	schloss	geschlossen	to shut
schneiden	schneidet	schnitt	geschnitten	to cut
schreiben	schreibt	schrieb	geschrieben	to write
schreien	schreit	schrie	geschrien	to cry out, scream
schweigen	schweigt	schwieg	geschwiegen	to be silent
*schwimmen	schwimmt	schwamm	geschwommen	to swim
sehen	sieht	sah	gesehen	to see
senden	sendet	sandte	gesandt	to send
singen	singt	sang	gesungen	to sing
*sinken	sinkt	sank	gesunken	to sink
sitzen	sitzt	sass	gesessen	to sit
sprechen	spricht	sprach	gesprochen	to speak
*springen	springt	sprang	gesprungen	to spring, jump
stehen	steht	stand	gestanden	to stand
stehlen	stiehlt	stahl	gestohlen	to steal
*steigen	steigt	stieg	gestiegen	to mount, climb
*sterben	stirbt	starb	gestorben	to die
stossen	stösst	stiess	gestossen	to push, thrust, pound
streiten	streitet	stritt	gestritten	to quarrel
tragen	trägt	trug	getragen	to carry
treffen	trifft	traf	getroffen	to meet, hit (a target)
treiben	treibt	trieb	getrieben	to drive
tun	tut	tat	getan	to do
†verderben	verdirbt	verdarb	verdorben	to spoil, to perish

† take **sein** when used without an object

ALPHABETICAL LIST OF IRREGULAR VERBS—(*Continued*)

INFINITIVE	PRESENT (3rd sing.)	IMPERFECT (1st & 3rd sing.)	PAST PARTICIPLE	ENGLISH
vergessen	vergisst	vergass	vergessen	*to forget*
verlieren	verliert	verlor	verloren	*to lose*
*wachsen	wächst	wuchs	gewachsen	*to grow*
waschen	wäscht	wusch	gewaschen	*to wash*
weisen	weist	wies	gewiesen	*to point out*
wenden	wendet	wandte	gewandt	*to turn*
werfen	wirft	warf	geworfen	*to throw*
wiegen	wiegt	wog	gewogen	*to weigh*
winden	windet	wand	gewunden	*to wind*
wissen	weiss	wusste	gewusst	*to know, to have know-*
ziehen	zieht	zog	gezogen	*to pull* [*ledge of*
zwingen	zwingt	zwang	gezwungen	*to force*

VERRÜCKT

In der Irrenanstalt in Dalldorf wird mitten in der Nacht die Hausglocke mit grösster Vehemenz gezogen. Ein Wärter öffnet das Fenster: "Ist da unten jemand?"

"Ja, ich möchte hinein, ich bin plötzlich wahnsinnig geworden und will mich hier behandeln lassen."

"Was? Mitten in der Nacht? Sie sind wohl verrückt!"

Verrückt, *mad;* **die Irrenanstalt, -en,** *lunatic asylum;* **Dalldorf,** *place near Berlin with famous asylum;* **die Hausglocke, -n,** *front bell;* **mit grösster Vehemenz,** *violently;* **ziehen,** *to pull;* **der Wärter, -,** *warder;* **ich möchte hinein,** *I want to get in;* **plötzlich,** *suddenly;* **wahnsinnig,** *insane;* **sich behandeln lassen,** *to be treated.*

SICHERHEIT

Ein Europäer wollte im Ganges baden und fragte einen Eingeborenen, ob er ihm nicht eine Stelle zeigen könnte, wo man vor Haifischen sicher wäre. Der Eingeborene wies ihm eine Bucht. Nach dem Bade setzte der Europäer die Unterhaltung fort: "Die Stelle muss man sich merken; die scheint wirklich ganz sicher zu sein."

"Ja, Herr," erwiderte der Eingeborene,

"hierher kommen die Haifische niemals, die haben hier zu grosse Angst vor den Krokodilen!"

Der Eingeborene, -n, *native;* **die Stelle, -n,** *place, spot;* **der Haifisch, -e,** *shark;* **sicher,** *safe;* **weisen,** *to point out;* **die Bucht, -en,** *bay;* **die Unterhaltung, -en,** *talk;* **fortsetzen,** *to continue;* **merken,** *to take note of;* **scheinen,** *to seem;* **wirklich,** *really;* **niemals,** *never;* **die Angst, ··-e,** *fear.*

IM ZIRKUS

Während der Vorstellung ruft eine Löwenbändigerin ihren grössten Löwen zu sich. Gehorsam kommt er—und nimmt ein Stück aus ihrem Munde.

"Das kann ich auch!" ruft ein junger Mann in der ersten Reihe.

"Das bezweifle ich", meint die Löwenbändigerin.

"Doch", ruft der Jüngling eifrig, "genau so gut wie der Löwe!"

Der Zirkus, -se, *circus;* **die Vorstellung, -en,** *performance;* **rufen,** *to call;* **die Löwenbändigerin, -nen,** *female lion-tamer;* **der Löwe, -n,** *lion;* **gehorsam,** *obedient(ly);* **die Reihe, -n** *row;* **bezweifeln,** *to doubt;* **doch,** *yes, indeed;* **eifrig,** *eagerly;* **genau so gut wie,** *just as well as.*

IN DER SÄCHSISCHEN SCHWEIZ

Die Sächsische Schweiz ist ein Teil des Elbsandsteingebirges südöstlich von Dresden zu beiden Seiten der Elbe. Das Gebirge ist nicht sehr hoch, aber reich an schroffen Sandsteinfelsen und tiefen Schluchten. Vielbesuchte Punkte auf dem rechten Elbufer : Liebethaler und Uttewalder Grund, Bastei, Amselgrund, Schandau, Kuhstall, Lilienstein; auf dem linken: Bärensteine, Königstein, Bielathal, u.a. (*Translation on page* 379)

die Sächsische Schweiz		**reich**	**schroff**	**der Felsen, -**	**die Schlucht, -en**
Saxon Switzerland		*rich*	*steep*	*rock*	*gorge*
vielbesucht	**der Punkt, -e**	**das Ufer, -**	**die Amsel, -n**	**u.a. (und andere)**
much-visited	*point, spot*	*river bank*	*blackbird*	*and others*

HINTS ON LETTER WRITING

The date (das Datum):
Berlin, W.8., den 8. Juli 1956
Dresden, den 21. August 1956
The following abbreviated form is also used:
3.V.54.   15.XI.55.   31.I.56.

Formal opening (formelle Anrede):
Sehr geehrter Herr!
Sehr geehrte, gnädige Frau!
Sehr geehrtes, gnädiges Fräulein!

Less formal (weniger formell):
Sehr geehrter Herr Meier!
Sehr verehrte Frau Schmidt!
Sehr verehrtes, gnädiges Fräulein!

Familiar opening (familiäre Anrede):
Lieber Herr Meier!
Liebe Frau Schmidt!
Liebes Fräulein Schulz!

Intimate (intim):

Lieber	Fritz! Freund! Vater! Onkel! Vetter!	Liebe	Grete! Freundin! Mutter! Tante! Kusine!

Miscellaneous (Verschiedenes):
Dear old boy
Lieber, alter Junge!

Darling
Liebling!

Dear Doctor Braun
Sehr geehrter (Lieber) Herr Doktor!

Dear Captain (Müller)
Sehr geehrter Herr Hauptmann!

Closing of letter (der Briefschluss):
I am, yours faithfully,
Ich verbleibe mit vorzüglicher Hochachtung, Ihr Karl Schmidt

Hoping to hear from you soon, we are, yours truly
In der Hoffnung, bald von Ihnen zu hören, zeichnen wir,
hochachtungsvoll
F. Stadler & Co.

With kind regards, yours sincerely
Mit freundlichen Grüssen,
Ihr ergebener (Ihre ergebene)
Heinz Schwarz (Grete Braun)

The envelope (der Briefumschlag):

Herrn
Walter SCHMIDT

BERLIN W16

Hansastrasse 36^{III}*

Frau
Gertrud WEISS

FRANKFURT a/M.

Kaiserallee 92
Linkes Gartenhaus ^{II}†

Fräulein
Anna HOLZ

bei¶ Schirmer

HEIDENHEIM
Bayern‡

---

* 3rd floor. † In large blocks of flats the part of the building is sometimes indicated.
¶ Care of. ‡ Bavaria.

The envelope (continued):

The following endorsements are commonly used on envelopes:

Eingeschrieben	Registered
Drucksache	Printed matter
Durch Luftpost	By Air Mail
Persönlich	Private and personal

Falls unbestellbar, bitte zurück an...	In case of non-delivery, please return to...
Bitte Nachsenden	Please forward
Per Adresse ... ⎱ Bei... ⎰	Care of ...
Postlagernd	⎰ To be called for ⎱ Poste restante
Muster ohne Wert	Sample(s) without value

LETTERS AND INVITATIONS

1. Einladung

Herr und Frau Schwarz bitten Herrn Weiss zu einem zwanglosen Abendessen am Montag dem 23. April um 7 Uhr 30. U.A.W.G.

die Einladung, -en =
invitation
zwanglos = *informal*
U.A.W.G. (Um Antwort wird gebeten) = *R.S.V.P.*

2. Annahme der Einladung

Herr Weiss dankt Herrn und Frau Schwarz für die freundliche Einladung und wird ihr mit grösstem Vergnügen Folge leisten.

die Annahme, -n =
acceptance
freundlich = *kind*
das Vergnügen = *pleasure*
Folge leisten = *to follow suit, to accept*

3. Absagen

Herr Weiss dankt Herrn und Frau Schwarz für die freundliche Einladung und bedauert ausserordentlich, dass eine frühere Verabredung es ihm unmöglich macht, ihr Folge zu leisten.

die Absage, -n = *refusal*
bedauern = *to regret*
ausserordentlich =
exceedingly
früher = *earlier, former*
die Verabredung, -en =
appointment, engagement

Sehr geehrte, gnädige Frau!

Ich danke Ihnen vielmals für Ihre liebenswürdige Einladung, der ich zu meinem grössten Bedauern nicht Folge leisten kann, da ich für einige Tage geschäftlich verreisen muss.

Ihr sehr ergebener,

vielmals = *many times*
liebenswürdig = *kind, charming*
das Bedauern = *regret*
geschäftlich = *on business*
verreisen = *to go away (on a journey)*

4. Anfrage

Ich verdanke Ihre Adresse meinem Geschäftsfreund Herrn Grün, der letztes Jahr seine Sommerferien mit seiner Familie bei Ihnen verbracht hat.

Ich beabsichtige mit meiner Frau am 18. d. Mts. für drei Wochen nach ... zu kommen und bitte Sie mir mitzuteilen, ob Sie für diese Zeit ein Doppelzimmer frei haben, und was Sie für volle Pension berechnen.

Ihrer umgehenden Antwort entgegensehend,

Hochachtungsvoll,

die Anfrage, -n = *inquiry*
verdanken = *to owe*
der Geschäftsfreund, -e =
business friend
Ferien (pl.) = *holidays*
verbringen = *to spend*
beabsichtigen = *to intend*
d. Mts. = *dieses Monats*
mitteilen = *to inform*
umgehend = *by return of post*
entgegensehen = *to look forward*

5. Antwort auf Nr. 4

Sehr geehrter Herr Braun!

In Erwiderung auf Ihr wertes Schreiben vom dritten d. Mts. freue ich mich, Ihnen mitteilen zu können, dass ich Ihnen am 18. d. Mts. ein schönes, grosses Vorderzimmer zur Verfügung stellen kann.

Der Preis pro Person beträgt 100 Mark pro Woche mit voller Pension (Frühstück, Mittagessen, Abendessen). Wir garantieren gepflegte Küche, sowie ein sonniges Zimmer mit jedem Komfort.

Mit der Bitte um Bestätigung, dass ich Sie am 18. erwarten darf,

Hochachtungsvoll,
Ihre sehr ergebene
L. Mittler

6. Bestätigung

Bitte mir ein grosses Doppelzimmer zu reservieren, möglichst mit Badezimmer. Wir kommen Dienstag abends um 8 Uhr.

Hochachtend,
Karl Braun

7. Privatbrief

Sehr geehrtes Fräulein Schneider!

Sie werden gewiss überrascht sein, dass ich Ihnen schreibe, denn wir kennen uns nicht.

Ein Geschäftsfreund meines Vaters, Herr Lehmann aus Leipzig, schrieb uns, eine deutsche Dame wünsche mit einer Engländerin in Briefwechsel zu treten. Da ich schon lange den Wunsch habe, meine deutschen Schulkenntnisse aufzufrischen, mache ich Ihnen folgenden Vorschlag.

Wir schreiben uns—Sie auf Englisch, ich auf Deutsch—alle 14 Tage und senden einander die verbesserten Briefe mit dem nächsten Brief zurück. Ist Ihnen das recht?

Zuerst will ich Ihnen schreiben, wer ich bin. Ich heisse Anne Warner, bin 23 Jahre alt und als Bibliothekarin in einer Volksbibliothek beschäftigt. Ich bemühe mich, meine Sprachkenntnisse zu verbessern, um später unsere fremdsprachliche Abteilung übernehmen zu können.

Ich war schon ein halbes Jahr in Frankreich und spreche Französisch ziemlich fliessend. Mein Deutsch ist aber noch sehr fehlerhaft, und es fehlt mir an Übung. Deshalb würde ich mich sehr freuen, wenn Ihnen mein Vorschlag gefällt.

Ich hoffe bald von Ihnen zu hören und sende Ihnen beste Grüsse.

Ihre
Anne Warner

---

die Erwiderung, -en = *reply*
wert = *esteemed*
das Vorderzimmer, - = *front room*
Ihnen zur Verfügung stellen = *place at your disposal*
betragen = *to amount to*
gepflegte Küche = *high-class cooking*
sowie = *as well as*
die Bestätigung, -en = *confirmation*

möglichst = *preferably*
das Badezimmer, - = *bathroom*

gewiss = *certainly*
überrascht = *surprised*
der Briefwechsel = *correspondence*
der Wunsch, ¨-e = *wish, desire*
Schulkenntnisse(pl.) = *knowledge acquired at school*
auffrischen = *to brush up*
der Vorschlag, ¨-e = *suggestion*
verbessern = *to correct*
zuerst = *first*
einander = *each other*
Bibliothekar(in) = *librarian*
die Volksbibliothek, -en = *public library*
beschäftigt = *employed*
sich bemühen = *to endeavour*
die fremdsprachliche Abteilung = *foreign language section*
übernehmen = *to take charge*
ziemlich = *rather, fairly*
fliessend = *fluent(ly)*
fehlerhaft = *faulty*
fehlen an = *to lack in*
die Übung, -en = *practice*
deshalb = *therefore*

FREIBURG IM BREISGAU : DER MARKTPLATZ

Freiburg im Breisgau, eine Stadt von nahezu hunderttausend Einwohnern, liegt am Fusse des Schwarzwaldes. Freiburg hat ein herrliches Münster (im Jahre 1122 begonnen), eine alte Universität (1457 gegründet) und viele sehenswerte, mittelalterliche Gebäude.

(*Translation on page* 379)

nahezu	**der Einwohner, -**	**herrlich**	**das Münster, -**	**gründen**	**sehenswert**
nearly	*inhabitant*	*glorious*	*cathedral*	*to found*	*worth seeing*

8. Geschäftsbrief
Ich verdanke Ihre Adresse einem meiner deutschen Geschäftsfreunde und erlaube mir die Anfrage, ob Sie bereit sind, ein Tee-exportgeschäft zu vertreten, vorausgesetzt dass Sie nicht schon eine ähnliche Vertretung haben.
Ich besitze eigene grosse Pflanzungen in Ceylon, die es mir ermöglichen, ausserordentlich vorteilhaft zu liefern.
Ihrer Antwort gern entgegensehend, zeichne ich,
Hochachtungsvoll

sich erlauben = *to beg to*
bereit = *prepared*
vertreten = *to represent*
die Vertretung, -en = *agency*
besitzen = *to possess*
eigen (adj.) = *own*
die Pflanzung, -en =
plantation
ermöglichen = *to enable*
vorteilhaft =
advantageous (ly)
liefern = *to supply, to deliver*
entgegensehend = *looking forward*

9. Auftrag
Einliegend sende ich Ihnen Auftrag auf sechs Dutzend Liebfrauenmilch 1923, den ich Ihrer schnellsten und besten Ausführung empfehle.
Ihre Rechnung und Versandanzeige erwartend, zeichne ich,
Hochachtungsvoll

6 Dutzend Liebfrauenmilch zu 56,00 M. das Dutzend.

Bedingungen: F.a.B. (Frei an Bord) Hamburg. Dreimonats-wechsel oder $2\frac{1}{2}\%$ Rabatt bei sofortiger Barzahlung.
Verschiffung: mit erstem Dampfer nach Hull.
Versicherung: wird von mir gedeckt.

der Auftrag, ··-e = *order*
das Dutzend, -e = *dozen*
Liebfrauenmilch, a famous Rhenish wine
die Ausführung, -en =
execution
empfehlen = *to recommend*
die Versandanzeige =
forwarding advice
die Bedingung, -en = *term, condition*
der Wechsel, - = *draft*
der Rabatt = *discount*
die Barzahlung, -en =
payment in cash
die Verschiffung, -en =
shipment
die Versicherung, -en =
insurance
decken = *to cover*
die Bestätigung, -en =
confirmation
empfangen (empfing, emp-fangen) = *to receive*
ausführen = *to carry out*

10. Bestätigung
Ich empfing Ihr Schreiben vom 24. ds. Mts., dem ich mit bestem Dank Ihren Auftrag auf 10 Dutzend Flaschen Liebfrauenmilch entnehme. Ich werde ihn so bald als möglich ausführen.

11. Mahnung
Unser Auftrag vom 24.d.Mts. ist noch nicht ausgeführt worden.
Sollte die Ware nicht binnen 14 Tagen abgesandt werden, werden wir zu unserm Bedauern gezwungen sein, den Auftrag rückgängig zu machen.
Hochachtungsvoll

die Mahnung, -en = *reminder*
ausführen = *to carry out*
binnen = *within*
das Bedauern = *regret*
rückgängigmachen =
to cancel

DAS ZIMMER MARTIN LUTHERS AUF DER WARTBURG

Die Wartburg, eine aus dem zwölften Jahrhundert stammende Festung, liegt hoch über der Stadt Eisenach in Thüringen. Hier fand Martin Luther 1521 Zuflucht und hier arbeitete er an seiner Übersetzung des Neuen Testaments. Das Bild zeigt das Fenster seines Arbeitsraums. In früheren Zeiten wurde die Wartburg viel von Minnesängern besucht, darunter Walther von der Vogelweide und Wolfram von Eschenbach.

(*Translation on page* 379)

stammen	die Festung, -en	die Zuflucht, -en	die Übersetzung, -en	darunter
to originate	*fortress*	*refuge, shelter*	*translation*	*among them*

STUDY GUIDE TO GERMAN LITERATURE

By R. FRIEDENTHAL

THE German language is among the four or five leading international languages of the world. English—spoken, according to estimates, by about 250 million people, and known to many more—takes first place. French, for many centuries universally accepted by the educated classes in all countries, and until recent times still the official language of international diplomacy, follows at a considerable distance, while German takes third place, above Spanish and Portuguese.

Where German is Spoken

Besides being the language of Germany proper (with an estimated population of seventy millions), German is spoken in Austria (nearly seven millions), and in large parts of Switzerland. There are, in addition, German-speaking communities in North and South America, in particular in Brazil.

German books are read in the Netherlands, in Scandinavia and in many countries at least some knowledge of German was long regarded as important for the understanding of philosophy and modern scientific progress. Prior to 1939 German textbooks, works of reference, scientific dictionaries and periodicals were widely distributed and played a prominent part in the cultural relations of the world.

Hitlerism played havoc with this precious heritage, yet interest in the German language and in German literature did not cease, even during the war. The German classics were read, in the original and in new translations, and some of the modern German authors, such as the poet Rainer Maria Rilke and the novelist Thomas Mann, the greatest of the many refugee writers, found a new public abroad.

After the downfall of the Nazi régime, the practical needs of participating in the administration or re-education of occupied Germany brought many more people into contact with the language. The revival of German literature, inevitably, has been a slow process, and the division of the country into two separate states, the Federal Republic in the West (Bundesrepublik Deutschland) and the German Democratic Republic (Deutsche Demokratische Republik) in the East, has added new difficulties, with Berlin in between as a third divided community. This state of affairs is reflected in literature as well

History of the Language

A certain knowledge of the history of the German language is useful for a better understanding, not only of literary developments in the past, but also of modern literature. The so-called Teutonic or Germanic languages comprise a number of languages: English, German, Dutch, the Scandinavian languages, and some extinct varieties such as Gothic. The German language, together with English and Frisian, belongs to the West Germanic part of that group, and for a considerable time the development of German and English had a common history.

Old High German and Old Low German, in use until about the year 1050 and sometimes called Old Saxon, are very near to Old English or Anglo-Saxon, and the great heroic poem *Beowulf*, the only surviving epic of the Germanic tribes, is regarded in Germany as a precious common heritage. The language of those times, however, is as alien to the German of to-day as is Anglo-Saxon to the modern English reader. He will read *Beowulf*, as well as the Old German heroic legend *Lay of Hildebrand*, and the Gospel story *Heliand*, in translation.

The next stage in the development of the language produced Middle High German (and Middle Low German), a form which lasted until the end of the Middle Ages. Modern High and Low German date from the time of Martin Luther, about 1500, although they had still to undergo many changes.

Low German, still spoken in many parts of North Germany and in the West, represents an older stage in the development of the language and has many words which are identical with the respective English expressions : *Water*, for instance (*Wasser* in High German). The people of the Waterkante are the inhabitants of the maritime districts who speak Low German, or Plattdeutsch as it is called in High German.

Low German is by no means confined to the lower classes of the population ; it has a rich literature throughout the ages, and a number of great German writers, such as Fritz Reuter, the novelist, and the South Schleswig poet Klaus Groth, wrote in Low German dialects.

There are many different dialects in both Low and High German, and some of them, like the Swiss High Alemannic, are regarded almost as languages of their own. They all have their poets and writers, and German literature is, indeed, to a far greater extent than any other European literature, built on those federal lines. The greatest modern German dramatist, Gerhart Hauptmann, wrote his most powerful plays in the Silesian dialect of his home province.

High German, however, mainly under the impact of the Bible translation of Martin Luther, became eventually the dominant language. It reached its culmination in the eighteenth century, and the literary language of the great German classics, Klopstock, Lessing, Herder, Goethe and Schiller, created finally a unified standard.

There are still many local differences with regard to pronunciation. In Germany, a universally accepted pronunciation, as in Britain or in the U.S.A., is unknown. Even highly-educated people, particularly in South Germany, will in daily life speak with a rather marked local accent. Some of these dialect accents, like Bavarian or the rather refined-sounding Hanoverian— by some regarded as the purest type of German—enjoy special favour with all other parts of the country, while others, like the accent of Saxony, are for no particular reason ridiculed in other regions.

During the last few decades, a certain amount of unification in pronunciation has been reached by the adoption of a special form of speech in the theatres, and the so-called Bühnenaussprache has become the standard for stage, film and radio.

History of German Literature

German literature, as known to the world, has had a comparatively late development. The Italians produced their greatest poet, Dante, in the thirteenth century, after which followed the English literature of Shakespeare's time, as the Elizabethan Age is invariably called in Germany. The Great Age of French literature was during the seventeenth century. The Germans did not reach that height until the middle of the eighteenth century.

There are, however, precious relics and fragments preserved from early times : charms, prayers, translations from the Gospels into Old High or Low German, and one solitary fragment of a national saga, *Das Hildebrandslied* (*The Lay of Hildebrand*). No other heroic poem of pre-Christian times survived the destruction of " heathen manuscripts " ordered by the Emperor Louis the Pious, son of Charlemagne.

Of medieval poetry, there is the great national epic *Das Nibelungenlied* (*The Lay of the Nibelungs*), written in its present form by an Austrian poet about the end of the twelfth century, and the other national epic, *Gudrun*, a saga of the North Sea coasts.

There are also the famous court epics, such as *Parzifal*, written about 1200 by Wolfram von Eschenbach, a Bavarian knight, and *Tristan*, by Gottfried von Strassburg, both based on French models ; and finally a wealth of lyrical poetry, the so-called Minnesang.

Walther von der Vogelweide (c. 1170-

1230), a poor knight from the Tyrol, wandering from court to court in South Germany and singing for his bread, was the greatest of the Minnesänger, encompassing in his work the whole range of human emotions, from love-songs to scathing political pamphlets in verse ; from fierce appeals for a new crusade to the moving poem of his old age in which he complains that life seems to wither away like a dream.

The whole poetry of chivalry came to a rapid end and was soon forgotten, only to be revived by the German romantic school in the nineteenth century. Literature passed during the next century into the hands of middle-class poets ; the Minnesang became the Meistersang.

These Meistersinger, who were immortalized later by Richard Wagner in his opera *The Mastersingers of Nuremberg*, were mostly craftsmen or artisans in the then highly prosperous cities of the Reich. They formed themselves into schools (Singschulen) and practised the art of singing and writing in a strong, guild-like spirit ; poetry could be taught and studied, but had to obey a great number of strict rules and laws, often difficult to observe. Hans Sachs of Nuremberg was the best known of these Meistersinger, and he was always proud to mention his profession as a shoemaker at the end of his poems, in the doggerel verse practised by him and his fellow-rhymesters :

So schreibt Hans Sachs, ein Schuhmacher und Poet dazu.

(Thus writes Hans Sachs, a shoemaker and a poet too).

At the same time, the anonymous folksong (Volkslied) flourished and was distributed by means of the newly invented art of printing in innumerable song-books

STADTTOR IN WOLFRAMS-ESCHENBACH

Dieses eigentümliche, von mittelalterlichen Wällen umgebene, bayerische Städtchen ist nach dem Verfasser des *Parzifal* benannt, dem Minnesänger Wolfram von Eschenbach, der im zwölften Jahrhundert dort lebte. (*Translation on page* 379)

eigentümlich	der Wall, ···e	umgeben	der Verfasser, -	benennen
queer, quaint	*rampart*	*to surround*	*author*	*to name*

DAS DENKMAL JOHANN SEBASTIAN BACHS IN EISENACH

Dieses Bronzedenkmal auf dem Marktplatz in Eisenach ist dem grossen Komponisten gewidmet, der 1685 in dieser Stadt geboren wurde. Über dem Eingang zu der Kirche stehen die Worte "Ein' feste Burg ist unser Gott" aus Martin Luthers bekannter Hymne, zu der Bach die Musik komponiert hat.

(Translation on page 379)

das Denkmal, -e	**der Komponist, -en**	**widmen**	**geboren** (p.p. of **gebären**)	**fest**
monument	*composer*	*to dedicate*	*born*	*firm*

and ballad-sheets. Popular jokes were collected, some of the best-known clustering round the figure of a certain baker's apprentice from the town of Brunswick, Till Eulenspiegel (Till Owlglass).

The beast fable, greatly in favour during the whole of the Middle Ages, enjoyed a new life, a popular example being *Reynard the Fox* (*Reinke de Vos* in the Low German version), which was later revived and rewritten by Goethe as *Reineke Fuchs*.

Luther's Bible Translation

The great literary event of the Reformation was, as already mentioned, Luther's translation of the Bible. Martin Luther (1483-1546), the son of a miner from Thuringia, took great pains to choose the most simple and plain language for his rendering of the Greek and Hebrew text of Holy Script. "To look the common man upon his mouth," as he expressed it in a famous phrase, was his avowed aim, and he succeeded to an extraordinary degree. There had been about a dozen translations before Luther, but his version soon became predominant and was the most powerful factor in building up the modern German language.

Luther's Bible is still the standard translation throughout Protestant Germany, although the text has undergone many alterations and modernizations. For many centuries it was The Book, read by high and low, by peasants and poets alike, and "Lutherdeutsch" became a byword for powerful and vigorous German.

Luther also exercised a lasting influence upon German literature as a hymn-writer. A keen musician himself, and in constant contact with some of the finest professional musicians of his time, he created a new form of religious poetry that reached its height in the next century: the poetry of the hymn-book (Gesangbuch). Some of his texts were not only sung as hymns in church but were also used by some of the great German composers, such as Johann Sebastian Bach, in their cantatas.

There was, however, another side to the Lutheran influence. Religious struggle led to civil war and finally to the disastrous Thirty Years' War (1618-1648), the greatest catastrophe in German life prior to the Hitler régime. After the conclusion of the peace, the population had decreased by one-third; industry and trade had been ruined and almost brought to a standstill in many parts of the country.

Cultural life had suffered still more. There is one solitary literary document from these times: Grimmelshausen's powerful novel *Simplicius Simplizissimus*, describing in stark realism the horrors perpetrated by the ravaging soldiery of the different parties and powers. But, generally speaking, intellectual life was at a low ebb as never before. The very language was in danger of being entirely swamped and suffocated.

The educated classes turned for more than a century from the vernacular to foreign languages. Latin was the language of the scholar; French, and sometimes Spanish, was employed at court and in higher society; Dutch, Swedish, and Italian words invaded the language in the fields of trade and industry.

The greatest German of the seventeenth century, the philosopher Gottfried Wilhelm Leibnitz (1646-1716), a truly universal mind (Bertrand Russell has devoted a special study to him in English), wrote and thought in French. Even Frederick the Great, more than a hundred years later, employed the German language only occasionally in his famous marginal remarks, displaying his disregard both for humanity and the most elementary rules of grammar. He usually wrote and conversed in French, and he surrounded himself with French men-of-letters. For the great German writers who had grown up during his lifetime and had created a new literature, he had nothing but scorn.

The Classical Age

The new German literature that was to produce the classical age had its roots not in national but in foreign sources. The most powerful influence, however, was not French but English, although in Germany knowledge of the English language was very limited at this period.

English strolling players, the so-called English comedians (die englischen Comödianten), had visited the country during the seventeenth century. They played in English to audiences who can have had very little knowledge of the language, but so skilful were their productions in stagecraft and team-work that their appearance marks the beginning of the modern German theatre and drama.

Troupes of professional players—as distinct from the earlier lay performers in Shrovetide plays, pageants or mummeries —formed themselves on the English model under a so-called principal. Some of these players produced versions of Shakespeare's plays, though in a rather garbled and mutilated form and without even mentioning the name of the author.

Shakespeare's Influence

For the German revival of the eighteenth century, William Shakespeare was to become the lodestar and battlecry. Lessing (1729-1781), the first of the great German critics, used his name to combat the prevailing French influence; some of the finest brains of the age translated Shakespeare's works in ever-renewed attempts to express their meaning, first in prose (Wieland) and then in the original metre (A. W. Schlegel), until the dramatist's work became fully adopted and absorbed.

This process went on during the following century, the translation by Schlegel-Tieck being regarded as the standard classical rendering. The history of the German theatre is to a great extent the history of Shakespeare's plays in Germany.

Next to Shakespeare, Milton, with his epic power, was the most influential poet. *Der Messias* (*The Messiah*), by Friedrich Gottlieb Klopstock (1724-1803), was regarded by his contemporaries as a worthy counterpart to *Paradise Lost* and inaugurated the new age. Lessing, in addition to his critical essays, gave the German stage its first great comedies and dramas. His comedy *Minna von Barnhelm* is still a stock play of the German stage, and its heroine, Minna, remains one of the gayest and most engaging figures in German classical comedy. Lessing's last drama, *Nathan der Weise* (*Nathan the Wise*), crowned his life-long struggle for tolerance and humanitarian ideals.

The eighteenth century produced a wealth of stimulating minds, among them J. G. Herder, who collected the folk-songs of all nations, and Lichtenberg, professor at Göttingen, revealing in his aphoristic fragments one of the most witty and elegant minds that ever adorned German university life. The latter lived for some time in England, and his *Briefe aus England* (*Letters from England*), containing his impressions and observations of mid-eighteenth century England, are, especially for English readers, among the most interesting of his writings. The same period, too, produced minor writers such as G. A. Bürger, whose vivid and dramatic ballads were imitated by Robert Burns and translated by Walter Scott, and poets like Hölty and Matthias Claudius.

Works of Goethe

The climax of this period was reached at a bound by the youthful Johann Wolfgang Goethe (1749-1832) of Frankfurt. His novel *Werthers Leiden* (*The Sorrows of Werther*) created a European sensation; Napoleon carried a copy throughout his campaigns. Published in 1774, the novel is both a sentimental story and a deep psychological study, describing with graphic effect the restless life of a sensitive, lovelorn youth who is driven to suicide by the pressure of worldly problems. Goethe's first drama, *Götz von Berlichingen*, reviving the colourful life of old-time Germany before the Thirty Years' War, was the model for a long series of historical plays by minor writers. The hero, originally a famous robber knight of the sixteenth century, is portrayed by Goethe as a noble character crusading against the wickedness of the world.

One can here merely hint at the almost immeasurable range of Goethe's work. This comprised not only the highest achievements in the field of drama (*Faust, Iphigenie, Tasso*), novel-writing (*Wilhelm Meister*, translated by Thomas Carlyle)

WILHELM TELL AUFFUHRÜNG IN INTERLAKEN

Eine Szene aus einer Freilichtaufführung von Schillers Drama *Wilhelm Tell*, das alljährlich in Interlaken (Berner Oberland) gespielt wird.   (*Translation on page 379*)

die Szene, -n   **die Freilichtaufführung, -en**   **alljährlich**
scene   *open-air performance*   *annually*

and poetry of all kinds, from simple little verses (*Heideröslein*) to finely-wrought poems in classical metres. Goethe's literary work also extended into science (optics and geology) and embraced nearly all the known literatures of the world.

When Goethe died, he had made Weimar, the little Thuringian town in which he had spent the greater part of his life, a kind of spiritual capital of Western civilization, to which young men and women from all countries, from England, Russia, Italy and Scandinavia went in pilgrimage.

Next to Goethe stands Friedrich Schiller (1759-1805), the greatest German dramatist and playwright. He, too, became famous almost overnight with his *Die Räuber* (*The Robbers*), a youthful protest against tyranny which cost him his career as a surgeon in the service of one of the South German princelings (and brought him, after the Revolution, the award of honorary citoyen of the French Republic). His trilogy *Wallenstein* (translated by Coleridge) is the most eminent work of the German stage and is, indeed, one of the greatest historical tragedies ever written in any language.

Schiller's last play, *Wilhelm Tell*, a fine drama of the Swiss people, celebrated again the struggle against oppression and despotism, and it is as a fighter for freedom and liberty that Schiller has been venerated for generations. His poetry was also very popular, in particular his ballads, and one of his famous lyrics *An die Freude* (*An Ode to Joy*) was used by Beethoven as the final and crowning chorus in his ninth symphony.

A pupil of Schiller's in his youth, Friedrich Hölderlin (1770-1843), the third

STÄTTEN DEUTSCHER KULTUR

Das obige Bild zeigt die efeuumrankte Ruine des Heidelberger Schlosses, das Wahrzeichen der alten Universitätsstadt. Das untere Bild zeigt das Nationaltheater in Weimar mit dem Denkmal Goethes und Schillers. Beide Dichter lebten in Weimar, und sie waren eng befreundet. Im Jahre 1919 fanden im Weimarer Nationaltheater die Sitzungen des ersten Parlaments der neuen deutschen Republik statt. (*Translation on page* 380)

die Stätte, -n	**der Efeu**	**umranken**	**der Dichter, -**	**sie waren eng befreundet**
place, centre	*ivy*	*to enclose*	*poet*	*they were close friends*

of the great classical poets, passed away almost unknown to his contemporaries. His works, however, became famous later and he is now regarded as one of the purest representatives of the German spirit.

German Philosophy

At the same time, German philosophy culminated in Immanuel Kant (1724-1804) and G. W. F. Hegel (1770-1831), whose theory of dialectical progress forms the basis of Marxism. The influence of German philosophy upon the world was even greater during the nineteenth century than the prestige of the classics. From the literary point of view, however, these German philosophers are difficult and often obscure writers, and reading them entails hard work, not only for a foreigner but for Germans themselves. Only in Arthur Schopenhauer (1788-1860) and Friedrich Nietzsche (1844-1900) did German philosophical language become supple, swift and easily understood by the layreader.

In general it may be said that the German literature of the classical epoch offers to the foreign student the considerable advantage that, in poetry as well as prose, the great writers are sufficiently near to present-day German to be read without difficulty. No special vocabulary is needed; few sentences require an explanation, although there is no lack of annotated editions, the notes often encumbering the text to a quite unnecessary degree. Goethe and Schiller can, and should, be read and enjoyed without the paraphernalia of the textbook.

Nineteenth Century

The next stage in literary development, already beginning in Goethe's lifetime, was the movement of the romantic school. A certain restlessness is a characteristic sign of most of these writers, and their way is strewn with broken fragments, unfinished works and unfulfilled promises. Yet their very restlessness bore fruit in a wealth of translations from all languages, from the English (Schlegel-Tieck), Italian, Spanish.

Portuguese; from the Arabian and Persian and Indian literatures; and even from then still unknown languages like the Serbian.

Other writers revived the German past. Brentano and Arnim collected the old German folk-songs, charming in their simplicity, and published them jointly under the curious title *Des Knaben Wunderhorn* (*The Boy's Wonder Horn*); the brothers Grimm gathered and retold the popular German fairy-tales (*Kinder- und Hausmärchen der Brüder Grimm*), still perennial favourites among children throughout the world. There is fine lyrical poetry by Eichendorff, Uhland, Chamisso (a Frenchman who became a naturalized German), by Rückert, Lenau and Mörike. Many of these poems were eminently suited for setting to music, and it is the German Lied, in particular in the compositions by Franz Schubert and Robert Schumann, that has made the names of these poets known to music-lovers in all countries.

The Role of Music

Music, in fact, plays a great role in the romantic movement, and the contemporary school of musicians is in constant contact with the literary trend of the times. Weber, in writing the libretto for his magnificent romantic opera, *Der Freischütz* (*The Marksman*), was the first German musician to express himself also in writing; he was followed by Schumann, a great journalist as well as composer, and Richard Wagner (1813-1883), who also wrote the libretti of his operas. Heinrich von Kleist (1777-1811) is the one dramatic genius of the epoch; Jean Paul (1763-1825), originally Jean Paul Friedrich Richter, master-novelist and a humorous writer of the first rank. Of the many fragmentists, Novalis (F. von Hardenberg, 1772-1801) stands out as the deepest thinker and most stimulating mind.

Heinrich Heine (1797-1856), decidedly a romantic in his poetry (*Das Buch der Lieder* and *Romancero*), belongs, according to the usual classification of the textbooks, to what was known as the "Young

Germany" school of writers. The revolutionary trend of the times, arrested for a while by the all-powerful reaction, found expression in their writings. They suffered persecution, in the same way as their successors a century later, and many of them had to leave the country.

Heine found a refuge in Paris; others, like Boerne or Herwegh, who had participated in the sadly miscarried German revolution of 1848, followed. Freiligrath lived for more than fifteen years in London. Georg Büchner, the most gifted of the young poets, fled to Switzerland; others emigrated to the U.S.A.

The writings of these authors, however, were never quite successfully suppressed by a comparatively clumsy censorship, and they remained famous and widely-read by the public. Even Bismarck, the Iron Chancellor, regarded Heine as the greatest poet of his time, and not some versifier of the official school who sang the praises of the temporal powers.

Birth of Modern Journalism

One result of the Young Germany movement is the birth of modern journalism. Heine was not only the leading poet, but also the foremost journalist of his time. His style, for better or worse, served as a model for a host of followers. Maga-

EIN BLICK AUF SALZBURG

Salzburg ist schön gelegen, zwischen dem Kapuzinerberg und dem Mönchsberg, im österreichischen Teil der Alpen. Die dort stattfindenden Musikfestspiele haben internationale Berühmtheit gewonnen.

(*Translation on page 380*)

der Blick, -e	das Musikfestspiel, -e	die Berühmtheit, -en	gewinnen
glimpse, view	*music festival*	*fame*	*to win*

zines and pamphlets became prolific. Karl Marx (1818-1883) started his amazing career as a journalist in these Young Germany circles (*Rheinische Zeitung*, 1842). He, too, became a refugee and wrote his *Kapital* in the reading-room of the British Museum. Ferdinand Lassalle (1825-1864), highly influential in the first years of German socialism (he founded in 1863 the Allgemeiner Deutscher Arbeiterverein, the workers' union which formed the nucleus of the German Social Democratic party), ended his short and brilliant life on Swiss soil in a duel arising from a love affair. George Meredith, in his *Tragic Comedians*, has made this subject familiar to English readers.

But schools and movements are only one side of the picture. Outside any classification, and often hidden in the provinces, lived some of the finest poets and writers of the century. Franz Grillparzer (1791-1872) in Vienna wrote the greatest tragedies after Schiller, among them *Des Meeres und der Liebe Wellen* (*Waves of the Sea and of Love*), which dramatizes the story of Hero and Leander and is sometimes regarded, in its classic simplicity and romantic wistfulness, as the finest of all German love tragedies. Nestroy and Raimund are the flower of Austrian popular play-writing, too often known to the outside world only by its last sentimental and flashy offspring, the Viennese operetta.

Friedrich Hebbel (1813-1863), a powerful dramatist who was born in Schleswig, also lived in Vienna. His *Tagebücher* (*Diaries*) are deeply moving documents of self-analysis and the struggles of a tortured mind. By the Lake of Constance, Annette von Droste-Hülshoff, the greatest German poetess, wrote her sharp-cut poems and realistic stories, notably *Die Judenbuche*, a sombre, vigorously-written story of rural crime.

Jeremias Gotthelf created in the Swiss vernacular a new type of village story. His novels are a mirror of peasant life unsurpassed in shrewd, realistic observation and epic grandeur. Adalbert Stifter, in Bohemia, is the master of miniature word-painting (*Bunte Stein* and *Der Nachsommer*).

In Mecklenburg, Fritz Reuter (1810-1874), the Low-German Dickens as he has been called with some justification, wrote semi-autobiographical novels full of humour and insight into human character. Klaus Groth in his Low-German poetry, and Theodor Storm in his delicately-drawn short stories represent South Schleswig. Even the German emigrants to America found expression in the writings of K. A. Postl, who wrote under the penname of Charles Sealsfield, his most popular work being *Das Kajütenbuch* (*The Cabin Book*).

Gottfried Keller (1819-1890) from Zürich and C. F. Meyer (1825-1898), although both Swiss by birth and consciously Swiss in their patriotism, belong rather to the general trend of German literature than to any local school. Both wrote the finest prose of the nineteenth century, and Keller's delicate autobiographical novel *Der grüne Heinrich* (*Green Henry*) is the one great novel of the time that can bear comparison with the great masters of other languages. Wilhelm Raabe, of Brunswick, may be mentioned as a third leading novelist; he is the master of quaint types and of a particularly ironic humour.

Social Realism

The growth of realism, already marked in the writings of many of these authors, led at the end of the century to a new development. Gustav Freytag, a Silesian, had placed middle-class life on the map in his novel *Soll und Haben* (*Debit and Credit*), a particularly realistic story of commercial life which brought him wide fame and was translated into most of the other European languages.

Another Silesian, Gerhart Hauptmann (1862-1946), created by his powerful plays a revolution in German theatrical life and became for many years the leader of the new movement. His *Die Weber* (*The Weavers*), depicting the conflict of capital and labour, is the first great social drama of the German stage; in other plays he explored individual human conflicts. His *Biberpelz* (*Beaver Skin*) is the best modern

DIE UNIVERSITÄTSSTADT GÖTTINGEN

Die 1737 von dem englischen König Georg II gegründete Universität Göttingen gilt als eine der besten Universitäten Deutschlands. Viele Häuser der Stadt tragen Gedenktafeln zum Andenken berühmter Gelehrter, die dort gelehrt oder studiert hatten. Der oben abgebildete Brunnen mit der Statue einer Gänsehüterin gehört zu den Sehenswürdigkeiten der Stadt.

(*Translation on page* 380)

gründen	gelten	die Gedenktafel, -n	das Andenken, -	die Gänsehüterin, -nen
to found	*to be esteemed*	*memorial tablet*	*remembrance*	*goose-girl*

German comedy. Hermann Sudermann was at the time linked with Hauptmann as the leader of the realistic school, and his plays were internationally known. They have faded, but his fine stories from his East Prussian home province, *Lithauische Geschichten* (*Lithuanian Tales*), showing a keen observation and a vivid touch, are a lasting achievement.

The novel found a new master in Theodor Fontane (1819-1898), most of whose stories dealt with contemporary life; in the field of poetry Arno Holz and Richard Dehmel became the protagonists of the realist school.

The Volksbühne

The last decades of the nineteenth century are marked by a steady growth of popular movements in connection with the new writers, the Volksbühne, as a theatre for the people, being the most powerful and lasting development in that line. Many of these authors were socialists, or at least in their youth influenced by socialist ideas.

The movement of realism, as with all literary movements, did not last very long. Gerhart Hauptmann himself, the leading spirit, developed soon a romantic and mystical strain in his work. Characteristic of his new style are his plays *Hanneles Himmelfahrt* (*Hannele's Journey to Heaven*), giving expression to the fantastic dreams of a dying child, and *Die versunkene Glocke* (*The Sunken Bell*), an allegorical, fairy-tale piece of somewhat vague symbolic character.

Under the influence of the French poets of the eighties, Stefan George emphasized again the value of pure poetry and art for art's sake, holding consciously aloof from the multitude and forming one of the self-contained, almost sectarian circles that became a feature of German cultural life.

Hugo von Hofmannsthal, for a short while his friend, wrote even in his teens some of the finest neo-classical poems in the language and developed a new type of short lyrical drama (*Der Tor und der Tod*). He then became a powerful influence in the new development of the German stage, re-writing Greek plays and the old English mystery play *Everyman* (*Jedermann*), besides producing libretti for his contemporary, the composer Richard Strauss (*Der Rosenkavalier*). His prose, in particular in his essays, is a model of classical German.

Twentieth Century

We have already entered the new century, a dominant feature of which is the extraordinary degree to which Germany has been open to foreign influence and to foreign personalities. There is little in the whole range of contemporary or classical literature of the world that has not been translated, analysed, or produced on the stage.

Russian authors (many of them, like Turgeniev or Dostoievski, lived for a considerable time in Germany) and French, British and Scandinavian writers were accepted with enthusiasm. Ibsen and Björnson started their European careers in Germany; and Bernard Shaw repeatedly acknowledged his indebtedness to the German theatre. Strindberg, the Swedish dramatist, spent his most impressionable years in Berlin; the Belgian poet E. Verhaeren was not only introduced to the German public in masterly translations by Stefan Zweig, but was printed in the original French by German publishers.

Yet German literature, in spite of bitter protests from the more old-fashioned or reactionary circles, was none the poorer for this lively interplay of forces.

The greatest of the modern German poets, Rainer Maria Rilke (1875-1926) lived in Paris up to the outbreak of the First World War, as secretary of the French sculptor Rodin. His work is full of French matter, and the greatest impression of his life was his visit to Russia. But it is in his poetry that Rilke shows himself to be the finest master of the language in his time, unsurpassed in the expression of the most intricate and interwoven feelings in all their shades and colours.

Thomas Mann (1875-1955), the most important prose writer, started as a pupil of the Russian and French novelists. His *Buddenbrooks*, the story of the decay of a family, covering the whole course of the nineteenth century, is the best picture of German upper middle-class life in a Hanseatic town. His *Der Zauberberg* (*The Magic Mountain*) is already a classic, representing European society at the crossways in the second decade of our century. His short stories are models of style, and his sequence of novels *Joseph*, re-moulding the old Biblical theme, is the nearest approach to the art of the old epic masters that modern literature can show.

There are many other representative and important writers. Among Austrian authors is Arthur Schnitzler, the dramatist of a Vienna that belongs now to the past, and Stefan Zweig, with his biographies of Marie Antoinette and Balzac, his short stories and essays (*Masterbuilders*).

Expressionism and Symbolism

Franz Werfel, hailing from Prague, became the leading poet of the new school of expressionism, and later a novelist of high rank (*The Song of Bernadette*). Another Bohemian, Franz Kafka, has won international fame as a writer of symbolist novels, anticipating in his dream-like world the terrors of a tortured age.

Switzerland produced in C. Spitteler a solitary bard of epic poetry in the old style; Hermann Hesse (born 1877), a South German, whose reputation as a novelist is now, in the view of many good judges, not far from that of Thomas Mann, became a Swiss citizen after the First World War. Jakob Wassermann, Leonhard Frank (*Karl und Anna*), and Lion Feuchtwanger (*Jew Süss*) were leading novelists. Hans Carossa wrote a series of fine auto-biographical books on his childhood (*Kindheit*) and his later development as a country doctor.

Arnold Zweig (*The Case of Sergeant Grischa*) wrote the most impressive, and Erich Maria Remarque the most widely read, war novel, *Im Westen nichts Neues* (*All Quiet on the Western Front*). A. Doeblin, the most experimental of the modern prose writers, reflected post-war Berlin in the mirror of a memorable and vivid novel, *Berlin Alexanderplatz*. Heinrich Mann, the brother of Thomas Mann, has painted social decay on a broad canvas. Ricarda Huch, the greatest German woman writer, is equally important as an historical novelist (*The Thirty Years' War*), biographer (*Bakunin*), and essayist.

Of modern dramatists, Frank Wedekind (*Der Erdgeist*), Carl Sternheim and Georg Kaiser were the leading playwrights of the expressionistic school. Ernst Toller was internationally known as a representative of the revolutionary German youth of 1919, and Bert Brecht was the strongest influence in the years between the two world wars, his *Dreigroschenoper* (*Threepenny Opera*) being a free adaptation of the English *The Beggar's Opera*.

After the War

The catastrophe that befell German cultural life with the advent of Hitlerism made an end to the whole development of literature and the arts along natural lines. Many poets and writers of renown had to leave the country. Others, who stayed at home, were silenced by the censorship. Some bowed to the reigning power.

After the War, the first years remained almost entirely under the shadow of struggle for bare existence and re-adaptation. With returning prosperity, in particular in West Germany, literary life began to revive again. The theatre, in its many local centres of old traditions, Berlin, Munich, Hamburg, Düsseldorf, was the first to become restored to former renown and splendour. The plays by Bert Brecht (*Mother Courage*) and Carl Zuckmayer (*The Devil's General*) became internationally known, and of the younger dramatists, the two Swiss authors, Friedrich Duerrenmatt and Max Frisch, presented powerful new plays. Philosophy has found in Karl Jaspers, one of the fathers of the Existentialist movement, a highly influential representative. In the field of modern children's literature, Erich Kaestner (*Emil and the Detectives*) is the undisputed master. New forms of writing, such as radio plays, are coming to the fore; Günter Eich has excelled in this branch of literature. Of the younger novelists,

TANZ DER SCHAFHIRTEN IN ROTHENBURG

Bei dem Rothenburger Pfingstfest, das alljährlich stattfindet, geben Schafhirten und Schafhirtinnen aus der Gegend um Rothenburg Vorführungen ihrer Volkstänze und tragen dabei ihre altherkömmlichen Trachten. *(Translation on page 380)*

der Schafhirt, -en	das Pfingstfest, -e	die Vorführung, -en	altherkömmlich
shepherd	*Whitsun festival*	*production, presentation*	*traditional*

Heinrich Böll, from Cologne, has made his mark. A new generation is trying to restore German literary life to its former place in the community of nations.

German Life

The extraordinary diversity of German cultural life and the striking differences between the many distinct regions are reflected in the daily life of the people. Germany is at the same time very old and very young.

There was, until the last war, an abundance of old castles and Gothic cathedrals, and whole towns, like Nuremberg or Rothenburg on the Tauber, that had been preserved like museum-pieces, with their wrinkled medieval streets and half-timbered houses. The war has destroyed a large proportion of the monuments of the past, although some reconstruction has taken place. Many of the oldest cities, however, such as Franfurt on the Main or Cologne, nearly entirely flattened by bombing, have become new towns, with new inhabitants, often refugees from the lost Eastern provinces, and new functional architecture. They compete with the industrial towns of the Ruhr basin in bustle and skyscraping austerity, and even in West Berlin, still to a large extent in ruins, a whole district has been rebuilt, by international competition of world-known architects, with huge blocks of flats of the most advanced type, subsidized by the government and at moderate rents.

There are still some regions where the peasants wear their old provincial costumes,

WORMS—DER DOM

Der aus dem zwölften Jahrhundert stammende Dom ist eines der markantesten Bauwerke des romanischen Baustils im Rheinland. Worms ist eine der ältesten Städte Deutschlands. Im Jahre 1521 verteidigte Martin Luther seine Lehren vor dem in Worms tagenden Reichstag. Die Stadt hat einen Hafen am Rhein und ist Mittelpunkt eines Weinbaubezirks.

(*Translation on page* 380)

markant	der Baustil, -e	verteidigen	die Lehre, -n	tagend
noteworthy	*style of architecture*	*to defend*	*doctrine*	*assembled*

346

and in Bavaria the peasant's dress, with knee-length leather breeches, short jackets and funny-looking felt-hats, adorned with a goat's beard or an eagle's feather, is almost the fashion for all classes. One may see a professor or a retired general walking in that strange garb to the Hofbräuhaus, the Royal Inn, or one of the other enormous beer-cellars of Munich, where the drinking of the national beverage amounts to a holy and serious rite.

The foreign visitor of the nineteenth century—typically represented by the American poet Longfellow—was quite naturally attracted in the first place by the associations with the romantic past. To him, Germany was the country of ruined castles on the Rhine, of colourful student life, of long-bearded, absent-minded professors pondering over some absurd theory of The Absolute.

To the contemporary mind, the German became known, not without very substantial reasons, as the tireless worker on innumerable deadly weapons and inventions, a uniform and uniformed people.

Post-war Germany presented again another picture: a people bewildered, in desperate need at first, and very soon staging an astounding recovery, hard-working, and almost dedicated to the task of forgetting the recent past as soon as possible.

All these aspects are true. The complexity of the German mind and of German life, moulded by the fateful events of history in violent swings of the pendulum, give the world at large the impression of something difficult to assess, dark, inscrutable at times, and easy, engaging and pleasant at other times. The Germans themselves, as reflected in the works of their great thinkers and poets, have never ceased to wonder and struggle with the problem of finding some unity in that diversity.

The Universities

Let us cast a glance at these different aspects. There is still the romantic past, although much of it has faded out of the daily life of the population since the time of Longfellow.

The modern student has become a hard-working trainee, often earning his living by half-time work in a factory. The many universities and high schools, however, are still a dominant feature of German life.

Heidelberg on the Neckar, one of the tributaries of the Rhine, with its famous castle, has always been best known abroad. There is Göttingen, with its many ties to Britain (in the eighteenth century the professors would bear the title of Royal British professor, Hanover then being united by personal union to the Kingdom of Great Britain); there are Jena, where the poet Schiller had been a teacher of history, Freiburg, Tübingen, Halle and many more.

Student life in Germany has always been different from that in Britain or the U.S.A. There are no residential colleges, no tutors; there is scarcely any supervision of private life. The student will take up his room—his Bude (den) as he calls it in student's slang—as a lodger in the town; he may work hard on his books, or he may spend his first terms in one of the innumerable inns and pubs, which have no licensing hours. There is only the dreaded time of the final examination to remind him of his duty as an "academic citizen".

He may change his university at will, and it was quite usual in normal times to spend the first year or two years in one of the smaller towns, where life was much easier, cheaper and more pleasant. In these small towns, the whole life of the population centres round the university; the term Universitätsstadt is their pride. Student life in East Germany, of course, has developed on entirely different lines and is under strictest supervision.

Architectural Styles

Heritages of the past are the great architectural monuments, reaching back in some cases to the dark ages. In Aachen, the minster preserves the memory of Charlemagne (Karl der Grosse); in Fulda the chapel founded by Bonifacius, the creator of the German church, who hailed from Devon, is still standing. On the Rhine, the churches at Worms, Speyer and

Mainz are witnesses of the times of the Holy Roman Empire, while the greatest glory of those South-German regions are the Gothic cathedrals of Cologne, Ulm and Freiburg.

There is a wealth of later architecture, ecclesiastical and temporal, of great merit, in particular in Bavaria: in Munich or in the Allgaeu.

In North Germany, buildings in brick instead of stone are predominant. Modern architectural development has taken up again this old tradition and has produced some fine results in Hamburg and Bremen.

Some towns, as mentioned already, had preserved their medieval character in its entirety, with their old walls, city gates, town halls and cobbled streets. Rothenburg, in Franconia, the most famous of these, has luckily escaped bombing and there are many more, such as Nördlingen, Dinkelsbühl or Memmingen, proud of their old tradition as former independent Reichsstädte (towns of the Realm).

In that part of Germany one may even come across some old village where the medieval Imperial eagle is painted in fading colours at the entrance to the village, as a sign that the place had been a free Reichs-village whose mayor had the right to participate in the sessions of the Imperial Diet (the Reichstag). He usually had to travel on foot to get there!

Local Costumes

In many regions, in addition to Bavaria, old local costumes are still worn, although mostly on Sundays only, or for weddings and festivals. In Berlin, women from the Spreewald, a marshy district to the south-east of the city, were popular as nurses until more recent years. They used to wear a wide-winged headgear, neck-cloths, wide skirts and aprons, often richly embroidered with flowers in many colours. In Hesse, the district of the Schwalm was famous for its provincial types, the women wearing short, almost ballet-like skirts, with white stockings, the men long smocks in dark blue with red velvet collars.

In Lower Saxony, many of the old farmhouses are preserved, uniting under one thatched roof the family of the farmer, the servants or labourers and the cattle. Even in quite recent times, it was the custom in such houses for wedding and other feasts to be held in the enormous main hall, with its bare rafters, the women displaying a most elaborate choice of broad velvet ribbons, silk aprons, and armlets worked in crochet and sometimes sewn with pearls. The animals participated in the celebration; the cows had their horns adorned with gold and carried little crowns on their heads and would look from their open boxes on both sides of the hall over the banquet table.

Folk-dances of many kinds are another survival, and the Bavarian Schuhplattler, a clog-dance, is the best known. It is an enormously exhausting performance in which the boys try to attract attention by leaping and jumping and by slapping the soles of their shoes on the ground while the girls are slowly and coyly turning round in the centre. In the Tyrol some yodelling is often thrown in to show that even these breath-taking antics have not quite exhausted the strength of the wooing male.

Many of these old traditions were revived by the German youth movement, the Wandervögel (birds of passage). Their little groups, consisting at first mostly of students, but later of people from all sections of the community, travelling on foot, with guitars or violins, singing folksongs and performing folk-dances, could be found at all romantic or picturesque spots until the Nazis suppressed the organization and took the growing generations into their official Hitler-Youth.

So much for the romantic past. The other side of the picture is represented by modern industrial Germany. There, too, old traditions are sometimes still kept. The German miners, for instance, still wear their traditional uniforms on special occasions. The miners from the salt mines near Halle, the Hallesche Pfännerschaft (so called from the salt-pans in which the salt was made), had the special privilege on festive occasions of appearing in Berlin in their picturesque garments as representatives of the miners.

Industrial Germany

In general, however, industrial Germany shows no great difference from the industrial regions in other European countries. There is the giant combine of the coal and steel towns in the Ruhr, comprising nearly sixteen per cent of the whole population of the country. In Saxony the textile industry is predominant. Leipzig is the seat of the well-known International Fair (Leipziger Messe) and the centre of German publishing and book-selling for Eastern Germany, Frankfurt on the Main being the equivalent centre for West Germany.

In the Black Forest (Schwarzwald) the clockmaking industry has its home. In the more leisurely past, innumerable cuckoo clocks (Kuckucks-Uhren) were shipped from there to all parts of the world, while in the times of austerity these have been replaced by alarm-clocks (Weckeruhren).

Nuremberg was peacefully employed on making toys and a special kind of gingerbread (Nürnberger Lebkuchen), before it became the unhappy town of the official Nazi party rallies.

A special feature of German industrial life, often overlooked, is the highly important role of waterways and canals. The

WINTER IM SCHWARZWALD

Im Winter verzaubern Schnee und Eis den Schwarzwald in ein weisses Elfenreich. Schlitten und Ski werden zeitweilig die Hauptverkehrsmittel auf den zahlreichen durch das Gebirge führenden Hochstrassen.
(*Translation on page* 380

verzaubern	der Schlitten, -	zeitweilig	das Hauptverkehrsmittel, -
to transform	*sleigh*	*for the time being*	*chief means of travel*

HEIMWEG VON DER SCHULE

Vier kleine Kinder auf dem Heimweg von der Schule in der ehemalig freien Reichsstadt Nördlingen. Mit seinen aus dem 14ten und 15ten Jahrhundert stammenden mittelalterlichen Mauern und Türmen ist Nördlingen eine der zahlreichen deutschen Städte, die ihren mittelalterlichen Charakter fast unverfälscht erhalten haben.

(Translation on page 380)

der Heimweg, -e	ehemalig	die Mauer, -n	fast	unverfälscht	erhalten
homeward way	*former*	*wall, battlement*	*almost*	*unspoilt*	*to preserve*

town of Duisburg, for instance, was at one time the largest inland harbour in Europe; Berlin, too, had an enormous water traffic serving its economic needs. The Rhine, the Danube, the Elbe, the Oder, are waterways of the first order, and also much in favour for tourist purposes.

Holiday Places

The German spas and holiday resorts (Kurorte) are now again prosperous and efficiently organized. Some of them have a tradition reaching back to Roman times. Wiesbaden, like Bath, in Somerset, was founded on the site of an old Roman thermal bath. Others were of more recent fame. To the British public of Victorian times, Baden-Baden and Homburg were the best-known names. Later the resorts on the North Sea and the Baltic coasts became popular.

The latest developments were the discovery of the lovely scenery of the Lüneburg Heath (Lüneburger Heide) and the winter sports movement, favouring the Bavarian Alps and other such districts.

Proximity to the German forests, the largest in central Europe, was often a special feature of these holiday resorts, as in the Harz Mountains or in the Erzgebirge on the Czechoslovakian border.

Town Life

Housing conditions in the larger towns developed along somewhat different lines from those in Britain, with the result that it became the custom for most families to live in huge blocks of flats, nicknamed Miets-Kasernen (rental barracks). Only the more well-to-do could afford their own homes in one of the Vororte (suburbs), which are often called Villen-Kolonie, although their villas consist mostly of rather modest little dwellings.

The equivalent to gardening in Britain is the widespread habit of owning some allotment on the fringe of the large towns. These plots are known as Schreber-Gärten, after one Dr. Schreber, who started the movement about 1870.

Recreation is available on a large scale for all classes of the community. The theatres and opera houses, not only in the big cities, but also in smaller towns, are subsidized by the state or the communities. There are many open-air theatres and festivals. Bayreuth, as the home of Wagner's operas, has kept up its old reputation under the management of the grandsons of the composer; special seasons in Munich or Salzburg attract many visitors from all parts of the country and from abroad. A very high proportion of stage entertainment is devoted to classical and serious literature of all nations. In Austria, the famous Burg-Theater and the Opera house, now restored in faithful adherence to its old plans, are regarded as national shrines. Hamburg, Düsseldorf, Frankfurt, Darmstadt, are other famous centres of theatrical activity in the West, and in Berlin the Deutsche Theater has preserved its old reputation.

No less vigorous is the musical life all over the country, with innumerable Philharmonic societies and smaller circles for chamber music. Thousands of choral societies (Gesangvereine) cultivated the German Lied, many of them being for male singers (Männergesangvereine) only. In addition, evening classes and the so-called People's Universities (Volkshochschulen), based on the Danish model, had sprung up after the First World War.

Radio entertainment, and, so far to a lesser degree, television has largely superseded these older forms of music-making, and the German Hausmusik, with the piano as the centre-piece of family life, is now more or less a thing of the past.

Sports

Football and other originally British games became very popular. Horse races were also based on the English model, the "Derby" at Hamburg being the great event of the year.

Skittle-alleys (Kegel-Bahnen) are in many regions the national amusement, and the typical skittle-player (nicknamed Kegel-bruder) represents the rather stout and heavy kind of German middle-class citizen.

The younger generation, however, has altered this picture to a considerable extent, and for some decades hiking, rowing, sailing and winter sports, in particular ski-ing in the many mountainous districts, have steadily gained ground.

Motorization has again altered the picture. The younger generation, in West Germany, is going to work and on pleasure trips on scooters, motor-bicycles or in cars. The famous Volkswagen is only one instance of the ubiquitous cheap vehicle. The roads, with the well-kept Autobahnen as long-distance communication, are excellent; driving discipline, however, is rather poor and the rate of accidents correspondingly high. Motor coaches and the modern diesel-trains serve the most remote parts of the country, and the greatest part of West Germany can now be reached by international air lines, with Frankfurt, Munich, Hamburg and Düsseldorf as the main air ports. Berlin too is connected with the outside world by several air lines.

Travelling not only inside the country but also abroad has become the sign of the newly-won freedom, and of the old Wanderlust, at least for West Germans; unfortunately, travel between the two parts of Germany is still beset with insuperable difficulties.

It is this division into two separate states, steadily moving apart not only in politics, but also in all aspects of cultural life, that makes it impossible to speak of Germany as a whole. Daily life is different in East and West. Literature and entertainment are different. Russian is taught as the first foreign language in the East, English in the West.

Reunification, if it should come in the foreseeable future, will pose new problems, and is one of the dominant problems of the day in both parts. And so, Germany is standing, as so often in her chequered history, on the crossways, powerful again, after an unprecedented downfall, and powerless at the same time, looking for its place in the development of civilization and her share in the general welfare of mankind.

SCHWEIZERISCHES RATHAUS

Fern von der Hast und dem Treiben des modernen Grosstadtlebens rattelt dieser alte Ochsenkarren gemächlich über das Steinpflaster des Dorfplatzes in Mayenfeld (Graubünden). Die Fresken auf dem Rathaus sind charakteristisch für die Ausschmückung derartiger Gebäude in Teilen der Schweiz und Süddeutschlands.

(*Translation on page* 380)

die Hast	**das Treiben**	**gemächlich**	**das Steinpflaster, -**	**die Ausschmückung, -en**
haste	*activity*	*steadily*	*stone paving*	*adornment*

352–354

KEY TO THE EXERCISES

You are advised to check your own answers carefully with those given below, and if necessary to repeat the same test at intervals of a few days until you are word-perfect.

Lesson One

I

Who is the father of Hans and Grete? Herr Schulz is the father. Who is the mother? Frau Schulz is the mother. Who are the parents? Herr and Frau Schulz are the parents. Who are the children? Hans and Grete are the children. What is Herr Schulz of Hans and Grete? He is the father. What is Frau Schulz of Hans and Grete? She is the mother. What is Hans of Grete? He is the brother of Grete. What is Grete of Hans? She is the sister of Hans. Where does the Schulz family live? The Schulz family lives in Hamburg. Where is Hamburg? It is in Germany. Where is Berlin? It is also in Germany. Is Berlin large? Yes, it is large. Is Hamburg also large? Yes, it is also large. Is Hans large (tall)? No, he is small. Is Herr Schulz stout? Yes, he is stout. Is Hans also stout? No, he is not stout, he is thin. Is Grete the sister of Frau Schulz? No, she is not the sister of Frau Schulz. What is Grete of Frau Schulz? She is the daughter. Who are the parents of Hans and Grete? Herr and Frau Schulz are the parents.

II

1. Vater. 2. Er. 3. Mutter. 4. Sie. 5. Sohn. 6. Er. 7. Tochter. 8. Sie. 9. Eltern. 10. Kinder. 11. der. 12. die. 13. der. 14. die. 15. die. 16. die.

III

1. Hans ist der Bruder von Grete. 2. Frau Schulz ist die Mutter von Hans. 3. Er ist der Vater von Hans. 4. Er ist der Bruder von Grete. 5. Ja, sie ist die Tochter von Frau Schulz. 6. Nein, er ist nicht der Vater von Grete. 7. Herr Schulz ist der Vater von Grete. 8. Grete ist die Schwester von Hans. 9. Herr und Frau Schulz sind die Eltern. 10. Ja, er ist dick. 11. Ja, sie ist auch dick. 12. Nein, er ist nicht gross. 13. Ja, sie ist klein. 14. Berlin ist in Deutschland. 15. Hamburg ist auch in Deutschland.

Lesson Two

I

1. That is the chair. It is brown. 2. That is the door. It is green. 3. That is the book. It is blue. 4. Is the wine white? No, it is red. 5. Hans is the brother of Grete. 6. He eats sausage. 7. The sausage is good. 8. Grete drinks water. 9. The water is cold. 10. The young lady drinks coffee. 11. What does the gentleman eat? 12. He eats meat. 13. Who eats fruit? 14. What does Frau Schulz eat? 15. Is the pencil blue? No, it is yellow.

II

1. Ja, er ist der Vater. 2. Ja, er isst Fleisch. 3. Sie isst Obst. 4. Sie trinkt Kaffee. 5. Hans trinkt Limonade. 6. Hans isst Brot mit Butter und Käse. 7. Sie isst Wurst mit Salat. 8. Nein, sie sind nicht gross. 9. Nein, sie ist nicht rot. 10. Der Wein ist rot. 11. Die Milch ist weiss.

III

1. der. 2. die. 3. das. 4. die. 5. die. 6. das. 7. der. 8. das. 9. der. 10. der. 11. das. 12. der. 13. die. 14. das. 15. die. 16. die. 17. die. 18. die. 19. der. 20. die.

IV

1. er. 2. sie. 3. er. 4. es. 5. er. 6. sie. 7. er.

Lesson Three

I

Herr Lessing is a man. Frau Lessing is a lady. Fräulein Lessing is a young lady. Fritz is a boy. Hilda is a girl. Herr Schulz drinks a glass of beer. Frau Schulz drinks a cup of coffee. Herr Lessing smokes a cigar. Frau Lessing does not smoke. Fräulein Lessing smokes a cigarette. Does

Fritz smoke? No, he does not smoke, he is too young.
Who is the father? Herr Lessing is the father. Who is the young man? He is Herr Lessing junior. Who is a schoolboy? Fritz is a schoolboy. Who is a student (female)? Fräulein Lessing is a student. Who is a Scotsman? Mr. Murdoch is a Scotsman. Who are you? I am Mr. Smith. What are you, Mr. Smith? I am an Englishman. Are you an English woman, Mrs. O'Connor? No, I am an Irish woman.

II

1. Er ist ein Mann. 2. Er ist ein Student. 3. Er ist ein Knabe. 4. Sie ist ein Mädchen. 5. Sie ist eine junge Dame. 6. Herr Lessing ist der Vater. 7. Hilde ist eine Schülerin. 8. Herr Lessing junior ist ein Student. 9. Herr Smith ist ein Engländer. 10. Frau Murdoch ist eine Schottin. 11. Er ist ein Schüler. 12. Es ist eine Schülerin. 13. Fräulein Lessing ist eine Studentin. 14. Herr O'Connor ist ein Ire. 15. Frau Lessing ist eine Deutsche.

III

1. ein. 2. ein. 3. ein. 4. ein. 5. eine. 6. ein, ein. 7. ein. 8. eine. 9. ein. 10. ein. 11. eine. 12. ein.

Lesson Four

I

Is this garden large? No, it is small. Is this street long? No, it is short. Is the red book thick or thin? It is thin. Is the stout man tall? No, he is small. Which pencil is long, the yellow one or the blue one? Which book is thick, the red one or the green one? Which street is beautiful, the long one or the short one? What is Fräulein Lessing like, stout or slim? She is slim. This gentleman drinks beer. That gentleman drinks wine. This lady plays the piano, that lady plays cards. This gentleman smokes a cigar, that gentleman smokes a cigarette. This child is a boy, that one is a girl.
Which lady is beautiful, the blonde or the brunette? The blonde is beautiful, but the brunette is ugly. Do you not agree? (do you not think so also)?

II

1. -es, -es. 2. -e, -e. 3. -er, -er, -er, -er. 4. -e, -e, -e. 5. -es, -es, -es. 6. -e. 7. -er. 8. -er. 9. -es. 10. -er.

III

1. Herr Schulz ist gross. 2. Frau Schulz ist klein und dick. 3. Grete ist dünn. 4. Die Strasse ist lang. 5. Der blaue Bleistift ist kurz. 6. Dieser rote Bleistift ist gut. 7. Er ist gross und dick. 8. Sie ist klein und dick. 9. Herr Schulz ist gross und dick. 10. Fräulein Lessing ist dünn.

Lesson Five

I

What are you drinking? I will take a cup of coffee. With milk or without milk? With a lot of milk, please. Do you take sugar? Two lumps, please. What are you eating? Meat with salad, please. Waiter, two cups of coffee, please. One cup without milk and one with a lot of milk. A portion of meat with salad and for me a slice of bread and butter with cheese.

II

1. Ich trinke (nicht) Milch. 2. Ich trinke (nicht) viel Tee. 3. Ich trinke Kaffee mit (*or* ohne) Milch und Zucker. 4. Herr Schulz isst viel Fleisch. 5. Ich esse (nicht) viel Fleisch. 6. Ich bin (nicht) Vegetarier. 7. Ich esse gern Gemüse. 8. Ich trinke (nicht) gern Bier. 9. Ich rauche (nicht) viel. 10. Milch mit Zucker schmeckt (nicht) gut. 11. Kaffee ohne Zucker schmeckt bitter. 12. Schokolade schmeckt süss. 13. Zitronen schmecken sauer. 14. Ich esse (nicht) gern Obst. 15. Ich habe (nicht) viele Bücher. 16. Ich habe dreiundzwanzig Bücher. 17. Sie haben vier Kinder. 18. Ich trinke (nicht) gern Kaffee. 19. Ich nehme zwei Stück Zucker. 20. Ich nehme (nicht) viel Milch.

III

1. die Tür, die Türen. 2. das Glas, die Gläser. 3. das Fenster, die Fenster. 4. die Tasse, die Tassen. 5. der Sohn, die Söhne. 6. die Tochter, die Töchter. 7. das Buch, die Bücher. 8. die Feder, die Federn. 9. die Zigarette, die Zigaretten. 10. der Stuhl, die

Stühle. 11. das Haus, die Häuser. 12. der Baum, die Bäume. 13. der Garten, die Gärten. 14. die Strasse, die Strassen.

Lesson Six

I

1. Ich habe drei Paar Schuhe. 2. Mein Mantel ist grau. 3. Meine Schuhe sind schwarz. 4. Nein, es ist nicht gelb. 5. Nein, sie sind braun. 6. Sie wohnt in Berlin. 7. Nein, ich wohne nicht in Berlin. 8. Ich wohne in London. 9. Sie ist die Tante von Hans und Grete. 10. Herr Schulz ist der Onkel von Fritz und Hilde. 11. Er ist ein Vetter von Hans. 12. Der alte Herr Schulz ist der Grossvater. 13. Sie ist die Grossmutter von Hans und Grete. 14. Sie ist seine Schwester. 15. Sie ist die Schwiegermutter. 16. Sie leben nicht mehr. 17. Er ist ein Schwager von Frau Schulz.

II

1. mein, meine, meine; Ihr, Ihre, Ihre; sein, seine, seine; ihr, ihre, ihre; ihr, ihre, ihre; unser, unsere, unsere. 2. mein; Ihr; sein; ihr; ihr; unser. 3. mein, meine; Ihr, Ihre; sein, seine; ihr, ihre; ihr, ihre; unser, unsere. 4, 5, 6. meine, Ihre, seine; ihre, ihre, unsere.

III

1. Dieses kleine Mädchen ist meine Nichte. 2. Dieser kleine Knabe ist mein Vetter. 3. Jener alte Mann ist unser Grossvater. 4. Er trinkt gern Wein. 5. Was isst er gern? 6. Er isst gern Fisch. 7. Essen Sie gern Bonbons? 8. Ich esse sie nicht gern, sie sind nicht gut für die Zähne. 9. Sie isst viel Fleisch. 10. Sie haben fünf Kinder, zwei Söhne und drei Töchter. 11. Welche Farbe hat Ihr Anzug? 12. Er ist grau. 13. Sind Ihre Schuhe auch grau? Nein, sie sind schwarz; aber mein Hut ist grau. 14. Mein Grossvater lebt nicht mehr. 15. Meine Eltern leben in Südengland. 16. Wo wohnen Sie? 17. Lebt Ihr Grossvater noch? 18. Haben Sie viele Brüder und Schwestern? 19. Meine Schwiegereltern wohnen nicht in einer Wohnung, sie haben eine Villa. 20. Ihre Grossmutter lebt nicht mehr.

Lesson Seven

I

To-day is Friday, the twenty-eighth of March. Yesterday was Thursday, the twenty-seventh. The day after to-morrow will be Sunday, the thirtieth. Friday is the sixth day. March is the third month. January is the first month. May is the fifth month. November is the eleventh (or next to last) month. We are now in summer. November is an autumn month. The winter months are called December, January and February.

II

1. Ich heisse .... 2. Es heisst "German— How to Speak and Write it". 3. Heute ist der .... 4. Vorgestern war der ... ... 5. Gestern war ..., der .... 6. Er hat einunddreissig Tage. 7. Nicht jeder Monat hat einunddreissig Tage. 8. Nicht jede Frau hat lange Haare. 9. Ja, jeder Schüler hat ein Buch. 10. Nicht alle Engländer sind gross. 11. Sie heissen Januar, Februar, März, April, Mai, Juni, Juli, August, September, Oktober, November und Dezember. 12. Es hat dreihundertfünfundsechzig oder dreihundertsechsundsechzig Tage. 13. Er hat achtundzwanzig Tage. 14. Dieses Jahr ist ein (or kein) Schaltjahr. 15. Sie heissen Sonntag, Montag, Dienstag, Mittwoch, Donnerstag, Freitag und Sonnabend.

III

1. Im September sind die Äpfel reif. 2. Jetzt sind wir im Sommer. 3. Die Tage sind im Sommer lang. 4. Im Winter sind die Tage kurz. 5. Im Winter sind die Bäume mit Schnee bedeckt. 6. Der vierte Monat ist der April. 7. Dreissig Tage hat dieser Monat. 8. Im Sommer reift das Getreide. 9. Walter Müller heisse ich. 10. Im Frühling blühen die Obstbäume.

Lesson Eight

I

1. Ein Tag hat vierundzwanzig Stunden. 2. Ich arbeite siebeneinhalb Stunden. 3. Ich arbeite (nicht) gern. 4. Ich arbeite (nicht) viel. 5. Meine Uhr zeigt (nicht) die Sekunden. 6. Es ist jetzt zehn Minuten

nach elf. 7. Ich esse um halb acht Frühstück. 8. Ich esse um ein Uhr zu Mittag. 9. Ich esse um sieben Uhr Abendbrot. 10. Ich lese oder spiele Karten. 11. Sie geht etwas vor (*is slightly fast*). 12. Sie hat zwei Zeiger. 13. Ich komme um halb sieben nach Hause. 14. Ich esse zu Hause. 15. Ich gehe um elf Uhr zu Bett. 16. Ich schlafe acht Stunden. 17. Ich stehe gewöhnlich um sieben Uhr auf. 18. Ich wasche mich im Badezimmer.

II

1. Was ist dies? Es ist ein Glas und es ist voll Wasser. 2. Nicht jedes Glas ist voll. 3. Wie viele Gläser haben Sie? Ich habe acht. 4. Wer ist er? Ein Engländer. Um wieviel Uhr kommt er her? 5. Wieviel Uhr ist es? Es ist zwanzig nach drei. 6. Um wieviel Uhr stehen Sie auf? Ich stehe um halb sieben auf, aber am Sonntag stehe ich um neun auf. 7. Was tun Sie dann? Ich wasche mich im Badezimmer. Ich wasche meine Hände und mein Gesicht. Dann gehe ich ins Schlafzimmer zurück und kleide mich an. 8. Um acht Uhr gehe ich ins Esszimmer und frühstücke. 9. Der wievielte ist heute? Es ist der einundzwanzigste März. 10. Wie viele Minuten hat eine Viertelstunde? Fünfzehn. Ist das richtig? 11. Wir essen um halb acht Frühstück, zu Mittag um eins und Abendbrot um drei Viertel sieben. 12. Ich arbeite von acht bis halb eins und von zwei bis ein Viertel sieben.

III

1. Fünf Minuten nach elf Uhr vormittags. 2. Viertel neun morgens. 3. Ein Uhr fünfundzwanzig nachmittags. 4. Drei Viertel acht Uhr abends. 5. Der Mittag *or* zwölf Uhr mittags. 6. Die Mitternacht *or* zwölf Uhr nachts. 7. Fünf Minuten vor zwölf Uhr mittags. 8. Fünf Minuten vor zwölf Uhr nachts.

Lesson Nine

I

1. Ja, er hat viel Geld. 2. Nein, ich habe nicht so viel Geld wie er. 3. Ich habe (nicht) viele Taschentücher. 4. Ein Herrentaschentuch ist grösser. 5. Damenschuhe sind

nicht so gross wie Herrenschuhe. 6. Kinderschuhe sind kleiner als Herrenschuhe. 7. Neuyork ist die grösste Stadt in Amerika. 8. Nein, die Donau ist länger als der Rhein. 9. Eine Taschenuhr ist grösser als eine Armbanduhr. 10. Sie geht (nicht) gut. 11. Die Rose ist schöner. 12. Die Rose ist die schönste. 13. Sie sind im Juli länger. 14. Der einundzwanzigste Juni ist der längste Tag. 15. Sie sind im Winter kürzer. 16. Der einundzwanzigste Dezember ist der kürzeste Tag.

II

1. Sie haben eine schöne Wohnung. 2. Mein Buch ist dicker als Ihr Buch. 3. Wie alt sind Sie? 4. Ich bin älter als Sie. 5. Sie sind jünger als meine Schwester. 6. Wer ist hier der älteste? 7. Sind Sie der jüngste? 8. Welcher ist besser, der Rotwein oder der Weisswein? 9. Ist dies das beste Buch? 10. Ist dies der kürzeste Weg? 11. Welcher Weg ist kürzer? 12. Dieser Weg ist so kurz wie jener. 13. Essen Sie eine ganze Apfelsine oder nur eine halbe? 14. Ist dies das grösste Hotel? 15. Es ist nicht das grösste, aber es ist das beste. 16. Wieviel kosten die Birnen? 17. Sie sind zu teuer. 18. Sind diese billiger?

III

1. älter. 2. jüngste. 3. länger. 4. längste. 5. interessanter. 6. grösste. 7. besser. 8. beste. 9. interessanteste. 10. jünger.

Lesson Ten

I

1. Do you speak German? 2. A little, not much. 3. Does your wife speak French? 4. She reads French books and newspapers, but she does not speak well. 5. She is taking French lessons. 6. Do you take German lessons? 7. I have a friend. He is a teacher. He gives German lessons. 8. Is he a German? 9. He is not a German, but he speaks German well. 10. He is a Scotsman. His name is Jock. But his wife is German. 11. They like eating strawberries. 12. My sister likes cherries best.

II

1. Ich lese (nicht) gern Romane. 2. Ich lese
... lieber. 3. Ich esse sie (nicht) gern. 4. Ich
esse ... lieber. 5. Ich esse am liebsten ...
6. Ich trinke am liebsten ... 7. Ich finde sie
(nicht) interessant. 8. Ich spreche ein wenig
Deutsch. 9. Ich habe (nicht) viele Bücher.
10. Ich lese (nicht) viel. 11. Ich fahre
(nicht) Rad. 12. Ich habe ein (or kein)
Fahrrad.

III

1. Ich liebe sie. 2. Sie liebt ihn. 3. Er liebt
sie. 4. Sie liebt mich nicht. 5. Ich liebe ihn
nicht. 6. Wir sprechen Deutsch. 7. Sie
sprechen nicht Französisch. 8. Was tun
Sie? 9. Ich lese. 10. Was tut sie? 11. Sie
liest ein Buch. 12. Ich esse gern Erdbeeren.
13. Ich esse Kirschen nicht gern (or nicht
gern Kirschen). 14. Ich habe ihn gern. 15.
Sie hat ihn nicht gern. 16. Wir haben sie
nicht gern. 17. Haben Sie ihn gern? 18.
Lesen Sie viel? 19. Schreiben Sie gern
Briefe? 20. Was trinken Sie lieber, Tee oder
Kaffee? 21. Ich trinke Tee lieber als
Kaffee. 22. Ich trinke Tee nicht gern ohne
Milch.

Lesson Eleven

I

1. Ich bin .. Jahre alt. 2. Ich habe einen
(keinen) or ich habe mehrere (several)
Brüder. 3. Sie heisst ... strasse. 4. Ich habe
eine (keine). 5. Sie ist (nicht) aus Gold. 6.
Er ist aus Holz. 7 (a). Der Schlüssel ist aus
Eisen. (b) Die Feder ist aus Stahl. (c) Das
Buch ist aus Papier. 8. Er kostet 20
Pfennig. 9. Er ist billig. 10. Eine goldene
ist teurer. 11. Ich schreibe (nicht) viele
Briefe. 12. Sie lieben die Kinder.

II

1. Er liebt ihn. 2. Sie nimmt sie. 3. Er
schliesst sie. 4. Sie öffnet es. 5. Sie trinken
sie. 6. Sie lieben sie. 7. Sie sieht es. 8. Er
bringt ihn. 9. Sie liest sie. 10. Sie lesen sie.

III

1. Steckt. 2. legt. 3. steckt. 4. stellt. 5.
legt. 6. steckt.

IV

1. Der Lehrer öffnet das Buch. 2. Auch die
Schüler öffnen ihre Bücher. 3. Ein Schüler
liest. 4. Er nimmt das Buch, öffnet es und
liest. 5. Bitte, öffnen Sie ein Fenster. 6.
Bitte, schliessen Sie die Tür. 7. Bitte,
nehmen Sie nicht meinen Hut, nehmen Sie
Ihren. 8. Stecken Sie diesen Brief in den
Briefkasten. 9. Nehmen Sie diesen Stuhl, er
ist besser. 10. Stellen Sie ihn hier. 11. Wie
heisst Ihr Lehrer? 12. Wo wohnt er? 13.
Bitte, schreiben Sie seine Adresse auf
dieses Stück Papier. 14. Stecken Sie dies in
Ihre Tasche. 15. Uhren sind jetzt teuer,
nicht wahr?

Lesson Twelve

I

1. I have to write letters. Can I have your
pen? 2. You can have it. Here it is. 3. I
want to read while you are writing. 4.
Have you anything to read? 5. Do you
want to read a book or the paper? 6. Here
is a German newspaper. Can you read it?
7. I can read German, but I can't speak it.
8. Can you understand me? 9. I can understand you if you don't speak too fast.
10. You must not speak so fast.

II

1. Ich kann (nicht) Russisch sprechen. 2.
Sie können Deutsch sprechen. 3. Ich kann
nur eine Sprache (. .Sprachen) sprechen. 4.
Ich will (nicht) Russisch lernen. 5. Es ist
nicht leicht zu lernen. 6. Ich finde es
(nicht) schwer. 7. Ja, ich muss Stunden
nehmen, wenn ich die Sprache lernen will.
8. Wir müssen ein Messer haben. 9. Ich
kann sie nicht aufschliessen, wenn ich
keinen Schlüssel habe. 10. Ich will heute
(nicht) ins Kino gehen.

III

1. Können Sie Deutsch sprechen? 2. Ich
kann Deutsch lesen, aber nicht sprechen.
3. Wollen Sie rauchen? 4. Was wollen Sie
trinken? 5. Müssen Sie gehen? 6. Ich will
nicht, aber ich muss. 7. Hier ist eine
Zeitung. Lesen Sie sie, während ich diesen
Brief schreibe. 8. Warum öffnen Sie jene

Tür nicht? Weil ich den Schlüssel nicht habe. 9. Warum essen Sie Ihr Fleisch nicht? 10. Ich kann es nicht essen, weil es zu kalt ist. 11. Ich kann meine Milch nicht trinken, weil sie zu heiss ist. 12. Sie können jetzt nicht herein.

Lesson Thirteen

I

1. Is there wine in this glass? 2. No, there is water in this glass but there is wine in the other glass. 3. Can I give you anything to drink? 4. What do you like to drink? What do you like best to drink? 5. Can you give me a glass of water, please? 6. Wait a moment, I'll bring you a cup of coffee. 7. Do you drink coffee with milk and sugar? With milk please, but without sugar. 8. Please fetch my mother a glass of milk and something to eat.

II

1. es, ihm. 2. ihr. 3. er, sie. 4. ihn. 5. sie, ihnen. 6. er, ihr. 7. ihm.

III

1. Was tun Sie? 2. Ich schreibe einen Brief. 3. Wem (*or* an wen) schreiben Sie? 4. Meinem Bruder, meiner Schwester und meinen Eltern. 5. Schreiben sie Ihnen oft? 6. Wem gehört diese Füllfeder? 7. Sie gehört mir. 8. Diese Handtasche gehört jener Dame. Geben Sie sie ihr. 9. Bringen Sie diese Flasche Ihrer Mutter. 10. Wie geht es ihr? 11. Wie geht es Ihrem Sohn? 12. Was fehlt ihrer Tochter?

Lesson Fourteen

I

1. dem. 2. dem. 3. dem. 4. der. 5. dem. 6. der. 7. ihren. 8. meiner. 9. den. 10. der. 11. der. 12. den. 13. der. 14. seinem. 15. ihrer. 16. einem, einer. 17. den. 18. den, diesem. 19. Ihren. 20. dieser, jener.

II

1. Auf dem Bild sind sechs Personen. 2. Sie hat eine Feder in der Hand. 3. Briefbogen und Umschläge. 4. Unter dem Tisch. 5.

Vor dem Fenster. 6. Der Mann steht neben dem Ofen. 7. Niemand steht an der Tür. 8. Nichts liegt auf dem Ofen. 9. Auf dem Tisch. 10. Sie geht aus dem Zimmer.

III

1 (a) Der Lehrer gibt es. (b) Er gibt es dem Schüler. (c) Er gibt ihm das Buch. 2 (a) Sie sendet es der Tochter. (b) Sie sendet ihr das Paket. (c) Ja, sie sendet es ihr. 3 (a) Sie zeigen ihnen Bilder. (b) Die Kinder zeigen sie ihnen. (c) Ja, sie zeigen sie ihnen.

Lesson Fifteen

I

1. Look, it's beginning to rain. You can't go out now. 2. But I have to go out. I am expected at my friends'. 3. Wait a few more minutes. Soon the rain will stop. 4. Won't you sit down? Sit down by the fire. 5. There is not enough coal on the fire. I shall put on some more coal. 6. Are you warm enough? Thank you, I am quite warm, but I must really go now. 7. But you can't go without an umbrella. 8. Have you got one? I haven't got one. 9. If you really have to go, take my umbrella. 10. Thank you very much. I'll bring it back to-morrow. 11. It is raining less now. Soon the rain will stop altogether.

II

1. Es ist jetzt (nicht) hell. 2. Wir sehen den Mond und die Sterne. 3. Nein, sie scheint nicht in der Nacht. 4. Sie scheint am Tage. 5. Am Mittag steht sie im Süden. 6. Um drei oder vier Uhr. 7. Im Mai geht er früher auf. 8. In der Nacht können wir nicht gut sehen. 9. Wir müssen Licht machen. 10. Wir setzen uns an den Ofen. 11. Nein, im Winter tragen wir dicke Kleider. 12. Weil uns kalt ist, wenn wir im Winter dünne Kleider tragen. 13. *See page* 130. 14. Es schneit (nicht). 15. Er ist weiss. 16. Wir nehmen einen Regenschirm mit, wenn wir im Regen ausgehen müssen.

III

1. Wie ist das Wetter heute? 2. Es ist ziemlich kalt. 3. Es regnet. 4. Mir ist kalt. 5. Ist Ihnen kalt? 6. Ich werde meinen Mantel anziehen. 7. Wie ist das Wetter

hier im Sommer? 8. Es ist gewöhnlich heiss. Manchmal regnet es. 9. Im Winter ist es windig, manchmal stürmisch. 10. Es wird dunkel. Wir müssen Licht machen. 11. Bitte schalten Sie das Licht ein. Der Schalter ist an der Tür. 12. Ich gehe spazieren. Wollen Sie mitkommen? 13. Ich werde mitkommen, aber nur für eine halbe Stunde. 14. Ich werde nachmittags im Garten arbeiten. 15. Die Sonne geht jetzt früh unter; es wird um fünf Uhr dunkel sein.

Lesson Sixteen

I

1. At what time did you have breakfast? I had breakfast at eight o'clock. 2. I drank coffee and ate rolls with marmalade. 3. What did you do afterwards? I read the newspaper and wrote letters. Then I worked in the garden until one. 4. At one o'clock I had lunch. In the afternoon I had a visitor. 5. A friend who speaks German well came to see me and we spoke German together. 6. At four o'clock we had tea. After tea we went for a walk. 7. In the evening my friend played the piano and we sang German songs.

II

1. Ich spiele (nicht) Tennis. 2. Ich habe heute (nicht) Tennis gespielt. 3. Ich habe ein Ei gegessen. 4. Ich schreibe (nicht) viele Briefe. 5. Ich habe diese Woche fünf Briefe geschrieben. 6. Ja, ich lese sie jeden Tag. 7. Ich habe heute den "Daily . . ." gelesen. 8. Ich tanze (nicht) gern. 9. Ich habe gestern (nicht) getanzt. 10. Herr und Frau Lessing haben sie eingeladen. 11. Ja, sie haben sie angenommen. 12. Zwei Tage vor der Abreise hat sie zu packen begonnen. 13. Für ihren Mann hat sie Anzüge, Hemden, Unterhosen u.s.w. eingepackt. 14. Die Toilettenartikel. 15. Sie werden um zehn Uhr vormittags abfahren.

III

1. Haben Sie die Fenster im Wohnzimmer geöffnet? 2. Haben Sie gestern abend eine deutsche Stunde gehabt? 3. Haben Sie heute früh die Zeitung gelesen? 4. Hat Ihre Schwester Ihnen geschrieben? 5. Sie hat in ihrem Brief gesagt: Der Zug fährt um 9 Uhr 30 ab und kommt um 5 Uhr nachmittags an. 6. Haben Sie Ihre Taschentücher eingepackt? 7. Der Zug kommt von Köln und fährt nach München. 8. Ist sie beim Frisör? 9. Ich habe im Garten gearbeitet. 10. Wir haben die Einladung angenommen. 11. Wir sind früh aufgestanden, haben gefrühstückt und unser Gepäck gepackt. 12. Ich habe es selbst getan.

Lesson Seventeen

I

1. When did you get up? I got up at half-past seven. 2. At a quarter past eight I left home. I went by tram to the station. 3. At nine o'clock I arrived at the station. I bought a ticket and went on the platform. 4. The train was there punctually. I got in and sat down in a corner by the window. 5. At the next stop several persons got in. 6. An old lady did not find a seat. I stood up and offered her my seat. 7. At half-past nine we arrived. I got out and walked to the factory. 8. There I worked till one o'clock. At one I went for lunch. 9. At two I was back at the office and worked for three-and-a-half hours. 10. In the evening I went to the cinema. 11. At ten I came home and went to bed immediately. 12. I fell asleep at once and dreamt a lot. I climbed a high mountain. There I fell and rolled down the mountain.

II

1. Gestern war Dienstag. 2. Ich bin gestern (nicht) im Theater gewesen. 3. Ich bin heute um sieben aufgestanden. 4. Ich bin um halb neun von Hause fortgegangen. 5. Ich bin mit dem Autobus gefahren. 6. Ich habe im Restaurant gegessen. 7. Ich gehe spät zu Bett. 8. Ich bin um halb zwölf zu Bett gegangen. 9. Sie ist um zwanzig nach neun am Bahnhof angekommen. 10. Der Vater hat sie gekauft. 11. Die Fensterplätze waren schon besetzt. 12. Der Stationsvorsteher.

III

1. Sie packte die Koffer. Sie hat die Koffer gepackt. 2. Er legte .... Er hat ... gelegt. 3. ... war voll. ... ist voll gewesen. 4. Fritz holte .... Fritz hat ... geholt. 5. Wir gingen zu Fuss. Wir sind ... gegangen. 6. Sie fuhren ... Sie sind ... gefahren. 7. ... kam und sie stiegen ein. ... ist gekommen und sie sind eingestiegen. 8. ... gab ... fuhr ab. ... hat das Zeichen zur Abfahrt gegeben und der Zug ist abgefahren. 9. Wir sangen und tanzten. Wir haben gesungen und getanzt. 10. Die Kinder spielten ... und kletterten ... Die Kinder haben ... gespielt und sind ... geklettert. 11. Ich setzte mich .... Ich habe mich ... gesetzt. 12. Er fand .... Er hat ... gefunden. Alle Plätze waren besitzt. Alle Plätze sind besitzt gewesen.

Lesson Eighteen

I

1. We have packed our trunks and are ready. 2. I fetch a taxi and we drive to the station. 3. A porter takes the trunks and registers them. 4. We go to the booking office to buy the tickets. Then we go on the platform. The train is not there yet. 5. We go into the waiting room to have a cup of coffee. 6. It is soon time to board the train. 7. We find two window seats. The station master shouts: "All aboard". The train leaves.

II

1. Wir fuhren in einem Taxi zum Bahnhof. 2. Der Zug fährt um vier Uhr fünfzehn nachmittags (16 Uhr 15) ab und kommt um sechs Uhr fünfunddreissig morgens an. 3. Ich sagte zu dem Gepäckträger: "Bitte, bringen Sie mein Gepäck zum Zug. Ich möchte diesen Koffer aufgeben". 4. In Deutschland muss man alles grosse Gepäck aufgeben. 5. Ich ging zum Schalter, die Fahrkarten zu kaufen. Viele Leute warteten vor dem Schalter. 6. Ich sagte: "Zwei Rückfahrkarten dritter Klasse nach Wien". 7. Dann folgten wir dem Gepäckträger nach dem Bahnsteig. Es waren viele Leute auf dem Bahnsteig. 8. Der Zug kam an und wir stiegen ein. 9. Das Abteil war voll. Es gab nur einen Platz in der Ecke an der Tür. Meine Schwester setzte sich und ich musste stehen. 10. Ihr gegenüber sass eine junge Engländerin. Sie ist nach Deutschland gekommen, um die Sprache zu lernen.

III

1. des, meiner. 2. Ihres. 3. dieser. 4. jener. 5. meiner. 6. meines, meiner. 7. Ihrer. 8. seiner.

Lesson Nineteen

I

1. Der Zug ist fünf Minuten nach eins in Berlin angekommen. 2. Herr Schulz ist zuerst ausgestiegen. 3. Er ist zum Bahnhof gekommen, um seine Verwandten zu begrüssen. 4. Weil Hans so gross geworden ist. 5. Er stellt ihm Herrn Brown vor. 6. Sie geben sie an der Sperre ab. 7. Der Hotelportier nimmt sie ihm ab. 8. Nur ein Zimmer ist frei. 9. Er will einige Monate bleiben. 10. Er macht einen Spaziergang, um die Stadt zu besichtigen.

II

1. Wird der Zug pünktlich ankommen? 2. Steigen Sie zuerst aus, ich werde mit den Koffern folgen. 3. Sie sehen nicht gut aus. Sie sind dünner geworden. 4. Ich habe Sie zuerst nicht erkannt. 5. Ich bin nach Deutschland gekommen, um die Sprache zu studieren. 6. Können Sie ein Restaurant empfehlen, wo man gut aber nicht zu teuer essen kann? 7. Bitte, halten Sie vor dem Bahnhof. 8. Ich werde in fünf Minuten unten sein. 9. Wollen Sie nicht Ihren Mantel abnehmen? 10. Darf ich Sie bitten heraufzukommen?

III

1. Er zerbrach ...; er hat ... zerbrochen. 2. Sie liebten sich; sie haben sich geliebt. 3. Ich stellte ihm meinen Freund vor; ich habe ... vorgestellt. 4. Sie dankte ihm; sie hat ihm gedankt. 5. Wir stiegen aus; wir sind ausgestiegen. 6. Ich freute mich; ich habe mich gefreut. 7. Sie sah gut aus; sie hat gut ausgesehen.

Lesson Twenty

I

1. Es hat drei Stockwerke. 2. Es ist im Erdgeschoss. 3. Man isst im Esszimmer. 4. Man kocht in der Küche. 5. Im Keller. 6. Unter dem Dach. 7. Es ist in der Diele. 8. Die englische Lehrerin der Kinder. 9. Man muss sie aufschliessen. 10. Er klingelt.

II

1. Wo wohnen Sie? 2. Ist es weit von hier? 3. Wie viele Zimmer hat Ihr Haus? 4. Ist in seinem Hause ein Badezimmer? 5. In welchem Stock ist das Kinderzimmer? 6. Es ist im zweiten Stock. 7. Ihre Koffer sind in dem Boden. 8. Sie haben schöne Blumenbeete in Ihrem Garten, nicht wahr? 9. Haben Sie Gemüse in Ihrem Garten? 10. Wir haben nur wenige Blumen. 11. Schläft dieses Kind? 12. Die Küche ist neben dem Esszimmer. 13. Das Herrenzimmer ist links. 14. Das Telefon ist rechts neben dem Kleiderständer. 15. Die erste Tür rechts führt in das Wohnzimmer, die zweite ins Esszimmer und die dritte in die Küche.

III

1. das. 2. der. 3. dem. 4. der, den. 5. die. 6. dem. 7. die, die. 8. das. 9. dessen. 10. das. 11. der. 12. die. 13. das. 14. die. 15. den. 16. dessen. 17. deren. 18. dem, der.

Lesson Twenty-one

I

1. Er schläft bei seinem Vetter. 2. Er klopft, um seinen Sohn aufzuwecken. 3. Weil er Ferien hat. 4. Weil er zur Schule gehen muss. 5. Er bleibt im Bett, bis sein Vetter sich gewaschen hat. 6. Zuletzt zieht er seine Jacke an. 7. Um ein Viertel zehn. 8. Sie bewahrt dort ihre Toilettenartikel auf. 9. In der untersten Schublade ihrer Kommode. 10. Neben ihrem Bett steht ein Nachttisch.

II

1. Bitte, kommen Sie herein. Bitte, komm (kommt) herein. 2. Spielen Sie Tennis? Spielst du (spielt ihr) Tennis? 3. Haben Sie (hast du, habt ihr) gut geschlafen? 4. Geben Sie (gib, gebt) mir Ihr (dein, euer) Buch. 5. Sind Sie (bist du, seid ihr) krank? 6. Werden Sie (wirst du, werdet ihr) kommen? 7. Wie geht es Ihnen (dir, euch)? 8. Ich habe Sie (dich, euch) gestern gesehen.

III

1. Wir stehen um sechs Uhr auf. 2. Gehen Sie (gehst du, geht ihr) nicht früh zu Bett? 3. Sie waschen sich nicht im Schlafzimmer. 4. Ich werde mich im Schlafzimmer. 5. Sind Stühle im Schlafzimmer? 6. Vergessen Sie (vergiss, vergesst) nicht mich zu wecken. 7. Alle schliefen (or jeder schlief). 8. Er wollte sich nicht vor dem Frühstück waschen. 9. Sie legte ihre Juwelen in die dritte Schublade ihres Toilettentisches. 10. Er las gern im Bett.

Lesson Twenty-two

I

1. In einer Bank kann man Geld umwechseln. 2. In einem Zigarettenladen. 3. Er kennt sie nicht. 4. Er hat vergessen, wie die Sorte heisst, für die man so viel Reklame macht. 5. Er kauft Tinte, Briefpapier und Ansichtskarten. 6. Er schreibt sie im Hotel. 7. Er geht zur Post. 8. Man muss ein Formular ausfüllen. 9. Weil schon viele Leute dort stehen. 10 (a). per Einschreiben; (b) als Drucksache; (c) durch Postanweisung.

II

1. Er steht auf, stand auf, ist aufgestanden. 2. Er geht fort, ging fort, ist fortgegangen. 3. Er kommt mit, kam mit, ist mitgekommen. 4. Er fährt ab, fuhr ab, ist abgefahren. 5. Er kommt an, kam an, ist angekommen. 6. Er kleidet sich an, kleidete sich an, hat sich angekleidet.

III

1. Meine Zigarren sind besser als Ihre (deine, eure) Zigaretten. 2. Der beste Tabak ist sehr teuer. 3. Deutsche Zigaretten sind billiger. 4. Sie kosten fünf Pfennig das Stück. 5. Wieviel kostet ein Paket mit zehn Stück? 6. Er muss viele Briefe schreiben. 7. Wollen Sie Ihre englischen

Geldscheine umwechseln? 8. Ich werde nicht vergessen, eine Schachtel Streichhölzer und Tinte zu kaufen. 9. Ist ein Papierwarengeschäft hier in der Nähe? 10. Ich möchte einige Ansichtskarten kaufen.

Lesson Twenty-three

I

1. Sie haben ihnen Eis versprochen. 2. In dem Erfrischungsraum eines Kaufhauses. 3. Ich esse es (nicht) gern. 4. Weil Frau Schulz dort nicht finden kann, was sie haben möchte. 5. Ja, es hat viele Abteilungen. 6. In einem Handschuhgeschäft oder in der Handschuhabteilung eines Kaufhauses. 7. Er geht in den Frisiersalon, sich die Haare schneiden zu lassen. 8. Er ist in dem Kaufhaus. 9. Nein, er lässt sich ihn nicht waschen. 10. Weil er seiner Frau versprochen hat, bald zurück zu sein.

II

1. Kommen Sie herein. 2. Sie können dort nicht hineingehen. 3. Sagen Sie ihr, dass sie heraufkommen soll. 4. Sie will nicht heraufkommen. 5. Kommen Sie jetzt nicht herein. 6. Wollen Sie nicht herunterkommen? 7. Bringen Sie Ihr Grammophon herauf. 8. Ich möchte einen Schirm kaufen. 9. Die Farbe gefällt mir nicht. 10. Das ist zu teuer. 11. Ich nehme diesen. 12. Wo kann ich meine Wäsche waschen lassen?

III

1. herauf. 2. hinauf. 3. herunter. 4. hinunter. 5. hinein. 6. her. 7. hinaus. 8. wohin. 9. heraus.

Lesson Twenty-four

I

I should like to eat something. I had breakfast rather early this morning. Do you know a good restaurant near here? There is quite a good one round the corner. Where would you rather sit, upstairs or down here? I think it's nicer upstairs. Please not too near the band. What will you have for hors d'oeuvre? What will you have for the next course? A knife (a fork, a spoon) is missing. How do you like it? Waiter, the bill please.

II

1. Es befindet sich in der Nähe des Büros von Herrn Lessing. 2. Herr Lessing hat Herrn und Frau Schulz eingeladen. 3. Weil sein Haus zu weit vom Büro ist. 4. Er hat sie am Ausgang der Untergrundbahn getroffen. 5. Sie nehmen Heringsalat. 6. Herr Lessing bestellt Schweinebraten und Herr Schulz Hasenbraten. 7. Er kann Hochheimer 1931 empfehlen. 8. Nein, er bestellt ihn nicht. 9. Es schmeckt ihr sehr gut. 10. Herr und Frau Schulz gehen in ein Museum, Herr Lessing geht zurück ins Büro.

III

1. Kennen Sie meinen Freund Karl? 2. Haben Sie ihn gern? 3. Wie gefällt Ihnen mein neuer Hut? 4. Ich ging gestern Abend ins Theater, aber das Stück hat mir nicht gefallen. 5. Tanzen Sie gern? 6. Möchten Sie tanzen? 7. Gefällt Ihnen diese Musik? 8. Möchten Sie etwas essen? 9. Ich möchte Eis essen. 10. Hat Ihnen das Eis geschmeckt?

Lesson Twenty-five

I

(a) 1. Er kommt von dem Bahnhof. 2. Er fährt nach dem Vorort. 3. Er hält vor dem Museum. (b) 1. Er stand an dem Tisch. 2. Sie nehmen ihn von dem Tisch. 3. An das Fenster. 4. An dem Fenster. (c) 1. Sie war in der Küche. 2. Aus der Küche. 3. In das Esszimmer. 4. Auf dem Tablett. 5. Auf den Tisch.

II

1. Können Sie mir ein Hotel empfehlen? 2. Ist dies der Weg zum Bahnhof? 3. Wie lange geht man zu Fuss? 4. Ich möchte lieber im Omnibus fahren. 5. Wo muss ich umsteigen? 6. Wohin wollen Sie? 7. Sie ist nicht zu Hause. 8. Ich werde später zurückkommen. 9. Ich kann Sie nicht verstehen. 10. Bitte, sprechen Sie langsamer.

Lesson Twenty-six

I

The body consists of the head, the trunk and the limbs. The front part of the head is called the face. In the middle of the face is the nose. We smell with the nose. Above the nose are the eyes, with which we see. Beneath the nose is the mouth, in which are the teeth and the tongue. We bite with the teeth and taste with the tongue. On the right and left of the head are the ears, with which we hear.

The neck connects the head with the trunk. In the trunk are the lungs, with which we breathe, the heart, through which the blood circulates, and the stomach, the organ of digestion. If all organs work well the person is healthy. If an organ is not in order the person is ill and must go to the doctor.

II

1. Der Körper des Menschen besteht aus dem Kopf, dem Rumpf und den Gliedern. 2. Er heisst das Gesicht. 3. Wir sehen mit den Augen. 4. Mit der Nase. 5. Wir hören mit den Ohren. 6. Es zirkuliert durch das Herz. 7. Der Magen. 8. Man geht zum Zahnarzt, wenn man Zahnschmerzen hat. 9. Ihre Schwägerin hat ihn empfohlen. 10. Nein, er zieht ihn nicht. 11. Sie ist froh, dass der Zahnarzt ihr keine Zähne gezogen hat. 12. Wir beissen mit ihnen (or damit).

III

(a) 1. Die Medizin wird von ihm dreimal täglich genommen. 2. Das muss von ihnen nicht wieder getan werden. 3. Die Briefmarken sind von mir verkauft worden. 4. Ich werde ans Telefon gerufen. 5. Er wurde von seiner Mutter begleitet. (b) 6. Ihre Eltern schlagen die Kinder oft. 7. Ihre Lehrerin begleitete sie. 8. Man wird ihn töten. 9. Man rief den Arzt zu dem Kranken.

Lesson Twenty-seven

I

1. Er hat Interesse für Fussballspiel und für Boxen. 2. Er hat sie zu einem Sportfest eingeladen. 3. Bekannte Weltmeister befanden sich unter ihnen. 4. Er sagte, dass er schlecht trainiert war. 5. Sie hat den Ehrgeiz, eine berühmte Schlittschuhläuferin zu werden. 6. Dreimal in der Woche. 7. Ihr Lieblingssport ist Radfahren. 8. Er macht gern Ausflüge in die Umgebung Berlins. 9. Wenn man sich verirrt, fragt man nach dem Weg. 10. Er muss die Lampen anzünden.

II

1. Dies ist (ich kenne) ein schönes Bild. 2. Dies ist ein begeisterter Sportsmann. Ich kenne einen begeisterten Sportsmann. 3. Dies ist (ich kenne) eine Berliner Zeitung, 4. Dies ist ein französischer Schlittschuhläufer. Ich kenne einen französischen Schlittschuhläufer. 5. Dies ist (ich kenne) meine amerikanische Tante. 6. Dies ist sein neuer Wagen. Ich kenne seinen neuen Wagen. 7. Dies ist ihr alter Lehrer. Ich kenne ihren alten Lehrer.

III

1. arme . . . kleines. 2. interessantes. 3. diesen langen . . . kurze. 4. neue, blaue. 5. neuen . . . meine alten. 6. reichen . . . grossen Haus. 7. alten. 8. guter. 9. gutes. 10. schöne. 11. gute. 12. grossen. 13. neue . . . neue . . . neue. 14. neuen. 15. neuen. 16. neue. 17. neues. 18. neue . . . neue.

Lesson Twenty-eight

I

1. Frau Schulz besucht sie gern. 2. Er zieht das Varieté vor. 3. Das Kino und der Zirkus. 4. Sie amüsieren sich über die Streiche der Clowns. 5. Weil er nicht gern stillsitzt. 6. Billardspielen. 7. Er geht wandern. 8. Sie liest, malt und spielt Tennis. 9. Sie beschäftigt sich am liebsten mit Handarbeiten oder Strickerei. 10. Lotte und Georg begleiten sie. 11. Man wirft ihnen Nüsse zu. 12. Er bringt sie für die Seehunde.

II

1. He owns several houses. 2. She has bad taste. 3. Skittles is very popular with the Germans. 4. Which is your favourite pastime? 5. If you want to get thinner you

must be more active physically. 6. She finds her greatest pleasure in looking at the masterpieces in the museums. 7. He paints, draws, does gymnastics and dances. 8. May I accompany you? 9. It is forbidden to feed the animals. 10. Catch what I am throwing to you.

III

1. Er musste es tun. 2. Werden Sie es wieder tun können? 3. Ich konnte gestern nicht kommen. 4. Ich werde in einem Restaurant essen müssen. 5. Die Kinder durften wegen des schlechten Wetters nicht ins Kino gehen. 6. Was wollen Sie lieber, Karten spielen oder zum Konzert gehen? 7. Ich werde in den Ferien ins Gebirge fahren. 8. Ich bewundere seine Gemälde. 9. Sie werden sich anstellen müssen. 10. Ich möchte die Löwen sehen.

Lesson Twenty-nine

I

1. darin. 2. damit. 3. davor. 4. daraus. 5. dahinter. 6. davon. 7. dazu. 8. darüber. 9. damit. 10. darin.

II

1. jung. 2. schlecht. 3. schmal, eng. 4. hässlich. 5. dunkel. 6. spät. 7. alt. 8. aufstehen. 9. hereinkommen. 10. unten. 11. sich auskleiden. 12. falsch. 13. schwach. 14. leer. 15. links. 16. schwer. 17. hell. 18. früh.

III

1. Ich habe beschlossen, meine Ferien an der See zu verbringen. 2. Sie wohnen in einem Vorort, eine halbe Stunde mit dem Autobus von der Stadtmitte. 3. Welches ist die Geschwindigkeitsgrenze in diesem Dorf? 4. Sie fahren zu schnell. Bitte, fahren Sie langsamer! 5. Halten wir für

kurze Zeit! 6. Versuchen wir, etwas zu essen zu bekommen! 7. Als wir ankamen, hatten sie schon die Kühe gemolken. 8. Wie lange wird es dauern, das Auto reparieren zu lassen? 9. Wir hatten eine Panne. 10. Diese Werkzeuge sind schmutzig. Können Sie mir helfen, sie zu säubern?

Lesson Thirty

I

1. When are you having your holidays this year? 2. Will you stay at home or will you go away? 3. Where are you going, to the seaside or to the mountains? 4. We are going to a seaside place on the South Coast of England. 5. We have taken rooms in a boarding house. 6. We shall bathe in the sea and go on excursions in the surrounding district. 7. We shall also go out on to the sea in a sailing boat. 8. Have you a room to let? 9. Unfortunately, there is none available. 10. I should like to take a furnished flat. 11. For how long? 12. For half a year. 13. How much is the rent? 14. Are light and heating included? 15. With breakfast or with full board? 16. The bathroom is on the first floor. 17. Will you please call me at half-past seven.

II

1. Was für ein herrlicher Anblick! 2. Wann wird das Schiff abfahren? 3. Er sagte, dass es morgen ankommen würde. 4. Sie fragte ihn, ob er krank wäre. 5. Als der Lehrer kam, setzten sich die Schüler. 6. Wie schade, dass er nicht mit uns kam (or mitkam)! 7. Können Sie mir bitte den Weg zum Strand zeigen? 8. Wie lange dauert es, nach Paris zu fliegen? 9. Ich habe ein Zimmer in einem Hotel bestellt (or ich bestellte). 10. Wir werden morgen abreisen. Kann ich, bitte, meine Rechnung haben?

*   *   *

KEY TO WORD-BUILDING PICTURES

Page 46

MEN'S CLOTHING. **Der Anzug,** suit: 1. collar; 2. jacket; 3. lapel; 4. sleeve; 5. waistcoat; 6. trousers. **Die Reitkleidung,** riding clothes: 1. sports jacket; 2. pocket; 3. breast pocket; 4. crop; 5. riding breeches; 6. riding boot. **Der Smoking,** dinner suit: with a dinner suit one wears a black tie. **Der Frack,** evening dress: with evening dress one always wears a white tie. **Der Mantel,** overcoat: this man is wearing a coat without a belt. **Die Krawatte,** tie: this is a striped tie. **Das Halstuch,** scarf: this is a woollen scarf. **Der Regenmantel,** raincoat: this man is wearing a raincoat with a belt.

Page 48

LADIES' CLOTHING. **Die Bluse,** blouse; **die Falte,** pleat; **der Rock,** skirt; **der Gürtel,** belt; **die Schnalle,** buckle; **der Sweater,** jumper; **das Jäckchen,** cardigan; **der Kragen,** collar; **der Armel,** sleeve; **das Kleid,** frock; **das Kostüm,** suit; **die Jacke,** jacket; **der Regenmantel,** raincoat; **die Kapuze,** hood; **der Wintermantel,** winter coat; **der Hut,** hat; **der Pelzkragen,** fur collar; **der Muff,** muff; **der Pelzmantel,** fur coat; **das Abendkleid,** evening dress.

Page 60

FRUIT AND NUTS. **Die Stachelbeere,** gooseberry; **die Brombeere,** blackberry; **der Apfel,** apple; **die Feige,** fig; **die Mandarine,** tangerine; **die Johannisbeere,** red currant; **die Weintraube,** grape; **der Pfirsich,** peach; **die Dattel,** date; **die Zitrone,** lemon; **die Himbeere,** raspberry; **die Birne,** pear; **die Aprikose,** apricot; **die Melone,** melon; **die Ananas,** pineapple; **die Erdbeere,** strawberry; **die Banane,** banana; **die Pflaume,** plum; **die Apfelsine,** orange; **die Walnuss,** walnut; **die Haselnuss,** hazel nut; **die Mandel,** almond.

Page 66

CLOCKS AND WATCHES. **Die Taschenuhr,** pocket watch: 1. winder; 2. watch chain; 3. dial; 4. watch case; 5. hour hand; 6.minute hand; 7. seconds hand. **Das Uhrwerk,** watch mechanism; **das Uhrarmband,** watch strap; **die Armbanduhr,** wrist watch; **die Kaminuhr,** mantelpiece clock; **die Stoppuhr,** stop watch; **der Schlüssel,** winder; **die Sanduhr,** hourglass; **die Standuhr,** grandfather clock; **das Gewicht,** weight; **das Pendel,** pendulum; **der Wecker,** alarm clock; **die Glocke,** bell; **die Sonnenuhr,** sundial; **das Gestell,** pedestal.

Page 70

GETTING UP. 1. Karl sleeps. 2. He wakes up. 3. He gets up. 4. He washes himself. 5. He has a bath. 6. He dries his face. 7. He cleans his teeth. 8. He brushes his hair. 9. He combs his hair. 10. He dresses himself. 11. Herr Schulz shaves himself. 12. He puts on his tie.

Page 88

FLOWERS. **Das Schneeglöckchen,** snowdrop; **das Stiefmütterchen,** pansy; **die gelbe Narzisse (die Osterglocke),** daffodil; **die Nelke,** carnation; **der Arum,** arum lily; **die Rose,** rose; **die Dahlie,** dahlia; **die Tulpe,** tulip; **das Veilchen,** violet; **der Flieder,** lilac; **die Winteraster (die Chrysantheme),** chrysanthemum; **die Kornblume,** cornflower; **das Gänseblümchen,** daisy; **der Jasmin,** jasmine; **das Maiglöckchen,** lily of the valley; **die Narzisse,** narcissus; **die Orchidee,** orchid; **der Goldlack,** wallflower; **die Azalie,** azalea; **der Blumenstrauss,** bunch of flowers; **der Blumentopf,** flower pot; **der Kranz,** wreath.

Page 92

JEWELLERY AND TRINKETS. **Der Ring,** ring; **der Trauring,** wedding ring; **der Siegelring,** signet ring; **Ring mit Stein,** ring with stone; **der Ohrring,** earring; **das Medaillon,** locket; **der Talisman,** charm; **die Krawattennadel,** tie pin; **die Diamantnadel,** diamond pin; **das Armband,** bracelet; **der Armring,** bangle; **die Uhrkette,** watch chain; **die Perlenkette,** string of pearls; **das Halsband (die Halskette),** necklace; **die Brosche,** brooch; **die Spange,** dress clip.

Page 110

THE COFFEE TABLE. 1. Coffee table; 2. coffee pot; 3. sugar basin; 4. sugar tongs; 5. cream jug; 6. tray; 7. salt cellar; 8. cup; 9. saucer; 10. coffee spoon; 11. egg cup; 12. egg spoon; 13. newspaper; 14. fork; 15. knife; 16. plate; 17. butter dish; 18. butter knife; 19. marmalade pot; 20. table mat; 21. bread basket; 22. bread roll; 23. cheese dish; 24. small fancy cake; 25. cake (plain or fruit); 26. cream cake; 27. maid; 28. apron; 29. doormat; 30. french window.

Page 118

THE SITTING ROOM. 1. Window; 2. curtain; 3. standard lamp; 4. lampshade; 5. writing desk; 6. drawer; 7. picture; 8. picture frame; 9. picture rail; 10. chandelier; 11. ceiling; 12. wall; 13. wireless set; 14. bookcase; 15. carpet; 16. mirror; 17. mantelpiece; 18. clock; 19. flower vase; 20. fireplace; 21. armchair; 22. table; 23. box; 24. tea trolley; 25. settee; 26. cushion; 27. piano; 28. piano stool.

Page 122

THE DINNER TABLE. 1. Table; 2. table leg; 3. tablecloth; 4. vegetable dish; 5. potato dish; 6. bread basket; 7. wine glass; 8. table napkin; 9. soup plate; 10. soup tureen; 11. salt cellar; 12. pepper pot; 13. mustard; 14. dinner plate; 15. decanter; 16. gravy dish; 17. soup spoon; 18. knife; 19. fish knife; 20. dessert spoon; 21. fork; 22. napkin ring; 23. sideboard; 24. fruit dish; 25. dessert dish; 26. dessert plate; 27. wine bottle; 28. meat dish; 29. carving fork; 30. carving knife.

Page 142

LUGGAGE. Der Reisekoffer, trunk; der Handkoffer, suitcase; der Stadtkoffer, attaché case; die Reisetasche, travelling bag; der Griff, handle, grip; das Reise-Necessaire, dressing case; die Thermosflasche, Thermos flask; die Handtasche, handbag; das Reisekissen, travelling cushion; die Reisedecke, travelling rug; der Rucksack, rucksack; der Bergstock, alpenstock; der Hutkoffer, hat box; das Luftkissen, air cushion; die Warmflasche, hot-water bottle; der Regenschirm, umbrella; die Kamera, camera; der Behälter, golf bag; der Golfschläger, golf club; der Feldstecher, fieldglasses; der Plaidriemen, strap; der Kofferzettel, label.

Page 144

UNDERCLOTHING. Das Unterkleid, slip; das Hemd, chemise; der Schlüpfer, pair of knickers; das Nachthemd, nightdress; der Schlafrock, dressing gown; der Büstenhalter, brassière; der Strumpf, stocking; der Schlafanzug (der Pyjama), pyjamas; die Hose, trousers; die Jacke, jacket; das Korsett, corset; der Unterrock, petticoat; das Taschentuch, handkerchief; der Strumpfhalter, stocking suspender; der Kragen, collar; der Kragenknopf, collar stud; das Oberhemd, shirt; das Nachthemd, night shirt; der Hosenträger, braces; die Manschette, cuff; die Socke, sock; das Unterhemd, undershirt; die Unterhose, pair of underdrawers; der Gürtel, belt; der Sockenhalter, sock suspender.

Pages 152-153

THE RAILWAY STATION. 1. Booking hall; 2. luggage label; 3. porter; 4. luggage registration office; 5. luggage forms; 6. Ladies; 7. advertisement; 8. letter box; 9. cloakroom; 10. shutters; 11. arrival indicator; 12. bookstall; 13. salesman; 14. newspaper; 15. platform; 16. train; 17. barrier; 18. station clock; 19. buffet; 20. revolving door; 21. ticket collector; 22. litter basket; 23. timetable; 24. railway guide; 25. waiting room; 26. information office; 27. luggage rest; 28. platform ticket machine; 29. telephone; 30. Gentlemen; 31. rucksack; 32. field glasses; 33. booking office; 34. booking clerk; 35. traveller (female); 36. traveller (male); 37. booking counter; 38. attaché case; 39. porter's truck; 40. pram; 41. luggage.

Pages 162-163

THE TRAIN (OUTSIDE). 1. Electric train; 2. driver's cabin; 3. overhead power conductor; 4. traveller (male); 5. rail; 6. sleeper; 7. buffer; 8. stationmaster; 9. disc signal; 10. locomotive; 11. lamp; 12. funnel; 13. smoke; 14. safety valve; 15. handrail; 16. boiler; 17. porter; 18. luggage; 19. porter's truck; 20. platform; 21. engine-driver; 22. fireman; 23. coal; 24. tender; 25. pillar; 26. train indicator (Passenger Train to Munich); 27. luggage van; 28. door; 29. door handle; 30. mail van; 31. passenger coach; 32. guard; 33. ventilator; 34. roof; 35. platform seat.

Pages 164-165

THE TRAIN (INSIDE). 1. First-class carriage; 2. restaurant car; 3. attendant (waiter); 4. napkin; 5. tray; 6. communication cord; 7. ventilator; 8. table lamp; 9. wall lamp; 10. window; 11. kitchen compartment; 12. chef; 13. shelf; 14. wheel; 15. bogie; 16. steps; 17. third-class carriage; 18. sleeping compartment; 19. upper berth; 20. lower berth; 21. wash basin; 22. suitcase; 23. partition, wall; 24. smoking compartment; 25. luggage rack; 26. seat; 27. ticket inspector; 28. ticket punch; 29. uniform; 30. non-smoking compartment; 31. rail; 32. sleeper.

Pages 178-179

THE HOTEL. 1. Entrance hall; 2. reception office; 3. counter; 4. telephone; 5. inkpot; 6. visitors' book; 7. reception clerk; 8. pigeon hole; 9. visitors' mail; 10. keyboard; 11. electric fan; 12. hotel guest; 13. wall clock; 14. chandelier; 15. curtain; 16. hall porter; 17. bellboy; 18. apron; 19. bell push; 20. suitcase; 21. mat; 22. lift; 23. lift boy; 24. lift gate; 25. pillar; 26. notice; 27. umbrella stand; 28. umbrella; 29. table; 30. ash tray; 31. plant pot; 32. palm; 33. clothes stand; 34. picture; 35. hotel lounge; 36. settee; 37. carpet; 38. armchair; 39. page boy; 40. bar; 41. barman; 42. bar stool.

Page 184

HOUSES. Das Bauernhaus, farmhouse; das Einfamilienhaus, cottage, one-family house; das Doppelhaus, semi-detached house; Reihenhäuser, row of houses; das einstöckige Haus, bungalow; das Mietshaus, block of flats; die Laube, summer house; das Bürohaus, office block.

Page 186

THE HOUSE (OUTSIDE). 1. Chimney; 2. smoke; 3. lightning conductor; 4. roof; 5. attic; 6. aerial; 7. guttering; 8. drain pipe; 9. upper floor; 10. ground floor; 11. cellar; 12. window; 13. window shutter; 14. balcony; 15. porch; 16. front door; 17. pillar; 18. steps; 19. garden path; 20. front gate; 21. garden wall; 22. garden; 23. side door; 24. trellis.

Page 188

THE HOUSE (INSIDE). 1. Loft; 2. rafter; 3. water cistern; 4. trap door; 5. attic; 6. wooden steps; 7. bathroom; 8. bedroom; 9. study; 10. desk; 11. nursery; 12. cot; 13. rocking horse; 14. sitting room; 15. radiogram; 16. hall; 17. clothes stand; 18. stairs; 19. banister; 20. dining room; 21. kitchen; 22. cellar; 23. coal bunker; 24. furnace.

Pages 190-191

THE KITCHEN. 1. Kitchen table; 2. scrubbing brush; 3. washing soap; 4. bowl; 5. kitchen chair; 6. dresser; 7. hourglass; 8. coffee grinder; 9. scales; 10. shelf; 11. salt cellar; 12. jug; 13. pastry cutter; 14. pastry; 15. rolling pin; 16. pastry board; 17. mixing bowl; 18. cook; 19. mincing machine; 20. kitchen towel; 21. sink; 22. window ledge; 23. water tap; 24. pail; 25. draining board; 26. dishcloth; 27. waste bin; 28. refrigerator; 29. handle; 30. wall clock; 31. larder; 32. bread bin; 33. flour bin; 34. bacon; 35. sausage; 36. ham; 37. gas cooker; 38. kettle; 39. gas ring; 40. paving tile; 41. kitchen stove; 42. oven; 43. poker; 44. frying pan; 45. cooking pot, saucepan; 46. ladle; 47. stove pipe; 48. saucepan lid.

Page 198

THE BATHROOM. 1. Water heater; 2. bath wrap; 3. bath; 4. soap; 5. sponge; 6. bath salts; 7. shower; 8. bath towel; 9. linen basket; 10. safety razor; 11. tumbler; 12. mouth wash; 13. razor; 14. soap dish; 15. wash cloth; 16. wash basin; 17. nail brush; 18. tap; 19. hand towel; 20. toothpaste; 21. toothbrush; 22. shaving brush; 23. shaving soap; 24. mirror.

BURG RHEINSTEIN AM RHEIN

Diese romantische, alte Burg ist eine der vielen auf dem steilen, linken Ufer des Rheins zwischen Koblenz und Bingen.

(Translation on page 380)

die Burg, -en   **steil**   **das Ufer**   **zwischen**
castle, stronghold   *steep*   *bank (of a river)*   *between*

Pages 202-203

THE BEDROOM. 1. Dressing table; 2. bedroom slipper; 3. dressing gown; 4. hand mirror; 5. hairbrush; 6. comb; 7. face cream; 8. mirror; 9. powder puff; 10. powder box; 11. scent spray; 12. lipstick; 13. flower vase; 14. curtain; 15. curtain cord; 16. lampshade; 17. screen; 18. electric light plug; 19. bedside table; 20. table lamp; 21. calendar; 22. alarm clock; 23. bedside rug; 24. rug; 25. bed; 26. eiderdown; 27. bedspread; 28. sheet; 29. mattress; 30. bolster; 31. pillow; 32. maid; 33. apron; 34. chest of drawers; 35. portrait; 36. ornamental figure; 37. drawer; 38. wardrobe; 39. divan; 40. cushion; 41. blanket; 42. pouffe.

Page 208

THE TOBACCONIST. Die Zigarre, cigar; die Zigarette, cigarette; die Manillazigarre, cheroot; die Zigarrenschere, cigar-cutter; die Pfeife, pipe; der Tabaksbeutel, tobacco pouch; der Aschenbecher, ash tray; das Streichholz (das Zündholz), match; die Schachtel Streichhölzer, box of matches; der Tabak, tobacco; das Feuerzeug, lighter; die Kiste Zigarren, box of cigars; das Päckchen Zigaretten, packet of cigarettes; der Zigarettenhalter, cigarette holder; das Zigarettenetui, cigarette case; die Zigarrentasche, cigar case.

Page 210

STATIONERY. Der Schreibblock, writing block; der Kalender, calendar; das Heft, exercise book; das Lineal, ruler; der Federha'ter, penholder; der Füllbleistift, propelling pencil; der Bleistift, pencil; der Füllfederhalter, fountain pen; das Tintenfass, ink stand; der Bleistiftanspitzer, pencil sharpener; die Schreibfeder, pen nib; das Notizbuch, notebook; die Tintenflasche, ink bottle; die Heftklammer, paper clip; der Radiergummi, eraser; der Brieföffner, paper knife; das Siegel, seal; der Siegellack, sealing wax; der Briefbogen, sheet of paper; das Briefpapier, notepaper; der Aufklebezettel, stick-on label; der Briefumschlag, envelope; die Postkarte, postcard; die Briefwaage, letter scales; die Ansichtskarte, picture postcard.

Pages 212-213

THE POST OFFICE. 1. Telephone box; 2. telephone directory; 3. stamp machine; 4. counter; 5. official; 6. partition; 7. finger sponge; 8. writing counter; 9. paper rack; 10. ink well; 11. blotting paper; 12. telegraph forms; 13. letter box; 14. lock; 15. mailbag; 16. letter; 17. postman; 18. briefcase; 19. light; 20. ceiling; 21. wall; 22. wall clock; 23. air mail letter box; 24. hinge; 25. pigeon hole; 26. door; 27. parcel scales; 28. form; 29. paste pot; 30. paste brush; 31. parcel; 32. label; 33. apron; 34. registered parcel; 35. string; 36. seal.

Pages 222-223

THE STORE. 1. Men's clothing; 2. drawer; 3. cupboard; 4. tailor's dummy; 5. display stand; 6. toilet article; 7. shelf; 8. toothbrush; 9. soap; 10. price card; 11. jar; 12. scoop; 13. bath salts; 14. scissors; 15. salesgirl; 16. wrapping paper; 17. string; 18. scales; 19. counter; 20. male customer; 21. lift girl; 22. lift; 23. pullover; 24. cashier (female); 25. cash desk; 26. cash register; 27. ladies' department; 28. material; 29. salesman; 30. tape measure; 31. curtain; 32. woman customer; 33. swinging door; 34. door handle; 35. commissionaire; 36. shop window; 37. dress material; 38. clothes brush; 39. showcard; 40. sponge; 41. hairbrush; 42. shaving set.

Page 224

SHOES AND BOOTS. Der Schnürstiefel, boot; 1. heel; 2. instep; 3. sole; 4. welt; 5. toecap; 6. boot lace; 7. tongue. Der Halbschuh, shoe; der Reitstiefel, riding boot; die Gamasche, spat; der Lackschuh, patent leather shoe; der Spangenschuh, strap shoe; die Pumps, court shoe; die Sandale, sandal; der Tennisschuh, tennis shoe; der Bergstiefel, climbing boot; der Langschäfter, wellington boot; der Überschuh, bootee; die Gamasche, gaiter; der Gummischuh, golosh; der Pantoffel, slipper; der Schneeschuh, snow shoe.

Page 230

MEAT. Das Rind, ox: 1. oxtail; 2. rump; 3. sirloin; 4. thin flank; 5. rib; 6. breast (brisket); 7. shoulder; 8. leg; 9. neck; 10. head. Das Kalb, calf: 1. head; 2. neck; 3. upper neck; 4. breast; 5. shoulder; 6. back; 7. loin; 8. belly; 9. leg; 10. foot. Das Schwein, pig: 1. ham; 2. loin; 3. foreloin; 4. belly; 5. neck, spare rib; 6. shoulder; 7. ear; 8. cheek; 9. trotter. Das Schaf, sheep (der Hammel, mutton): 1. head; 2, neck; 3. upper neck; 4. breast; 5. shoulder; 6. saddle; 7. belly; 8. leg.

Page 232

VEGETABLES. Die Erbse, pea; die Bohne, bean; die grüne Bohne, runner bean; die Tomate, tomato; der Kohl, cabbage; die Mohrrübe (die Karotte), carrot; die Gurke, cucumber; der Spargel, asparagus; die Zwiebel, onion; der Sellerie, celery; der Rosenkohl, brussels sprout; die rote Rübe, beetroot; die Kohlrübe, turnip; der Spinat, spinach; der Kopfsalat, lettuce; die Kartoffel, potato; der Blumenkohl, cauliflower.

Page 234

GAME AND POULTRY. Die Ente, duck; der Hahn, cock; das Huhn, hen; die Pute, turkey; die Taube, pigeon; die Gans, goose; der Hase, hare; das Kaninchen, rabbit; der Hirsch, stag; der Fasan, pheasant; das Rebhuhn, partridge; das Reh, roebuck; die Waldschnepfe, woodcock; die Schnepfe, snipe; das Waldhuhn, grouse.

Page 236

FISH. Der Hering, herring; die Makrele, mackerel; die Flunder, flounder; der Aal, eel; die Sardine, sardine; die Forelle, trout; der Lachs, salmon; der Rochen, skate; der Schellfisch, haddock; der Hummer, lobster; die Krabbe, crab; die Uferschnecke, winkle; die Auster, oyster; die Garnele, shrimp; die Muschel, mussel; die Trompetenschnecke, whelk; die Herzmuschel, cockle; der Kabeljau, cod; die Seezunge, sole.

Pages 242-243

THE STREET. 1. Main street; 2. tramline; 3. crossing; 4. kerb; 5. pavement; 6. roadway; 7. woman pedestrian; 8. beggar; 9. crutch; 10. shop signboard; 11. barrow; 12. peddler; 13. housewife (making purchases); 14. shopping basket; 15. pram; 16. tram; 17. driver; 18. destination board; 19. power conductor; 20. power cable; 21. cyclist; 22. policeman; 23. cross roads; 24. omnibus; 25. conductor; 26. lower deck; 27. upper deck; 28. advertisement kiosk; 29. sunblind; 30. roof; 31. lamp; 32. lamp standard; 33. side street; 34. lorry; 35. street corner; 36. male pedestrian; 37. pillar box; 38. shop window; 39. shop; 40. shutter; 41. traffic sign; 42. shop entrance; 43. motor car; 44. refuge; 45. litter box.

Pages 250-251

THE TOWN. 1. Canal; 2. barge; 3. fence; 4. school; 5. playground; 6. shelter; 7. market; 8. advertisement kiosk; 9. street lamp; 10. square; 11. statue; 12. main street; 13. side street; 14. town hall; 15. steps; 16. turret; 17. bell tower; 18. town gate; 19. fire station; 20. fire engine; 21. flat roof; 22. park; 23. lake; 24. block of flats; 25. church; 26. church tower; 27. flying buttress; 28. churchyard; 29. tombstone; 30. path; 31. gate; 32. flower bed; 33. car park; 34. embankment; 35. river; 36. castle; 37. castle tower; 38. bridge; 39. arch; 40. parapet; 41. café; 42. railway station; 43. signal; 44. railway track; 45. factory; 46. factory chimney; 47. water tank; 48. suburb.

Page 264

SPORT. Das Schwimmen, swimming; das Fischen, fishing, angling; das Segeln, sailing, yachting; das Tennis, tennis; das Rudern, rowing; das Fussballspiel, football; das Boxen, boxing; das Ringen, wrestling; das Fechten, fencing; das Golfspiel, golf; das Skilaufen, ski-ing; das Schlittschuhlaufen, skating; das Schiessen, shooting; die Jagd, hunting; das Wettlaufen, running; das Springen, jumping.

Page 266

FOOTBALL. 1. Spectator; 2. playing field; 3. corner flag; 4. goal line; 5. goal; 6. goalkeeper; 7. goalpost; 8. goal area; 9. penalty area; 10. left back; 11. right back; 12. left half; 13. centre half; 14. right half; 15. outside left; 16. inside left; 17. centre forward; 18. inside right; 19. outside right; 20. linesman; 21. referee; 22. ball; 23. touch line; 24. stand.

Page 270

TENNIS. 1. Tennis court; 2. tennis player; 3. tennis racquet; 4. tennis ball; 5. service line; 6. flannel trousers; 7. centre line; 8. net; 9. post; 10. ball-boy; 11. service court; 12. base line; 13. linesman; 14. roller; 15. sideline; 16. stand; 17. spectator; 18. umpire; 19. score book; 20. table tennis; 21. bat; 22. ball; 23. clamp; 24. trestle.

Pages 272-273

THE THEATRE. 1. Stage; 2. curtain; 3. props; 4. actress; 5. actor; 6. supporting player; 7. scenery; 8. wing; 9. stage hand; 10. proscenium; 11. footlight; 12. prompter's box; 13. orchestra; 14. conductor; 15. rostrum; 16. violinist; 17. flautist; 18. clarinettist; 19. saxophonist; 20. trumpet player; 21; drummer; 22. music stand; 23. music score; 24. stage manager; 25. emergency exit; 26. box; 27. front row; 28. orchestra stall; 29. stall; 30. barrier; 31. gangway; 32. pit; 33. programme; 34. opera glasses; 35. usherette; 36. dress circle; 37. fire extinguisher; 38. chocolate seller; 39. exit; 40. upper circle; 41. gallery; 42. light.

Pages 278-279

THE ZOOLOGICAL GARDENS. 1. Snake; 2. branch; 3. palm leaf; 4. crocodile; 5. tail; 6. claw; 7. tortoise; 8. tortoise-shell; 9. cage; 10. ape; 11. monkey; 12. leopard; 13. tiger; 14. lion; 15. mane; 16. lioness; 17. cliff; 18. brown bear; 19. polar bear; 20. mountain goat; 21. keeper; 22. elephant; 23. trunk; 24. giraffe; 25. buffalo; 26. horn; 27. paddock; 28. camel; 29. hump; 30. aviary; 31. hippopotamus; 32. kangaroo; 33. stork; 34. beak; 35. ostrich; 36. seal; 37. fin; 38. pond; 39. pelican; 40. wing; 41. penguin; 42. peacock.

Page 282

MUSICAL INSTRUMENTS. Das Fagott, bassoon; die Flöte, flute; die Geige (die Violine), violin; die Bassgeige (der Contrabass), double-bass; die Klarinette, clarinet; die Trompete, trumpet; die Tuba, tuba; das Saxophon, saxophone; die Posaune, trombone; die Laute, lute; die Trommel, drum; die Harfe, harp; die Guitarre, guitar; das Klavier, upright piano; die Mandoline, mandolin; die Mundharmonika, mouth organ; die Ziehharmonika, accordeon; der Flügel, grand piano.

Page 284

THE MOTOR CAR. 1. Bumper; 2. number plate; 3. tail lamp; 4. luggage rack; 5. hood; 6. wing; 7. back wheel; 8. tyre; 9. running board; 10. spare wheel; 11. hand brake; 12. gear lever; 13. clutch pedal; 14. foot brake; 15. accelerator; 16. steering wheel; 17. horn button; 18. dashboard; 19. starter; 20. speedometer; 21. windscreen; 22. windscreen wiper; 23. bonnet; 24. direction indicator; 25. radiator; 26. headlamp; 27. front wheel.

Page 288

THE VILLAGE. 1. Chick; 2. feeding trough; 3. hen house; 4. ladder; 5. barn; 6. pond; 7. milestone; 8. signpost; 9. common; 10. school; 11. church; 12. church spire; 13. windmill; 14. thatched roof; 15. cart; 16. stable; 17. farmhouse; 18. cowshed; 19. cow; 20. calf; 21. pump; 22. water trough; 23. shaft (of cart); 24. peacock.

Pages 290-291

ON THE ROAD. 1. Two-seater; 2. bicycle; 3. handlebar; 4. pedal; 5. chain; 6. traffic sign; 7. hill; 8. hiker; 9. fence; 10. breakdown; 11. tricycle; 12. limousine; 13. omnibus; 14. gas; 15. gas station; 16. garage; 17. mechanic; 18. truck; 19. racing car; 20. hedge; 21. castle; 22. wood; 23. tandem; 24. cabriolet; 25. major road; 26. road corner; 27. first aid kiosk; 28. motorcycle; 29. pavement; 30. racing cycle; 31. caravan trailer; 32. saloon car; 33. sidecar; 34. bend; 35. field; 36. footpath; 37. wall; 38. pillar box; 39. barrier; 40. level crossing; 41. railway attendant; 42. flag.

Pages 296-297

AT THE SEASIDE. 1. Tent; 2. tent peg; 3. sailing boat; 4. bather (female); 5. bucket; 6. bathing wrap; 7. bathing trunks; 8. beach ball; 9. deck chair; 10. beach; 11. breakwater; 12. wave; 13. sea; 14. sandbank; 15. sand castle; 16. rowing boat; 17. pier; 18. seagull; 19. pleasure steamer; 20. pavilion; 21. landing stage; 22. hotel; 23. boathouse; 24. bathing hut; 25. beach stall; 26. bandstand; 27. promenade; 28. cliff; 29. rock; 30. covered wicker beach chair; 31. lifesaving station; 32. life belt; 33. life jacket; 34. sunshade; 35. bathing towel; 36. bathing cap; 37. bathing costume; 38. bathing shoe; 39. oar; 40. boatman; 41. anchor; 42. rowlock.

Pages 302-303

THE HARBOUR. 1. Paddle steamer; 2. train ferry; 3. ventilator; 4. searchlight; 5. davit; 6. tarpaulin; 7. lifeboat; 8. rope; 9. rudder; 10. ship's officer; 11. captain; 12. binoculars; 13. captain's bridge; 14. handrail; 15. tug; 16. sailing boat; 17. sail; 18. cargo steamer; 19. bows; 20. derrick; 21. stern; 22. crane; 23. fishing boat; 24. ferry; 25. passenger liner; 26. funnel; 27. hull; 28. floating dock; 29. quay; 30. shed; 31. factory; 32. wagon; 33. jetty; 34. barge; 35. motor launch; 36. wake; 37. bollard; 38. forecastle; 39. porthole; 40. cargo hold; 41. sailor; 42. mast; 43. crow's nest; 44. promenade deck; 45. upper deck; 46. passenger; 47. rowing boat; 48. oar.

Pages 306-307

THE AIRPORT. 1. Aeroplane; 2. propeller; 3. engine; 4. undercarriage; 5. landing wheel; 6. tyre; 7. wing; 8. cockpit; 9. cabin; 10. loop aerial (direction finder); 11. glider; 12. air speed indicator; 13. nose; 14. pilot; 15. helmet; 16. goggles; 17. flying suit; 18. air passenger; 19. policeman; 20. aerodrome building; 21. control tower; 22. balcony; 23. windsock; 24. aerial; 25. wireless mast; 26. biplane; 27. seaplane; 28. float; 29. parachute; 30. parachutist; 31. crane; 32. hangar; 33. refuelling tank; 34. motor trolley; 35. customs officer; 36. transport plane; 37. truck; 38. crate; 39. fuselage; 40. tail fin; 41. oxygen cylinder,

TRANSLATION OF CAPTIONS

Below and on the following pages are given translations of the German captions to the photographic illustrations in this book. They are provided not in order that you may refer to them systematically as you progress through the book, but as a last resort in cases of doubt and difficulty.

Page 12

IN THE HARBOUR OF HAMBURG. Hamburg is the largest commercial port in Germany and one of the principal ports of the European continent. Hamburg lies on the lower Elbe and Alster, about 100 kilometres from the North Sea. At high tide ships sail right into the harbour of Hamburg. The city has over a million inhabitants and is also an important industrial city.

Page 16

VINE HARVEST. The vine harvest in Germany takes place in October and November. The grapes are crushed in the grape mill and then pressed in the wine-press. The workers have much to do and they have to cut grapes and carry them to the mill from early morning until late evening.

Page 24

BAVARIAN INN. This is an inn in Dinkelsbühl, a little Bavarian village which, on account of its beautiful old houses, is visited by many tourists. Although this inn is hardly one of the ancient buildings, with its high gables it still fits into the framework of the medieval town.

Page 29

WHAT IS THE PRICE OF CABBAGE? Cabbage is healthy and cheap. This greengrocer certainly looks well nourished and is a good advertisement for his goods.

Page 31

WHERE TIME STANDS STILL. Here is the market place of Gengenbach, a small town in the Black Forest with beautiful old houses. A bell tower rises over the town gate at the end of the market place, across which the long morning shadows still lie.

Timber work and high gables are characteristic of the Black Forest house. Motor car and bicycle hardly fit into the medieval picture.

Page 35

CAFE TERRACE ON THE KURFÜRSTENDAMM, BERLIN. People are still wearing their winter coats, it is true, but already they are sitting on the café terrace in order to enjoy the first sunshine of spring.

Page 38

AFTER HARD WORK THE MEAL TASTES ALL THE BETTER. This photograph comes from the Bernese Oberland in Switzerland. The farmer's family eat their midday meal together with the farmworkers. They seem to enjoy it (*lit.*, it seems to them to taste good) because they have worked since early morning in the fields and on the hillsides.

Page 51

NATIONAL COSTUME. In many regions of Germany the old national costumes are still preserved. The upper picture shows the headdress of the Bückeburg peasant women. The lower picture is of a fashion show in a café on the Kurfürstendamm in Berlin.

Pages 54-55

IN THE BAVARIAN ALPS: GENERAL VIEW OF OBERAMMERGAU. Oberammergau is a village in Upper Bavaria in which a school for wood carving is situated. The village is famous for the Passion Plays which, following a vow given during a plague, are performed by the inhabitants every ten years. Here one sees a general view of the village, with the church on the left and the Passion theatre on the right. In the background rise the steep tree-covered slopes of the Alps. The three mountain peaks are called Not, Kofel and Rappenkopf.

Page 62

HERE NO ONE NEEDS TO DIE OF THIRST. The cart with the beer barrels stops in front of the Post-Stiftsstube in the Stiftstrasse in Stuttgart. Another cart has already unloaded ice, in order to keep the beer cool. Whoever prefers to drink something warm can sit next door in the café on the first floor of the inn.

Page 64

BERNE: THE CLOCK TOWER. The clock tower, the old landmark of the Swiss capital, Berne, was until the thirteenth century the West Gate of the city. It was restored several times and in the year 1930 was decorated with frescoes. On the east side is a curious clock, which announces every full hour with the crowing of a cock.

Page 74

STREET SCENE IN VIENNA. The traffic policeman brings the traffic to a stop to enable the pedestrians to cross. The dress of the girl with braids is characteristic of the pretty national costumes of which the Austrian people are very fond.

Page 78

NEUSCHWANSTEIN CASTLE. This castle, which lies near Hohenschwangau in Southern Bavaria, is one of the most beautiful of the Bavarian royal castles. Like other castles, it owes its existence to the romantic inclinations of Ludwig II. The position of the castle is incomparably lovely, with a wide view of the Bavarian Alps, which form a magnificent background.

Page 84

THE STRUGGLE FOR THE DAILY BREAD. The Swiss farmer has many unusual tasks to perform. He has to plough and harrow on dangerously steep mountain slopes; for every bit of earth that is capable of producing a crop must be laboriously cultivated in order that the food supply of the country may be maintained.

Page 94

WIESBADEN: THE FLOWER GARDEN IN FRONT OF THE PUMP ROOM. The Latin inscription over the entrance to the Pump Room proclaims that here one is in the region of the healing springs which were known even to the Romans. The famous spa is visited annually by thousands from all countries who seek in its warm springs a cure for gout, rheumatism and catarrh.

Page 99

ZONS ON THE RHINE. The little town of Zons, north-east of Dormagen on Rhine, is with its numerous towers and gates one of the best-preserved medieval fortresses of the Rhineland. Like most of the towns on the left bank of the river, it is of Roman foundation. The Romans called it *Sontium*. Cologne was originally called *Colonia Agrippina*, Trier *Augusta Treverorum*, Mainz *Mogontiacum*, and Coblenz *Confluentes*, i.e. the town founded at the confluence of several rivers (Rhine, Moselle, Lahn).

These towns were connected by land routes and had aqueducts, baths and bridges. Their occupation by the Romans was primarily military and had the object of guarding the extended frontiers of the Roman Empire.

The cultivation of the vine, for which the Rhineland is so famous, is supposed to have been introduced by the Romans.

Page 103

GOBELIN TAPESTRY WEAVERS. The art of hand-weaving has not quite died out. In many parts of Germany it is still practised. The picture shows Thuringian Gobelin weavers at work.

Page 104

IN THE BLACK FOREST. The Black Forest is divided into two parts by the deep Kinzigtal. The northern part has an average height of 700 metres. The highest mountain, the Feldberg (1,493 metres) lies in the south. The Black Forest is thickly covered with woods. Oaks and beeches in the lower regions, and fir trees in the upper, provide the material for the famous timber and clock industries.

Page 106

CYCLE RACING THROUGH THE ALPS. The participants in a cycle race through Germany and Austria approach the hardest part of their task: the ride over the Arlberg Pass (1,802 metres) on the road from Innsbruck to Friedrichshafen.

Page 114

COAL MINERS AFTER THE DAY'S WORK. In the Ruhr Germany possesses a complex industrial centre. Factories and mines of every kind are scattered throughout this region. The picture shows coal miners at the change of the shift leaving a coalmine in the neighbourhood of Gelsenkirchen.

Page 117

SPRING IN THE UPPER ENGADINE. The Engadine is a 60-mile-long valley which stretches from the Maloja Pass as far as the Tyrol and is surrounded by high mountains. The higher part of the valley, the Upper Engadine above St. Moritz, is the most beautiful part, with its snow-covered mountain peaks and deep, clear lakes.

Page 125

THE MARKET PLACE IN TRIBERG. Triberg is a little Black Forest town of 4,500 inhabitants. It is a spa, winter sports resort and centre of the clock industry.

Page 126

THE MARKET PLACE IN HAMELN. Hameln, an ancient county town near Hanover, has become well known through the legend of the rat-catcher (pied piper): a stranger, by the charm of his piping, is said to have allured the souls of the children, as well as the rats, so that the children were obliged to keep on following him and the rats.

Page 134

ON THE ICE-RINK NEAR GARMISCH-PARTENKIRCHEN. Garmisch-Partenkirchen, in Upper Bavaria, are neighbouring resorts at the foot of the Zugspitze (2,962 metres), the highest mountain in Germany. Both places are popular as summer resorts and as winter sports centres. Skating, tobogganing and ski-ing are the most popular kinds of winter sport.

Page 138

VIENNA: KÄRNTNERSTRASSE WITH ST. STEPHEN'S CATHEDRAL. The Kärntnerstrasse is one of the most fashionable streets of Vienna. In front, on the right, is the fashionable Hotel Bristol and in the background the church of St. Stephen, with its famous tower. The church was built in the fourteenth and fifteenth centuries and i 108 metres long. The tower, 137 metres hig' carries a bell weighing 22,626 kilograr (22¼ tons).

Page 141

LIVING CHESS. This living game of che was played in the market place of Villinge in the province of Baden. The chess-m were represented by Black Forest people their national costumes.

Page 145

SECOND-HAND MARKET IN NUREMBERG. Here you can sell your old things and buy used articles of clothing and furniture cheaply.

Page 148

FROM THE GOOD OLD TIMES. While today our furniture is manufactured by mass production, formerly it was produced by craftsmen, who endeavoured to create with beauty even the common articles destined for everyday use. Above, a dining room in the Bernese Oberland with beautifully carved furniture; below, an old Franconian farmhouse room.

Page 151

AUTOBAHN WITHOUT SPEED LIMIT. On the autobahns which connect the important towns with each other there is no speed limit to observe. Pedestrians may not set foot on the autobahns, but must use overhead crossings.

HEUERNTE IN BAYERN

Im Schatten der Bergriesen in den Bayerischen Alpen wird das Heu aufgeladen. Die Männer und Frauen tragen die für das bayerische Alpenland charakteristische Tracht.

(Translation on page 380)

das Heu	**die Ernte, -n**	**der Schatten, -**	**der Riese, -n**
hay	*harvest*	*shadow*	*giant*

Page 158

FRIEDRICHSTRASSE STATION, BERLIN. The train running into Platform A is an electric train which formerly operated on the route Berlin-Cologne and had an average speed of 81 miles an hour. The train was Diesel-electrically driven and reached on a trial run a speed of 116 miles an hour.

Page 167

THE SUSPENSION RAILWAY AT WUPPERTAL. In order to ease the traffic in the principal streets, the Wuppertal municipality has built a suspension railway. The picture shows the railway over an ordinary tram in the Sonneborner Strasse.

Page 170

IN THE HARBOUR. In North Germany fishing is of special importance. The catch of the boats which have just come in is examined by experts.

Page 173

BERLIN STREET SCENE. In front of much-visited shops, guards are established to keep watch on cycles, prams and such-like things.

Page 174

CAFÉ IN BERLIN. Just as on a Parisian boulevard, here in the Kurfürstendamm there is a succession of one café after another. In fine weather one sits on the terrace.

Page 177

THE SPREE FROZEN OVER. During the winter the cold in Berlin sometimes reaches many degrees below freezing point. Then the Spree, like most of the North German rivers, becomes frozen over. In the picture one sees ice-bound ships in the harbour of the German capital.

Page 183

GATHERING WOOD IN THE WOODS. These women are seeking their fuel in the woods, in order to prepare for the winter.

Page 195

A SUNDAY MORNING RIDE IN GRUNEWALD. These Berliners are in the fortunate position of being able to go for a Sunday morning ride. They are riding through Grunewald, the fashionable villa suburb in the west of Berlin.

Page 196

SCHOOL IN THE OPEN AIR. The upper picture shows Berlin schoolchildren playing "ring o' roses". The lower picture shows a class taking an English lesson in an open-air school in the Grunewald, near Berlin. One of the pupils writes on the blackboard while the teacher asks the others questions.

Page 215

AT THE CHRISTMAS MARKET. Motto-hearts, i.e. gingerbread shapes with a motto in sugar-icing are a traditional feature of the German Christmas market.

Page 227

A SAUSAGE STALL IN FRANKFURT. The Germans are well known as sausage-eaters. In large towns one sees innumerable shops and stalls of this kind, where there are sausages of every variety for sale and one can eat small hot sausages on the spot. Frankfurt sausages are especially favoured.

Page 239

ZELL AM SEE. Zell am See, in the Salzburg district, is favoured as a summer resort. The Zell lake lies 753 metres above sea level.

Page 241

WORKERS' FLATS IN SIEMENSSTADT, NEAR BERLIN. The Siemens works employed many thousands of workmen and clerks. In order to accommodate them near the factory, hundreds of huge buildings equipped with modern workers' flats were erected. Thus arose a new suburb in the north of Berlin: the Siemensstadt.

Page 245

POLICEMAN AND CIVILIAN. The man with the rucksack, as well as the policeman with his helmet, is a frequent sight in the street life of Berlin.

Page 246

MODERN BLOCKS OF FLATS IN BERLIN. In large German towns, houses for single families are not common and the great majority of people live in flats. This block of buildings contains hundreds of flats.

Page 249

THE ARMOURY, BERLIN. This stately building, which formerly contained a museum of army equipment, stands in the famous street called Unter den Linden ("beneath the lime trees").

Page 261

IN THE SPREEWALD. The Spreewald is an extensive woodland south-east of Berlin. It is crossed by the River Spree, which is split up into many arms.

Pages 262-263

BLACK FOREST PICTURE: GLOTTER VALLEY AND GLOTTERBAD. The Black Forest is a dark wooded range of mountains in south-west Germany. It is divided by deep valleys and is separated into northern and southern Black Forest by the Kinzig Valley. In the southern Black Forest lie the highest mountains: the Feldberg (1,493 metres), the Herzogenhorn (1,417 metres), the Belchen (1,414 metres) and others. Both parts possess lakes and numerous mineral springs. The picture shows Glotterbad, which lies in the Glotter Valley. In the right foreground we see Black Forest women in their characteristic dress.

Page 295

THE BATHING BEACH AT WANNSEE, NEAR BERLIN. Only half-an-hour's rail journey from Berlin lies the Wannsee. On its extensive bathing beach innumerable crowds of people sunbathe, bathe and swim on fine summer Sundays. Deck chairs and covered wicker beach chairs have become scarce. Most of the people lie in the sand and let themselves become tanned by the sun.

Page 308

WÜRZBURG: VINE HARVEST ON THE "STEIN", WITH VIEW OF STEIN CASTLE. The vine harvest in Germany usually takes place from October to November. The vine is grown only in south-west Germany, on the Rhine, the Moselle, the Neckar and the middle Main. In these localities wine is cheap and more often drunk than beer.

Page 312

MOUNTAIN FESTIVAL IN THE BERNESE OBERLAND. Wrestling, music and dancing are the chief attractions at this annual mountain festival in the Bernese Oberland. Often the wrestlers have to be brought from the dance floor when their turn comes for the next wrestling match.

Page 316

IN THE MUNICH ZOOLOGICAL GARDEN. The Zoological Garden in Munich is one of the largest and most modern in Europe and is highly popular with both children and adults. As everywhere, the elephant, with its gigantic body, long trunk and funny tricks, is one of the principal attractions.

Page 320

HAYMAKING IN THE SWISS PLAIN. While the hay wagon is being loaded and all the farm workers and harvest helpers are toiling under the hot summer sun, the ox can rest itself. It makes use of the break to partake of a snack.

Page 324

IN SAXON SWITZERLAND. Saxon Switzerland is part of the sandstone mountain range south-east of Dresden on both sides of the Elbe. The range is not very high but is rich in steep sandstone rocks and deep gorges. Much-visited spots on the right bank of the Elbe: Liebethaler and Utte-walder Grund, Bastei, Amselgrund, Schandau, Kuhstall, Lilienstein; on the left: Bärensteine, Königstein, Bielathal, and others.

Page 328

FREIBURG IM BREISGAU: THE MARKET PLACE. Freiburg im Breisgau, a town of nearly 100,000 inhabitants, lies at the foot of the Black Forest. Freiburg has a glorious cathedral (begun in the year 1122), an old university (founded 1457) and several medieval buildings which are worth seeing.

Page 330

MARTIN LUTHER'S ROOM IN THE WARTBURG. The Wartburg, a fortress dating from the twelfth century, lies high above the town of Eisenach, in Thuringia. Here Martin Luther found refuge in 1521 and here he worked on his translation of the New Testament. The picture shows the window of the room in which he worked. In earlier times the Wartburg was visited by many of the Minnesänger, including Walther von der Vogelweide and Wolfram von Eschenbach.

Page 333

TOWN GATE IN WOLFRAM'S-ESCHENBACH. This quaint little Bavarian town, surrounded by medieval walls, is named after the author of Parzifal, the minstrel Wolfram von Eschenbach, who lived there in the twelfth century.

Page 334

MONUMENT TO JOHANN SEBASTIAN BACH IN EISENACH. This bronze monument in the market place of Eisenach is dedicated to the great composer, who in 1685 was born in this town. Over the entrance to the church are inscribed the words of Martin Luther's famous hymn "A fortress firm is our Lord", which Bach set to music.

Page 337

WILLIAM TELL PLAY AT INTERLAKEN. A scene from an open-air performance of Schiller's drama William Tell, which is produced annually in Interlaken (Bernese Oberland).

Page 338

CENTRES OF GERMAN CULTURE. The top picture shows the ivy-covered ruins of Heidelberg Castle, the landmark of the old university town. The bottom picture shows the National Theatre at Weimar, with the Goethe and Schiller monument. Both poets lived in Weimar and they were close friends. In the year 1919 the sittings of the first Parliament of the new German Republic took place in the National Theatre of Weimar.

Page 340

A GLIMPSE OF SALZBURG. Salzburg is beautifully situated between the Kapuziner-berg and the Mönchsberg in the Austrian part of the Alps. The music festivals which take place there have won international fame.

Page 342

UNIVERSITY TOWN OF GÖTTINGEN. The University of Göttingen, founded in 1737 by King George II of England, ranks as one of the best German universities. Many houses in the town bear memorial tablets in remembrance of famous scholars who taught or studied there. The fountain depicted above, incorporating the statue of a goose-girl, is one of the places worth seeing in the town.

Page 345

SHEPHERD DANCE IN ROTHENBURG. At the Rothenburg Whitsun festival, which takes place every year, shepherds and shep-herdesses from the area around Rothen-burg give performances of folk dancing in their traditional costumes.

Page 346

WORMS—THE CATHEDRAL. The twelfth century cathedral is one of the most out-standing examples of Romanesque archi-tecture in the Rhineland. Worms is one of the oldest towns in Germany. In the year 1521 Martin Luther defended his doctrines before the Imperial Diet assembled in Worms. The town has a harbour on the Rhine and is the centre of a vine-growing district.

Page 349

WINTER IN THE BLACK FOREST. In winter snow and ice magically transform the Black Forest into a white fairyland. Sleigh and ski become for the time being the chief means of travel on the highroads leading across the mountains.

Page 350

HOMEWARD BOUND FROM SCHOOL. Four little children on the way home from school in the former Imperial town of Nördlingen. With its battlements and towers dating from the fourteenth and fifteenth centuries, Nördlingen is one of many German towns preserving their medieval character almost unspoilt.

Page 354

SWISS TOWN HALL. Far from the bustle and activity of modern city life, this old ox-cart rumbles steadily over the stone-paved village square of Mayenfeld (Grisons). The frescoes on the town hall are characteristic of the way in which buildings of that kind in parts of Switzerland and South Germany are adorned.

Page 370

RHEINSTEIN CASTLE ON THE RHINE. This romantic old castle is one of many on the steep left bank of the Rhine between Coblenz and Bingen.

Page 377

HAYMAKING IN BAVARIA. The hay is loaded in the shadow of the mountain giants of the Bavarian Alps. The men and women are wearing the characteristic cos-tumes of the Bavarian highlands.

INDEX

ACKNOWLEDGEMENTS

The Publishers wish to express their thanks to the following for their courtesy in supplying many of the photographs reproduced: Messrs. Thos. Cook & Son, Ltd., Berkeley Street, London, W.1. Swiss Federal Railways, 458, Strand, London, W.C.2.

A CATALOG OF SELECTED
DOVER BOOKS
IN ALL FIELDS OF INTEREST

A CATALOG OF SELECTED DOVER
BOOKS IN ALL FIELDS OF INTEREST

CONCERNING THE SPIRITUAL IN ART, Wassily Kandinsky. Pioneering work by father of abstract art. Thoughts on color theory, nature of art. Analysis of earlier masters. 12 illustrations. 80pp. of text. 5⅜ x 8½.   23411-8 Pa. $4.95

ANIMALS: 1,419 Copyright-Free Illustrations of Mammals, Birds, Fish, Insects, etc., Jim Harter (ed.). Clear wood engravings present, in extremely lifelike poses, over 1,000 species of animals. One of the most extensive pictorial sourcebooks of its kind. Captions. Index. 284pp. 9 x 12.   23766-4 Pa. $14.95

CELTIC ART: The Methods of Construction, George Bain. Simple geometric techniques for making Celtic interlacements, spirals, Kells-type initials, animals, humans, etc. Over 500 illustrations. 160pp. 9 x 12. (Available in U.S. only.)   22923-8 Pa. $9.95

AN ATLAS OF ANATOMY FOR ARTISTS, Fritz Schider. Most thorough reference work on art anatomy in the world. Hundreds of illustrations, including selections from works by Vesalius, Leonardo, Goya, Ingres, Michelangelo, others. 593 illustrations. 192pp. 7⅛ x 10¼.   20241-0 Pa. $9.95

CELTIC HAND STROKE-BY-STROKE (Irish Half-Uncial from "The Book of Kells"): An Arthur Baker Calligraphy Manual, Arthur Baker. Complete guide to creating each letter of the alphabet in distinctive Celtic manner. Covers hand position, strokes, pens, inks, paper, more. Illustrated. 48pp. 8¼ x 11.   24336-2 Pa. $3.95

EASY ORIGAMI, John Montroll. Charming collection of 32 projects (hat, cup, pelican, piano, swan, many more) specially designed for the novice origami hobbyist. Clearly illustrated easy-to-follow instructions insure that even beginning papercrafters will achieve successful results. 48pp. 8¼ x 11.   27298-2 Pa. $3.50

THE COMPLETE BOOK OF BIRDHOUSE CONSTRUCTION FOR WOODWORKERS, Scott D. Campbell. Detailed instructions, illustrations, tables. Also data on bird habitat and instinct patterns. Bibliography. 3 tables. 63 illustrations in 15 figures. 48pp. 5¼ x 8½.   24407-5 Pa. $2.50

BLOOMINGDALE'S ILLUSTRATED 1886 CATALOG: Fashions, Dry Goods and Housewares, Bloomingdale Brothers. Famed merchants' extremely rare catalog depicting about 1,700 products: clothing, housewares, firearms, dry goods, jewelry, more. Invaluable for dating, identifying vintage items. Also, copyright-free graphics for artists, designers. Co-published with Henry Ford Museum & Greenfield Village. 160pp. 8¼ x 11.   25780-0 Pa. $12.95

HISTORIC COSTUME IN PICTURES, Braun & Schneider. Over 1,450 costumed figures in clearly detailed engravings–from dawn of civilization to end of 19th century. Captions. Many folk costumes. 256pp. 8⅜ x 11¾.   23150-X Pa. $12.95

STICKLEY CRAFTSMAN FURNITURE CATALOGS, Gustav Stickley and L. & J. G. Stickley. Beautiful, functional furniture in two authentic catalogs from 1910. 594 illustrations, including 277 photos, show settles, rockers, armchairs, reclining chairs, bookcases, desks, tables. 183pp. 6½ x 9¼. 23838-5 Pa. $11.95

AMERICAN LOCOMOTIVES IN HISTORIC PHOTOGRAPHS: 1858 to 1949, Ron Ziel (ed.). A rare collection of 126 meticulously detailed official photographs, called "builder portraits," of American locomotives that majestically chronicle the rise of steam locomotive power in America. Introduction. Detailed captions. xi+129pp. 9 x 12. 27393-8 Pa. $13.95

AMERICA'S LIGHTHOUSES: An Illustrated History, Francis Ross Holland, Jr. Delightfully written, profusely illustrated fact-filled survey of over 200 American lighthouses since 1716. History, anecdotes, technological advances, more. 240pp. 8 x 10¾. 25576-X Pa. $12.95

TOWARDS A NEW ARCHITECTURE, Le Corbusier. Pioneering manifesto by founder of "International School." Technical and aesthetic theories, views of industry, economics, relation of form to function, "mass-production split" and much more. Profusely illustrated. 320pp. 6⅛ x 9¼. (Available in U.S. only.) 25023-7 Pa. $10.95

HOW THE OTHER HALF LIVES, Jacob Riis. Famous journalistic record, exposing poverty and degradation of New York slums around 1900, by major social reformer. 100 striking and influential photographs. 233pp. 10 x 7⅞. 22012-5 Pa. $11.95

FRUIT KEY AND TWIG KEY TO TREES AND SHRUBS, William M. Harlow. One of the handiest and most widely used identification aids. Fruit key covers 120 deciduous and evergreen species; twig key 160 deciduous species. Easily used. Over 300 photographs. 126pp. 5⅜ x 8½. 20511-8 Pa. $3.95

COMMON BIRD SONGS, Dr. Donald J. Borror. Songs of 60 most common U.S. birds: robins, sparrows, cardinals, bluejays, finches, more–arranged in order of increasing complexity. Up to 0 variations of songs of each species. Cassette and manual 99911-4 $8.95

ORCHIDS AS HOUSE PLANTS, Rebecca Tyson Northen. Grow cattleyas and many other kinds of orchids–in a window, in a case, or under artificial light. 63 illustrations. 148pp. 5⅜ x 8½. 23261-1 Pa. $7.95

MONSTER MAZES, Dave Phillips. Masterful mazes at four levels of difficulty. Avoid deadly perils and evil creatures to find magical treasures. Solutions for all 32 exciting illustrated puzzles. 48pp. 8¼ x 11. 26005-4 Pa. $2.95

MOZART'S DON GIOVANNI (DOVER OPERA LIBRETTO SERIES), Wolfgang Amadeus Mozart. Introduced and translated by Ellen H. Bleiler. Standard Italian libretto, with complete English translation. Convenient and thoroughly portable–an ideal companion for reading along with a recording or the performance itself. Introduction. List of characters. Plot summary. 121pp. 5¼ x 8½. 24944-1 Pa. $3.95

TECHNICAL MANUAL AND DICTIONARY OF CLASSICAL BALLET, Gail Grant. Defines, explains, comments on steps, movements, poses and concepts. 15-page pictorial section. Basic book for student, viewer. 127pp. 5⅜ x 8½. 21843-0 Pa. $4.95

THE CLARINET AND CLARINET PLAYING, David Pino. Lively, comprehensive work features suggestions about technique, musicianship, and musical interpretation, as well as guidelines for teaching, making your own reeds, and preparing for public performance. Includes an intriguing look at clarinet history. "A godsend," *The Clarinet,* Journal of the International Clarinet Society. Appendixes. 7 illus. 320pp. 5⅜ x 8½. 40270-3 Pa. $9.95

HOLLYWOOD GLAMOR PORTRAITS, John Kobal (ed.). 145 photos from 1926-49. Harlow, Gable, Bogart, Bacall; 94 stars in all. Full background on photographers, technical aspects. 160pp. 8⅜ x 11¼. 23352-9 Pa. $12.95

THE ANNOTATED CASEY AT THE BAT: A Collection of Ballads about the Mighty Casey/Third, Revised Edition, Martin Gardner (ed.). Amusing sequels and parodies of one of America's best-loved poems: Casey's Revenge, Why Casey Whiffed, Casey's Sister at the Bat, others. 256pp. 5⅜ x 8½. 28598-7 Pa. $8.95

THE RAVEN AND OTHER FAVORITE POEMS, Edgar Allan Poe. Over 40 of the author's most memorable poems: "The Bells," "Ulalume," "Israfel," "To Helen," "The Conqueror Worm," "Eldorado," "Annabel Lee," many more. Alphabetic lists of titles and first lines. 64pp. 5³⁄₁₆ x 8¼. 26685-0 Pa. $1.00

PERSONAL MEMOIRS OF U. S. GRANT, Ulysses Simpson Grant. Intelligent, deeply moving firsthand account of Civil War campaigns, considered by many the finest military memoirs ever written. Includes letters, historic photographs, maps and more. 528pp. 6⅛ x 9¼. 28587-1 Pa. $12.95

ANCIENT EGYPTIAN MATERIALS AND INDUSTRIES, A. Lucas and J. Harris. Fascinating, comprehensive, thoroughly documented text describes this ancient civilization's vast resources and the processes that incorporated them in daily life, including the use of animal products, building materials, cosmetics, perfumes and incense, fibers, glazed ware, glass and its manufacture, materials used in the mummification process, and much more. 544pp. 6⅛ x 9¼. (Available in U.S. only.) 40446-3 Pa. $16.95

RUSSIAN STORIES/PYCCKNE PACCKA3bl: A Dual-Language Book, edited by Gleb Struve. Twelve tales by such masters as Chekhov, Tolstoy, Dostoevsky, Pushkin, others. Excellent word-for-word English translations on facing pages, plus teaching and study aids, Russian/English vocabulary, biographical/critical introductions, more. 416pp. 5⅜ x 8½. 26244-8 Pa. $9.95

PHILADELPHIA THEN AND NOW: 60 Sites Photographed in the Past and Present, Kenneth Finkel and Susan Oyama. Rare photographs of City Hall, Logan Square, Independence Hall, Betsy Ross House, other landmarks juxtaposed with contemporary views. Captures changing face of historic city. Introduction. Captions. 128pp. 8¼ x 11. 25790-8 Pa. $9.95

AIA ARCHITECTURAL GUIDE TO NASSAU AND SUFFOLK COUNTIES, LONG ISLAND, The American Institute of Architects, Long Island Chapter, and the Society for the Preservation of Long Island Antiquities. Comprehensive, well-researched and generously illustrated volume brings to life over three centuries of Long Island's great architectural heritage. More than 240 photographs with authoritative, extensively detailed captions. 176pp. 8¼ x 11. 26946-9 Pa. $14.95

NORTH AMERICAN INDIAN LIFE: Customs and Traditions of 23 Tribes, Elsie Clews Parsons (ed.). 27 fictionalized essays by noted anthropologists examine religion, customs, government, additional facets of life among the Winnebago, Crow, Zuni, Eskimo, other tribes. 480pp. 6⅛ x 9¼. 27377-6 Pa. $10.95

FRANK LLOYD WRIGHT'S DANA HOUSE, Donald Hoffmann. Pictorial essay of residential masterpiece with over 160 interior and exterior photos, plans, elevations, sketches and studies. 128pp. 9¼ x 10¾. 29120-0 Pa. $14.95

THE MALE AND FEMALE FIGURE IN MOTION: 60 Classic Photographic Sequences, Eadweard Muybridge. 60 true-action photographs of men and women walking, running, climbing, bending, turning, etc., reproduced from rare 19th-century masterpiece. vi + 121pp. 9 x 12. 24745-7 Pa. $12.95

1001 QUESTIONS ANSWERED ABOUT THE SEASHORE, N. J. Berrill and Jacquelyn Berrill. Queries answered about dolphins, sea snails, sponges, starfish, fishes, shore birds, many others. Covers appearance, breeding, growth, feeding, much more. 305pp. 5¼ x 8¼. 23366-9 Pa. $9.95

ATTRACTING BIRDS TO YOUR YARD, William J. Weber. Easy-to-follow guide offers advice on how to attract the greatest diversity of birds: birdhouses, feeders, water and waterers, much more. 96pp. 5³⁄₁₆ x 8¼. 28927-3 Pa. $2.50

MEDICINAL AND OTHER USES OF NORTH AMERICAN PLANTS: A Historical Survey with Special Reference to the Eastern Indian Tribes, Charlotte Erichsen-Brown. Chronological historical citations document 500 years of usage of plants, trees, shrubs native to eastern Canada, northeastern U.S. Also complete identifying information. 343 illustrations. 544pp. 6½ x 9¼. 25951-X Pa. $12.95

STORYBOOK MAZES, Dave Phillips. 23 stories and mazes on two-page spreads: Wizard of Oz, Treasure Island, Robin Hood, etc. Solutions. 64pp. 8¼ x 11. 23628-5 Pa. $2.95

AMERICAN NEGRO SONGS: 230 Folk Songs and Spirituals, Religious and Secular, John W. Work. This authoritative study traces the African influences of songs sung and played by black Americans at work, in church, and as entertainment. The author discusses the lyric significance of such songs as "Swing Low, Sweet Chariot," "John Henry," and others and offers the words and music for 230 songs. Bibliography. Index of Song Titles. 272pp. 6½ x 9¼. 40271-1 Pa. $10.95

MOVIE-STAR PORTRAITS OF THE FORTIES, John Kobal (ed.). 163 glamor, studio photos of 106 stars of the 1940s: Rita Hayworth, Ava Gardner, Marlon Brando, Clark Gable, many more. 176pp. 8⅜ x 11¼. 23546-7 Pa. $14.95

BENCHLEY LOST AND FOUND, Robert Benchley. Finest humor from early 30s, about pet peeves, child psychologists, post office and others. Mostly unavailable elsewhere. 73 illustrations by Peter Arno and others. 183pp. 5⅜ x 8½. 22410-4 Pa. $6.95

YEKL and THE IMPORTED BRIDEGROOM AND OTHER STORIES OF YIDDISH NEW YORK, Abraham Cahan. Film Hester Street based on Yekl (1896). Novel, other stories among first about Jewish immigrants on N.Y.'s East Side. 240pp. 5⅜ x 8½. 22427-9 Pa. $7.95

SELECTED POEMS, Walt Whitman. Generous sampling from Leaves of Grass. Twenty-four poems include "I Hear America Singing," "Song of the Open Road," "I Sing the Body Electric," "When Lilacs Last in the Dooryard Bloom'd," "O Captain! My Captain!"—all reprinted from an authoritative edition. Lists of titles and first lines. 128pp. 5³⁄₁₆ x 8¼. 26878-0 Pa. $1.00

THE BEST TALES OF HOFFMANN, E. T. A. Hoffmann. 10 of Hoffmann's most important stories: "Nutcracker and the King of Mice," "The Golden Flowerpot," etc. 458pp. 5⅜ x 8½. 21793-0 Pa. $9.95

FROM FETISH TO GOD IN ANCIENT EGYPT, E. A. Wallis Budge. Rich detailed survey of Egyptian conception of "God" and gods, magic, cult of animals, Osiris, more. Also, superb English translations of hymns and legends. 240 illustrations. 545pp. 5⅜ x 8½. 25803-3 Pa. $13.95

FRENCH STORIES/CONTES FRANÇAIS: A Dual-Language Book, Wallace Fowlie. Ten stories by French masters, Voltaire to Camus: "Micromegas" by Voltaire; "The Atheist's Mass" by Balzac; "Minuet" by de Maupassant; "The Guest" by Camus, six more. Excellent English translations on facing pages. Also French-English vocabulary list, exercises, more. 352pp. 5⅜ x 8½. 26443-2 Pa. $9.95

CHICAGO AT THE TURN OF THE CENTURY IN PHOTOGRAPHS: 122 Historic Views from the Collections of the Chicago Historical Society, Larry A. Viskochil. Rare large-format prints offer detailed views of City Hall, State Street, the Loop, Hull House, Union Station, many other landmarks, circa 1904-1913. Introduction. Captions. Maps. 144pp. 9⅜ x 12¼. 24656-6 Pa. $12.95

OLD BROOKLYN IN EARLY PHOTOGRAPHS, 1865-1929, William Lee Younger. Luna Park, Gravesend race track, construction of Grand Army Plaza, moving of Hotel Brighton, etc. 157 previously unpublished photographs. 165pp. 8⅞ x 11¾. 23587-4 Pa. $13.95

THE MYTHS OF THE NORTH AMERICAN INDIANS, Lewis Spence. Rich anthology of the myths and legends of the Algonquins, Iroquois, Pawnees and Sioux, prefaced by an extensive historical and ethnological commentary. 36 illustrations. 480pp. 5⅜ x 8½. 25967-6 Pa. $10.95

AN ENCYCLOPEDIA OF BATTLES: Accounts of Over 1,560 Battles from 1479 B.C. to the Present, David Eggenberger. Essential details of every major battle in recorded history from the first battle of Megiddo in 1479 B.C. to Grenada in 1984. List of Battle Maps. New Appendix covering the years 1967-1984. Index. 99 illustrations. 544pp. 6½ x 9¼. 24913-1 Pa. $16.95

SAILING ALONE AROUND THE WORLD, Captain Joshua Slocum. First man to sail around the world, alone, in small boat. One of great feats of seamanship told in delightful manner. 67 illustrations. 294pp. 5⅜ x 8½. 20326-3 Pa. $6.95

ANARCHISM AND OTHER ESSAYS, Emma Goldman. Powerful, penetrating, prophetic essays on direct action, role of minorities, prison reform, puritan hypocrisy, violence, etc. 271pp. 5⅜ x 8½. 22484-8 Pa. $8.95

MYTHS OF THE HINDUS AND BUDDHISTS, Ananda K. Coomaraswamy and Sister Nivedita. Great stories of the epics; deeds of Krishna, Shiva, taken from puranas, Vedas, folk tales; etc. 32 illustrations. 400pp. 5⅜ x 8½. 21759-0 Pa. $12.95

THE TRAUMA OF BIRTH, Otto Rank. Rank's controversial thesis that anxiety neurosis is caused by profound psychological trauma which occurs at birth. 256pp. 5⅜ x 8½. 27974-X Pa. $7.95

A THEOLOGICO-POLITICAL TREATISE, Benedict Spinoza. Also contains unfinished Political Treatise. Great classic on religious liberty, theory of government on common consent. R. Elwes translation. Total of 421pp. 5⅜ x 8½. 20249-6 Pa. $10.95

MY BONDAGE AND MY FREEDOM, Frederick Douglass. Born a slave, Douglass became outspoken force in antislavery movement. The best of Douglass' autobiographies. Graphic description of slave life. 464pp. 5⅜ x 8½. 22457-0 Pa. $8.95

FOLLOWING THE EQUATOR: A Journey Around the World, Mark Twain. Fascinating humorous account of 1897 voyage to Hawaii, Australia, India, New Zealand, etc. Ironic, bemused reports on peoples, customs, climate, flora and fauna, politics, much more. 197 illustrations. 720pp. 5⅜ x 8½. 26113-1 Pa. $15.95

THE PEOPLE CALLED SHAKERS, Edward D. Andrews. Definitive study of Shakers: origins, beliefs, practices, dances, social organization, furniture and crafts, etc. 33 illustrations. 351pp. 5⅜ x 8½. 21081-2 Pa. $12.95

THE MYTHS OF GREECE AND ROME, H. A. Guerber. A classic of mythology, generously illustrated, long prized for its simple, graphic, accurate retelling of the principal myths of Greece and Rome, and for its commentary on their origins and significance. With 64 illustrations by Michelangelo, Raphael, Titian, Rubens, Canova, Bernini and others. 480pp. 5⅜ x 8½. 27584-1 Pa. $10.95

PSYCHOLOGY OF MUSIC, Carl E. Seashore. Classic work discusses music as a medium from psychological viewpoint. Clear treatment of physical acoustics, auditory apparatus, sound perception, development of musical skills, nature of musical feeling, host of other topics. 88 figures. 408pp. 5⅜ x 8½. 21851-1 Pa. $11.95

THE PHILOSOPHY OF HISTORY, Georg W. Hegel. Great classic of Western thought develops concept that history is not chance but rational process, the evolution of freedom. 457pp. 5⅜ x 8½. 20112-0 Pa. $9.95

THE BOOK OF TEA, Kakuzo Okakura. Minor classic of the Orient: entertaining, charming explanation, interpretation of traditional Japanese culture in terms of tea ceremony. 94pp. 5⅜ x 8½. 20070-1 Pa. $3.95

LIFE IN ANCIENT EGYPT, Adolf Erman. Fullest, most thorough, detailed older account with much not in more recent books, domestic life, religion, magic, medicine, commerce, much more. Many illustrations reproduce tomb paintings, carvings, hieroglyphs, etc. 597pp. 5⅜ x 8½. 22632-8 Pa. $12.95

SUNDIALS, Their Theory and Construction, Albert Waugh. Far and away the best, most thorough coverage of ideas, mathematics concerned, types, construction, adjusting anywhere. Simple, nontechnical treatment allows even children to build several of these dials. Over 100 illustrations. 230pp. 5⅜ x 8½. 22947-5 Pa. $8.95

THEORETICAL HYDRODYNAMICS, L. M. Milne-Thomson. Classic exposition of the mathematical theory of fluid motion, applicable to both hydrodynamics and aerodynamics. Over 600 exercises. 768pp. 6⅛ x 9¼. 68970-0 Pa. $20.95

SONGS OF EXPERIENCE: Facsimile Reproduction with 26 Plates in Full Color, William Blake. 26 full-color plates from a rare 1826 edition. Includes "TheTyger," "London," "Holy Thursday," and other poems. Printed text of poems. 48pp. 5¼ x 7. 24636-1 Pa. $4.95

OLD-TIME VIGNETTES IN FULL COLOR, Carol Belanger Grafton (ed.). Over 390 charming, often sentimental illustrations, selected from archives of Victorian graphics—pretty women posing, children playing, food, flowers, kittens and puppies, smiling cherubs, birds and butterflies, much more. All copyright-free. 48pp. 9¼ x 12¼. 27269-9 Pa. $9.95

PERSPECTIVE FOR ARTISTS, Rex Vicat Cole. Depth, perspective of sky and sea, shadows, much more, not usually covered. 391 diagrams, 81 reproductions of drawings and paintings. 279pp. 5⅜ x 8½. 22487-2 Pa. $9.95

DRAWING THE LIVING FIGURE, Joseph Sheppard. Innovative approach to artistic anatomy focuses on specifics of surface anatomy, rather than muscles and bones. Over 170 drawings of live models in front, back and side views, and in widely varying poses. Accompanying diagrams. 177 illustrations. Introduction. Index. 144pp. 8⅜ x11¼. 26723-7 Pa. $9.95

GOTHIC AND OLD ENGLISH ALPHABETS: 100 Complete Fonts, Dan X. Solo. Add power, elegance to posters, signs, other graphics with 100 stunning copyright-free alphabets: Blackstone, Dolbey, Germania, 97 more–including many lower-case, numerals, punctuation marks. 104pp. 8⅛ x 11. 24695-7 Pa. $9.95

HOW TO DO BEADWORK, Mary White. Fundamental book on craft from simple projects to five-bead chains and woven works. 106 illustrations. 142pp. 5⅜ x 8. 20697-1 Pa. $5.95

THE BOOK OF WOOD CARVING, Charles Marshall Sayers. Finest book for beginners discusses fundamentals and offers 34 designs. "Absolutely first rate . . . well thought out and well executed."–E. J. Tangerman. 118pp. 7¾ x 10⅝. 23654-4 Pa. $7.95

ILLUSTRATED CATALOG OF CIVIL WAR MILITARY GOODS: Union Army Weapons, Insignia, Uniform Accessories, and Other Equipment, Schuyler, Hartley, and Graham. Rare, profusely illustrated 1846 catalog includes Union Army uniform and dress regulations, arms and ammunition, coats, insignia, flags, swords, rifles, etc. 226 illustrations. 160pp. 9 x 12. 24939-5 Pa. $12.95

WOMEN'S FASHIONS OF THE EARLY 1900s: An Unabridged Republication of "New York Fashions, 1909," National Cloak & Suit Co. Rare catalog of mail-order fashions documents women's and children's clothing styles shortly after the turn of the century. Captions offer full descriptions, prices. Invaluable resource for fashion, costume historians. Approximately 725 illustrations. 128pp. 8⅜ x 11¼. 27276-1 Pa. $12.95

THE 1912 AND 1915 GUSTAV STICKLEY FURNITURE CATALOGS, Gustav Stickley. With over 200 detailed illustrations and descriptions, these two catalogs are essential reading and reference materials and identification guides for Stickley furniture. Captions cite materials, dimensions and prices. 112pp. 6½ x 9¼. 26676-1 Pa. $9.95

EARLY AMERICAN LOCOMOTIVES, John H. White, Jr. Finest locomotive engravings from early 19th century: historical (1804–74), main-line (after 1870), special, foreign, etc. 147 plates. 142pp. 11⅜ x 8¼. 22772-3 Pa. $12.95

THE TALL SHIPS OF TODAY IN PHOTOGRAPHS, Frank O. Braynard. Lavishly illustrated tribute to nearly 100 majestic contemporary sailing vessels: Amerigo Vespucci, Clearwater, Constitution, Eagle, Mayflower, Sea Cloud, Victory, many more. Authoritative captions provide statistics, background on each ship. 190 black-and-white photographs and illustrations. Introduction. 128pp. 8⅞ x 11¾. 27163-3 Pa. $14.95

LITTLE BOOK OF EARLY AMERICAN CRAFTS AND TRADES, Peter Stockham (ed.). 1807 children's book explains crafts and trades: baker, hatter, cooper, potter, and many others. 23 copperplate illustrations. 140pp. 4⅝ x 6.

23336 7 Pa. $4.95

VICTORIAN FASHIONS AND COSTUMES FROM HARPER'S BAZAR, 1867–1898, Stella Blum (ed.). Day costumes, evening wear, sports clothes, shoes, hats, other accessories in over 1,000 detailed engravings. 320pp. 9⅜ x 12¼.

22990-4 Pa. $16.95

GUSTAV STICKLEY, THE CRAFTSMAN, Mary Ann Smith. Superb study surveys broad scope of Stickley's achievement, especially in architecture. Design philosophy, rise and fall of the Craftsman empire, descriptions and floor plans for many Craftsman houses, more. 86 black-and-white halftones. 31 line illustrations. Introduction 208pp. 6½ x 9¼.

27210-9 Pa. $9.95

THE LONG ISLAND RAIL ROAD IN EARLY PHOTOGRAPHS, Ron Ziel. Over 220 rare photos, informative text document origin (1844) and development of rail service on Long Island. Vintage views of early trains, locomotives, stations, passengers, crews, much more. Captions. 8⅞ x 11¾.

26301-0 Pa. $14.95

VOYAGE OF THE LIBERDADE, Joshua Slocum. Great 19th-century mariner's thrilling, first-hand account of the wreck of his ship off South America, the 35-foot boat he built from the wreckage, and its remarkable voyage home. 128pp. 5⅜ x 8½.

40022-0 Pa. $5.95

TEN BOOKS ON ARCHITECTURE, Vitruvius. The most important book ever written on architecture. Early Roman aesthetics, technology, classical orders, site selection, all other aspects. Morgan translation. 331pp. 5⅜ x 8½. 20645-9 Pa. $9.95

THE HUMAN FIGURE IN MOTION, Eadweard Muybridge. More than 4,500 stopped-action photos, in action series, showing undraped men, women, children jumping, lying down, throwing, sitting, wrestling, carrying, etc. 390pp. 7⅞ x 10⅝.

20204-6 Clothbd. $29.95

TREES OF THE EASTERN AND CENTRAL UNITED STATES AND CANADA, William M. Harlow. Best one-volume guide to 140 trees. Full descriptions, woodlore, range, etc. Over 600 illustrations. Handy size. 288pp. 4½ x 6⅜.

20395-6 Pa. $6.95

SONGS OF WESTERN BIRDS, Dr. Donald J. Borror. Complete song and call repertoire of 60 western species, including flycatchers, juncoes, cactus wrens, many more–includes fully illustrated booklet. Cassette and manual 99913-0 $8.95

GROWING AND USING HERBS AND SPICES, Milo Miloradovich. Versatile handbook provides all the information needed for cultivation and use of all the herbs and spices available in North America. 4 illustrations. Index. Glossary. 236pp. 5⅜ x 8½.

25058-X Pa. $7.95

BIG BOOK OF MAZES AND LABYRINTHS, Walter Shepherd. 50 mazes and labyrinths in all–classical, solid, ripple, and more–in one great volume. Perfect inexpensive puzzler for clever youngsters. Full solutions. 112pp. 8⅛ x 11.

22951-3 Pa. $5.95

PIANO TUNING, J. Cree Fischer. Clearest, best book for beginner, amateur. Simple repairs, raising dropped notes, tuning by easy method of flattened fifths. No previous skills needed. 4 illustrations. 201pp. 5⅜ x 8½. 23267-0 Pa. $6.95

HINTS TO SINGERS, Lillian Nordica. Selecting the right teacher, developing confidence, overcoming stage fright, and many other important skills receive thoughtful discussion in this indispensible guide, written by a world-famous diva of four decades' experience. 96pp. 5³/₈ x 8¹/₂. 40094-8 Pa. $4.95

THE COMPLETE NONSENSE OF EDWARD LEAR, Edward Lear. All nonsense limericks, zany alphabets, Owl and Pussycat, songs, nonsense botany, etc., illustrated by Lear. Total of 320pp. 5⅜ x 8½. (Available in U.S. only.) 20167-8 Pa. $7.95

VICTORIAN PARLOUR POETRY: An Annotated Anthology, Michael R. Turner. 117 gems by Longfellow, Tennyson, Browning, many lesser-known poets. "The Village Blacksmith," "Curfew Must Not Ring Tonight," "Only a Baby Small," dozens more, often difficult to find elsewhere. Index of poets, titles, first lines. xxiii + 325pp. 5⅝ x 8¼. 27044-0 Pa. $12.95

DUBLINERS, James Joyce. Fifteen stories offer vivid, tightly focused observations of the lives of Dublin's poorer classes. At least one, "The Dead," is considered a masterpiece. Reprinted complete and unabridged from standard edition. 160pp. 5³⁄₁₆ x 8¼. 26870-5 Pa. $1.50

GREAT WEIRD TALES: 14 Stories by Lovecraft, Blackwood, Machen and Others, S. T. Joshi (ed.). 14 spellbinding tales, including "The Sin Eater," by Fiona McLeod, "The Eye Above the Mantel," by Frank Belknap Long, as well as renowned works by R. H. Barlow, Lord Dunsany, Arthur Machen, W. C. Morrow and eight other masters of the genre. 256pp. 5⅜ x 8½. (Available in U.S. only.) 40436-6 Pa. $8.95

THE BOOK OF THE SACRED MAGIC OF ABRAMELIN THE MAGE, translated by S. MacGregor Mathers. Medieval manuscript of ceremonial magic. Basic document in Aleister Crowley, Golden Dawn groups. 268pp. 5⅜ x 8½. 23211-5 Pa. $9.95

NEW RUSSIAN-ENGLISH AND ENGLISH-RUSSIAN DICTIONARY, M. A. O'Brien. This is a remarkably handy Russian dictionary, containing a surprising amount of information, including over 70,000 entries. 366pp. 4½ x 6⅛. 20208-9 Pa. $10.95

HISTORIC HOMES OF THE AMERICAN PRESIDENTS, Second, Revised Edition, Irvin Haas. A traveler's guide to American Presidential homes, most open to the public, depicting and describing homes occupied by every American President from George Washington to George Bush. With visiting hours, admission charges, travel routes. 175 photographs. Index. 160pp. 8¼ x 11. 26751-2 Pa. $13.95

NEW YORK IN THE FORTIES, Andreas Feininger. 162 brilliant photographs by the well-known photographer, formerly with *Life* magazine. Commuters, shoppers, Times Square at night, much else from city at its peak. Captions by John von Hartz. 181pp. 9¼ x 10¾. 23585-8 Pa. $13.95

INDIAN SIGN LANGUAGE, William Tomkins. Over 525 signs developed by Sioux and other tribes. Written instructions and diagrams. Also 290 pictographs. 111pp. 6⅛ x 9¼. 22029-X Pa. $3.95

ANATOMY: A Complete Guide for Artists, Joseph Sheppard. A master of figure drawing shows artists how to render human anatomy convincingly. Over 460 illustrations. 224pp. 8⅜ x 11¼. 27279-6 Pa. $11.95

MEDIEVAL CALLIGRAPHY: Its History and Technique, Marc Drogin. Spirited history, comprehensive instruction manual covers 13 styles (ca. 4th century through 15th). Excellent photographs; directions for duplicating medieval techniques with modern tools. 224pp. 8⅜ x 11¼. 26142-5 Pa. $12.95

DRIED FLOWERS: How to Prepare Them, Sarah Whitlock and Martha Rankin. Complete instructions on how to use silica gel, meal and borax, perlite aggregate, sand and borax, glycerine and water to create attractive permanent flower arrangements. 12 illustrations. 32pp. 5⅜ x 8½. 21802-3 Pa. $1.00

EASY-TO-MAKE BIRD FEEDERS FOR WOODWORKERS, Scott D. Campbell. Detailed, simple-to-use guide for designing, constructing, caring for and using feeders. Text, illustrations for 12 classic and contemporary designs. 96pp. 5⅜ x 8½. 25847-5 Pa. $3.95

SCOTTISH WONDER TALES FROM MYTH AND LEGEND, Donald A. Mackenzie. 16 lively tales tell of giants rumbling down mountainsides, of a magic wand that turns stone pillars into warriors, of gods and goddesses, evil hags, powerful forces and more. 240pp. 5⅜ x 8½. 29677-6 Pa. $6.95

THE HISTORY OF UNDERCLOTHES, C. Willett Cunnington and Phyllis Cunnington. Fascinating, well-documented survey covering six centuries of English undergarments, enhanced with over 100 illustrations: 12th-century laced-up bodice, footed long drawers (1795), 19th-century bustles, 19th-century corsets for men, Victorian "bust improvers," much more. 272pp. 5⅝ x 8¼. 27124-2 Pa. $9.95

ARTS AND CRAFTS FURNITURE: The Complete Brooks Catalog of 1912, Brooks Manufacturing Co. Photos and detailed descriptions of more than 150 now very collectible furniture designs from the Arts and Crafts movement depict davenports, settees, buffets, desks, tables, chairs, bedsteads, dressers and more, all built of solid, quarter-sawed oak. Invaluable for students and enthusiasts of antiques, Americana and the decorative arts. 80pp. 6½ x 9¼. 27471-3 Pa. $8.95

WILBUR AND ORVILLE: A Biography of the Wright Brothers, Fred Howard. Definitive, crisply written study tells the full story of the brothers' lives and work. A vividly written biography, unparalleled in scope and color, that also captures the spirit of an extraordinary era. 560pp. 6⅛ x 9¼. 40297-5 Pa. $17.95

THE ARTS OF THE SAILOR: Knotting, Splicing and Ropework, Hervey Garrett Smith. Indispensable shipboard reference covers tools, basic knots and useful hitches; handsewing and canvas work, more. Over 100 illustrations. Delightful reading for sea lovers. 256pp. 5⅜ x 8½. 26440-8 Pa. $8.95

FRANK LLOYD WRIGHT'S FALLINGWATER: The House and Its History, Second, Revised Edition, Donald Hoffmann. A total revision–both in text and illustrations–of the standard document on Fallingwater, the boldest, most personal architectural statement of Wright's mature years, updated with valuable new material from the recently opened Frank Lloyd Wright Archives. "Fascinating"–*The New York Times*. 116 illustrations. 128pp. 9¼ x 10¾. 27430-6 Pa. $12.95

PHOTOGRAPHIC SKETCHBOOK OF THE CIVIL WAR, Alexander Gardner. 100 photos taken on field during the Civil War. Famous shots of Manassas Harper's Ferry, Lincoln, Richmond, slave pens, etc. 244pp. 10⅝ x 8¼.　　22731-6 Pa. $10.95

FIVE ACRES AND INDEPENDENCE, Maurice G. Kains. Great back-to-the-land classic explains basics of self-sufficient farming. The one book to get. 95 illustrations. 397pp. 5⅜ x 8½.　　20974-1 Pa. $7.95

SONGS OF EASTERN BIRDS, Dr. Donald J. Borror. Songs and calls of 60 species most common to eastern U.S.: warblers, woodpeckers, flycatchers, thrushes, larks, many more in high-quality recording.　　Cassette and manual 99912-2 $9.95

A MODERN HERBAL, Margaret Grieve. Much the fullest, most exact, most useful compilation of herbal material. Gigantic alphabetical encyclopedia, from aconite to zedoary, gives botanical information, medical properties, folklore, economic uses, much else. Indispensable to serious reader. 161 illustrations. 888pp. 6½ x 9¼. 2-vol. set. (Available in U.S. only.)　　Vol. I: 22798-7 Pa. $10.95
Vol. II: 22799-5 Pa. $10.95

HIDDEN TREASURE MAZE BOOK, Dave Phillips. Solve 34 challenging mazes accompanied by heroic tales of adventure. Evil dragons, people-eating plants, bloodthirsty giants, many more dangerous adversaries lurk at every twist and turn. 34 mazes, stories, solutions. 48pp. 8¼ x 11.　　24566-7 Pa. $2.95

LETTERS OF W. A. MOZART, Wolfgang A. Mozart. Remarkable letters show bawdy wit, humor, imagination, musical insights, contemporary musical world; includes some letters from Leopold Mozart. 276pp. 5⅜ x 8½.　　22859-2 Pa. $9.95

BASIC PRINCIPLES OF CLASSICAL BALLET, Agrippina Vaganova. Great Russian theoretician, teacher explains methods for teaching classical ballet. 118 illustrations. 175pp. 5⅜ x 8½.　　22036-2 Pa. $6.95

THE JUMPING FROG, Mark Twain. Revenge edition. The original story of The Celebrated Jumping Frog of Calaveras County, a hapless French translation, and Twain's hilarious "retranslation" from the French. 12 illustrations. 66pp. 5⅜ x 8½.　　22686-7 Pa. $4.95

BEST REMEMBERED POEMS, Martin Gardner (ed.). The 126 poems in this superb collection of 19th- and 20th-century British and American verse range from Shelley's "To a Skylark" to the impassioned "Renascence" of Edna St. Vincent Millay and to Edward Lear's whimsical "The Owl and the Pussycat." 224pp. 5⅜ x 8½.　　27165-X Pa. $5.95

COMPLETE SONNETS, William Shakespeare. Over 150 exquisite poems deal with love, friendship, the tyranny of time, beauty's evanescence, death and other themes in language of remarkable power, precision and beauty. Glossary of archaic terms. 80pp. 5³⁄₁₆ x 8¼.　　26686-9 Pa. $1.00

THE BATTLES THAT CHANGED HISTORY, Fletcher Pratt. Eminent historian profiles 16 crucial conflicts, ancient to modern, that changed the course of civilization. 352pp. 5⅜ x 8½.　　41129-X Pa. $9.95

THE WIT AND HUMOR OF OSCAR WILDE, Alvin Redman (ed.). More than 1,000 ripostes, paradoxes, wisecracks: Work is the curse of the drinking classes; I can resist everything except temptation; etc. 258pp. 5⅜ x 8½. 20602-5 Pa. $6.95

SHAKESPEARE LEXICON AND QUOTATION DICTIONARY, Alexander Schmidt. Full definitions, locations, shades of meaning in every word in plays and poems. More than 50,000 exact quotations. 1,485pp. 6½ x 9¼. 2-vol. set.
Vol. 1: 22726-X Pa. $17.95
Vol. 2: 22727-8 Pa. $17.95

SELECTED POEMS, Emily Dickinson. Over 100 best-known, best-loved poems by one of America's foremost poets, reprinted from authoritative early editions. No comparable edition at this price. Index of first lines. 64pp. 5$\frac{3}{16}$ x 8¼.
26466-1 Pa. $1.00

THE INSIDIOUS DR. FU-MANCHU, Sax Rohmer. The first of the popular mystery series introduces a pair of English detectives to their archnemesis, the diabolical Dr. Fu-Manchu. Flavorful atmosphere, fast-paced action, and colorful characters enliven this classic of the genre. 208pp. 5$\frac{3}{16}$ x 8¼. 29898-1 Pa. $2.00

THE MALLEUS MALEFICARUM OF KRAMER AND SPRENGER, translated by Montague Summers. Full text of most important witchhunter's "bible," used by both Catholics and Protestants. 278pp. 6⅝ x 10. 22802-9 Pa. $12.95

SPANISH STORIES/CUENTOS ESPAÑOLES: A Dual-Language Book, Angel Flores (ed.). Unique format offers 13 great stories in Spanish by Cervantes, Borges, others. Faithful English translations on facing pages. 352pp. 5⅜ x 8½.
25399-6 Pa. $9.95

GARDEN CITY, LONG ISLAND, IN EARLY PHOTOGRAPHS, 1869–1919, Mildred H. Smith. Handsome treasury of 118 vintage pictures, accompanied by carefully researched captions, document the Garden City Hotel fire (1899), the Vanderbilt Cup Race (1908), the first airmail flight departing from the Nassau Boulevard Aerodrome (1911), and much more. 96pp. 8⅞ x 11¾. 40669-5 Pa. $12.95

OLD QUEENS, N.Y., IN EARLY PHOTOGRAPHS, Vincent F. Seyfried and William Asadorian. Over 160 rare photographs of Maspeth, Jamaica, Jackson Heights, and other areas. Vintage views of DeWitt Clinton mansion, 1939 World's Fair and more. Captions. 192pp. 8⅞ x 11. 26358-4 Pa. $14.95

CAPTURED BY THE INDIANS: 15 Firsthand Accounts, 1750-1870, Frederick Drimmer. Astounding true historical accounts of grisly torture, bloody conflicts, relentless pursuits, miraculous escapes and more, by people who lived to tell the tale. 384pp. 5⅜ x 8½. 24901-8 Pa. $9.95

THE WORLD'S GREAT SPEECHES (Fourth Enlarged Edition), Lewis Copeland, Lawrence W. Lamm, and Stephen J. McKenna. Nearly 300 speeches provide public speakers with a wealth of updated quotes and inspiration–from Pericles' funeral oration and William Jennings Bryan's "Cross of Gold Speech" to Malcolm X's powerful words on the Black Revolution and Earl of Spenser's tribute to his sister, Diana, Princess of Wales. 944pp. 5⅜ x 8⅜. 40903-1 Pa. $15.95

THE BOOK OF THE SWORD, Sir Richard F. Burton. Great Victorian scholar/adventurer's eloquent, erudite history of the "queen of weapons"–from prehistory to early Roman Empire. Evolution and development of early swords, variations (sabre, broadsword, cutlass, scimitar, etc.), much more. 336pp. 6⅛ x 9¼.
25434-8 Pa. $9.95

AUTOBIOGRAPHY: The Story of My Experiments with Truth, Mohandas K. Gandhi. Boyhood, legal studies, purification, the growth of the Satyagraha (nonviolent protest) movement. Critical, inspiring work of the man responsible for the freedom of India. 480pp. 5⅜ x 8½. (Available in U.S. only.)   24593-4 Pa. $9.95

CELTIC MYTHS AND LEGENDS, T. W. Rolleston. Masterful retelling of Irish and Welsh stories and tales. Cuchulain, King Arthur, Deirdre, the Grail, many more. First paperback edition. 58 full-page illustrations. 512pp. 5⅜ x 8½.   26507-2 Pa. $9.95

THE PRINCIPLES OF PSYCHOLOGY, William James. Famous long course complete, unabridged. Stream of thought, time perception, memory, experimental methods; great work decades ahead of its time. 94 figures. 1,391pp. 5⅜ x 8½. 2-vol. set.
Vol. I: 20381-6 Pa. $14.95
Vol. II: 20382-4 Pa. $16.95

THE WORLD AS WILL AND REPRESENTATION, Arthur Schopenhauer. Definitive English translation of Schopenhauer's life work, correcting more than 1,000 errors, omissions in earlier translations. Translated by E. F. J. Payne. Total of 1,269pp. 5⅜ x 8½. 2-vol. set.
Vol. 1: 21761-2 Pa. $12.95
Vol. 2: 21762-0 Pa. $12.95

MAGIC AND MYSTERY IN TIBET, Madame Alexandra David-Neel. Experiences among lamas, magicians, sages, sorcerers, Bonpa wizards. A true psychic discovery. 32 illustrations. 321pp. 5⅜ x 8½. (Available in U.S. only.)   22682-4 Pa. $9.95

THE EGYPTIAN BOOK OF THE DEAD, E. A. Wallis Budge. Complete reproduction of Ani's papyrus, finest ever found. Full hieroglyphic text, interlinear transliteration, word-for-word translation, smooth translation. 533pp. 6½ x 9¼.
21866-X Pa. $12.95

MATHEMATICS FOR THE NONMATHEMATICIAN, Morris Kline. Detailed, college-level treatment of mathematics in cultural and historical context, with numerous exercises. Recommended Reading Lists. Tables. Numerous figures. 641pp. 5⅜ x 8½.
24823-2 Pa. $11.95

PROBABILISTIC METHODS IN THE THEORY OF STRUCTURES, Isaac Elishakoff. Well-written introduction covers the elements of the theory of probability from two or more random variables, the reliability of such multivariable structures, the theory of random function, Monte Carlo methods of treating problems incapable of exact solution, and more. Examples. 502pp. 5³⁄₈ x 8¹⁄₂.   40691-1 Pa. $16.95

THE RIME OF THE ANCIENT MARINER, Gustave Doré, S. T. Coleridge. Doré's finest work; 34 plates capture moods, subtleties of poem. Flawless full-size reproductions printed on facing pages with authoritative text of poem. "Beautiful. Simply beautiful."–Publisher's Weekly. 77pp. 9¼ x 12.   22305-1 Pa. $7.95

NORTH AMERICAN INDIAN DESIGNS FOR ARTISTS AND CRAFTSPEOPLE, Eva Wilson. Over 360 authentic copyright-free designs adapted from Navajo blankets, Hopi pottery, Sioux buffalo hides, more. Geometrics, symbolic figures, plant and animal motifs, etc. 128pp. 8⅜ x 11. (Not for sale in the United Kingdom.)   25341-4 Pa. $9.95

SCULPTURE: Principles and Practice, Louis Slobodkin. Step-by-step approach to clay, plaster, metals, stone; classical and modern. 253 drawings, photos. 255pp. 8⅛ x 11.
22960-2 Pa. $11.95

THE INFLUENCE OF SEA POWER UPON HISTORY, 1660–1783, A. T. Mahan. Influential classic of naval history and tactics still used as text in war colleges. First paperback edition. 4 maps. 24 battle plans. 640pp. 5⅜ x 8½. 25509-3 Pa. $14.95

THE STORY OF THE TITANIC AS TOLD BY ITS SURVIVORS, Jack Winocour (ed.). What it was really like. Panic, despair, shocking inefficiency, and a little heroism. More thrilling than any fictional account. 26 illustrations. 320pp. 5⅜ x 8½. 20610-6 Pa. $8.95

FAIRY AND FOLK TALES OF THE IRISH PEASANTRY, William Butler Yeats (ed.). Treasury of 64 tales from the twilight world of Celtic myth and legend: "The Soul Cages," "The Kildare Pooka," "King O'Toole and his Goose," many more. Introduction and Notes by W. B. Yeats. 352pp. 5⅜ x 8½. 26941-8 Pa. $8.95

BUDDHIST MAHAYANA TEXTS, E. B. Cowell and others (eds.). Superb, accurate translations of basic documents in Mahayana Buddhism, highly important in history of religions. The Buddha-karita of Asvaghosha, Larger Sukhavativyuha, more. 448pp. 5⅜ x 8½. 25552-2 Pa. $12.95

ONE TWO THREE . . . INFINITY: Facts and Speculations of Science, George Gamow. Great physicist's fascinating, readable overview of contemporary science: number theory, relativity, fourth dimension, entropy, genes, atomic structure, much more. 128 illustrations. Index. 352pp. 5⅜ x 8½. 25664-2 Pa. $9.95

EXPERIMENTATION AND MEASUREMENT, W. J. Youden. Introductory manual explains laws of measurement in simple terms and offers tips for achieving accuracy and minimizing errors. Mathematics of measurement, use of instruments, experimenting with machines. 1994 edition. Foreword. Preface. Introduction. Epilogue. Selected Readings. Glossary. Index. Tables and figures. 128pp. 5³/₈ x 8¹/₂. 40451-X Pa. $6.95

DALÍ ON MODERN ART: The Cuckolds of Antiquated Modern Art, Salvador Dalí. Influential painter skewers modern art and its practitioners. Outrageous evaluations of Picasso, Cézanne, Turner, more. 15 renderings of paintings discussed. 44 calligraphic decorations by Dalí. 96pp. 5⅜ x 8½. (Available in U.S. only.) 29220-7 Pa. $5.95

ANTIQUE PLAYING CARDS: A Pictorial History, Henry René D'Allemagne. Over 900 elaborate, decorative images from rare playing cards (14th–20th centuries): Bacchus, death, dancing dogs, hunting scenes, royal coats of arms, players cheating, much more. 96pp. 9¼ x 12¼. 29265-7 Pa. $12.95

MAKING FURNITURE MASTERPIECES: 30 Projects with Measured Drawings, Franklin H. Gottshall. Step-by-step instructions, illustrations for constructing handsome, useful pieces, among them a Sheraton desk, Chippendale chair, Spanish desk, Queen Anne table and a William and Mary dressing mirror. 224pp. 8⅛ x 11¼. 29338-6 Pa. $16.95

THE FOSSIL BOOK: A Record of Prehistoric Life, Patricia V. Rich et al. Profusely illustrated definitive guide covers everything from single-celled organisms and dinosaurs to birds and mammals and the interplay between climate and man. Over 1,500 illustrations. 760pp. 7½ x 10⅛. 29371-8 Pa. $29.95

Prices subject to change without notice.

Available at your book dealer or write for free catalog to Dept. GI, Dover Publications, Inc., 31 East 2nd St., Mineola, N.Y. 11501. Dover publishes more than 500 books each year on science, elementary and advanced mathematics, biology, music, art, literary history, social sciences and other areas.